· SCHUBERT'S VIENNA·

An Aston Magna Academy Book

Schubert's

YALE UNIVERSITY PRESS/NEW HAVEN & LONDON

Vienna

EDITED BY RAYMOND ERICKSON

Published in association with the Aston Magna
Foundation for Music and the Humanities,
Inc. (www.astonmagna.org)

Frontispiece: Krafft, the triumphant return of
Francis I to Vienna (see plate 1).

Designed by Nancy Ovedovitz and set in
Monotype Bembo type by The Marathon
Group, Inc., Durham, North Carolina. Printed
in the United States of America by Vail-Ballou
Press, Binghamton, New York.

Library of Congress Cataloging-in-Publication Data
Schubert's Vienna / edited by Raymond
Erickson.
    p.   cm.
"An Aston Magna Academy book."
Includes bibliographical references and index.
ISBN 0-300-07080-2 (cloth : alk. paper)
 1. Schubert, Franz, 1797–1828.
 2. Music—Austria—Vienna—19th
century—History and criticism.
 3. Vienna (Austria)—Politics and gov-
ernment.   4. Vienna (Austria)—Social
life and customs.   5. Arts, Austrian—
Austria—Vienna.   I. Erickson, Raymond.
ML410.S3S29975   1997
780'.92—dc21
[B]   97-10707

A catalogue record for this book is available
from the British Library.

10 9 8 7 6 5 4 3 2 1

In appreciation, to the professional staff
of the National Endowment for the Humanities.

• CONTENTS •

Acknowledgments ix

Introduction xiii

Sources of Illustrations xvii

PART ONE
Politics and Social Life

1 Vienna in Its European Context 3
Raymond Erickson

2 People, Class Structure, and Society 36
Waltraud Heindl

3 The Congress of Vienna 55
Enno Kraehe

PART TWO

Musical Life

4 "Classic" and "Romantic," Beethoven
and Schubert 79
Leon Plantinga

5 Vienna, City of Music 98
Alice M. Hanson

6 Social Dancing in Schubert's World 119
Elizabeth Aldrich

PART THREE

The Other Arts

7 Architecture and Sculpture 143
Thomas DaCosta Kaufmann

8 Viennese Biedermeier Painting 174
Gerbert Frodl

9 The Poetry of Schubert's Songs 183
Jane K. Brown

10 The Viennese Theater 214
Simon Williams

Afterword Vienna's Schubert 246
Ernst Hilmar

List of Contributors 257

Index 259

Color plates follow page 76

• A C K N O W L E D G M E N T S •

This is less a book about Schubert than it is about Vienna. On the other hand, the essays should give the reader—whether student, music lover, history buff, musician, scholar, museum goer, or would-be tourist eager to visit or revisit Vienna—the kind of background leading to an enriched view of Schubert and his older contemporary Beethoven, and of the city in which they resided.

In the summer of 1993 at the Mason Gross School of the Arts, Rutgers University (New Brunswick), the authors and about fifty other scholars and musicians gathered to study for three intensive weeks the Vienna that Schubert knew, that Vienna over which reigned, from 1792 to 1806, the Holy Roman Emperor Francis II—who, because of historical circumstances explained in Chapter 1, also ruled as Francis I, Emperor of Austria, from 1804 to 1835. The gathering was the eleventh interdisciplinary academy sponsored since 1978 by the Aston Magna Foundation for Music and the Humanities. Funding came principally from the Division of Education of the National Endowment for the Humanities, with additional support from the Austrian Cultural Institute in New York City.

The Aston Magna Academies have as their purpose the fostering of intellectual exchange among humanities scholars of different disciplines and the development of mutual understanding between scholars and performing artists. Unlike many worthy programs that set out to enhance further the competency of professionals in their specialties, the Academy program has sought to provide leading-edge interpretations of *basic* knowledge in many fields that the participants know they need but—especially because of the high level of specialization in higher education today—have not had the opportunity to acquire. Appropriately then, those chosen as Academy faculty not only must have studied and reflected deeply upon their respective areas of research, but also must be willing to share their expertise to an eager but sophisticated audience from largely outside their own discipline. This book, in a similar spirit, offers essays intended for a broad, nonspecialist public by some of these same experts.

There are many debts that the editor is happy to acknowledge. The contributors have been extraordinarily cooperative in shaping their essays to be logical and necessary pieces of a coordinated whole. I have also consulted them on some aspects of the illustration captions, for which I am nonetheless to be held responsible. The belief of the collaborators in the value of the Academy program and their collegial generosity are further evidenced by the fact that all have agreed that any royalties from this publication will go to support the educational activities of the Aston Magna Foundation.

I have also benefited from the constructive contributions of many others: the anonymous outside reader for Yale University Press; my Queens College colleagues Rolf Kieser and Hermann Haller, who reviewed my translations from the German of Chapter 7 and the Afterword, and Rufus Hallmark, who suggested some readings for Chapter 9; Professor Kristina Muxfeldt of Yale University, Professor Enno Kraehe of the University of Virginia, and Catherine Gasper Jessup, whose observations have improved the opening chapter; John M. Gingerich, who was kind enough to send me a copy of his insightful 1996 Yale dissertation on Schubert; Rita Steblin in Vienna, who generously shared with me unpublished information concerning a recently discovered Schubert archive; and Professor Paula Fichtner of Brooklyn College, to whom I have often turned, over many years, for precise information and thoughtful perspectives on various aspects of Habsburg history and culture. Last, but hardly least, is the debt I owe to my wife, Carole DeSaram, who has sacrificed not a little so that this book might appear in the Schubert anniversary year.

To reach its audience and accomplish its purpose, a book like this one requires generous visual documentation. Helping to underwrite the cost of the illustrations were Christopher H. Murray and Edwin McAmis, present and past members of the Aston Magna Foundation Board. Michael Spudic, a doctoral candidate at the Graduate School of the City University of New York, assisted me early on with the picture research. The necessary burden of contacting and negotiating with more than twenty institutions or independent departments therein for visual materials was substantially lightened by the unfailingly helpful cooperation of the staffs of these institutions. In the first instances I must cite Claudia Oesterreicher, Adelbert Sussler, and Helmut Selzer of the Historisches Museum der Stadt Wien, the source of more than half of our illustrations, and Gerbert Frodl of the Österreichische Galerie, who provided most of the color negatives and gave advice on a number of important matters. But I also wish to acknowledge specifically the following for their personal assistance (all in Vienna, except where noted): Eckart Vancsa (Bundesdenkmalamt), Otto Biba (Gesellschaft der Musikfreunde), Renata Antoniou (Graphische Sammlung Albertina), Gottfried Mraz and Christiana Thomas (Hof-, Haus-, und Staatsarchiv), Robert Rill (Österreichisches Staatsarchiv), Sandra Mikulczik (Kunsthistorisches Museum), Christian Witt-Dörring and Gabriele Fabiankowitsch (Museum der angewandten Künste), Mary Doherty, Laurence Libin, and Stuart Pollens (Metropolitan Museum of Art, New York), Charles Eubanks (New York Public Library), Franz Albrecht Graf Metternich-Sándor (Schloß Grafenegg), Elisabeth Wagner (Österreichische Nationalbibliothek, Musiksammlung), Reinhard Strohm and Humaira Ahmed (Department of Music, Oxford University), Gwyneth Campling (Royal Collection Enterprises, Windsor Castle), Petra Schneider (Stiftung Weimarer Klassik, Weimar), and Otto Brusatti and Johann Ziegler (Wiener Stadt-und Landesbibliothek). I am also indebted to Director Wolfgang Waldner, Thomas Stelzer, Peter Mikl, and Friederike Zeitlhofer of the Austrian Cultural Institute in New York for their various contributions that have furthered this enterprise; moreover, the former deputy director of the Institute, Ernst Aichinger, now based in Vienna at the Federal Ministry for Foreign Affairs, arranged for the Institute's cosponsorship of the 1993 Aston Magna Academy and has actively supported this book project. Finally, I owe a debt of continuous gratitude to Aston Magna Executive Director Ronnie Boriskin and her assistant Florence Lynch for handling and facilitating various financial and legal transactions associated with this publication.

Much of my writing, editing, and research associated with this book was facilitated by the resources and helpful staffs of several libraries near to home. In particular I would like to acknowledge the Rosenthal Library and Music Library at Queens College; the New York Public Library's Center for the Humanities (Fifth Avenue at 42d Street) and the Research Divisions of the Library for the Performing Arts at Lincoln Center; and the Thomas J. Watson Library of the Metropolitan Museum of Art. During working vacations, I have always found myself welcome at the Old Forge (N.Y.) Library, nestled in the beauties of the Adirondack Mountains.

It was my pleasure to work with Harry Haskell, music editor of Yale University Press, on a previous, unrelated book. It was he who made a compelling case that Yale University Press should publish this volume as the first of an anticipated series deriving from the Aston Magna Academies; his diplomatically expressed yet candid opinions and editorial judgment, not to say patience, have had no little influence on the overall shape of the present publication. Furthermore, I have enjoyed jousting verbally with the manuscript editor, Dan Heaton, whose sharp eye, mind, and wit have earned my deep respect and have even persuaded me to yield on some points of contention.

In conclusion, I wish to acknowledge the extraordinary quality of the many program officers of the National Endowment for the Humanities with whom I have been privileged to work since 1976 on matters relating to the twelve Aston Magna Academies to date (a thirteenth has been funded for 1997). It was the early encouragement by Adrienne Gyongi to pursue what was then an unusual educational concept that led to the first Academy proposal in 1977. After that, Peter Patrikis, Charles Meyers and, for the last several Academies, Barbara Ashbrook, have overseen the projects from Washington, with Jean Hughes assuming this responsibility for 1997. In addition to reaching hundreds of college teachers and musicians throughout the nation and involving scholars and artists from abroad as well, the Academy program has also been able to reach out to the general public, thanks to funding from the National Endowment for the Humanities' Division of Public Programs, by means of over thirty multidisciplinary weekend programs presented all over the United States at museums and libraries; Malcolm Richardson and Wilsonia Cherry, both of whom have gone on to important positions elsewhere, served as NEH program officers for these undertakings. The nation owes all of these professionals, as well as their unnamed colleagues, a profound debt of gratitude for their understanding of how the study of the humanities enriches our culture and informs our citizenry.

The Aston Magna Academy program has explicitly sought from the beginning to build bridges between diverse areas of learning, with a view to expanding knowledge and understanding of those roots of American culture found in Europe. It has also sought to foster an appreciation of how the arts and humanities generally, but differently, serve society by providing a conduit between the present and the past. This book is but one way in which the aspirations of that enterprise can be shared with the American public as well as with the larger English-reading citizenry of music and Vienna lovers the world over.

Of all of Europe's major cities, Vienna has the image of being the most comfortable and among the most enchanting. Sachertorte, coffee with globs of whipped cream, a central historic district that can be easily traversed on foot, a New Year's celebration that is televised the world over—and above all, music, music, music. That is the image projected by the travel posters and other advertisements, and it is all true.

It is not the whole truth, of course. There are also dark times to be reckoned with in Vienna's history, and it may come as a surprise to today's casual tourist or music lover to know that these include the periods in which Joseph Haydn (1732–1809), Ludwig van Beethoven (1770–1827), and Franz Schubert (1797–1828) lived there. This was an era of war and deprivation, of bombardment and occupation of the city by Napoleon's army, of the dissolution after a thousand years of the Holy Roman Empire, of political oppressiveness sufficiently great that it would lead to revolution in 1848.

What is remarkable is the artistic and cultural vitality that can still be discovered under such circumstances. It was at this time that Vienna became *Musikstadt Wien*— Europe's great center of music, the many facets of which are delineated in Chapter 5 by Alice M. Hanson. Perhaps, as Waltraud Heindl suggests in Chapter 2, music was not as dangerous for the artist as painting or writing—even though public concert programs had to pass the censor. Perhaps another contributing factor was that music provided family entertainment in a patriarchal and family-centered society. Whatever the reasons, it is almost as though music was seized upon not only for the sake of its own pleasures but as a means of escape in what was in fact a repressive (although not violent) police state ruled over, with good intentions, by Emperor Francis (r. 1792–1835), who was not a little influenced by his minister Clemens Metternich.

The Moravian-born former Habsburg subject Charles Sealsfield (born Karl Postl), a liberal-thinking émigré to America who returned to gather information for a polemical book about Austria's authoritarian state, related in his *Austria As It Is* (London, 1828) that music held a predominant position in Vienna—in the church (where it overpowered worship), in public concerts, and at home, especially on Sunday, when, Sealsfield wrote, "from three o'clock till eleven the city is literally in a musical and sensual uproar. Wherever you go, the sound of musical instruments will reach your ears." And yet the most important aspect of music is the legacy of two great composers, Beethoven and Schubert—the former the dominant musical personality of the age, and indeed the century, and the latter, unlike Haydn, Mozart, and Beethoven, a true Viennese. The last thirty years of Beethoven's life overlap with virtually the whole of Schubert's, yet they likely met but once and lived in different social spheres. A book about Beethoven's Vienna, therefore, would be somewhat different from this one.

Schubert's Vienna was less the Vienna of imperial and high aristocratic activity than that of the so-called Biedermeier milieu of the middle class, which in this book is described in social terms by Waltraud Heindl and in visual terms by Gerbert Frodl (Chapter 8). Schubert, who adopted a modest, more or less bohemian lifestyle, did not demand as much of Vienna as Beethoven did, so he did not receive as much. During his lifetime there was only one major concert devoted solely to his music, none of his symphonies were publicly performed or published, and his many operas went mostly unperformed. Still, as Ernst Hilmar points out in the Afterword, Schubert was hardly unknown in Vienna, nor as poor as the popular literature would like to paint him. Moreover, while it is fruitless to speculate how Schubert's career might have developed had he lived longer, the evidence suggests that he was on the verge of a major leap forward into public consciousness and that, in any case, the output of his thirty-one years is in many ways more impressive than that of the first three decades or so of Beethoven's life.

Whereas the (mostly eighteenth-century) palaces of the great were frequented by Beethoven, the most characteristic new architecture of Schubert's Vienna, as explained by Thomas DaCosta Kaufmann in Chapter 7, was embodied in utilitarian and functional buildings aimed at the general welfare—apartment complexes, institutions of research and higher learning, parks with their coffeehouses. This represented the resumption of the imperial public works policy of the reform-minded Joseph II (r. 1780–90) by Joseph's nephew Francis, whose reign covers the whole of Beethoven's Vienna period and Schubert's entire life.

Schubert had, of course, a few noble friends and patrons who lived in grand palaces, but his circle consisted mainly of artists, writers, and bureaucrats. Thus a volume like this must treat the various arts of the time and Schubert's relation to them. The composer's attitude toward poetry, painting, theater, and the dance is of more importance to understanding Schubert the man and artist than it is for the antisocial and iconoclastic Beethoven, who came to embody Kant's description of a genius as someone who gives rules to art, hence someone operating almost independent of society. Whereas Beethoven provided the romantic model of the artist seemingly existing in an empyreal realm, Schubert, dying as he did at age thirty-one—an age at which Beethoven was still in his "early" period—had no chance to be seen in that light. In fact, his contemporaries saw him as existing on the margins of human society, not above it or in control of it—and this is not so different from Mozart, who was also fated to die young. Thus Franz Grillparzer, arguably Austria's greatest dramatist, could write an epitaph for Schubert decrying the loss of talent unfulfilled.

That said, we must also recognize that Schubert lived a life that put him in touch with a remarkable number of important cultural currents, events, places, and personalities of his time, as the illustrations in this volume help to document. He had the advantage, as an imperial choirboy, of a first-class education and the connections that came with it. He loved the theater, which, as Simon Williams shows us in Chapter 10, was experiencing a golden age, and he knew many important people in the Viennese theater world besides Grillparzer. Moreover, his many operas, also freshly assessed by Williams, are distinctly Viennese in their style and content. Some of his close artist friends (Leopold Kupelwieser, Moritz von Schwind), as well as some only peripherally associated with him (Joseph Danhauser, Johann Nepomuk Hoechle, Joseph Kriehuber, and Ferdinand Waldmüller), turned out to be among the more important Austrian painters of the nineteenth century. His huge volume of danceable dance music (not to mention his frequent improvising of same) is evidence that it was not only during the Congress of Vienna—whose importance not only for Schubert's Vienna but for all Europe is conveyed by Enno Kraehe in Chapter 3—that the city waltzed, although, as Elizabeth Aldrich explains in Chapter 6, the Viennese waltz at this time is not quite what we think of today.

But there are other, less tangible factors in Schubert's world to be considered, such as the intellectual and aesthetic currents that coursed through Europe in the later eighteenth century—the results of such diverse factors as the discovery of lava-encrusted Pompeii and Herculaneum, the writings of Rousseau, the French Revolution (and its attempt to emulate republican Rome), and a growing fascination with the Middle Ages—not to mention the singularly powerful impact, especially in the German-speaking world, of Johann Wolfgang von Goethe (Schubert's favorite poet, as we learn from Jane K. Brown in Chapter 9). Measuring the direct and indirect impact of these and other forces on Schubert and on the arts of his time provides useful means of assessing them in both their Viennese and European contexts.

It follows, therefore, that several chapters in this book consider the meaning(s) of terms like *classicism, neoclassicism, romanticism, sensibility,* and *Biedermeier.* Some of these were used at the time in very specific contexts (*classical* and *romantic,* for example, in a series of important lectures on literature delivered in Vienna in 1808 by August Wilhelm Schlegel, brother of the politically active Friedrich Schlegel). Others, like *neoclassicism* and *Biedermeier,* have been applied retroactively to a particular style or milieu.

All these terms are common parlance, yet a reading of the essays by Jane K. Brown, Gerbert Frodl, Thomas DaCosta Kaufmann, and Leon Plantinga will reveal something important: that the arts do not necessarily move in concert, that the same term can have quite different connotations when applied to different arts, and therefore that different arts often cannot even be profitably compared with one another.

By treating the arts in their own terms and not attempting to find facile comparisons among them, however, these essays clarify for us both the origins of style-critical terms and the limits of their use. Thus, we see that *classicism,* which was understood to imply emulation of antiquity, can be reasonably applied to architecture and the fine arts and even to poetry and literature, because there are antique models to be imitated, but that it is hard to justify the term when speaking of music. Likewise, *romantic,* understood in an aesthetic sense, was common from the early years of the nineteenth century, yet was used differently for music and literature and has never really caught on as a meaningful style designation for architecture.

Moreover, although music appreciation students typically learn that the "classic" period of Haydn, Mozart, and at least some of Beethoven was succeeded by the "romantic" nineteenth century, Plantinga argues in Chapter 4 instead for a single classic-romantic period (c. 1750–1900) that has coexisting "classic" and "romantic" style traits; this position enables us to recognize and accept both of these tendencies in the music of Schubert (and other composers, too).

Schubert's Vienna is thus to be seen as a time and place conditioned by concrete historical events and ethereal, artistic sensibilities. To convey some of these and their relationship to Schubert the man and artist is the purpose of this book.

BDA	Bundesdenkmalamt, Vienna		Sándor, Schloß Grafenegg,
GNM	Germanisches Nationalmu-		Haitzendorf
	seum, Nuremberg	NYPL:	S. P. Avery Collection,
GdMf	Archive, Gesellschaft der	Avery	Miriam and Ira D. Wallach
	Musikfreunde, Vienna		Division of Art, Prints,
GSA	Graphische Sammlung Al-		and Photographs, the
	bertina, Vienna		New York Public Library,
HHSa	Haus-, Hof-, und Staats-		Astor, Lenox, and Tilden
	archiv, Vienna		Foundations
HM	Historisches Museum der	NYPL:	Dance Collection, Dance
	Stadt Wien, Vienna	Dance	Committee Purchase Funds,
KHM	Kunsthistorisches Museum,		the New York Public Library
	Vienna		for the Performing Arts,
MAK	Museum der angewandten		Astor, Lenox, and Tilden
	Künste, Vienna		Foundations
MMA	Metropolitan Museum of	NYPL:	Music Division, the New
	Art, New York	Music	York Public Library for the
MS	Franz Albrecht Metternich-		Performing Arts, Astor,

PART ONE

Politics and Social Life

Vienna in Its European Context

RAYMOND ERICKSON

It was June 16, 1814, and all Vienna turned out to welcome home their beloved ruler—"Francis the Good," they called him—after nearly two years away (see plate 1). The Schubert family home at Säulengasse 10 sported a banner hailing "The Best of Emperors."[1] The Viennese had enthusiastically welcomed him home before—even in 1809, following the disastrous defeat that resulted in the Treaty of Pressburg. But this time he was the victor, the victor over that once–seemingly invincible colossus that had been on everyone's mind and lips for almost twenty years: Napoleon Bonaparte. Francis I's arrival was, in fact, but one of several grand monarchical entrées that were to entertain the Viennese in 1814, when the leaders of all Europe gathered in Vienna at a great Congress to decide just what to do with Europe in the post-Napoleonic era (see chapter 3).

The Congress of Vienna, lasting from September 1814 to June 1815, provides a convenient dividing point within Francis's reign. From his accession as head of the Habsburg dynasty and election as Holy Roman Emperor in 1792 until 1815, his capital and empire were threatened by the ideas and ideals of the French Revolution and the military might of Napoleon's armies. But after 1815 until his death in 1835, Francis's reign was blessed by the absence of major European wars, due in great part to the diplomatic achievements of Prince Clemens Metternich, the preeminent minister at the emperor's side (see fig. 3.4). It was during this latter period also that virtually the whole of Franz Schubert's musical legacy was created (see plate 2).

Francis was born in February 1768 in Florence, the oldest son of Leopold, Grand Duke of Tuscany. Benign and enlightened, the father was fated to reign as Emperor Leopold II for only two years. He had succeeded his childless brother Joseph II, a brilliant man, whose ten-year reign from 1780 to 1790 had attempted too many Enlightenment reforms too fast for the population to digest. Leopold also inherited from Joseph a war with the Turks and the revolution in France, the latter threatening their sister, Queen Marie Antoinette.

Leopold thus had his hands full—too full. It is likely that his death in 1792 was at least partly due to overwork while trying to solve these and other serious problems. But suddenly, on March 1, 1792, all the unsolved problems fell to the twenty-four-year-old Francis, who, conscious of his youth, felt overwhelmed and inadequate.

The future looked terribly grim and threatening to young Francis, yet he had the benefit of the education and training arranged by his father and then by his uncle in Vienna. As a boy in Florence, Francis had learned intimately the geography of the widely scattered Habsburg possessions and became fascinated by history and the lessons derived from it. He had acquired fluency in what his father termed "essential languages": Italian, French, German, and Latin, and later he would master Viennese dialect, to the delight of the denizens of the capital city. In fact, despite the international use of French at courts and in diplomacy, and even among the noble and polite society in Vienna, Francis as emperor preferred German, the language his father had termed "the most difficult." Among other subjects Francis had studied were philosophy, physics, astronomy, chemistry, botany, and anatomy.

Perhaps more important to Leopold, however, was that Francis be inculcated with an Enlightenment view of the responsibility of a monarch: "The princes must, above all, be convinced of the equality of man. . . . They should be made to realize . . . that their entire existence must ever be subordinate to their duties. They must regard it as their highest duty to listen and to comfort. . . . They must understand that one may never receive individuals in a bored, disdainful, distracted, ill-humored, or choleric manner; that one must give one's full attention to such persons, whatever their station."[2]

That Francis the monarch absorbed at least some of these principles is evident by his behavior at the later Friday public audiences he held (fig. 1.1). Two hundred to three hundred petitioners, gathered in the designated anteroom in the imperial residence, the Hofburg, had come the preceding Monday to obtain a number guaranteeing a place on line that Friday, the numbers being issued in order of application, regardless of station. One chronicler described the crowd as "all kinds of people, in rags and in riches, as the case happened to be. Mingling with the refined odors of perfumed elegance were the ramlike stench of befurred shepherds and the peculiar poverty smell

1.1 Schubert's entire life (1797–1828) was played out within the reign of Francis I (r. 1792–1835), shown here receiving a petitioner at one of his regular audiences. Francis's genuine but patriarchal concern for the welfare of the people, who had great affection for him (see plate 1), expressed itself not only in his modest demeanor and great generosity, but also in rigid strictures affecting intellectual and social freedoms. Sepia drawing by Alexander Clarot (1831). [HM]

of the needy."[3] Entering in groups of twenty-five or so and spaced around the room to preclude eavesdropping, the petitioners were approached in turn by their simply dressed monarch, accompanied by a secretary. Francis politely listened to each plea and answered in the petitioner's own language; each petition was duly noted, and many were granted. But any extravagant gestures of obeisance, such as falling to the knees, angered the emperor, who in known to have shouted, "Kneel before *God!* I am but a man!" That this abhorrence of obsequiousness was widely known is reflected in a popular play of the day; there, a Francis-like king responds in kind to a groveling subject: "Ich bitt recht sehr, stehen Sie auf, ist alles zu viel!" ("I beg you, stand up! This is unnecessary!").[4]

In 1784, Joseph II had ordered Archduke Francis and his tutors to Vienna so that there might be regular contact between the sovereign-in-training and the various peoples of the Habsburg hereditary lands (fig. 1.2). Francis began to acquire military experience (working his way up from the lowest commissioned officer rank). He also started a personal library (which became part of the Austrian National Library after World War I) and a portrait collection—both of which grew to enormous size. As he undertook various travels or military commissions, he maintained detailed notebooks;

he kept track of everything just as later his government would keep track of everybody. Finally on January 6, 1788, the archduke married the first of his four wives, but she died in 1790 after giving birth to one daughter. This blow to the loving and apparently faithful husband was doubled when his beloved if difficult uncle Joseph II died the very next day.

Now began an intensive and unexpectedly short final phase of Francis's training, as his father, now Emperor Leopold II, assigned him real responsibilities in the government. He got involved in a number of public welfare projects. More ominous, however, was his developing interest in the police and censorship, the political use of which was, of course, nothing new. But Francis was aware that antimonarchical ideas were finding their way into the Habsburg lands—ideas that, in his view, had to be suppressed.

Francis's period of apprenticeship abruptly ended when Leopold II died. Francis was now the head of the House of Austria, which controlled an area of about the size of Texas and 27–29 million people. This area included—roughly speaking—today's Austria and Czech Republic (the latter then comprising Bohemia and Moravia), Hungary, Croatia, and Slavonia. In addition to these essentially contiguous areas there were bits of Poland, the Austrian Netherlands (today's Belgium and Luxembourg), and scattered Austrian possessions in Italy, including the cities of Milan and Mantua.

Francis's title as ruler varied among these territories. He was a king several times over, for he was "by the grace of God, King of Hungary, Bohemia, Dalmatia, Croatia, Slavonia, Galicia, Lodomeria, and Jerusalem." Next in rank was his Austrian title, "Archduke of Austria," and then such titles as Duke of Milan and Mantua.

Francis's grandest title was that of Kaiser (emperor) of the Holy Roman Empire, a venerable institution founded in 962 (fig. 1.3).[5] The Empire had once incorporated almost all of central Europe, but by Francis's time it was mostly limited to German-speaking Europe—and not all of that. About half of the Habsburg lands were included in the Empire, excluding Hungary and most of the Slavic territories to the east. The imperial title was not hereditary but elective by a college of the seven or eight most powerful princes of Germany, including three archbishops of the Catholic Church. Successive generations of Habsburg sons had had to bargain for the title, each surrendering a bit more of the imperial prerogatives to assure election.

And thus Francis was accepted as hereditary ruler of lower Austria on April 25, 1792, was crowned King of Hungary on June 6, was elected Holy Roman Emperor on July 7, was crowned Emperor Francis II in Frankfurt am Main a week later, was crowned King of Bohemia on August 7, and so on. Characteristically, he authorized minimal state expenditure and made generous contributions to the poor in connection with these affairs.

However, Francis had little opportunity to savor all these coronation honors, for, in the midst of them, France declared war on him.

1.2 The influence of Emperor Joseph II (r. 1789–90; see plate 4) on his nephew the Archduke Francis as well as the reverence that the future emperor had for his uncle are suggested by this painting, possibly by Joseph Hickel, of 1785, the year the Florence-born archduke was called to Vienna by his imperial uncle. [KHM]

1.3 In 1792, Archduke Francis succeeded his father Leopold II (r. 1790–92) as Holy Roman Emperor Francis II and became, as it turned out, the last to attain the title. In 1806 circumstances forced him to abdicate, bringing an official end to the Holy Roman Empire, but he maintained his imperial dignity, having assumed the title of Francis I, Emperor of Austria, in 1804. [HM]

AUSTRIA, THE FRENCH REVOLUTION, AND NAPOLEON

The French Revolutionary Wars

Leopold II had not originally wanted to meddle in France's internal affairs. Nonetheless, after the French royal couple were caught trying to flee France in June 1791 and were forcibly brought back to Paris as prisoners, Leopold had taken action, issuing with the King of Prussia the Declaration of Pillnitz, whereby all European royalty were exhorted to use appropriate and necessary means to protect Louis XVI.

The French government, growing ever more radical, took the Declaration of Pillnitz as a serious threat. Thus, stirred partly by fear of invasion and partly by a proselytizing fervor to export revolutionary ideas, France declared war on Austria a few weeks after Leopold's death. This inaugurated more than two decades of almost constant war spread over several continents and involving all the major European powers—and even the newly born United States of America. These wars were the single most present fact of life for Francis and Vienna—and thus also for Beethoven (b. 1770 and a Viennese resident since 1792) and the young Schubert (b. 1797).

At the outset, in 1792, a lengthy military engagement with France seemed unlikely. With France in political, economic, and social upheaval, European leaders expected a relatively easy victory against the revolutionary upstart. Thus it was a shock when the allied forces turned heel at Valmy, France, in September. Stunning both sides, this retreat, strategically correct though it was, nonetheless saved the Revolution, doomed

Louis XVI and Marie Antoinette, and gave French troops the heart to push the Prussian and Austrian forces back across the Rhine and to invade the Austrian Netherlands.

In 1793 the deposed king and queen were executed. France issued further declarations of war but also suffered military reverses. The year might have ended with French defeat but for the situation in Poland, where Austria and Prussia were compelled to keep the bulk of their armies against Russia. Also important was a brilliant idea of the French war minister Carnot: a *levée en masse*—universal compulsory male military service. Within a year, France had an army of 700,000, and the nation was gearing up for total war of the kind never seen before in Europe. Stirred to action by the regicide and France's military aggressiveness, Austria, Prussia, Spain, the United Provinces (Holland), and Britain formed the First Coalition; before the end of 1795, however, the French would settle to their advantage with all but Britain and Austria.

In 1796 the tone changed. Historians refer to the "French Revolutionary wars" of 1792–95 but to the wars from 1796 to 1815 as "Napoleonic."

Austria and the Napoleonic Wars

Born on the French-controlled island of Corsica in 1769, the year after Francis's birth, Napoleon was educated in France and graduated in the bottom fifth of his class at the École militaire in Paris. In 1791 he was a prorevolutionary Jacobin, becoming increasingly radical with time and moving up in rank: by 1793 he was a brigadier general.

The political instability in France was precisely what gave the ambitious Napoleon his chance. In May 1795 he put down a royalist revolt in Paris, saving both the National Convention and the Republic, and was rewarded with command of the Army of the Interior; then, under the Directory, the next government, he was made commander in chief of the French Army of Italy.

Now began the real struggle between France and Austria, one-sided though it was. In 1796, Napoleon swept across northern Italy, which was largely Austrian territory, while another French army headed for Vienna. Frightened, the authorities in Vienna sought ways to whip up public courage and patriotism. What better way, thought Franz Josef, Count of Saurau, than through song? Beethoven had already provided his "Abschiedsgesang an Wiens Bürger" (Farewell-Song to the Citizens of Vienna) in honor of the volunteer corps in 1796 and was to compose a "Kriegslied der Österreicher" (War-Song of the Austrians) the next year. But the most powerful symbol to rally around was the popular emperor himself, so a song in praise of Francis II was needed. Entrusted to write the text was a Francophobe who had, as had so many other Austrian intellectuals and bureaucrats, originally been an enthusiastic supporter of the ideals of the French Enlightenment; now, disillusioned with the French Revolution, he was churning out such hate songs as "Verwünschungen der Franzosen" (Curses on the French!) and "Blutrache über die Franzosen" (Bloody Revenge on the French!). His paean of praise to Francis, who was out of sympathy with the French philosophes' point of view, was in turn given over to Vienna's leading musical citizen, who then

1.4 This autograph of Haydn's four-part setting of his patriotic melody "Kaiserhymne" (hymn for the emperor), with text by Lorenz Leopold Haschka (1796) symbolizes how music, along with the other arts, was conscripted into service during the Austrian wars against Napoleon. The melody was later used as a series of variations in Haydn's "Emperor" Quartet and is still today the tune of the German national anthem. [ÖNb:Mus]

produced the most famous melody he ever wrote, although he modestly entitled it a Volkslied—folk song. The result of this collaboration was, of course, the famous *Kaiserhymne* "Gott erhalte" (God preserve [the Emperor]!), its text by Lorenz Leopold Haschka and music (still the melody of the German national anthem) by Josef Haydn (fig. 1.4). First sung on February 12, 1797, on the emperor's birthday in theaters all over the Habsburg lands, it soon acquired the status of a standard.

Poets and musicians were not the only ones who contributed to the war effort. There is a stirring account of how the students of the Academy of Fine Arts responded to the call to arms in 1797. They assembled in the hall of antiquities to hear (according to one student) the "splendid, stately Füger, reading the call to arms with deep pathos in his sonorous voice. Hundreds of voices cheered him, we joined hands in an oath for life and for fatherland and emperor"—this while tears ran down the faces of the professors.[6]

These things happened the year Franz Schubert was born in Vienna. Considering the military situation, it was not a good year to arrive on the scene. Although the

French decided not to attack Vienna on this occasion, Napoleon did extract from Austria, in the Treaty of Campo Formio, the first and least humiliating of four agreements to be cited here, the Austrian Netherlands in exchange for Venice, Istria, and Dalmatia on the Adriatic.

In 1798, Napoleon invaded Egypt. But other French armies continued southward, capturing the Papal States and Naples. The Second Coalition—consisting of England, Russia, the Ottoman Empire (Turkey), Naples, and Portugal—began to form, but it foundered because of internal divisions. Austria joined the coalition in March 1799, when the French armies invaded Tuscany, where Francis had been born. During this year the allies did have some success in overthrowing some of the French puppet states, but then, in October, who should show up in Paris (having abandoned his defeated army in the Middle East) but Bonaparte, and just in time to coengineer a coup d'état. He was named first consul, effectively the ruler of France, in December 1799. France, having revolted against absolutism, now embraced it anew.

It did not take Napoleon long to finish off the Second Coalition, and Austria in particular. In a spectacular move, he crossed the Alps via the Great St. Bernard Pass, catching the Austrians by surprise and defeating them at Marengo. When this was followed by other French victories over Austrian armies in Germany, Austria had to endure the Peace of Lunéville in 1801. Austria ceded all territory west of the Rhine to France, fortifications on the Rhine's eastern bank were razed, leaving western and central Germany essentially defenseless. Hitting Austria even harder was the sharp reduction of its territory and influence in Italy, which Austria had worked harder to protect than it had the German-speaking area. Moreover, because the Habsburg Duke of Modena and the Grand Duke of Tuscany were now without territory, Austria was forced to agree to giving pieces of the Reich to the Habsburg dukes displaced from Italy. This, of course, undermined the Reich. No wonder that the Austrian foreign minister Thugut, who had acquired the unflattering nickname Thunichtgut—"do no good"—had to resign.

The Creation of the Austrian Empire and the Dissolution of the Holy Roman Empire

A general peace in Europe was temporarily achieved in 1802. In tribute and gratitude for his accomplishments, France bestowed life tenure on its first consul Napoleon and gave him the right to name his successor. In the same month, the *Reichsdeputation,* a committee of the German imperial legislature or *Reichstag,* met at Regensburg under the shadow of Napoleon's fist and in consequence of the Treaty of Lunéville. Its purpose: to reorganize the Holy Roman Empire, of which Francis was nominal head.

This was effected through the so-called *Reichsdeputationshauptschluß* or Imperial Recess of 1803. Reflecting Napoleon's anticlericalism, this constitutional resolution wiped out virtually all of the states of the Reich headed by ecclesiastics—including Salzburg, ruled by a prince archbishop, as Mozart had known it—and reapportioned the territories to secular states. Similarly, almost all of the fifty-one imperial cities lost

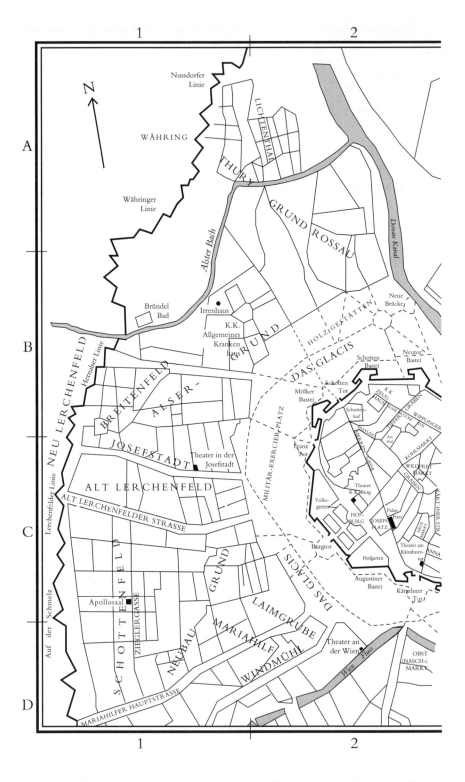

Am Hof C2–B2
Apollosaal C1
Burgtor C2
Das Glacis C2, B2, C3
Donaukanal C4–A2

Freyung B2-C2
Graben C2
Hohe Markt C2–C3
Josefsplatz C2
Josefstadt C1

Kaffeehäuser B4
Kärnthner Tor C2
Kettenbrücke B3
K. K. Augarten A3

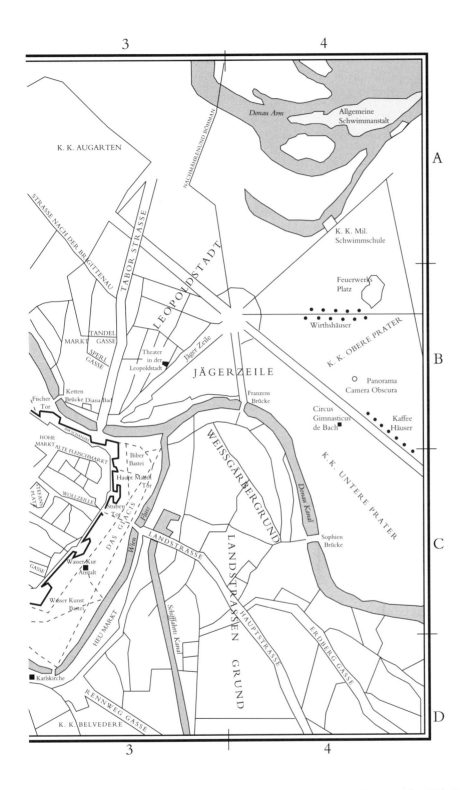

	3	4	

K. K. AUGARTEN

STRASSE NACH DER BRIGITTENAU

NACHMAHRENUND BOHMAN

Donau Arm

Allgemeine Schwimmanstalt

K. K. Mil. Schwimmschule

TABOR STRASSE

LEOPOLDSTADT

Feuerwerks Platz

• • • • • • •
Wirthshäuser

K. K. OBERE PRATER

TANDEL GASSE
MARKT
SPERL GASSE

Theater in der Leopoldstadt

Jäger Zeile

JÄGERZEILE

○ Panorama
Camera Obscura

Ketten Brücke Diana Bad
Fischer Tor

Franzens Brücke

Circus Gimnasticus de Bach ■

Kaffee Häuser
• • • •
• • •

HOHE MARKT ALTE FLEISCHMARKT
AM SCHANZL

Biber Bastei

WEISSGÄRBERGRUND

K. K. UNTERE PRATER

STEFANS PLATZ
WOLLZEILE
Haupt Mauth Tor

Donau Kanal

Stuben Tor
DAS GLACIS
Wien Fluss

LANDSTRASSE

GASSE
Wasser Kur Anstalt ■

LANDSTRASSEN GRUND

Sophien Brücke

Wasser Kunst Bastel

HEU MARKT

LANDSTRASSE HAUPTSTRASSE

ERDBERG GASSE

Schiffahrts Kanal

■ Karlskirche

RENNWEG GASSE

K. K. BELVEDERE

K. K. Belvedere D3	Neue Markt C2	Theater an der Wein D2
K. K. Obere Prater B4	Schottenhof B2	Theater in der Josefstadt C1
K. K. Untere Prater C4	Stefansplatz C3	Theater in der Leopoldstadt B3
Leopoldstadt B3	Straße nach der Brigittenau A2	Theater K. K. Burg (Burgtheater) C2
Lichtenthal A2	Theater am Kärnthnertor C2	Volksgarten C2

their independence and came under secular princes. Both measures facilitated Napoleon's control over the territories and princes of the Reich. But worst of all for Austria was the modification of the college of electors that chose the emperor; now Protestants were in the majority, and chances that the next emperor would be a Habsburg were almost nil.

When Francis realized that the imperial title was almost certain to be lost—and that his successor would be a mere archduke within the Reich—and when Napoleon was proclaimed emperor in May 1804, he knew that he would have to take action. First, he tried to have the Holy Roman Empire converted into a hereditary entity under the Habsburgs. Not surprisingly, this failed, so, in a stroke of *Realpolitik,* Francis took the additional title Francis I, Emperor of Austria, on August 14, 1804. Although the legal basis for this was not unimpeachable, the title was not challenged; for the first time, the head of the House of Habsburg had a single title that covered all of the various Habsburg territories.

In 1805 England, Russia, Austria, Sweden, and Naples formed the Third Coalition against France. Again, it was mostly in Italy that Austria got involved, prompted by Napoleon's having crowned himself King of Italy in Milan and by France's having swallowed parts of Italy. This time Napoleon was determined to reach the Habsburg capital; he did so on November 13, 1805, finding the city deserted by everyone who could afford to leave (fig. 1.5). This explains why the sparse audience at the premiere of Beethoven's opera *Fidelio* on November 20 consisted mainly of French soldiers. A rout of allied forces at Austerlitz followed in early December, and Austria was subjected to the crushing Peace of Pressburg. By this treaty, Austria was completely shut out of Italy and further weakened in Germany. Wrote Metternich, then ambassador to Paris, to Friedrich Gentz about the treaty of Pressburg: "The world is lost. Europe is burning out and only out of its ashes will a new order of things arise."[7] Metternich had, in fact, suffered personal indignity as a result of the French victory: while at Austerlitz, Napoleon had used Metternich's new house, the Schloss Kaunitz, as his headquarters.

The Pressburg agreement also contained an ominous mention of Bavaria and Württemberg, to which Napoleon doled out some surrendered Austrian territory, as members of "the Confédération Germanique." What, then, was this?

It did not take long to find out. In July 1806 the *Rheinbund* or Confederation of the Rhine was created, with Napoleon as "protector." Following close upon this, sixteen German princes announced they were seceding from the Reich. The legality of this move is highly doubtful, but de facto if not de jure, this was the end of the Holy Roman Empire established in the tenth century. On August 6, 1806, Francis, as Holy Roman Emperor Francis II, abdicated, giving up all pretense to stature and influence in western and southern Germany, now under Napoleon's thumb. As Francis I of the *Austrian* Empire, though, he was determined to rule with more real power than he had had before.

1.5 Twice during the Napoleonic wars, in 1805 and 1809, Vienna suffered the indignity and hardship of occupation by French troops. This etching by Pierre Adrien LeBeau after Thomas Charles Naudet depicts the entry of the French army into Vienna on November 13, 1805. At the time, Schubert was eight years old. [HM]

Shortly thereafter Napoleon crushed Prussia. He had reached the apogee of his power, now controlling all of Italy, most of the German-speaking world, and most of Europe west of the Rhine. He had imposed social and political change in most of his conquered territories, eliminating feudalism and church control and modernizing and consolidating political units. Furthermore, by means of his so-called "Continental system," he was trying to eliminate all European commerce with England, which had beaten him at sea.

Meanwhile, in Vienna, the Treaty of Pressburg had led to a major reorganization of the government and to thoughts of revenge. Over the next three years, inspired and pushed on by the new foreign minister Johann Philipp Stadion (like Metternich, a German-speaking non-Austrian), Austria prepared for renewed war with France. The military was reformed by the Emperor's brother Karl, and a military reserve army or *Landwehr* was formed in 1808—the Austrian version of the French levée en masse. Moreover, there was a concerted campaign, especially as war approached, in which the arts were enlisted, to whip up not just Austrian but pan-German patriotism. Here another imperial brother, Archduke Johann, played an especially important role. He believed that the moment was approaching when Providence would give to Austria the means of rescuing distressed humanity, by which he meant especially the Germans in the French-controlled Confederation of the Rhine. He encouraged artists to choose national themes for their paintings and had anti-Napoleonic literature translated and published.

The foreign minister Stadion, recognizing the power of the press to instill national feeling, persuaded the emperor—who in 1792 had complained that too many people were reading newspapers—to loosen the manacles on the press and on the educational system. The goal was not freedom of expression, of course, but rather the education of the people about their culture, history, geography, heroes, customs, arts, and literature. The results ranged from the founding of new newspapers to encyclopedic enterprises such as that undertaken by the Archduke Johann's friend Joseph Hormayr, who devoted himself over many years to publishing popular works on virtually every topic of German culture. In the same nationalistic spirit was the commission and installation of the equestrian statue of Joseph II in the Josefsplatz of the Hofburg, a work of the important Austrian sculptor Franz Anton Zauner (see Chapter 7). That artists were considered useful for the state's purposes is also evident from Francis's 1809 decree that freed artists from military service—which may explain in part the flood of students entering the Academy of Fine Arts after the Treaty of Pressburg.

A flood of pamphlets also appeared, many written by professional propagandists in state service, such as Friedrich Gentz and the German nationalist writer Friedrich Schlegel. The latter, with his brother August Wilhelm, had come to Vienna, along with a string of other German romantics from the north, around 1808; in the same year Schubert, who was later to set some of Friedrich Schlegel's poetry to music, entered the *Stadtkonvikt,* the select and strict school for nonnoble boys closely connected to the court; his acceptance indicates that Schubert was recognized from the start as having special potential.

All the military reforms and propaganda efforts were intended to help realize a plan to push the French out of central Germany in the hope of restoring the Empire and of punishing those German lords who had given in so easily to Napoleon. This time Austria would be the aggressor. As Metternich concluded in a communication to Stadion on April 27, 1808: "Peace with Napoleon is not peace."[8]

That all Austria was geared up for war was recognized by the French chargé d'affaires in Vienna, who wrote to the foreign minister: "In 1805, war was wanted by the government, but not the army nor the people; in 1809, it is wanted by the government, by the army, and by the people."[9] Even the emperor's third wife, Maria Ludovica, driven from northern Italy with her parents by Napoleon in 1796, contributed by encouraging the cultivation of national customs and traditional costume. The Viennese came to call her *Unsere liebe Landesmutter*—the dear mother of our country.

And so on April 10, 1809, inspired by an emotional declaration penned by Friedrich Schlegel, the Austrians attacked. However, all the preparations had been for naught. Napoleon pushed the Habsburg forces back and reentered Vienna on May 13, this

1.6 This image captures the fierceness of the bombardment of Vienna on May 11–12, 1809, which preceded the second occupation of the city by Napoleon's troops. During this bombardment, a shell penetrated the Stadtkonvikt, where Schubert and other scholarship students of the Imperial Choir boarded. Engraving by Franz Gerasch after a painting by Schubert's friend Johann Nepomuk Hoechle. [HM]

time after an artillery bombardment that destroyed lives and property and undoubtedly hastened the demise of the aged Haydn only two weeks later (fig. 1.6). A week after the occupation Napoleon took a hard blow from the Austrian army at Essling-Aspern, but on July 5, less than two months after the Austrian attack, he defeated the same army at Wagram, leading to the Treaty of Schönbrunn three months later.

This time Napoleon demanded no less than Francis's abdication as ruler of Austria, desiring to replace him with one of Francis's more malleable brothers. The other alternative was that Austria accept terms comparable to the Treaty of Pressburg. Francis would not abdicate, so on October 14 at the Habsburg palace at Schönbrunn—now Napoleon's headquarters—Austria lost about 3.5 million more subjects in German lands to the Rheinbund, as well as part of Poland and territories on and around the Adriatic, eliminating Austria's last direct access to the sea. Furthermore, Francis was forced to pay a heavy cash indemnity, reduce his army, and—a humiliating provision—cashier and even expel many of the non-Austrian aristocratic refugees fleeing French-controlled territory. As a further taunt, Napoleon had imperial art and other treasures carted off to Paris. Austria was at the nadir of its fortunes.

Nonetheless, something had occurred about a week before the Treaty of Schön-brunn was signed that would lift Austria out of its ignominy: on October 8, 1809, Count Clemens Metternich replaced Stadion as foreign minister; he was to control Austrian foreign policy for almost the next forty years.

At this point, in fact, Austria might be said to have entered the Age of Metternich, for the new foreign minister quickly made his presence felt: only five months later Austria had outnegotiated Russia (Napoleon's initial favorite) in the contest to provide a wife for Napoleon. This was part of Metternich's strategy to protect Austria by temporary cooperation and alliance with France, even if it meant sacrificing an arch-duchess. The designated bride was Marie-Louise, Francis's daughter; she could not only provide Napoleon with an heir, but coursing through her veins was Habsburg blood, than which there was no nobler in Europe (fig. 1.7). The couple were married by proxy—and amid mixed public opinion—in Vienna on March 11, 1810, after which the hapless bride went to Paris to meet her husband for the first time and have a splendiferous state wedding. The upstart Corsican could now qualify for any social register. The efficacy of Metternich's diplomacy in this matter was confirmed the next year, when a son was born to the French imperial couple. His name is revealing— Napoleon Franz Karl Joseph—all names of emperors—and he was immediately made King of Rome.

If 1811 brought joy to Napoleon and Marie-Louise, it was not so for Austria. Contrary to Metternich's hopes, Napoleon did not lighten Austria's obligations under the Treaty of Schönbrunn, and the state went bankrupt, reducing the value of its currency by 80 percent. Life in Vienna was hard.

The Defeat of Napoleon

The next year, however, Napoleon made his fateful decision to extend his empire north and east. Assembling an army of 600,000, he headed toward Moscow in June 1812, arriving there in mid-September. Forced to double back, the army came under the attack of the Russian winter. With temperatures plummeting to minus 30 degrees Fahrenheit, the once-proud French army was reduced to about 30,000. Napoleon, getting wind of potential problems at home, acted as he had with his defeated Egyptian army—he left the troops to get home on their own. But his star was falling. Wellington's victory at Vittoria on June 21, 1812, in northern Spain, dealt the seemingly invincible Bonaparte a devastating blow, leading to an invasion of France and the Battle of Leipzig on October 16–19, by which time Austria had abandoned its alliance with France (figs. 1.8, 1.9).

All these events were celebrated in music, of course. Beethoven's "Wellington's Victory" gave the composer the biggest popular success of his life and led to a revival of

1.7 Johann Nepomuk Hoechle, pictorial chronicler of many important events and activities occurring in Schubert's Vienna, here shows the Archduchess Marie-Louise being handed over on March 16, 1810, to be the bride of Napoleon. The marriage was one of the important early diplomatic triumphs of the foreign minister Metternich and is indicative of his influence over the bride's father, the emperor. [HM]

Fidelio. Franz Schubert celebrated the victory at Leipzig with a song for voice and strings, "Auf den Sieg der Deutschen" (On the Victory of the Germans), D.81; he may even have written the rather artless text himself.[10]

Finally, in March 1814, the allies—Prussia, Russia, Austria, and Great Britain—joined forces effectively. Heading for Paris, Emperor Francis and his cohorts forced Napoleon's abdication on April 6 and triumphantly entered the city on April 15, the news of which caused Schubert to write a song for bass, "Die Befreier Europas in Paris" (The Liberators of Europe in Paris), D.104. Napoleon was sent off to Elba in exile.

In a matter of weeks, at Tsar Alexander's suggestion and in recognition of Austria's sacrifices over the previous two decades and Metternich's shrewd diplomacy, representatives of the various nations involved in the wars, as well as various interest groups, assembled in Vienna to redraw the map of Europe. This work—and the play for which the Congress was equally famous—was interrupted with the terrifying news that on March 1, Napoleon had returned to fight again. And so yet another alliance—the seventh since 1792—was formed to crush "the enemy and disturber of the peace of the world."

1.8 Title page of Ludwig van Beethoven's piano arrangement of his sensational success, "Wellington's Victory or the Battle of Vittoria," which commemorated in music the decisive defeat of Napoleon on July 21, 1813. (See also fig. 3.2.) Beethoven's popularity was so enhanced by this piece that it helped bring about in 1814 a revival of his previously unsuccessful opera *Leonore* in a revised (now standard) version entitled *Fidelio,* which Schubert heard. [WSLb]

In June 1815, after the famous "hundred days," it was finally over. Napoleon's last battle was at Waterloo, where he was defeated by English, Dutch, and Prussian forces. Six days later, Napoleon abdicated again in Paris and was sent this time to St. Helena, where he died in 1821 at the age of fifty-one.

"TRANQUILITY AND ORDER": AUSTRIA AFTER NAPOLEON

Wars dominated the first half of the reign of Francis I, and he and Metternich were determined that life in Vienna and the Austrian Empire would be less tumultuous in the future. *Ruhe und Ordung*—Tranquility and Order—was to become the motto of the second half of Francis's reign. It was necessary, felt Metternich, that revolution never show its demonic head again, and this required, first of all, a division of post-Napoleonic Europe that would keep all of the major powers in check. Austria gained some land, of course—it got more than its share of Italy back, for example—but Met-

1.9 The Battle of Leipzig, which was waged October 16–19, 1813, was one of the major events of the Napoleonic wars. It was depicted in music (see fig. 5.2) as well as in such pictures as this Artaria engraving by Carl Rahl after J. A. Klein. Artaria also published some of Schubert's compositions during the later part of the composer's life. [HM]

ternich felt that a balance of power in Europe would benefit Austria more than any temporary territorial gain. For this reason also the partitioning of the map took little account of local feelings but considered rather only what was acceptable to the rulers. It has been said that the resulting division of Europe was reasonable, but not necessarily just or moral.

Second, Metternich strove to persuade all parties to suppress revolution immediately so as to preserve the new status quo permanently. Although all governments of the time were repressive to some degree, Austria became known especially for the ubiquity and omnipresence of its police surveillance and its swift and hard suppression of an uprising that occurred in northern Italy. Thus was Ruhe und Ordung achieved in the Habsburg territories, at least until 1848.

The Austrian Police State

It may come as a surprise to many readers that the aged Haydn as well as Beethoven and Schubert lived in a Vienna cloaked in an atmosphere of political repression and suspicion, so a few words of explanation are in order.

The simplified account of the French Revolutionary and Napoleonic wars that I have offered really is but one side of the coin. Parallel with a war against the French armies was a war against ideas, many but not all of which were associated with France. For Francis, that war seems to have been the more important; he gave away his daughter to the enemy general, but he never tolerated free expression of opinion, at least on political matters. His course had been set early, by the restoration of the notorious Count Pergen to a position of power in the police ministry; Pergen had previously worked for Joseph II but had fallen out of favor with the more open-minded Leopold (fig. 1.10). Writing to the provincial governors in 1793, he had declared war against dangerous ideas: "In the present conditions when the cult of liberty has gained so much ground and all monarchical governments face great unrest, the ordinary arrangements for peace and security are inadequate. Every government must secretly set all forces in motion for the good of the state, in order to convert those in error and to wipe out through effective countermeasures all dangerous impressions that might have been instilled in any class of subjects by sneaking agitators."[11]

In 1794 a two-year resident of Vienna reported: "Several important persons have been arrested here. It is said that a revolution was to break out—but I believe that as long as the Austrian has some dark beer and little sausages he will not revolt. Briefly, the gates to the suburbs must be closed at ten in the evening. The soldiers have loaded muskets. One doesn't dare raise his voice here, otherwise the police find lodging for you."[12] The writer was Beethoven, and he was probably referring to the arrests, in July 1794, of members of the prorevolution political clubs. Determined to stop the spread of such groups, Francis restored the death penalty (abolished for civilians by Joseph II), and, after a public trial, the so-called Jacobins were executed, thereby sending the intended message to the populace.

But the police were not limiting their surveillance to genuine revolutionaries. From this point throughout the reign of Francis—he died in 1835—the police were everywhere in search of the slightest hint of unorthodox ideas among the citizenry. The state's suspicion of intellectuals was such that many citizens who desired careers in government avoided higher education in the belief that it would work against their obtaining a position. The emperor was finally informed in March 1810 that the heavy censorship was actually working *against* the welfare of the state. Francis, paternalistically devoted to his subjects yet ever wary of free thought and speech, ordered a loosening of the censorship, as long as naïve hearts and heads were protected "from the poisonous aspirations of self-seeking seducers, and from the dangerous illusions of crazed heads."[13] Of course, the conditions to be met for this—spelled out in detail—effectively kept the censorship in force.

In the Vienna of Francis I, then, it was dangerous to speak and write freely. Although the police did not employ systematic brutality and terror in enforcing the censorship or suppressing ideas, the possibility of arrest, the loss of one's job, and other deterrents made that unnecessary. Franz Schubert was himself arrested in 1820 with one of his former schoolmates, the poet Johann Senn. Senn, the principal target of the po-

1.10 Johann Anton Graf Pergen, pictured in this engraving by Johann Ernst Mansfeld as a Knight of the Order of St. Stephen, symbolized the omnipresence of the Austrian police before and during the reign of Francis I as well as the unrelenting search for evidence of republican tendencies among the Viennese population. [ÖNb:Ba]

lice in this instance, was suspected of being a member of a student organization like those recently outlawed as part of a general crackdown throughout Germany on universities and student freedoms as a result of the assassination of the reactionary poet and dramatist August Kotzebue. He was also accused—along with Schubert and some others present—of insulting the police. Senn was imprisoned and exiled; Schubert seems not to have been further punished, but apparently he was traumatized by this unpleasant contact with the dark forces of the new Austrian chief of police, Sedlnitzky, who was extremely concerned about "political fanaticism" (fig. 1.11). It has even been proposed that this incident may explain a significant change in his handwriting at this time.[14] In any event, Schubert never saw his friend again.

Less traumatic perhaps but nonetheless sobering was the fate of a rather funny organization called the *Ludlamshöhle,* the name of an inn near the Stefansplatz that took its name from a play performed in Vienna in 1817. Its one hundred or so members, led by Ignaz Castelli, were all connected to the arts and included some luminaries, imperial court composer Antonio Salieri for one. Fully one fourth of the membership was connected with Schubert in some way. The Ludlamites banned talk of politics or business, took parodistic nicknames, published witty and sarcastic newspapers, made fun of those junior members unable to pass the test to senior status, sang songs, and held their meetings openly. (Moreover, the rules stipulated that the society's head had to be the stupidest member of all.) Perhaps only in Vienna could such an organization flourish, but flourish it did from 1818 to 1826. From Schubert's friend Eduard von Bauernfeld, a member, we know that the composer wanted to join. But before this happened someone reported that secret and dangerous things were going on—something having to do with political and religious connections to India—so one foggy night the

1.11 Joseph Graf Sedlnitzky was Johann Anton Pergen's successor as head of the Austrian police. It was in 1820, during his term of office, that Schubert was arrested with his student activist friend Johann Senn, who was confined and then exiled. [Önb:Ba]

police descended upon the club's meeting place and confiscated all the papers, music, smoking pipes, and the like. This was followed by searches of the houses of members who were writers, notably Franz Grillparzer, a dramatist and an official of the Treasury Archives, who was interrogated, had his papers taken, and was confined to his house for a day (see fig. 10.14). When the police investigation turned up nothing, the organization was permitted to continue (as long as a representative of the police was present), but that was the end of the Ludlamshöhle.[15]

Schubert may not have made it into the Ludlamshöhle, but in 1817–18 he had been a member of a younger group of Viennese and German intellectuals who created something similar: the *Unsinns-Gesellschaft* (*Gesellschaft:* society; *Unsinn:* folly or absurdity). The activities of this long-unknown group, recently discovered by Rita Steblin, included the staging of original plays and publication of members-only newsletters that spoofed contemporary politics as well as scientific discoveries, drama, and literature.[16] Like the Ludlamshöhle, members had code names; Schubert's was Don Giovanni of the Keyboard. The membership included not only some persons long known to have been Schubert's friends (such as the Kupelwieser brothers) but also some not heretofore associated with him, like the artist Johann Nepomuk Hoechle. Schubert's involvement in the secret Unsinns-Gesellschaft is the newest piece of evidence pointing to his dissatisfaction with the political system under which he lived. That the Unsinns-Gesellschaft could have existed at all may prove that the clamp on free expression was not as tight as it would be after the assassination of Kotzebue. However, Schubert's later friend Eduard Bauernfeld was to write in *Aus Alt-und Neu-Wien* (1872) that in these same years some of his favorite teachers were being persecuted for their unduly liberal political or religious views and that ultimately the oppression of the Austrian system caused him to flee into the ideal world of poetry.

Biedermeier Pleasures

Generally speaking, then, Viennese society was forced to turn inward, to home and family, to innocent and nonpolitical activities. The result was a quiet, bourgeois culture that later was looked back on ironically as the good old days *(die gute alte Zeit)* and was denominated by the term *Biedermeier,* which at first carried negative connotations.[17] The middle-class ideals of this culture manifested themselves in everything from furniture to social dance. The family, perhaps in imitation of the truly exemplary first family of Austria, became even more central and, if possible, more patriarchal than before, and this was represented and idealized in the paintings and plays of the period (fig. 1.12; see Chapter 8).

Although recently there have been challenges to the traditional notion that noble patronage was sharply declining, it is clear that *Hausmusik* (music for/in the home), for example, was clearly in the ascendance. The *Vaterländische Blätter,* a publication founded to stir up patriotic pride before Austria attacked Napoleon, reported that "here on any given evening there is hardly a family that does not derive entertainment

1.12 This painting by Leopold Fertbauer not only shows how Francis I projected himself as the head of the imperial family in Austria's patriarchal society but also suggests how the ideals of domestic happiness and simple comforts associated with the Biedermeier lifestyle came to influence even the highest levels of Habsburg society. All these values are reflected also in plates 11 and 12. [HM]

from a string quartet or a piano sonata."[18] This applied as well to the imperial family, for Francis continued the family tradition of amateur music making.

Gatherings of family and friends probably represented the most common venue for music making during Francis's reign. Higher on the social scale were private salons—formerly often political but now more simply cultural, in the broad sense of the term. Traditionally, salons had been hosted by women, and this continued after the Congress. From the perspective of brain power, undoubtedly the premiere Viennese salon was that of Caroline Pichler, who surrounded herself with the leading poets, playwrights, and thinkers of the day (see fig. 2.8). From 1808 on, for example, the likes of Friedrich and Dorothea Schlegel, Clemens Brentano, Heinrich Josef and Matthäus von Collin, Grillparzer, Theodor Körner, and Joseph Hormayr were found there; previously Mozart and Haydn had visited, and Schubert also made Pichler's acquaintance.

If one wished to leave the house, there were public concerts (see Chapter 5) and especially the theater (see Chapter 10), which was experiencing one of its greatest moments in European history. In late 1810, the two privileged imperial theaters, the Burgtheater (then located just opposite the imperial palace or Hofburg) and the Kärntnertortheater became more specialized: the Burgtheater became the official venue for German spoken drama, the Kärntnertortheater the principle place for opera and ballet. That is why Schubert intended his operas for the latter. The Theater an der Wien, a private theater just outside of the inner city, offered everything—spoken theater, opera, ballet, magic plays; during the Congress of Vienna Mozart's *Die Zauberflöte (The Magic Flute)* had its 340th performance there. Then, for sheer fun, there were two suburban theaters that specialized in homegrown Viennese popular comedies. In connection with the Theater in der Leopoldstadt, especially, the actor and playwright Ferdinand Raimund must be mentioned, although he got his start at the other theater, in the Josefstadt.

Schubert's Friends and the Schubertiade

Franz Schubert's adult life mirrors this early Biedermeier culture. Among the great composers of the so-called first Viennese School—of which Mozart, Haydn, and Beethoven are considered the primary members—Schubert was the only true Viennese.[19] Moreover, Schubert lived among the middle classes, without the kind of regular intercourse with the highest echelons of Viennese nobility that Beethoven enjoyed. It may justly be said that the two composers, who met only once, lived at the same time in different Viennas.

If Beethoven could have his *Eroica* symphony first performed in a grand palace of the Lobkowitz family, Schubert in the main offered songs as well as piano and chamber music to a somewhat less distinguished but perhaps more appreciative audience in the intimate company of the *Schubertiade,* a term used to describe informal musical gatherings centered around the composer (fig. 1.13). On these occasions his friends and admirers (and strangers, too) came to hear his music, dance to his improvised accompaniments, and otherwise entertain themselves with those innocuous pleasures permitted in Biedermeier Vienna (see also fig. 11.6).

1.13 Ferdinand Georg Waldmüller's pencil drawing of 1827, showing Schubert at the piano with his singing friends Josephine Fröhlich and Johann Michael Vogl, documents the kind of informal
music making that was characteristic not only of Schubert's circle
but of Viennese Biedermeier society in general. (For Waldmüller,
see Chapter 8 and plates 12 and 18.) [GSA]

It is worthwhile to reflect briefly on Schubert's companions, for there is sometimes
a tendency to regard them as a group of bright but flighty bourgeoisie of little consequence. We tend to forget that most of them were just starting their careers, too. But
if we consider a bit just who these people were, we learn something about Schubert
the person and his position in the Viennese cultural scene—which, because of the
awesome, overshadowing presence of Beethoven, has tended to be underestimated.

There were many literary figures around Schubert during his short maturity. Johann
Mayrhofer, ten years older, was the oldest; Schubert set to music more of his poems
(forty-seven) than anyone else except Goethe and Schiller, and they collaborated on

two operas (see fig. 9.4). Another poet was the libertine Franz von Schober, librettist of Schubert's opera *Alfonso and Estrella* (see fig. 10.17).[20] Although Schober failed as a dramatist, he went on to lead a very interesting life, among other things serving as Franz Liszt's secretary in 1841–47. A third literary figure was Eduard von Bauernfeld (see fig. 10.16). Born in 1802 and living until 1890, this physicist's son was in his mid-twenties when a member of the Schubert circle. Thereafter he went on to become an important playwright of the Viennese theater, so important that he was made a corresponding member of the Imperial Academy of Sciences in 1848, an honorary citizen of Vienna, and a doctor *honoris causa* of the University of Vienna. Finally, we should mention Schubert's school chum Johann Senn, who tangled with the secret police, and Theodor Körner, poet of the War of Liberation and a member of the Pichler salon circle, who provided poetry for some early songs; both were individuals of real talent.

There were painters, too. The most important was Moritz von Schwind, a brilliant draughtsman, whose later, idealized depictions of Schubert's social life have come down to us (fig. 1.14). Schwind went on to become an important late romantic painter, whose

1.14 Moritz von Schwind, younger than Schubert by seven years and a close and true friend from 1823, sketched dancing (presumably by the Schubertians) outside the manor house in Atzenbrugg. The estate was owned by the great monastery of Klosterneuberg but was in the charge of relatives of Schubert's friend Franz von Schober, whose magnetic (but not always benign) character pulled both Schubert and Schwind into his circle. Many years later Schwind used the sketch as the basis for a finished picture. [GSA]

1.15 Excursions into the countryside were popular among the Viennese. Leopold Kupelwieser's watercolor of an outing of the Schubertians from Atzenbrugg to Aumühl in 1820 shows Schubert and Kupelwieser walking behind the wagon, Josef von Spaun's hat being crushed by the wagon wheel, and Franz von Schober, whose relatives had invited the group to Atzenbrugg, standing on the rear running board to the right. [HM]

work has been characterized as having a certain unaffected, happy, fairy-tale quality. His eminence was sufficient to win him the contract for the murals at the Vienna Opera House in the 1860s, and it was in this period that he did his famous *Schubert Evening at Spaun's,* which combines the audiences of different Schubertiades into one.

Another important painter, and a friend from 1815, was Leopold Kupelwieser (figs. 1.15, 1.16). He is one of those who recorded the fun-filled excursions of one Schubert circle to Atzenbrugg. Later he was especially noted for his religious paintings and his portraits. When he went to Rome in 1823, he kept up a lively correspondence with Schubert and Schwind. He later decorated the University Church of Vienna, and in 1836 he was named Professor at the Academy of Fine Arts.

There were no composers among Schubert's close friends, but there were professional musicians, notably the eminent singer Johann Michael Vogl, who had been a member of the Viennese court opera for about twenty years when he met Schubert; despite the age difference, the two became fast friends, often performing and traveling together.

The most important figure in contact with the Schubert circle, however, was Franz Grillparzer, considered the greatest of all Austrian dramatists (fig. 1.17). It is he who wrote the much discussed epitaph on Schubert's tomb:

The art of music here entombed a rich possession but even fairer hopes.

1.16 Leopold Kupelwieser portrayed here in 1821 the Schubertians at Atzenbrugg in a game of cha-
rades depicting the "fall" of "Rheinfall" by reference to the sin of Adam and Eve. In the center,
between "Adam" and "Eve," is Schober ("the Serpent"), clinging to Kupelwieser ("the Tree of
Knowledge"). Among those trying to decipher the scene are Schubert (at the piano) and Schubert's
oldest and most loyal friend, Joseph von Spaun (seated second from right). [HM]

It probably reflects Grillparzer's sincere belief that Schubert had not yet achieved the
full greatness as a composer of which he was capable.

The popular literature, perhaps unduly influenced by the extant pictorial evidence,
often describes the activities of the Schubert circle as lighthearted and sociable. To be
sure, they included reading evenings, occasions for listening to Schubert's compositions
and for dancing to his improvisations, party games, and outings into the countryside.
But there was also a more serious side to things, especially in the early 1820s, when
Schubert and Schober, together with Schwind, Kupelwieser, Bauernfeld, and the later-
estranged Franz von Bruchmann shared a common nonconformist attitude toward life
and art similar to, and somewhat inspired by, German romantics of a generation earlier.[21] They felt alienated by what they considered the hypocritical norms of the world
in which they lived, and they looked to art as the salvation of society. In reaction to the
rigorously hierarchical, controlled environment imposed by Metternich's "Austrian
system," the Schubertians therefore practiced and celebrated egalitarianism and intel-

lectual honesty among themselves, tolerated sexual behavior of their comrades that was condemned or at least discouraged by society, and committed themselves genuinely to the free creation of art that was frankly critiqued within the circle.[22] Their noncon-formity did not take outwardly brazen forms of political or religious opposition, but perhaps Schubert gave vent to that which could not be expressed explicitly by deleting the phrase "[I believe] in one, holy, catholic church" from the Credo of all six of his masses; by his friendship with the singer Katherine von Lászny, who, according to Schwind, flaunted her promiscuity in the face of societal conventions; and by his in-tensive work setting Bauernfeld's opera libretto *Der Graf von Gleichen* to music, even though a performance was precluded because the story, involving a bigamous mar-riage, could not get by the censor. More positively, his likely belief in a deistic or pan-theistic God (also shared by early romantics) found expression in his song "Die All-macht," wherein Schubert pours out a paean of praise from the depths of his soul.[23]

Along with the police and censorship, another essential element of the state influ-enced Viennese life during the reign of Francis I: the bureaucracy. Bureaucrats had a status quite different from that of U.S. government employees today; in Schubert's Vi-enna, a title and a uniform to go with it guaranteed the owner at least some respect, not to mention a regular paycheck. Many of Schubert's friends, in fact, were part of this byzantine system, with its infinite gradations and complex protocol. Josef von Spaun, Schubert's most faithful friend, who introduced him to Mayrhofer, Schober, Kupelwieser, and Körner, among others, worked in the Vienna lottery office. Mayrhofer was high in the censor's office and apparently, despite his liberal leanings,

1.17 Thugut Heinrich's 1826 chalk drawing of Schubert's acquaintance Franz Grillparzer shows the dramatist after his reputation had become established but before his full artistic maturity. In the next two years he provided the text for a substantial piece programmed on Schubert's one benefit concert, composed the eulogy delivered at Beethoven's funeral by Schubert's actor friend Heinrich Anschütz (see fig. 10.13), and wrote the epitaph that graces Schubert's tombstone. [HM]

took his work very seriously; this may have set up a conflict of values that contributed to his suicide. Grillparzer, too, chafing at the bit in his desire for real political freedom, nonetheless had a respectable position as head of the Imperial Treasury Archives. Kupelwieser, as professor at the Academy of Fine Arts, was a kind of bureaucrat, too, for Metternich himself was the true head of the Academy.

Although bureaucrats had to be extremely careful to avoid political activity, their work may not always have been demanding. Grillparzer writes in his diary: "Came to the office about noon . . . found nothing to do . . . so I read Thucydides." But when he becomes director of the Treasury Archives things get rougher: "This work will put me under the ground, especially because it robs me of the valuable morning hours."[24]

As we have seen, Viennese culture in the Age of Francis I was at first buffeted by war, then repressed in some but by no means all of its parts. The inhabitants of the Habsburg lands had little or no say in the policies of their government, yet they loved their dedicated if humorless "Franzl" (an affectionate nickname for Francis) and feared Metternich. It was in this environment, shaped not a little by the Napoleonic wars of his youth, that Franz Schubert created a musical legacy of exceptional beauty in his tragically short life. We can be grateful, moreover, that, as was true of Mozart, Schubert's fecundity was extraordinary. In 1814, with Napoleon down but not yet out, the seventeen-year-old Schubert began "an outburst of composition without parallel in the history of music," turning out his first completed opera and mass and the masterful "Gretchen am Spinnrade."[25] The next year nearly two hundred works flowed from his pen, including four operas and thirty songs on Goethe, among them "Erlkönig." When it was all over only twelve years later, there were a thousand works for Otto Erich Deutsch to catalog. Schubert's achievement in thirty-one years can be best appreciated when compared with Beethoven at age thirty-one: both had completed a dozen or so major sonatas, but Schubert had eight symphonies to Beethoven's one, eight operas to none for Beethoven, six hundred songs to Beethoven's three dozen. And although the inner feeling of Schubert's music is different from Beethoven's, the quality is just as extraordinary.

It makes one reflect, with Grillparzer, on what might have been.

NOTES

1. Ernst Hilmar, *Franz Schubert in His Time,* translated by Reinhard G. Pauly (Portland, Ore.: Amadeus, 1985), 13; and O. Biba and Ernst Hilmar, *Franz Schubert und seine Zeit,* exhibition catalog (Vienna: Universal Edition, 1978), 60, citing J. Rossi, *Denkbuch für Fürst und Vaterland* (1814).

2. Quoted in Walter C. Langsam, *Francis the Good: The Education of an Emperor, 1768–92* (New York: Macmillan, 1949), 12.

3. F. A. von Schönholz, *Traditionen zur Charakteristik Österreichs, seines Staats- und Volkslebens unter Franz I* (Leipzig, 1844), 2: 320, quoted by Langsam, *Francis the Good,* 154.

4. The play is Ferdinand Raimund's *Der Diamant des Geisterkönigs.* See Dorothy Prohaska,

Raimund and Vienna: A Critical Study of Raimund's Plays in Their Viennese Setting (Cambridge: Cambridge University Press, 1970), 68.

5. *Empire* is *Reich* in German; to later generations the Holy Roman Empire was sometimes known as the "first" Reich, as opposed to Bismarck's second and Hitler's pretentious third.

6. Heinrich Füger was director of the Academy of Fine Arts in Vienna and the most important figure in Austrian painting of his generation.

7. Letter to Gentz of January 21, 1806. Quoted in Enno Kraehe, *Metternich's German Policy,* vol. 1, *The Contest with Napoleon, 1799–1814* (Princeton: Princeton University Press, 1963), 43. Friedrich Gentz was a political theorist and propagandist who became Metternich's secretary in 1812 and was later also the secretary of the Congress of Vienna. He translated Edmund Burke's polemical and antirevolutionary *Reflections on the Revolution in France* into German.

8. Clemens Wenzel Lothar, Furst von Metternich, *Memoirs of Prince Metternich,* 5 vols. (1880; rpt. New York: H. Fertig, 1970), 2: 208.

9. March 18, 1809. Quoted in Langsam, *The Napoleonic Wars and German Nationalism in Austria* (New York: Columbia University Press; London: P. S. King & Son, Ltd., 1930), 31, n. 3.

10. Schubert's works are conventionally identified by "D" numbers, referring to the chronological catalog of his works by Otto Erich Deutsch, *Franz Schubert: Thematisches Verzeichnis seiner Werke in chronologischer Folge* (Basel: Bärenreiter Verlag, 1978).

11. Quoted in Donald E. Emerson, *Metternich and the Political Police: Security and Subversion in the Habsburg Monarchy, 1815–1830* (The Hague: Martinus Nijhoff, 1968), 22–23. The phrase *cult of liberty* is the translation of *Freiheitsschwindel* suggested by Paul P. Bernard, *From the Enlightenment to the Police State: The Public Life of Johann Anton Pergen* (Urbana: University of Illinois Press, 1991), 191.

12. Beethoven to his publisher Simrock, August 2, 1794. Printed in *Ludwig van Beethoven: Letters,* coll., trans., and ed. Emily Anderson (New York: St. Martin's, 1961), 1: 18.

13. Emerson, *Metternich and the Political Police,* 29.

14. Hilmar, *Franz Schubert in His Time,* 21.

15. This account of the Ludlamshöhle is based on L. Porhansl, "Auf Schuberts Spuren in der 'Ludlamshöhle,'" *Schubert durch die Brille* 7 (June 1991), 52–78.

16. Rita Steblin in *Babette und Terese Kunz: Neue Forschungen zum Freundeskreis um Franz Schubert und Leopold Kupelwieser* (Vienna: Pasqualatihaus, 1996). For an English-language summary of the matter, see the *Österreichische Zeitschrift* 52 (1997), 52–61.

17. In his 1872 memoir *Aus Alt- und Neu-Wien,* in *Gesammelte Schriften von Bauernfeld* 12 (Vienna: Wilhelm Braumüller, 1873), vol. 4, Schubert's close friend Eduard von Bauernfeld speaks sarcastically of the "so-called good old days," dominated by the "so-called Austrian system of Metternich." See also the section "Die gute alte Zeit" in Rupert Feuchtmüller and Wilhelm Mrazek, *Biedermeier in Österreich* (Vienna: Forum Verlag, 1963), 67–70.

[Like many style terms used by historians and critics of the arts (among them *medieval* and *baroque*), *Biedermeier* was used initially in a pejorative fashion and was applied to a cultural mileau that was already over. For a native speaker of German, in fact, *Biedermeier* has inherently comical implications, being a compound of *bieder* (honest, upright, but also ordinary) and *Meier* (a family name so common as to lend itself to deprecation and jokes).

The introduction of the word bears this out. A collection of poems, riddles, games, and the like for all occasions written by a village schoolmaster came into the hands of the country physician Adolf Kussmaul, who found in the materials a potential for hilarious parody. From 1855 to 1875,

Kussmaul, using the pseudonym Gottlieb Biedermaier, published in Munich's *Fliegende Blätter* his own comical reworkings of the serious efforts of the schoolmaster. Kussmaul was inspired by earlier publication in the same organ of poetry with titles like "Biedermanns Abendgemütlichkeit" ("Everyman's Evening Pleasures") and "Bummelmaiers Klage" (*Bummel* implies laziness, sloth, carelessness; *Klage* means complaint or lament). In 1869 yet another collection of such poetry appeared under the title *Biedermaiers Liedenkunst* (roughly translatable as *The Common Man's Art of Song*).

From such precedents *Biedermeier* took on implications of lack of sophistication, of provincialism, of simple if well-meaning thinking, of pleasure taken in ordinary creature comforts. Only in the twentieth century did the term lose most of its pejorative connotations as a style-critical concept in the arts, being used to denote the culture, in all its facets, of German-speaking Europe (especially southern Germany and Austria) between the close of the Congress of Vienna (1815) and the Revolution of 1848.

See Gerbert Frodl, *Wiener Malerei der Biedermeierzeit* (Rosenheim: Rosenheimer Verlagshaus, 1987), 1–6, 264 n. 1. Ed.]

18. Quoted in Feuchtmüller and Mrazek, *Biedermeier in Österreich,* 46.

19. For the origin of this term, see Chapter 4. Although Schubert was not originally counted among the composers of the Viennese classical school, it is not unreasonable to include him.

20. Schubert's operas are discussed in Chapter 10.

21. The material in this paragraph is largely drawn from John M. Gingerich's 1996 Yale University dissertation, "Schubert's Beethoven Project: The Chamber Music, 1824–1828," 1–75. But see also Ilija Dürhammer, "Schlegel, Schelling und Schubert: Romantische Beziehungen und Bezüge in Schuberts Freundeskreis, *Schubert durch die Brille* 16 (1996), 59–93.

22. Schober was a dissolute womanizer and Schubert, although his death was hastened by syphilis, may have engaged in homosexual activity. Schubert's sexuality has been at the center of a stormy musicological controversy for some years, beginning with Maynard Solomon's "Franz Schubert and the Peacocks of Benvenuto Cellini," *Nineteenth-Century Music* 12 (1989), 193–206. The first issue of volume 17 (1993) of the same journal was devoted to various opinions on the matter. Gingerich, "Schubert's Beethoven Project," 51–60, finds credible the hypothesis that Schubert was homosexual but does not see this as determining the character and outlook of Schubert's circle.

23. Maurice J. E. Brown, *Schubert: A Critical Biography* (New York: Da Capo, 1958, 1978), 255.

24. Quoted in Waltraud Heindl, *Gehorsame Rebellen: Bürokratie und Beamte in Österreich, 1780 bis 1848* (Vienna: Böhlau Verlag, 1991), 229.

25. Quotation from Maurice J. E. Brown, "Franz Schubert," *The New Grove Dictionary of Music and Musicians,* ed. Stanley J. Sadie (London: Macmillan, 1980), 16: 754.

FOR FURTHER READING

There is no good, comprehensive biography of Francis I. However, Walter C. Langsam's venerable *Francis the Good: The Education of an Emperor, 1768–92* (New York: Macmillan, 1949) is to be recommended for information on the future monarch's education, personality, and character. A basic but excellent survey especially of eighteenth-century Austria and the background leading to the reign of Francis is Ernst Wangermann, *The Austrian Achievement* (London: Thames and Hudson, 1973). A well-illustrated and fairly comprehensive treatment of Napoleon intended for the general reader is *The Horizon Book of The Age of Napoleon* (New York: American Heritage, 1963). For German and Austrian politics and diplomacy see Hajo Holborn, *A History of Modern Germany, 1648–1840,* vol. 2 (New York: Alfred A. Knopf, 1964), especially chapters 10 and 12; Robert A. Kann, *A History of the Habsburg Empire, 1526–1918* (Berkeley: University of California Press, 1974), chapters 5 and 6; Enno Kraehe, *Metternich's German Policy,* vol. 1, *The Contest with Napoleon, 1799–1814* (Princeton: Princeton University Press, 1963); and James J. Sheehan, *German History, 1770–1866* (Oxford: Clarendon, 1989), especially 235–50, 274–91, and 393–410. On the concept of Austria itself see Erich Zöllner, *Der Österreichbegriff: Formen und Wandlungen in der Geschichte* (Vienna: Verlag für Geschichte und Politik, 1988). Legal aspects of the dissolution of the Holy Roman Empire and attempts at reviving it at the Congress of Vienna are found in Walter Gero, *Der Zusammenbruch des Heiligen Römischen Reichs deutscher Nation und die Problematik seiner Restauration in den Jahren 1814–15* (Heidelberg: C. F. Müller Juristischer Verlag, 1980).

Studies of the police and of censorship include Paul P. Bernard, *From the Enlightenment to the Police State: The Public Life of Johann Anton Pergen* (Urbana: University of Illinois Press, 1991), especially 180–229 (for the early part of Francis's reign); Donald E. Emerson, *Metternich and the Political Police: Security and Subversion in the Habsburg Monarchy, 1815–1830* (The Hague: Martinus Nijhoff, 1968); Edda Ziegler, *Literarische Zensur in Deutschland, 1819–48* (Munich: C. Hanser, 1983); Dieter Breuer, *Geschichte der literarischen Zensur in Deutschland* (Heidelberg: Quelle und Meyer, 1982), 98–113 and 145–70; and Walter Obermaier, "Schubert und die Zensur," *Schubert-Kongreß Wien, 1978,* ed. Otto Brusatti (Graz: Akademische Druck- und Verlagsanstalt, 1979), 117–25.

Basic accounts of Schubert's life include Maurice J. E. Brown, *Schubert: A Critical Biography* (New York: Macmillan, 1958; rpt. New York: Da Capo, 1977) and his article on the composer, with an annotated list of Schubert's works by Eric Sams, in *The New Grove Dictionary of Music and Musicians,* ed. Stanley J. Sadie (London: Macmillan, 1980), 16: 752–811, republished in revised form as *The New Grove Schubert* (New York: W. W. Norton, 1983). The most recent biographical study is Elizabeth Norman McKay, *Franz Schubert: A Biography* (New York: Oxford University Press, 1996). An insightful if brief assessment of Schubert is Ernst Hilmar, *Franz Schubert in His Time,* trans. Reinhard Pauly (Portland, Ore.: Amadeus, 1985). Documentary evidence about the composer and his circle is collected in Otto Erich Deutsch, *The Schubert Reader,* trans. Eric Blom (New York: W. W. Norton, 1947); this will eventually be superseded by a four-volume collection being published in German as *Franz Schubert: Dokumente, 1817–1830,* ed. Till Gerrit Waidelich with Renate Hilmer-Voit and Andreas Mayer (Tutzing: Hans Schneider, 1993–). The journal of the International Franz Schubert-Institut in Vienna, *Schubert durch die Brille,* has a wide range of information on Schubert research and current events concerning the composer. A short account of Schubert's life within the Viennese context, written for the general reader, is Charles Osborne, *Schubert and His Vienna* (New York: Knopf, 1985).

For some other sources of additional reading, see the notes above.

· 2 ·

People, Class Structure, and Society

WALTRAUD HEINDL

The thirty-one years of Schubert's life fall within a crucial period in Austrian history, a time of crisis and of transition from the old European social system to the modern world. It was a time of changes and catastrophes—political, social, economic, and cultural, as well as psychological.

In 1797, when Schubert was born, Emperor Francis II was in the fifth year of his reign. Francis's uncle Joseph II, who had reshaped the Empire through his reforms, had been dead for seven years, Haydn was sixty-five years of age and Salieri forty-seven, and Beethoven—who had been living in Vienna for five years already—was twenty-seven. Two central figures of the Viennese theater, Franz Grillparzer and Ferdinand Raimund, were six and seven, respectively.

But it was not the best of times into which to be born. Seventeen days before Schubert entered the world on January 31, Austria had lost battles against Napoleon near Castiglione, Bassano, Arcole, and Rivoli in Italy. France had been at war with the twenty-nine-year-old Emperor Francis for five years—in fact, since the very beginning of his reign—and under the shock of the French Revolution the Emperor had begun to oppress the peoples of his multinational realm. Low spirits permeated Austrian society.

The first seventeen years of Schubert's life were thus marked by wars and their bitter consequences: general anxiety, poverty, and a confined cultural life. The great enemy was Napoleon: consul in 1799, emperor in 1804, conqueror, and finally prisoner on St. Helena after 1815. The last thirteen years of Schubert's life were marked by the dread words *police, secret police,* and *censorship.* Nevertheless, the new era into which Schubert was born was shaped by three important political factors that affected the Habsburg Empire and Austria up to our own time. These were, first, the political, social, ecclesiastical, and educational reforms of Joseph II, motivated by the ideals of the Enlightenment and the continuing influence of the "Josephinian spirit" on the further development of the Habsburg Empire—the so-called "Revolution from above"; second, the French Revolution and its influence in the Habsburg Empire—the "revolution from below"; and, third, the measures of the authoritarian Austrian state against all revolutionary movements, and even against cultural change itself.

SOCIAL DEVELOPMENT

Two other factors influenced Habsburg society and daily life in the late eighteenth century: the industrial revolution, which began to have its visible impact on all social strata, and the growth of population in the Habsburg Empire (fig. 2.1). From the fif-

2.1 In this view by Jakob Hyrtl after Joseph Fischer, looking north toward Vienna, the steeple of St. Stephen's Cathedral is visible in the distance, center; closer and to the left, but outside the city walls, is the Karlskirche (see also fig. 7.4), seen from the rear. Between the viewer and the city proper can be seen some of the suburbs in which much growth of population and industry was taking place. [NYPL:Print]

teenth to the seventeenth centuries, Europe had been characterized by a more or less stagnant population. But in the eighteenth century, governments began to take measures to stimulate growth in the populace. According to Enlightenment thought, the "happiness" of the state was dependent on the number of its inhabitants.

In Austria the enlightened Emperor Joseph II took distinctive measures in this regard (see plate 4). The state set conditions that made getting married difficult or impossible for many. For example, members of the lower classes, such as servants and journeymen who lived in the households of their masters, were not allowed to marry.[1] One consequence of these "marriage inhibitions" was a high rate of illegitimacy. Other consequences were widespread child abandonment and infanticide.

Joseph II improved the rights of illegitimate children. In Vienna and other cities he founded "birth houses," where a woman could give birth without being forced to tell her name. The children could then be adopted by others or be placed in foundling homes. Special workhouses were created to teach those children. Child labor was common, although a law promulgated in the 1770s forbade it before the age of nine.

In the city of Vienna the population grew slowly in spite of all new measures (fig. 2.2). (There was much greater growth in the suburbs, where a number of factories, forbidden in the city, were built.) In fact, not until the first half of the nineteenth century was there a real population boom. Nevertheless, Vienna at the end of the eighteenth century was the only true capital in the so-called "German-speaking" countries; after London and Paris, it was the most important capital in Europe.[2]

Thus, just at the time when Schubert was born, the city and the suburbs changed their faces. Although the suburbs grew much faster than the city because of industrialization and urbanization, Vienna developed into a true city, characterized by administrative buildings, shops, stores, and banking houses. Because numerous houses with apartments were converted into commercial or governmental use, rents soared, and only those people with a high income could afford to live in the city; many families, even those from the well-off middle classes, had to move to the suburbs, some of which consequently became overcrowded. Schubert himself was born at the Himmelpfortgrund, and he spent his childhood in Liechtental, one of those overpopulated suburbs, where craftsmen and low-ranking officials lived. Among them was Schubert's father, Franz Theodor, the headmaster of a primary school.

The infrastructure of the old city of Vienna was adequate, but roads in the suburbs were unpaved, and after a day of rain they turned into a mudbath; even neighbors were barely able to visit each other. It is easy to understand why everybody dreamed of living in the city. That privilege was enjoyed by the feudal aristocracy from all parts of the monarchy, who were accustomed to spending the winter in their palaces near the Hofburg, the imperial palace. Indeed, still standing from this period are the palaces of the Esterhazy, Kinsky, Wilczek, Palffy, Pallavicini, Lobkowitz, Fries, and other noble families. In summer the nobility lived on their estates. Very well-off middle-class people, such as some merchants, and high-ranking officials also could afford an apartment

2.2 House and silk factory of Joseph Göbel in the suburb of Schottenfeld. The growth of factories, and of the silk industry in particular, was one of the eighteenth- and early-nineteenth-century developments linked to the growth of the suburbs around Vienna in which Schubert lived at various times during his life. The family of Schubert's one-time love Theresa Grob (ca. 1815) was in the silk-weaving business at a modest level, but some entrepreneurs, such as Rudolf von Arthaber (see plate 11), accumulated considerable wealth. [HM]

or a house in the city. Members of the lower classes lived in the city, too, but these were often servants staying in the palaces and homes of the rich.

Socially, the Habsburg Empire comprised four "estates" or official classes that were generally represented in the Diets (parliaments) of the provinces of the Empire. These estates consisted of the landowning aristocracy, the Catholic high clergy (bishops and abbots of the greater monasteries), the burghers of the cities and market-towns, and free peasants.[3]

The peasants were officially represented only in the Diet of the Tyrol; in the other kingdoms and provinces of the monarchy the peasants were not free. Even after serfdom had been abolished by Joseph II in 1781, the peasants were bound to the landowners on whose land they lived. In Hungary and in Galicia, the numerous petty nobility (up to 10 percent of the population) formed a sort of free peasantry with full political rights. Only the first estate, the aristocratic families, could send a woman into the Diet, and then only if no man was left in the family. The first estate was socially predominant as well. Until the middle of the eighteenth century, aristocrats not only possessed money and real estate but had great influence in politics and society.

As a consequence of industrialization and urbanization in the second half of the eighteenth century, society became more dynamic. Middle-class people were given the chance to make a career and to become rich. Eventually a wealthy bourgeoisie arose out of the middle class, one of the great social changes taking place between the mid-eighteenth and the mid-nineteenth century. Thus at the time of Schubert's birth we find in Vienna a well-established middle class that had become a force for societal reform. Joseph II had promoted the development of this social stratum, and he used its members to break the power of the aristocracy and to further his reforms. Not surprisingly, members of the aristocracy were generally opposed to Joseph's program.

One of Joseph's best instruments in encouraging the middle classes was the university (fig. 2.3). He made university studies obligatory for a number of professions, especially for the bureaucracy. As a consequence, middle-class intellectuals became more and more influential in state and society. The role that the Third Estate had played in the French Revolution strengthened the self-confidence of the Austrian middle class. But because educated middle-class people were frequently suspected of being "Jacobins" in sympathy with the French Revolution, they were often put under surveillance or their voices suppressed. One of the victims was Schubert's friend Johann Senn, who was arrested and then exiled. In the years of peace following the Congress of Vienna, police and censorship were the most powerful institutions. Nevertheless, the numbers of bourgeoisie, intellectuals, and burghers continued to increase, all the while menacing the old social order through their expanding influence in society and the economy.

In the old system a peasant's son invariably lived and died a peasant, but the new system with its variety of professions allowed for a career, mostly by means of university studies. Most parents could not afford to send a child to the university, but there were a number of scholarships and fellowships offered by the state, the universities, and the Church. Thus, the sons of poor people could become officials or teachers or could gain wealth by founding manufactories and factories. Still, because of the relative lack

2.3 The University of Vienna, seen here as it looked in 1790, was the training ground for the civil service bureaucracy of the Austrian government. The Stadtkonvikt, where Schubert resided 1808–13 as a scholarship student, was just across the street. Colored engraving by Carl Schütz. [HM]

of capital in Austria, it was much more difficult to become a rich businessman than to make a career through university studies.

The steady growth of the middle class could not be stopped, much less reversed. Francis I tried to integrate the "nouveaux riches"—high-ranking bureaucrats, intellectuals, doctors, and so on—into the old system by ennobling them. From the beginning of the nineteenth century to 1918, an extraordinary number of ennoblements took place. But this practice did not lead to a breakdown of long-standing social barriers: the ennobled doctors, bureaucrats, and writers, with their minor aristocratic titles such as "Edler von" or "Ritter von," were rarely raised to the ranks of "Freiherr" or, in Hungary, "Baron." With their small incomes they remained middle class and were in no way socially accepted by the old and high aristocracy. Without feudal property and without belonging to one of the old families, these newly ennobled burghers were unable to marry into the old aristocratic families. Then as now, intermarriage was a measure of the degree to which people were accepted socially.

EVERYDAY LIFE IN VIENNA

In part because the educated middle class and the high aristocracy did not mix, Schubert's Vienna was far different socially from Beethoven's. This was quite unlike France, where bourgeois artists and intellectuals were invited to aristocratic salons. Thus Schubert's circle, although it changed over time, did not include high aristocrats, for Schubert's friends were mainly artists or officials coming from the middle class and minor nobility. Although Schubert spent the summers from 1818 to 1824 in Hungary at the Esterhazy residence in Zseliz, we can hardly assume that his hosts treated him as a social equal. Schubert's modesty and shyness made the problem worse. (Beethoven's more relaxed relationship with his aristocratic patrons was atypical for his time.)

The aristocratic lifestyle remained the ideal, and those middle-class people who could afford it imitated the aristocracy. Yet 1815 marks a change in the lifestyle of the middle classes. In the absolutist state that controlled and kept watch on Austrian society after the Congress of Vienna, the middle classes turned their attention to their homes and culture. Public life was impossible, and it had become dangerous to discuss public affairs even in a private salon. Schubert himself learned firsthand about the danger of association with political activists like his friend Johann Senn—he was arrested along with Senn, though not incarcerated. Such conditions caused people to consider their homes and their families the center of their lives. The new middle-class home was designed to create an embracing, comfortable *(gemütlich)* ambiance. Furnishings were meant to express this *Gemütlichkeit* as much as possible.

Three styles of furniture were popular: Empire, Biedermeier, and historicist (figs. 2.4, 2.5). The aristocracy preferred the Empire style, developed in the French Empire, with monumental furniture and clear classic forms designed for the large rooms they enjoyed. The middle classes after 1815 preferred the Biedermeier style, characterized

2.4 Biedermeier furniture was characterized by simple, graceful, curving lines as opposed to, on the one hand, the straight-line neoclassicism and antique motifs of Empire furniture and, on the other, the baroque or gothic elements found in the historicist style. [MAK]

by small houses, small rooms, small furniture, and clear, unornamented, if often curvaceous forms, such as those produced by the Danhauser Furniture Factory. On the other hand, the avant-garde bought furniture in the historicist style, which united elements of Gothic, Renaissance, and other historical traditions.

This development of the much simpler Biedermeier style had a practical origin: there was not enough space left in the city to build big houses. Vienna was small and its roads twisted; besides, it was too expensive for the middle classes. But the style had a more ideological basis as well: the bourgeois often detested the Empire style because they considered it French and aristocratic. For all the quiet admiration they had for the aristocracy and its way of life, the new middle classes also harbored hostile feelings toward the aristocrats—as well as toward such members of the lower classes as workers and servants. From the beginning, therefore, the new bourgeoisie set up defenses against all outsiders. Their new way of life eventually became dominant and in some respects began even to influence the aristocratic lifestyle, thus reversing the flow of ideas and taste that had prevailed up to the end of the eighteenth century.

Eventually, middle-class life changed profoundly, especially after 1815. New professions, which were proliferating because of industrialization and urbanization, required a different organization of the day. The old European society had been characterized by country life. The rural way of life—of both peasants and aristocrats—dominated European society, without separation of home and work and without occupational division of labor. Men and women toiled side by side within the household domain but

2.5 This painting of the Emperor Francis I hard at work in his simply furnished study shows a clock in historicist style over the window. [MAK]

were responsible for different things: men for the woods, the fields, the cattle; women for the house, the cooking, the clothes, and other domestic duties. This type of pre-industrial collaboration influenced the relationship between men and women. They needed each other for survival: marriage was more a necessity than a question of love.

But now urbanization, industrialization, and the growth of the middle classes in and around the city caused a new division of labor. This meant that men of the middle class left the house every morning to work in factories, offices, or stores, and women stayed at home, responsible for the house and the children. Middle-class men became the breadwinners, and women were left without an income of their own.

This new kind of work necessitated a new concept of marriage for the middle classes, with love becoming a moral condition for it. The middle class began to consider marriage for money, possession, rank, or preservation of the family as immoral. The association of romantic love with marriage thus became predominant among the bourgeoisie, and in time it was even adopted by some of the aristocracy. This shift is even perceivable in opera: in *The Marriage of Figaro* by Mozart (1786), the marriage between the Count Almaviva and Countess Rosina is based not on love but on convenience, though the Countess comes to demand love and fidelity from her unfaithful husband. The middle classes of Schubert's day despised this older model of marriage as aristocratic, French, and frivolous. Thus, about twenty years after *Figaro,* Beethoven's *Fidelio* praises matrimonial love, an ideal clearly in the ascendancy.

Love was equated with sentiment, and this sentimentality is evident in the arts of the time—for example, in the poetry of Schubert's songs. But in spite of the extraordinary idealization of the genders, the reality was that many middle-class men could not afford to marry a woman of a good house because their salaries were too small. The law required the vast majority of them to live as bachelors until the age of forty, as we can see in Schubert's circle. Little wonder that prostitution was a thriving trade in Vienna. Divorce was forbidden to Catholics, for whom the Church intended marriage to be a lifetime commitment. Yet an average marriage lasted only five years because many people died young of such diseases as typhoid fever, cholera, and syphilis. (Schubert, who died at thirty-one, suffered from syphilis, then a terminal disease.) Many women died in childbirth, and men often married two or three times.

The division of labor and the different responsibilities of the genders had serious consequences for the domestic roles of men, women, and children. Work organized for many people at one place, as in the factories and offices, necessitated new habits, such as punctuality and diligence. Order gained importance, and time began to be associated with money. Middle-class women were banished from the workplace and effectively confined to their homes. The roles of the sexes were more clearly defined and further polarized. In the philosophical and literary publications of the time, men are described as strong, public-minded, brave, and rational, whereas women are depicted as weak, pleasant, beautiful, emotional, or home-centered. The small family became the focus of their lives, while for the men—required to work outside the house in a sometimes hostile world—family and home became the symbol of peace, tranquility, privacy, and male authority. Biedermeier paintings reflect the importance of this domestic ideal. Children became increasingly important in the lives of their parents, and family paintings depicting that reality became the fashion (see Chapter 8). This importance may seem obvious to us today, but it has been maintained that childhood began to be treated as a cultural phenomenon and as a special period in life only in the seventeenth and eighteenth centuries.[4]

Compulsory education had been introduced only in 1774, and it did not yet embrace all social strata by the time Schubert was born, more than twenty years later (fig. 2.6). Many parents refused to send their children to school: most of the peasants and workers depended on the contribution of their children's work to family income. But ambitious lower-class and lower-middle-class people furthered their children's chances of social mobility either by giving them an education at home or sending them to school. Franz Theodor Schubert, for example, not only sent his sons to school but helped arrange for his musically precocious son Franz to take the examination for the imperial chapel choir, which guaranteed its members an excellent education. Franz

2.6 In Biedermeier Austria, education often took place in the home, as Joseph Danhauser indicates in this scene of a grandmother teaching her grandson. Danhauser was not only an important Biedermeier painter (see also plate 13) but also a skilled violinist and undoubtedly an acquaintance of Schubert's. After his father's death in 1830, he took over for a few years the family's style-setting furniture factory. [HM]

Theodor himself—coming from a poor country family in Silesia—had seized the opportunity to become a schoolteacher, a new profession.

Daily life of Viennese middle-class families in Schubert's time was characterized by many new social developments. New working hours influenced family life, from which men were now normally excluded during the day except for lunchtime. Lunch was typically an extensive meal, especially for middle-class families in Vienna, with up to four dishes being served. Evenings were reserved for the family and for such pleasant diversions as theater, opera, concerts, or social visits.

The Viennese bourgeoisie by Schubert's time had developed their special culture of everyday life, which was less refined than the aristocracy's but reflected the shifting social norms. Their innocuous forms of communication sought to circumvent the curiosity of the secret police. People now avoided political topics, but they read together (Schubert participated for years in a reading circle), discussed such cultural topics as books, theater, and the opera, or indulged in gossip.

One of the most characteristic middle- and upper-class cultural institutions of the early nineteenth century was the salon. This elevated form of social gathering provided a forum for lively human interaction. It brought together people of common intellectual qualities and interests to discuss leading topics of the day.

The concept of the salon originated in Renaissance Italy. Italian aristocratic ladies who were married to French citizens brought the fashion to seventeenth-century France. The first famous example was the salon of Mme de Rambouillet in the Palais Rambouillet in Paris.

The French salon was primarily a literary circle, open to educated men and women of different social levels: thus it was both a microcosm of polite society and a venue for female emancipation. The French slogan *savoir et savoir vivre* (to be informed and know how to live) nicely characterizes the tone of the French salon. The widely varied subjects discussed both educated and amused the members of the salon; topics embraced philosophy, literature, science, theater, opera, and music, among other things. Yet the focus of the salon was conversation itself: speaking and discussing became an art of its own, demonstrating the elegant way of life and *bon goût* (good taste). *Jeu d'esprit* (wit) and *préciosité* (mannered sophistication) became the valued characteristics of language. An extraordinary enthusiasm for elegant speech developed. Salons took place in the palaces and townhouses in the city, not the castles in the country, so the salon became a feature of urban life. A salon took place regularly once or twice a week, always on the same day and at the same time; no special invitations were sent out. One would imagine that French aristocratic salons, whose guests were unrestricted by working hours, would favor daytime sessions. In fact, though, most houses opened the salon in the evenings, after dinner.

The heart of every salon was the *salonière*, the lady of the house and hostess, who defined the cultural and social direction of her salon. Thus, the salon was the place where women could demonstrate their intellectual abilities. In the eighteenth century, salons became the stage for female culture. Mme d'Epinay, Mme du Deffands, Mme Geoffrin, Julie de Lespinasse, Mme de Lambert, Mme de Tencin, Mme Necker (mother of Mme de Staël) were famous salonières in Paris. Eroticism and love also found a place in the salon.

A number of salons flourished in Vienna in the last two decades of the eighteenth century. These had characteristics that to some extent distinguished them from the Paris salons. We learn from diaries and memoirs, for example, that music—performed, not merely discussed—played an important role from very beginning in these Viennese salons (see also Chapter 5). Salons of the middle class also became important for intellectual and cultural development in Vienna. Finally, some of the salons were hosted by men.

The salon of Gottfried van Swieten vividly exemplifies these Viennese traits. Van

Swieten was a Freiherr, but he came from a newly ennobled family. His father, Gerard, was the physician of Empress Maria Theresa (r. 1740–80), who granted him a title. Gottfried himself was a high state official, responsible for education under Joseph II, and was one of the most educated and learned men of his time. A poet, he wrote the words for Josef Haydn's *The Creation*. Mozart was invited to van Swieten's salon, and his music was played there, often for the first time. Another striking example is the salon of Hofrat Franz (later von) Greiner, also a state official and a man of middle-class background. He was married to a highly educated woman, the former reader *(Vorleserin)* for Maria Theresa, who spoke Latin and several other languages and who had a scholarly interest in all religions, as well as in geography and astronomy.

The Greiner family members were devoted to the ideas of Enlightenment; they were liberal in thinking (and, it seems, libertine in their erotic lifestyle). They were suspected, as were all liberals, of having favored the Jacobins. Viennese poets and authors attended the Greiner salon, as did Haydn and, presumably, Mozart. Music was evidently important in the salon of Franz Greiner; his daughter Caroline Pichler offers a vivid picture in her famous memoirs of the salon of her parents in the final decades of the eighteenth century. In the salon of Johann Georg Obermayer, secretary of Prince Kaunitz, music played an important role as well.[5] The lady of the house, who was a good musician and singer, entertained her elegant guests by playing the piano and singing.

The most famous salon in Vienna was that of Fanny Arnstein, a Jewish Prussian woman from the rich Itzig family of Berlin (fig. 2.7). The home of her father, who was the banker of Friedrich II of Prussia, was the center of social life in Berlin; his friends were artists, scientists, and philosophers, and Fanny herself was influenced by Moses Mendelssohn, the Jewish philosopher of the Enlightenment. In 1776 she married the Viennese banker Nathan Adam (later Baron) Arnstein, and in 1780 she founded her salon. Her invitations were very fashionable and elegant, with balls and midnight *soupées* for four hundred. Fanny could afford to give wonderful orchestra concerts, and she emulated an aristocratic lifestyle. Her salon was enormously successful in spite of the tradition of anti-Semitism, which was officially abated in 1781, when Joseph II issued his Edict of Toleration. But even when Jews were tolerated by law, they remained social outsiders. Fanny Arnstein's was the first Jewish salon in Vienna. Its cosmopolitan milieu drew philosophers and artists not only from Austria but from all of Europe.

Fanny Arnstein eventually closed her elegant salon for private reasons, but she founded a second salon in 1803. The new salon, quite different from the first, was a true literary salon. Colloquys no longer took place within the shining framework of great social events: now literary discussion and a simple style were predominant. This salon, which was again soon a magnet for Viennese as well as other European intellectuals, became politically important, too: during the Napoleonic wars, Fanny Arnstein developed an intense Austrian patriotism, and her salon came to be known as a center of conspiracy against Napoleon even after the emperor's daughter Marie Louise

2.7 Fanny Arnstein, originally from Berlin, was one of the
great Viennese *salonières* of the late eighteenth and early
nineteenth centuries. Her social position, which reached its
ıcme at the time of the Congress of Vienna, also reflects the
relatively emancipated state of Viennese Jews from the time
of Joseph II. During 1781–82 Mozart lived for eight months
in the Arnstein residence. Engraving by Vincenz Kininger
after P. Guérin. [HM]

was married to the French leader. Understandably, the court did not sanction the Arnstein salon's reservations about this politically expedient decision (see Chapter 1), but
after Napoleon's defeat the salon enjoyed even greater renown. Moreover, it became a
special attraction of the Congress in Vienna, luring not only such statesmen as the
Duke of Wellington, the Prussians Wilhelm von Humboldt and Chancellor Prince
Hardenberg, and the Austrian State Chancellor Metternich but also intellectuals and
writers like Mme de Staël, Friedrich Gentz, and the brothers August Wilhelm and
Friedrich Schlegel. When Fanny Arnstein died in 1818, the salon rapidly declined in
importance.

Fanny Arnstein's salon was the last distinguished salon associated with the elegant
style of eighteenth-century Vienna even though Fanny herself, though ennobled, in

no way belonged to the aristocracy. The salon represented an exception: the old aristocracy and the new intellectual bourgeoisie actually mixed there, probably because of the richness and intellectual distinction of Fanny's gatherings. The Biedermeier salons, beginning after 1815, were generally different in style. Although the salon of Fanny's daughter Henriette Eskeles continued the tradition of her mother, the more modest salon of the Greiners' daughter Caroline Pichler was more typical for Vienna of that era.

Biedermeier salons were typically bourgeois in comparison to their forerunners. The old salon had been open and liberal, and manners were aristocratically elegant even in the absence of riches. Often, middle-class people like Greiner did not have enough money to offer their guests more than tea or water with sugar, which was then quite expensive. Yet in gesture and behavior salon attendees had imitated the aristocracy. The hostesses were highly educated. They spoke several languages, were interested in politics, arts, and science; they were, for their time, emancipated women. Social life was open and cosmopolitan, without national prejudices. Yet after 1815 most of these qualities began to change. The salon gradually lost its reputation as a socially open meeting place. The Baroness de Montet, who lived in Vienna from 1810 to 1824 as the wife of a French diplomat, wrote in her memoirs: "There is a deep gap between the first and the second society—and this some day could lead to a terrible revolution. The arrogance of the aristocracy does not allow the poet and the genius to pass over the border that separates him from the first society."[6]

In fact, intellectual society in Vienna became split. The first society and the second—the old aristocratic families and the intellectuals, artists, officials, and officers of the middle class, some of them newly ennobled—were separated socially in Vienna by tradition and met only in the middle-class salon: the aristocracy hardly ever opened their salons to middle-class intellectuals.

After 1815 the separation became even more strict and the nationalistic element in the salon even more pronounced. The languages spoken in the salons reflected this: whereas in the former Viennese salon French was generally used as the language of conversation and Italian and Spanish were occasionally employed, the members of the new salon changed to German, not because they did not know French but because a new patriotism made them despise French. In deportment, the style of the new salon was typically bourgeois; grandness was excoriated as aristocratic. The new ideal of social behavior was to be jovial and comfortable, not elegant; discussion tended toward harmony rather than intellectual provocation. The world outside was politically dangerous, so private life, home, and social contacts were restricted to a circle of true and reliable friends. It was a time of the forming of great friendships, such as those that Schubert ardently enjoyed within his own harmonious group.

As can be imagined, the hospitality dispensed in middle-class salons was modest, despite generally improved economic conditions after 1815, but this necessary modesty became a fashionable virtue to display. Even Emperor Francis wore a tailcoat, the garment of the middle class (Joseph II had worn a uniform), and his wife, the empress, presented the image of a good housewife. So the Habsburg Court at that time demonstrated an odd bourgeois pose.

In the salon of Mme Caroline Pichler we find a model of the post-1815 Viennese form (fig. 2.8). It was called the literary tea table, another reflection of the prevailing modesty. Caroline's parents, the Greiners, had conducted a highly attractive salon from the 1770s to the 1790s. Caroline had grown up in a liberal atmosphere, educated according to the doctrines of the Enlightenment and presumably indoctrinated by her emancipated mother. She had married Andreas Pichler, an undistinguished state official working in her father's office. He had a modest income, much of which he spent on his indebted brother. Caroline took up writing novels, especially historical novels, and in so doing became one of Vienna's first famous female writers. The literati Franz Grillparzer, Adalbert Stifter, the Schlegel brothers August Wilhelm and Friedrich, and Ludwig Tieck were among the guests at Caroline Pichler's tea societies, along with the German statesman and scholar Wilhelm von Humboldt and Schubert himself. Guests read new literature and discussed theater, books, and music. Politics, philosophy, and the great questions of the world were mostly excluded in favor of the arts, if we are to trust Caroline's memoirs. But can we really? Perhaps she carefully avoided mention of those topics because she wanted her memoirs, written between 1837 and 1841, to pass the censor.

When we compare Caroline Pichler's salon to that of Fanny Arnstein, we see that what had really changed was deportment: good manners but not elegance, harmony instead of provocation had become the rule. Another obvious change in the post-1815 Biedermeier world was the Viennese philosophy of life. Caroline Pichler's parents had been liberal cosmopolitans; but Caroline was an Austrian patriot who demonstrated an abundance of enthusiasm for the dynasty, for Emperor Francis, and for Metternich. Her mother had been an emancipated woman, yet Caroline emphasizes on every page of her book that she was a loving wife and mother. Caroline's recommendation for marriage—love of and fidelity and obedience to the husband—was an expression of what then was considered modern thinking.

Over time Caroline Pichler's salon became a little old-fashioned, as other kinds of social intercourse claimed the term *modern*. Schubert's now-renowned circle represented a new social dynamic that included not only literary and intellectual discussions but lighthearted pursuits as well: walking in the countryside, visiting inns, and coming together for dancing and making music. What clearly did not change, what indeed became stronger, was the need for communication. We can perhaps recognize in this strong need for interaction a middle-class substitute for a public or political role. The philosopher Friedrich Daniel Ernst Schleiermacher analyzed the salon as an expression of early bourgeois demands for a changing society. To him, the salon represented a kind of utopia. Although Biedermeier social intercourse was more concerned with personal matters than with social theories, it still provided a forum for

2.8 Caroline Pichler, diarist, writer, and well-known
Viennese hostess, was captured in oils by Carl von Sales
in 1818. One of Pichler's friends, Anton Prokesch,
wrote in 1822 of being at Pichler's for lunch; according
to his account, Schubert played (and probably also sang)
several of his songs with a wealth of feeling and
profundity. [HM]

open discourse, tolerance, and stimulating debate. In this respect, the salon had some
democratic functions.

The years after 1815 are characterized by the introduction of new amusements in
Viennese social life. After the sufferings brought on by the wars, there was a mood of
renewal. At the same time, a reactionary political trend caused disappointment as well.
The new conviction that utopian hopes had no bearing on reality and that everyone
was dependent on the political power of the state induced passive resignation. Therefore, because one's fate would be decided by the authorities and not by the individual,
people avoided getting entangled in public affairs and learned to bear fate patiently.
Adalbert Stifter's *Nachsommer,* though published in 1857, expresses the escapism prevailing in Biedermeier society, in which innocuous amusement took on an exaggerated importance.

Not surprisingly, therefore, the Biedermeier period is known for its eating and drinking habits. (Schubert's nickname *Schwammerl* may reflect his own capacities in this regard.[7]) All those different kinds of soups, the carefully spiced meat dishes, the cakes (mostly of Bohemian origin) surprised foreign visitors to Vienna. They were stupefied by the Viennese capacity for food and drink. Hand in hand with the new amusements went the joys of discovering nature, of walking in the Prater park and the Viennese woods. The wanderings of Schubert's circle reflect this fashion. Of course, there were numerous inns and coffee shops to be found in the Prater and the woods, offering refreshments and repose that made hiking still more agreeable. Biedermeier was also an era of balls, of an increasing number of concerts and theater presentations. Diaries and memoirs of the time convey the impression that average middle-class people engaged in extensive social intercourse, going to the theater or to concerts virtually every day. Yet there was an underlying fear of life. As we can see from Grillparzer's dramas (see Chapter 10), a sunny cheerfulness lined by melancholy and the longing for death were twin sentiments propelling Biedermeier society.

In the framework of this desperate need for meaningful social intercourse, music played an extraordinarily important role (fig. 2.9; see Chapter 5). Barrel organmen on the street popularized opera melodies, as did the harpists in the inns and the musicians in the coffeehouses, the favored rendezvous of artists and intellectuals. Ordinary cafes were transformed into concert cafes. In the 1820s Josef Lanner and Johann Strauss began to play in the coffeehouses in the Prater and elsewhere. "House music" *(Hausmusik)*—the practice of playing music at home, in groups or singly—became a central factor in home life and afforded great pleasure to a society dependent largely on itself for entertainment. Piano playing and singing were essential parts of the education of middle-class daughters and sons. It was commonplace for people not only to listen to music but to play themselves, a tradition still partly alive in Vienna today in spite of radio, recordings, and television.

Schubert's life, his education, and the musical life of the society to which he belonged reflect quite typically the social, economic, and cultural patterns of early-nineteenth-century Vienna. It is rewarding to speculate why Viennese culture, and especially music, could flourish in a city that had hardly recovered from the Napoleonic wars. Vienna was economically poor (only between 1818 and the beginning of the thirties was the economy relatively strong) and socially divided. The status of the Viennese middle class could not be compared with that of its counterparts in England, France, and even some of the German states. The life of the bourgeoisie was regulated and watched over by the representatives of the reactionary state, the police, and the censors, while moral standards were dictated by the Catholic Church.

That music should flourish in such an atmosphere might seem astonishing, but some conditions of the time actually fostered its cultivation. In a multicultural city, where so many languages were spoken—German, French, Spanish, Italian, and Latin

2.9 A distinctive characteristic of salons in Vienna was the important role played by music, as indicated by this painting by Nikolaus Moreau (c. 1830) of a musical soirée at the home of Baron Denis Eskeles. (See also fig. 5.12.) [HM]

among both aristocracy and the middle classes, as well as Hungarian, Czech, Slovak, Ukrainian, Serbian, Croatian, Slovene, and Greek, some of which were spoken by the lower classes only—music may have seemed to some inhabitants the easiest form of communication. Moreover, the censorship controlling cultural production may have unwittingly promoted music because revolutionary motifs in music are less easy to discern than in literature. "Does the censor know what you think while you are composing?" asked Grillparzer in Beethoven's guestbook. His question is significant. Music was less dangerous for the artist than were writing and painting. Then, too, the Habsburgs themselves were very interested in music. Emperors Leopold I, Joseph I, and Charles VI were composers themselves, and creating music was given prominence at the Court of Vienna. The aristocrats imitated their emperors, and the developing bourgeoisie imitated the aristocracy. But members of the middle classes economized by playing the instruments themselves instead of hiring an orchestra.

Of course, there are always much more complicated reasons for special and unusual creativity in a given area than can be addressed in so short a cultural survey. Clearly, though, music was a potent social force that alleviated the often oppressive atmosphere of early-nineteenth-century Vienna. Indeed, music and Biedermeier Vienna are inseparable.

NOTES

1. Discussions of the marriage laws in relation to Schubert are found in Rita Steblin, "Franz Schubert und das Ehe-Consens Gesetz von 1815," *Schubert durch die Brille* 9 (1992), 32–42, and "The Peacock's Tale: Schubert's Sexuality Reconsidered," *Nineteenth-Century Music* 17 (Summer 1993), 6–8, as well as Maynard Solomon, "Schubert: Some Consequences of Nostalgia," *Nineteenth-Century Music* 17 (Summer 1993), 36.

2. Vienna's population grew only about 5,000 from an estimated 54,000 between 1754 and 1797; the increase in the suburbs, however, was much greater, from 121,000 to 169,000. Strong growth in the city in the early nineteenth century is inferable from the fact that the number of houses doubled between 1765 and 1821. See Maren Seliger and Karl Ucakar, *Wien: Politische Geschichte, 1740–1934* (Vienna: Jugend und Volk, 1985), 1: 165.

3. In Vienna itself the population about 1825 was distributed as follows: nobility, 8.5 percent; middle classes (bureaucrats, artists, craftsmen, and businessmen), 26.1 percent; servants, 45.9 percent; and members of households without a profession, 19.5 percent; ibid., 1: 166.

4. Philippe Ariès, *Centuries of Childhood: A Social History of Family Life* (New York: Knopf, 1970).

5. Wenzel Anton, Prince of Kaunitz, was one of the most important ministers of the eighteenth-century Habsburg rulers Maria Theresa, Joseph II, and Leopold II. He rose to the positions of foreign minister and chancellor.

6. Quoted in Waltraud Heindl, *Gehorsame Rebellen* (Vienna: Böhlau Verlag, 1991), 244.

7. Otto Erich Deutsch, *The Schubert Reader*, trans. Eric Blom (New York: W. W. Norton, 1947), 297, thinks that Schubert's nickname *Schwammerl* alluded to his figure and hence translates it Tubby. The word presumably derives from the German *Schwamm*, which can mean mushroom (hence implying a certain bulginess) but also means sponge, suggesting also a possible relation to Schubert's capacity to consume food and drink. *Schwammerl* is also the title of a romanticized novel about Schubert by R. H. Bartsch (Leipzig, 1912). [Ed.]

FOR FURTHER READING

Several exhibition catalogs provide much pictorial as well as factual information about the social environment of Schubert's time, among them *Biedermeiers Glück und Ende: Die gestörte Idylle, 1815–1848,* ed. H. Ottomayer with Ulrike Laufer (Munich: Hugendubel, 1987), and *Bürgersinn und Aufbegehren: Biedermeier und Vormärz in Wien, 1815–1848* (Vienna: Historisches Museum der Stadt Wien, 1987). On education, see Helmut Engelbrecht, *Geschichte des österreichischen Bildungswesens: Erziehung und Unterricht auf dem Bodem Österreichs,* vol. 3, *Von der frühen Aufklärung bis zum Vormärz* (Vienna: Österreichischer Bundesverlag, 1984). On gender roles, see also Karin Hausen, "Die Polarisierung der 'Geschlechtscharaktere': Eine Spiegelung der Dissoziation von Erwerbs- und Familienleben," in Werner Conze, ed., *Sozialgeschichte der Familie in der Neuzeit Europas: Neue Forschung* (Stuttgart: Klett Verlag, 1976), 363–93. On salons, see Hilde Spiel, *Fanny von Arnstein: A Daughter of the Enlightenment, 1758–1818,* trans. Christine Shuttleworth (Oxford: Berg, 1991); and Waltraud Heindl, "Caroline Pichler oder der bürgerliche Fortschritt: Lebensideale und Lebensrealität von österreichischen Beamtenfrauen," *Von Bürgern und ihren Frauen,* ed. Margret Friedrich and Peter Urbanitsch (Vienna: Böhlau, 1996), 197–207; and Waltraud Heindl, "Amt und Salon: Bildung und Kultur der Wiener Beamten zur Zeit Mozarts," *Genie und Alltag: Bürgerliche Stadtkultur zur Mozartzeit,* ed. Gunda Barth-Scalmani, Brigitte Mazohl-Wallnig, and Ernst Wangermann (Salzburg: O. Müller, 1994), 221–42.

The Congress of Vienna

ENNO KRAEHE

The most spectacular political event during the lifetime of Franz Schubert was the great international congress that convened in his Vienna from September 1814 to June 1815 to cope with the wreckage left by the Napoleonic wars (fig. 3.1). Peace conferences, to be sure, were nothing new, but this one was different—in scope, in duration, in the epochal consequences of its decisions, and in the indelible impression it has left on our imaginations. To this day the Congress of Vienna calls to mind the brilliant picture of Europe's high aristocracy at play. The lavish balls, the canters through the Prater, the sleigh ride to Schönbrunn, the hunts in the Vienna Woods, the coquetry of beautiful women, the chamber music at Prince Razumovsky's, the heaping buffets and sumptuous banquets—these are all permanently enshrined in the legend of Vienna (figs. 3.2, 3.3; see plate 5). The Viennese like to think of every summit conference there today, every gathering to deal with arms control or human rights, as but another revival of the mother of all congresses.

Host to this extravaganza were the Austrian emperor, Francis I, himself a dour and frugal man devoted to hard work, and the vivacious empress, Maria Ludovica; their master of ceremonies, so to speak, was the handsome and gifted foreign minister, Clemens von Metternich, now aged forty-one and just recently elevated in rank from

3.1 This famous 1819 engraving of the Congress of Vienna by Jean Godefroy, based on an 1815 drawing by Jean-Baptiste Isabey, shows the principal participants in the agreement to reshape Europe after
the Napoleonic wars. Among those seated are Hardenberg of Prussia, far left and looking at England's Castlereagh, third from left, with France's Talleyrand second from the right; those standing
include the British commander Wellington, far left; Austria's Metternich, sixth from left; Prussia's
Wilhelm von Humboldt, second from right; and Austria's Friedrich Gentz, third from right.
Standing in the rear as a pair just right of center are General Lord Stewart of England and
Prince Rasumofsky of Russia. [HM]

count to prince (fig. 3.4). Never before had so many crowned heads assembled in one
place: two emperors (Francis and the dashing Alexander I of Russia), four kings (of
Prussia, Bavaria, Württemberg, and Denmark), and dozens of dukes and grand dukes,
mainly from Italy and Germany. Virtually all the absent sovereigns were represented by
envoys, usually the best their services could produce, like the able papal delegate Cardinal Ercole Consalvi or the veteran French plenipotentiary Prince Charles Talleyrand, who had mediated with the allies the return of Louis XVIII to the throne.
With them came countless advisers and ministers, smart guard units camping in the
suburbs, and large staffs of secretaries, copyists, technical experts, and security agents.

There were as well hundreds of petitioners with assorted grievances to redress,
property to recover, or causes to press: abolition of the slave trade, for example, or uniform copyright conventions, concordats with the papacy, regulation of river navigation, civil rights for the Jews of Bremen and Hamburg, and, perhaps most important,
the restoration of autonomy to hundreds of noble families whose estates had been absorbed with Napoleon's aid by the greater sovereigns of Germany. The famous Baron

3.2 A musical highlight during the Congress of Vienna was a benefit concert for Beethoven in the large Redouten Hall. The program
featured the Symphony No. 7, the celebratory cantata "Der glorre-
iche Augenblick" ("The Glorious Moment"), and the orchestral
arrangement of "Wellington's Victory." (See also fig. 1.8.) [WSLb]

Karl Heinrich vom Stein, once minister-president of Prussia, spearheaded this group,
and Metternich's own father, Franz Georg, was an active lobbyist. Even the field mar-
shals of France had lawyers on the scene to see that they kept the rich endowments
that Napoleon had bestowed on them in foreign lands.

Among the embassy personnel were such notables as the budding folklorist Jakob
Grimm of Hesse-Cassel and the lesser-known Johann Michael Gries of Hamburg,
who translated the Spanish dramatist Calderón in his spare time. Metternich himself
employed the eminent romantic writers Friedrich Schlegel (see fig. 4.2) and Adam
Müller in his publicity service to spread the Austrian view of things in the newspapers
of north Germany, and his principal aide was the conservative publicist Friedrich
Gentz, who, as keeper of the minutes, came to be known as "the secretary of Europe."
The second plenipotentiary for Prussia was the great scholar Wilhelm von Humboldt,
the pioneer of the science of comparative philology and the founder of the University
of Berlin. The intellectuals did not set the tone of the Congress, perhaps, but they remind us that all was not frivolity, amorous trysts, and all-night dancing. Gentz, for one,
often despaired of his boss for putting trysts with "that damnable woman," the duchess

3.3 Vestiges of medieval chivalric rituals lasted long into the modern period, as demonstrated in J. N. Hoechle's depiction of the imperial carousel in the Hofburg on the evening of November 23, 1814, one of the most spectacular events organized for the benefit of those attending the Congress of Vienna. Before an audience of 2,500, twenty-four spectacularly clothed cavaliers, organized into four quadrilles of six (on quadrille, see fig. 6.8 and Chapter 6) and paired with female spectators in corresponding colors, executed a series of equestrian battle maneuvers. The carousel proper was followed by a banquet and masked ball. [GSA]

Wilhelmina von Sagan, ahead of business or for wasting time in planning personally some of the magnificent fêtes at his home.

Outside official circles the Congress also attracted hordes of tradesmen hawking their wares in hastily built street stalls, mountebanks preying on gullible visitors, and venturesome evangelists like the dramatist-preacher Zacharia Werner, saving souls in the streets and in the salons alike. Not far removed was the American physician, Justus Erich Bollmann, his medical bag filled with miraculous cures for the Austrian economy—a Danubian steamship line, perhaps, or a coinage based on platinum or an Austrian national bank, none of which materialized, despite his good connections.

On a loftier plane artists and musicians discovered at the Congress opportunities beyond their most delirious dreams. The eminent portraitists Thomas Lawrence from England and Jean-Baptiste Isabey, once a court painter to Napoleon, for a few hours at a time could give the orders as some of the grandest personages sat obediently before them (see figs. 3.4, 3.1). Lesser but locally important artists like Friedrich Johann Lieder and Johann Hoechle also did their bit (see figs. A.4, 1.7, 3.3), contributing to a pictorial record of the Congress unmatched for public events until the age of the photograph, Isabey's group painting of the assembled plenipotentiaries being the most fa-

3.4 Thomas Lawrence, the eminent English painter, was kept busy in Vienna during the Congress capturing the likeness of several of the great figures of the time, among them Clemens Metternich. This was about the time that Schubert began to turn out his early masterpieces. Although Metternich's nominal area of responsibility was foreign policy, he nonetheless had great impact on life and art in Schubert's Vienna. [RC]

mous example. Musicians also prospered. Think of Antonio Salieri, head of the imperial musical establishment (see fig. 5.14), leading a chorus of five hundred voices and one hundred pianos, or Beethoven, under imperial patronage, conducting a series of concerts before six thousand people packed into the Redouten Hall, to say nothing of all the ensembles necessary to giving successful balls. Beethoven, in fact, emerged from the Congress a rich man, benefiting not only from steady concert bookings but also from the institutional backing of the Gesellschaft der Musikfreunde, which had only recently been founded and has provided invaluable support for music ever since. Unfortunately, Schubert, who had hardly begun his career, spent those giddy days teaching for meager pay in his father's school while the Congress danced.

The culinary arts likewise prospered. Nine months of dinners and buffets jaded appetites and inspired innovation. Beef Wellington, beef Stroganov, Nesselrodetorte, and Esterhazytorte were so baptized in honor of these participants in the Congress. Talleyrand brought his own chef, the distinguished Antonin Carème, together with a fully equipped kitchen. Saucepans, he told his king as he departed for the fray, were more important than secretaries. With all the invitations and savoring of delicacies from other lands, Vienna became the birthplace of international cuisine. At every level, then, from the foreign trinkets sold in the street stalls to the extravagant exchange of exotic gifts and decorations, the Congress was a bubbling melting pot, truly the first world's fair. Only the giant Ferris wheel was missing: that came later in the century.

THE FOUR GREAT POWERS AND THE REORGANIZATION OF CENTRAL EUROPE

Today we know, of course, that the gaiety was superficial, less an expression of jubilance than the natural result of hospitality liberally dispensed, coupled with the enforced idleness brought about by political stalemate. While the many played, the statesmen of the great powers worked; and they gambled for high stakes.

The Congress of Vienna was not primarily about making peace. That had already been accomplished with the Treaty of Paris (May 31, 1814), by which France had returned essentially to its 1792 boundaries, and with them its great-power standing. In return France had forfeited the right to a voice in settling all the questions beyond its borders, the central business of the Congress. Europe, it seemed, would be reorganized without the participation of the French—a shocking humiliation to inflict on a great power, in the minds of some. Hence, when the victorious allies drafted Article 32 of the treaty, which provided for a general European congress to meet in Vienna and to be attended by all the powers engaged on either side in the present war, they assumed that the assembly would be largely ceremonial, a gala celebration of the victory, the occasion for the solemn affixing of signatures to agreements privately negotiated beforehand. In Metternich's words, the Congress was not for negotiating, just for signing. Only on this basis could the defeated power be included. But when the delegates began to arrive in September, they found that few understandings had been reached. On the contrary, despite earnest informal discussions in London, where the first victory celebration was held in June, relations among the victors were more embittered than ever.

Although the acrimony focused on the concrete issue of the fate of Saxony and Poland, its ultimate source was sharply divergent views on the new European order. From the wreckage of the French Empire there had emerged two superpowers that, had they collaborated, could have dictated the terms of settlement to the rest. Britain was now dominant on the high seas and determined to shore up its monopoly with maritime and colonial acquisitions around the world. On the Continent, however, the British foreign minister and head of the Congress delegation, Robert Stewart, Viscount Castlereagh, aimed only at a balance of power, a pattern of forces that would hem in France while containing Russia to the far side of the Vistula River in Poland

3.5 Robert Stewart, Viscount Castlereagh, served as British foreign secretary from 1812 to his suicide in 1822. He helped engineer the defeat of Napoleon by coordinating an alliance with Austria and Prussia, and his role at the Congress of Vienna was comparable in importance to that of Metternich. He was the prime mover behind the concert of Europe, an idea that was embraced in 1814 and confirmed in the Quadruple Alliance of 1815: that European sovereigns or their representatives should meet occasionally to maintain peace, prosperity, and mutual understanding. Engraving by Blasius Höfel based on a painting by Thomas Lawrence. [HM]

(fig. 3.5). Russia, conversely, was the dominant Continental power, and Tsar Alexander sought to consolidate this advantage by rallying the lesser sea powers and the other Continental states in undertakings of international cooperation (fig. 3.6). There was probably a strain of idealism in these plans, but the other powers understandably dreaded a European union in which Russia could not help but dominate the action, much as the Third World in our day has distrusted the American role in the United Nations. Power itself is suspect, even if directed toward benevolent ends. Castlereagh, for one, was not willing to allow Continental ports, fleets, and river mouths to fall under the influence of a single power.

The Austrians took a similar view of the threat, perhaps with even more alarm, as they were the first in the line of march, their flanks in Germany, Italy, and the Balkans exposed to Russian agents and undermined by frightened monarchs who were apprehensive of Austrian and Prussian intentions and often turned to the tsar for help. Metternich's solution—a grand design, it is not too much to say—was to organize all of central Europe in collective arrangements of his own, hoping that the lesser states would view Austria, in its weakened condition, as a partner rather than as a threat. Ideally, in both Italy and Germany he hoped to create loose confederations that would accept Austrian leadership in a regional barrier strong enough to block Russia and France without itself constituting a threat to either. Thus, his view of the balance of power harmonized almost perfectly with Castlereagh's, providing the basis of their close collaboration during the Congress and for some years after.

The main obstacle to the plan was Prussia, which had its own aspiration to dominate Germany, or at least the northern half of it, and which was in a position to play Austria and Russia against each other. King Friedrich Wilhelm III and his chancel-

3.6 Tsar Alexander I, an enlightened despot who emerged
from the Napoleonic wars as Europe's most powerful sovereign
and whose idea it was to convene a congress in Vienna, was
naturally feared by the other powers. Indeed, Austria, Britain,
and even France concluded a secret defense pact against Russia
in January 1815. Unlike the other rulers, he participated personally in the Vienna negotiations, and emerged with Poland
in the bargain. (See also fig. 3.12.) Engraving by Woltener
after E. Lami. [HM]

lor, Prince Karl August von Hardenberg, came to the Congress with a secret weapon,
so to speak—a treaty signed with Russia the year before that essentially awarded
Prussia the entire state of Saxony, its traditional buffer with Austria, in return for ced-
ing all its former Polish provinces to Russia (fig. 3.7). Rumors of the deal, which
would have made Prussia too strong in Germany and Russia too strong in Europe,
triggered alarms all over Europe. Even during the war, while there was still a French
army in the field and a separate peace conceivable, Metternich and Castlereagh tried
to bring the tsar to relent, but to no avail; by the opening of the Congress he had still
not declared himself.

3.7 Friedrich Wilhelm III, badly beaten by Napoleon in 1806–7, later came under the thumb of Tsar Alexander I. Becoming increasingly reactionary and fearing a recurrence of revolution, Friedrich Wilhelm failed to deliver on his promise to give his people a constitution and supported Metternich's policy of a rigid enforcement of the status quo after the Congress of Vienna. Etching by Ludwig Mayer after Franz Krüger. [HM]

FRANCE AND THE COMMITTEE OF EIGHT

While all eyes were on the tsar, the first initiative came from an unexpected quarter: Prince Talleyrand, the seasoned expert at fishing in troubled waters (fig. 3.8). Technically, he was only an observer, but until the Congress officially opened, that did not set him apart. In crowded corridors and snuff-filled rooms he sought bargaining power by taking up the cause of the myriad lesser states, likewise excluded from the deliberations. Perhaps his most famous contribution to the Congress was the doctrine of legitimacy, a principle according to which the rights of all historically established governments and the provisions of freely negotiated treaties were to be recognized, whereas the products of conquest and revolution were not. On this basis, of course, not only was Bourbon France the equal of any other power, but she might also insist on preserving the existing king of Saxony and restoring the exiled Bourbon line in Naples, where Napoleon's brother-in-law, Joachim Murat, still clung to power under Austrian protection. The doctrine was also calculated to ingratiate France with the many German rulers across the Rhine, who watched with horror as Alexander and Friedrich Wilhelm applied the right of conquest to their fellow monarch in Saxony. Whatever Talleyrand's true beliefs about the sanctity of legitimacy, the doctrine served French interests, and the other powers did not take it seriously—except when it served their purposes in turn.

The allies had barely addressed the problem of adopting proper procedure when Talleyrand, with a phalanx of the other dissidents behind him, faced the opposition. The Congress, he argued, was nothing less than a parliament of Europe and should assign seats to all legitimate rulers, including Friedrich Augustus III of Saxony and Fer-

3.8 One of the shrewdest diplomats at the Congress was Prince Charles Talleyrand of France, an excommunicated bishop whose chameleon-like changes of position throughout his career kept him powerful and rich through the French Revolution, the Napoleonic period, the Congress of Vienna, and the Bourbon Restoration of Louis XVIII. He played an important role in negotiating the marriage of Francis I's daughter Marie-Louise to Napoleon (see fig. 1.8). Line and stipple drawing by Marie-Thérèse Noireterre. [NYPL:Avery]

dinand of Naples. Seeing that decision making was slipping from their hands, especially on such a fundamental issue as the recognition of Saxony, the allies preferred to delay a formal opening indefinitely and in the meantime to get along as before with private conferences. In the final compromise, however, they grudgingly consented to establish a steering committee composed of the eight signatories of the Treaty of Paris—the four allied powers plus France, Sweden, Spain, and Portugal—on condition that even it would be consulted only on matters previously decided among the four. In Humboldt's words, this was not a congress at all but merely the site of many individual negotiations, "Europe without distances." As a result, the only official meeting of the Congress was its last, taking place on June 9, 1815, when at last there was a treaty to sign. Even then the signing was confined to the same eight powers.

THE CRISIS OVER RUSSIA'S DEMANDS

With France apparently sidelined on the innocuous Committee of Eight, the tsar at last deemed the time ripe to reveal his demands. They were even more onerous than previously imagined, amounting to the transfer of Napoleon's former Duchy of Warsaw intact to Russia, in effect extending its territory to the Oder River, deep into central Europe. To be sure, Alexander justified the move as a matter of simple justice for the Poles, as he intended to add Russia's own Polish provinces and give a constitution to the whole. In fact, however, he was to become the king, and Poland, though administratively separate, would function as an extension of his empire. With garrisons at Thorn and Cracow on the lower and upper stretches of the Vistula, the tsar could threaten Prussia's ties to East Prussia and command the heights over the "Moravian gateway," the key invasion route to Vienna. In the worst case he might well have replaced Napoleon as the protector of all the medium and small states in Germany; indeed, King Friedrich of Württemberg was already imploring him to do so.

To forestall these dire possibilities Metternich accelerated his efforts to construct his central barrier, supported from the outside by England. With the latter he was, if anything, almost too successful; Castlereagh, his goals in western Europe brilliantly achieved by the Treaty of Paris, was determined to press the Russians back beyond the Vistula, urging Prussia and Austria to demand more than they really deemed desirable. The key to the problem remained Prussia, and Metternich redoubled his efforts to appease Berlin, even at the risk of alienating the lesser German states as well as powerful factions at home, who decried any softness in dealing with the successors to Frederick the Great. In October Metternich endorsed a program presented by Hardenberg for a German federation dominated jointly by Austria and Prussia and in desperation finally acquiesced in Prussia's annexation of Saxony, the latter on condition that Prussia demand the return of its former Polish provinces as well—anything to halt the Russian advance into central Europe. Hardenberg, who had his own reasons to escape subservience to Russia if he could, accepted the offer—only to be overruled by his king, who feared that Russia was already too strong to be resisted. In a stunning reversal, made independent of Castlereagh, Metternich himself turned to Alexander, offering to recognize his Polish claims if he repudiated Prussia's right to Saxony. The tsar refused. War clouds gathered, and the business of the Congress came to a halt. France now appeared the only hope.

Talleyrand himself was no problem. In opting for legitimacy and the preservation of Saxony he had already signaled his preference for alignment with Austria and Britain, in contrast to the traditional French policy of allying with eastern states against the center. The greater problem was Castlereagh, who had been goading Austria to dangerous confrontations without once guaranteeing military support should war occur. The breakthrough came in an unexpected way. On New Year's Day, 1815, the day after a spectacular fire at the palace of Prince Razumovsky, a still greater sensation occurred: news of the Treaty of Ghent, which ended Britain's second war with the United States, reached Vienna. In every salon and ballroom overheated imaginations visualized countless British warships sailing again to European waters, British mercenaries once more deployed on the Continent. Castlereagh knew better, but the news was enough to permit the commitment for which Metternich had waited so long. On January 3, Austria, Britain, and France concluded a secret alliance pledging to resist Russian and Prussian pretensions by armed force if necessary. With renewed confidence Metternich and Castlereagh demanded the admittance of Talleyrand to the inner deliberations. Alexander, convinced that his gains in Poland were already secure, saw no reason to antagonize still another power solely for the sake of Prussia. He yielded, and the crisis was over.

In the compromise that followed, Russia was driven back from the military heights that it coveted. Thorn and the fortresses of Posen were awarded to Prussia, while Cra-

65
The Congress
of Vienna

cow became a free city. With these exceptions, Alexander kept all the territory he claimed and was able to conduct in the Congress Kingdom of Poland the constitutional experiments he dared not try at home. The compromise on Saxony consisted of maintaining the "legitimate" monarch on his throne, awarding about half of his territory (the less desirable half) to Prussia, and compensating Prussia with a much larger block of territory in western Germany, in the Rhineland and Westphalia. This outcome was especially disappointing to the Prussian generals, men like Neihardt von Gneisenau and old Gebhardt von Blücher, the heroes of the campaign against Napoleon. Instead of the territorial compactness and strong frontiers that Saxony would have given them, they now had to defend western territories that not only adjoined France but were separated from the main body of Prussia by the states of Hanover and Hesse-Cassel—precisely as Castlereagh wanted it. "The pen has lost what the sword has won" was the lament of Prussian patriots, who could not foresee the day when factories along the Rhine and the coal fields of the Ruhr would provide Prussia with the base of its industrial greatness.

Metternich, too, was roundly criticized. Although the result was the most that could reasonably have been expected, the price paid was high, as he himself knew more than anyone. Congress Poland represented a thrust into central Europe that placed Russia in a strong position to influence German affairs and to threaten Austria's flank in any clash in the Balkans. The generals, led by the army chief, Prince Karl zu Schwarzenberg, deplored the concessions made, placing reliable buffers and solid frontiers ahead of general European alignments as the bedrock of Austrian security. The compromise, moreover, awarded Prussia so much territory in Westphalia and the Rhineland that it was to take four more years of tedious negotiation to satisfy the claims of Austria's clients among the south German states. Talleyrand's policy has likewise had its critics, precisely because it brought the powerful Hohenzollern state westward, directly up against the French frontier, and ignored the alternative of a Franco-Russian combination.

NONTERRITORIAL AGREEMENTS

Little wonder, then, that the Congress, instead of resuming its labors with feelings of relief, did so amid recriminations, fatigue, and a grim determination to be done with the tarnished spectacle. Except for a brief revival during the carnival, the old gaiety was gone. One by one the emperor's personal guests left the Hofburg, until only the tsar and his disillusioned ally, the king of Prussia, were left. In February, Castlereagh himself departed Vienna to defend his policy before Parliament and turned his duties over to the duke of Wellington. Some of the other plenipotentiaries spent hours sitting for their portraits while lower-echelon deputies and technicians did much of the laborious work that remained. To expedite the vast territorial exchanges required by the agreements, they established a statistical commission to ascertain the exact population of each province and devise equitable formulas for weighing the value of rich and poor provinces. Thus, for example, each "soul"—as persons were then called in the jargon of the trade—in Prussia's ceded Polish territories was counted as worth only two-thirds of a soul in the Rhineland, an invidious and exasperating calculus. Another commission dealt with Swiss affairs, and the important committee on the German constitution, established at the opening of the Congress, now resumed its deliberations without the previous burden of Saxony's uncertain status.

A committee on international waterways succeeded in bringing orderly regulation to navigation and toll collection on the several rivers where traffic had been dislocated by the complex territorial exchanges. Similarly, a committee on diplomatic protocol laid down rules of conduct and precedence in the accrediting of envoys; the guidelines ended centuries of sterile bickering on these matters and are still observed today. Significantly, there was no committee on Italy, mainly because Metternich insisted that the country was merely a "geographical expression." He desired an Italian defense league, to be sure, but only if he could be the architect of it. Similarly, British proposals to set up a committee on abolition of the slave trade were blocked by Spain and Portugal, the powers with the most to lose.

THE RETURN AND FINAL DEFEAT OF NAPOLEON

By the end of February the last details of the Saxon-Polish settlement were in place and a draft treaty ready for signature. At another grueling conference of the five powers on March 6, Metternich was delegated to convey the terms to the Saxon king. At 3 A.M. he finally trudged off to bed, only to be awakened at six by an urgent dispatch from the Austrian consul in Livorno. Napoleon, it said briefly, had disappeared from Elba and could not be found. Corroborating information soon came from British sources. Alerts went out to all the army commanders in the field, but otherwise little could be done until Bonaparte's destination was clear. By March 9 it was: he had landed in France, and on the twenty-first he entered Paris—at the head of the very troops sent to capture him. The strains of the Marseillaise swelled anew in the land, summoning citizens to rally round the tricolor (figs. 3.9, 3.10).

In Vienna, everyone agreed that the Treaty of Paris must be upheld, but beyond that the situation was unclear. As expected, Talleyrand wanted to declare Napoleon an outlaw with a bounty on his head and make the restoration of the Bourbons the central aim of a military campaign. The other powers preferred to limit war aims to resisting aggression, should it actually occur, and to refrain from dictating the nature of a successor regime. Napoleon, after all, was still the son-in-law of Emperor Francis, and Alexander was not inclined to forgive Louis for his betrayal in the Saxon crisis. Under the pressure of events and mounting evidence of Napoleon's bellicose intentions, the powers closed ranks, issuing a bland statement that denounced Bonaparte for his illegal actions and vaguely implied a preference for Louis XVIII.

The most pressing business became the redeployment of the allied armies, at the

3.9 Napoleon's landing at Antibes in March 1815 threw the Congress of Vienna into panic but led within a few months to the final defeat and permanent exile of the once self-proclaimed emperor of the French. Watercolor by Friedrich Phillip Reinhold. [HM]

moment still intact but positioned not against France but against each other—in Saxony, Bohemia, Poland. Wellington, the preeminent general, the powerful British plenipotentiary, and the prospective dispenser of subsidies, was the man of the hour. With his approval the plan adopted was essentially the same as in the previous campaign: an Austrian army in Italy to cope with Murat, who had opted for Napoleon; a second force in Flanders that combined British, Dutch, and German troops under Wellington's command, with a large Prussian corps under Blücher in support; and a third army, intended as the main striking force, deployed on the Upper Rhine under Schwarzenberg. A Russian army of 200,000, lumbering westward from Poland, provided a strategic reserve, which many hoped would never be used. Ironically, this was a strategy of attrition, of encirclement and slow strangulation, not a preparation for one decisive battle, as Waterloo proved to be. It was, moreover, weakened by a ferocious dispute between Wellington, who felt entitled to hire all the mercenaries he wanted in north Germany, as Britain had always done, and the Prussians, who wanted all those troops integrated into their own formations—a thinly veiled scheme to seize control of north Germany after all. In the final agreement, the lesser German rulers did not sell their troops as mercenaries but joined the alliance as accessory members and fielded contingents supported by British subsidies. Those with dynastic ties to the British and Dutch crowns sent their units to Wellington; the rest reluctantly placed theirs under

3.10 A page from the declaration of the allied powers condemning Napoleon after his escape from exile. [HHSa, Staatskanzlei Kongreßakten 2 = alt 3, fol. 103a (Fotostudio Otto, Vienna)]

Prussian command. On March 29, Wellington left for the front, leaving Lord Richard Trench Clancarty in charge in Vienna.

Meanwhile, the Congress style, once so convivial, turned grim and spartan. The imperial court, in keeping with Francis's personal tastes, ceased all entertainment, and the aristocracy naturally did the same. With hostilities impending, the remaining sovereigns went home to supervise preparations, leaving their envoys to settle outstanding issues before the fighting began. Who could tell whether there would ever again be a sense of common purpose? A single lost battle might shatter the consensus and reshape the alignments of Europe.

By early June the task was done. On the ninth the Committee of Eight, trunks packed and coaches waiting, met one last time to affix signatures to the great Treaty of Vienna or the Vienna Final Act, as it was officially called (fig. 3.11). The signing was in alphabetical order by country, as just recently prescribed by the committee on protocol. All that was left of Talleyrand's original scheme to give voice to the lesser sovereigns was a terse invitation to sign as accessories if they wished. Metternich stayed on a few more days in the virtually deserted chancellery building, once the scene of so many boisterous conferences and bargains quietly struck. Then, at 1 A.M. on June 13, he, too, left the darkened city, bound for allied headquarters at Heidelberg and the news of Waterloo. The Congress of Vienna was, so to speak, a fête accomplie.

Given the earlier wrangling between Wellington and the Prussians, it is a fitting tribute to soldierly virtues that the stunning victory in Flanders on June 18 was their shared achievement, featuring Wellington's stubborn goal-line defense throughout the day and Blücher's surprise assault on Napoleon's flank, despite fading daylight and his own severe wounds, just when the outcome hung in the balance. The much larger force far to the south under Schwarzenberg saw no significant action, but its mere presence on the Rhine probably helped to convince the retreating emperor that the game was up. On June 25 he abdicated a second time, ending a coda of imperial glory known as the Hundred Days.

THE PEACE OF PARIS AND THE "VIENNA FINAL ACT"

The Second Peace of Paris, which followed on November 20, did indeed restore Louis XVIII but under harsher terms than before, stripping France of many frontier

3.11 Within the covers of the Final Act of the Congress of Vienna, signed on June 9, 1815, by seven of the eight powers (Spain declining), were provisions that to a large extent determined the shape of Europe for generations to come. The Final Act was actually completed shortly before the Battle of Waterloo, which brought Napoleon down after his return from exile. It also set down principles of international navigation, rules of diplomatic protocol, a loose confederation for the German-speaking world, and a new constitution for Switzerland, among other provisions. [HHSa, AVR 1815 VI 9 (Fotostudio Otto, Vienna)]

fortresses and strategic strong points, forcing it to indemnify its neighbors with 700 million francs for new fortifications to be constructed against it, and subjecting it to occupation by allied armies until the indemnity was paid. The return of purloined works of art, previously unmentioned, was still not demanded outright but was made a legitimate subject of later bilateral negotiations.

The harder line toward France had already been foreshadowed in the 121 articles of the Vienna Final Act, and these can best be understood as erecting a system of containment against future French aggression. In the north, the former Dutch Republic was renamed the Kingdom of the Netherlands under the House of Orange and was reinforced by the annexation of Belgium, which included the "barrier fortresses" along the French frontier. In return, the Netherlands ceded the colonies of Ceylon and the Cape of Good Hope to England. These, together with the acquisition of the islands of Heligoland in the North Sea and Malta in the Mediterranean, as well as a protectorate over the Ionian Islands, made England undisputed mistress of the seas. The southern anchor of the system against France, the Kingdom of Sardinia-Piedmont, was strengthened by the addition of the great port of Genoa and a stronger western frontier, including Nice and parts of Savoy. Behind Piedmont, moreover, stood the power of Austria, which not only annexed the rich provinces of Lombardy and Venetia (compensation for its losses in Poland) but also placed Habsburg relatives on the thrones of Parma, Modena, and Tuscany. In southern Italy, Murat, who had been defeated by the Austrians, was replaced by a Bourbon prince after all: Ferdinand I, who ruled Naples and Sicily jointly as the Kingdom of the Two Sicilies. He was, however, required to bind himself by treaty to Austria's military and foreign policies—just like the Habsburg princes of the north.

Between the Netherlands and Sardinia the barrier against France was completed by recognizing the perpetual neutrality of the confederated Swiss cantons, bringing Prussia westward into the Rhineland, and organizing the thirty-seven German states into a defense league called the German Confederation. The Confederation was a compromise between the loosely joined, neutral body that Metternich had envisioned in 1813 and Hardenberg's plan for a tighter union dominated by Austria and Prussia. Austria was made president, but otherwise all states were said to be equal. A federal diet was created, which was not a parliament but rather a diplomatic assembly of envoys appointed by the member states. No new states were created, but several that had disappeared during Napoleonic times were restored, notably Hanover, whose king was also king of England, and Hesse-Cassel, whose ruler, though a notorious dealer in mercenary soldiers, at least had never done business with Napoleon. The Confederation was a disappointment to those who believed that the common culture of the Germans entitled them to greater national unity. It was likewise a disappointment to the hundreds of petty princes, like the Steins and Metternich's father, who had hoped to restore the Holy Roman Empire and with it their former autonomous status. The most they achieved was the promise of certain aristocratic privileges in the states that had annexed them and a voice in state government through the establishment of old-fashioned assemblies based on the traditional estates.

The purpose of the Confederation was defined as "the preservation of the external and internal security of Germany," to which end all members were pledged to aid each other in the event of invasion. It is important to observe, however, that only the German provinces of Austria and Prussia were included—that is, their "possessions previously belonging to the Holy Roman Empire"; their eastern lands did not share in the provisions for mutual aid unless the diet decided to render it. Some generals in Berlin and Vienna considered this arrangement unfair because it meant that their countries, while automatically obligated to defend all Germany against France, could not count on the aid of the German states against a Russian attack on East Prussia or Hungary. Other observers, however, pointed out that the total absorption of Austria and Prussia into the Confederation might impair their independence as great powers. The overall effects, in any case, were beneficial for the European equilibrium. France was deterred from attacking Germany, and Austria and Prussia were restrained both from attacking each other and from adopting irresponsible policies against Russia. The latter in turn could never be sure how the diet would respond to aggression. Central Europe, consisting of the German and Italian states and the Austrian Empire, thus became a sprawling buffer zone between the two great military powers on the flanks.

Other decisions of the Congress were less concerned with the balance of power. In Central Italy the pope was restored to his temporal rule over the Papal States, with Rome as his capital. In northern Europe another famous principle of the Congress can be seen at work: that of compensation. Sweden, having lost Finland to Russia, was indemnified by the annexation of Norway, which was taken from Denmark. Denmark, in turn, was given Swedish Pomerania, which it promptly ceded to Prussia for the duchy of Lauenburg and a cash payment. Territorial compactness was usually the reason for these complicated deals.

THE HOLY ALLIANCE AND THE QUADRUPLE ALLIANCE

The "Vienna settlement," as the various treaties are collectively called, was supplemented by two instruments that laid the foundation for a system of international cooperation. The first of these was the Holy Alliance, signed by Russia, Prussia, and Austria and announced by Alexander at an awe-inspiring army review in Belgium on September 26, 1815, an imposing demonstration of Russian might that the success of Waterloo had denied him (fig. 3.12). As originally drafted by the tsar, the treaty called for abandoning the old ways of politics in favor of new guides based on religion. It spoke of the brotherhood of *peoples* and declared that all national armies were but one army in the service of Christ. Clearly it was no conservative document, and it is likely that Alexander intended it as the foundation of a popular international order that looked to Russia for moral guidance. But Metternich, who had risked war to prevent

3.12 The Holy Alliance, depicted allegorically in this watercolor, resulted mainly from Tsar Alexander's ideal of a united Christian Europe. But Metternich converted this notion of a brotherhood of peoples into a fraternity of monarchs. The alliance nominally bound Russia (Alexander I, left), Prussia (Friedrich Wilhelm III, center), and Austria (Francis I, right) to enforce Christian morality within their borders. In reality, it resulted in the enforcement of the status quo and the strengthening of the monarchy in each nation. [HM]

Russia's military domination of Europe, was determined to frustrate the tsar's new venture as well. He was also suspicious of the German religious mystics who hovered around Alexander—notably Franz Baader and the Baroness Julie von Krüdener. Metternich therefore amended the Russian draft so that it proclaimed not the brotherhood of peoples but the fraternity of monarchs and admonished their subjects to seek happiness in religion rather than in political reform. Though the meaning was vague, the sentiments appeared harmless enough to induce most of the European monarchs eventually to sign the Holy Alliance, the main exceptions being the king of England, who begged out because of parliamentary difficulties; the understandably affronted sultan of the Ottoman Empire; and the pope, who snorted that "from time immemorial the papacy has been in possession of Christian truth and needs no new interpretation of it."[1]

To the hard-headed Castlereagh the document appeared a "piece of sublime mysticism and nonsense," and even Metternich referred to it as a "loud-sounding nothing." It is doubtful, however, that they were as contemptuous as they pretended to be, for Alexander's bid for the moral leadership of Europe was plain to anybody who knew about the first version. If the Holy Alliance did nothing else, it pointed up the diversity of views about the peace and cast doubt on the solidarity of the coalition. To repair the damage, and to be sure that France remained isolated, Castlereagh insisted that the four allied powers renew the Quadruple Alliance, pledging men, money, and arms against France in the event of new disturbances emanating from Paris. The alliance, which was signed on November 20, 1815, the same day as the Second Peace of Paris, also provided for periodic conferences to consider "such measures as at each of these epochs shall be judged most salutary for the peace and prosperity of the nations and for the maintenance of the peace of Europe." Alexander would have preferred a stronger statement, one granting the powers the right to police the internal affairs of France, but once again Castlereagh suspected the tsar's motives and substituted weaker wording. The powers agreed, in effect, to act in concert to defend the peace they had devised—creating a procedure known to history as the Concert of Europe. In varying degrees it has been practiced off and on ever since. The divergent views of Castlereagh and Alexander, however, exposed a profound issue that also remains to this day: whether and under what circumstances it is justifiable to intervene in the internal affairs of other states.

It is unlikely that the Concert could have kept the peace for long without a foundation in the stable equilibrium of power achieved by the Congress of Vienna. Although no power was completely satisfied, all obtained more from the system than they could realistically attain without it. Prussia, despite its complaints, did after all receive some of Poland, some of Saxony, and extensive territories in the west that proved more valuable in the long run than any that it lost. Russia did not achieve the preponderance over Europe to which Alexander evidently aspired, but its influence for half a century was greater than that of any other power. Austria's gains were less impressive, but considering a chronic state of near bankruptcy, a polyglot population, and general exhaustion, its domination of central Europe seems almost a miracle. Indeed, the overlapping of Austrian Empire and German Confederation, combined with the control of Italy through Lombardy-Venetia, dynastic ties with the lesser states, and a defensive alliance with the Kingdom of the Two Sicilies, constituted a triumph of diplomatic ingenuity that marks Metternich as one of the greatest masters of this art.

For Great Britain one need only observe that the Congress of Vienna inaugurated a century of world leadership. In possession of dozens of strategic islands and beach-heads around the world, Britain had control of the sea, and as long as the Continental powers checked each other, no danger loomed for the island homeland. In the face of powerful opposition at home, Castlereagh risked the financial and military commitments on the Continent necessary to bring about such results. In this sense his performance, too, was masterly. Even France had reason to be satisfied with the outcome, for though its relative position was diminished, it remained a great power, the beneficiary of a peace milder by any standard than it had a right to expect. If the century that followed was on the whole more peaceful than any in Europe's history, the main reason is to be found in the fact that none of the great powers—the states that had it most in their power to break the peace—was seriously aggrieved by the settlement.

That same century, while enjoying the blessings of peace in righteous innocence, was merciless in its condemnation of the Congress. To intellectuals who believed that national self-determination or, for some, proletarian solidarity were the keys to earthly paradise, the Congress appeared as a cynical conspiracy of frightened monarchs and beleaguered aristocrats to hold on to their thrones and their property, content to adjust their own differences but heedless of everyone else. Only a few years ago this view still reigned among the historians of Communist Eastern Europe. It is true, of course, that in repartitioning Poland, in assigning Belgians to Dutch rule and Italians to Austrian without consulting the inhabitants, the powers made future trouble for themselves. Yet who today, in surveying the savage record of unrestrained national passions in the twentieth century, would be ashamed to shed a nostalgic tear for the peace-makers of 1815 and their lilting Congress? It danced, yes, but not on the backs of corpses.

NOTE

1. Quoted in Frederick B. Artz, *Reaction and Revolution, 1814–1832* (New York: Harper and Brothers, 1934), 118.

FOR FURTHER READING

There are several books in English devoted to the Congress of Vienna. Harold George Nicolson, *The Congress of Vienna: A Study in Allied Unity, 1812–1822* (London: Constable, 1946), is a lively account by a British diplomat writing with the problems of the 1940s in mind. Henry Kissinger, *World Restored: Metternich, Castlereagh, and the Problems of Peace, 1812–1822* (London: 1955; Boston: Houghton Mifflin, 1973), is a profound discussion of the subject, though opinionated and not based on the best sources. Dorothy G. McGuigan, *Metternich and the Duchess* (Garden City, N.Y.: Doubleday, 1975), which gives a rich account of social life at the Congress, is based on Metternich's correspondence with Wilhelmina von Sagan. Charles K. Webster, *The Congress of Vienna, 1814–1815* (1919; rpt. New York: Barnes and Noble, 1969), was written by the great biographer of Castlereagh to guide the British delegation at the Paris Peace Conference of 1919, and Enno

Kraehe, *Metternich's German Policy,* vol. 2, *The Congress of Vienna, 1814–1815* (Princeton: Princeton University Press, 1983), although centered on Metternich, deals with other aspects of the Congress, using reliable sources. Two useful biographies are Alan Palmer, *Metternich* (London: Weidenfeld and Nicolson, 1972), and Paul Sweet, *Friedrich von Gentz, Defender of the Old Order* (Madison: University of Wisconsin Press, 1941; rpt. Westport, Conn.: Greenwood, 1970), the latter on Metternich's chief aide, who served as secretary to the Congress.

An exhibition catalog devoted to the Congress of Vienna is *Der Wiener Kongress, 1814–15* (Vienna: Bundesministerium für Unterricht, 1965).

1. The triumphant return of Emperor Francis I to Vienna on June 16, 1814, as all Vienna celebrated victory over Napoleon, was preserved in pictorial form by several artists. This representation of the event by Peter Krafft, although done in the late 1820s, is nonetheless the most famous, and captures better than any other the loyalty and love the Viennese felt toward their "Franzl." Oil on canvas. [ÖG]

2. Wilhelm August Rieder's 1825 portrait of Franz Schubert was considered by his friends to be the best likeness of the composer. It also served as the basis of an engraving, copies of which were sold in Vienna during Schubert's lifetime. Watercolor over pencil. [HM]

3. François-Pascal-Simon Gérard was a pupil and follower of Napoleon's principal painter, Jacques-Louis David. His full-length portrait of the French ruler, who crowned himself emperor, captures well the arrogant self-assurance of Napoleon during the time that all Europe feared him. Napoleon's assumption of the imperial title caused Beethoven, who harbored republican sympathies, to retitle his Third Symphony—which the composer had originally called "Bonaparte"—simply *Sinfonia eroica*. [GNM]

4. Joseph II was sole ruler from 1780 to 1790 but was coregent with his mother, Maria Theresa, from 1765, the year he was crowned Holy Roman Emperor. A strong-willed ruler, he was determined to improve secular and religious institutions in need of reform. But Joseph's policies, now collectively referred to as Josephinism, were not always welcomed by the people affected by them. At the beginning full of idealism and tolerance, Joseph tightened the reins on Habsburg society at the end of his once-promising yet ultimately tragic reign. This anonymous oil painting (c. 1770) shows him with his most important symbols of authority: left to right, the imperial crown, the Hungarian crown of St. Stephen, and the archducal cap. (See also fig. 1.2.) [KHM]

5. Perhaps the most celebrated social and recreational highlight of the Congress of Vienna was the grand sleigh ride of the imperial family and Austrian and foreign dignitaries on November 23, 1814. The event, which traversed the distance from the center of the city to Schönbrunn palace some miles away, was captured for posterity in this colored engraving by Friedrich Phillip Reinhold. [HM]

6. In 1808 the aula of the University of Vienna was the venue for a grand performance of *The Creation* by Joseph Haydn, which turned out to be the last public appearance of the aged master. This was the year that the boy Franz Schubert was admitted to the court chapel school (Stadtkonvikt or City Seminary) located nearby. [HM]

7. Corpus Christi, a Eucharistic feast that ranks among the most important of the Catholic Church year, has traditionally been an occasion for elaborate processions in Catholic countries. Here one proceeding down the Graben c. 1840 is depicted in a gouache by Balthasar Wigand. [HM]

8. This view of Vienna, painted by Jacob Alt, father of Rudolf von Alt (fig. 7.1), looks north from the Rampe of Schwarzenburg Palace c. 1820. On the far left is the Karlskirche and on the right in the distance the tower of St. Stephen's rises high into the sky. This picture shows clearly that both the Karlskirche and the Schwarzenburg Palace were outside the city of Vienna proper. Compare this with plate 9, an earlier view showing approximately the same area and perspective. [HM]

9. Bernardo Bellotto, nephew and pupil of Canaletto, the great Venetian painter of vedute ("views") whose name he also took, continued in his uncle's vein, as seen in this view of Vienna from the Belvedere in the mid-eighteenth century. On the left, one sees the rear of the Karlskirche; in the middle is the Schwarzenberg Palace, and, just to the right behind it (but in the city proper), the steeple of St. Stephen's cathedral. See also the later view of Jacob von Alt (plate 8). [KHM]

10. Josef Kornhäusel was commissioned to design Vienna's famous synagogue (finished 1825), for which Schubert composed a Hebrew setting of Psalm 92. Schubert's Vienna continued the era of toleration of Protestants and Jews initiated by Joseph II, though it was necessary to position the synagogue so that it was not prominently visible. Colored engraving. [HM]

11. Friedrich Amerling, one of the most prolific and most traveled of Biedermeier portrait painters, here depicts Rudolf von Arthaber and his children looking on a picture of the late Frau Arthaber (1837). Arthaber was the wealthy owner of a silk factory—silk weaving being one of greater Vienna's most important industries (see fig. 2.2)—as well as an important patron of the arts. Oil on canvas. [ÖG]

12. Ferdinand Georg Waldmüller, the most universal of Biedermeier master artists in terms of subject matter, here portrays in oils the family of the Viennese notary Dr. J. A. Eltz in Ischl (1835). His realistic, honest art has been called the prototype and essence of Biedermeier. That Waldmüller, a few years older than Schubert, had contact with the composer and his circle is evidenced by fig. 1.14.
Oil on canvas. [ÖG]

13. Painted for the industrialist and art collector Rudolf von Arthaber (see plate 8), Josef Danhauser's
The Rich Reveler (1838) was the first of a pair of pictures; the second, *The Monastery Supper,*
showed the now lonely, poverty-stricken reveler reduced to receiving charity. Danhauser was a
furniture designer as well as painter, and through his father's famous furniture factory had a
significant impact on Biedermeier interior design. He also played the violin and had
contact with the Schubert circle. Oil on canvas. [ÖG]

14. Franz Eybl was, like Danhauser (see plate 13), a student of Krafft (see plate 1), although he specialized
in portraiture. His earliest training, however, was in engraving and then lithography, which he later put to
good use in collaboration with Schubert's acquaintance Josef Kriehuber (see figs. 5.11, 10.8, 10.16). His
painting of Frau Nadassy shows her in mourning clothes (a complementary picture shows her husband
similarly attired), suggesting the death of a child or other close family member. [ÖG]

15. According to a notation in the diary of Friedrich von Amerling, who here depicts Emperor
Francis I of Austria in the uniform of a Prussian general (1834), this picture was intended for Berlin,
but the Empress Karolina Augusta, Francis's fourth and last wife, found it too old-looking and
depressing, so it was not sent there. Oil on canvas. [ÖG]

16. In the late 1820s, when he lived in Salzburg, Friedrich Loos turned to oil painting from engraving. This view from the Mönchsberg to the Hohensalzburg Fortress (1826) is an early product of this artistic turn. Just the year before, Schubert (with his singer-companion Johann Michael Vogl) had been in Salzburg and had climbed the Mönchsberg. In a description written for (and edited by) his brother Ferdinand, Schubert describes how "the city [of Salzburg] itself made a rather gloomy impression on me . . . because the fortress, situated on the highest summit of the Mönchsberg, sends its ghostly message into every street in the town." However, after climbing the Mönchsberg the next day, he could not help being amazed at the number of wonderful buildings, palaces, and churches in Salzburg to be seen from the heights. Oil on cardboard. [ÖG]

17. In 1798 the German-born Friedrich Gauermann, then in his mid-twenties, came to study at the Vienna Academy. In time his patrons included Moritz Graf von Fries (see fig. 7.7), Albert of Sachsen-Teschen (see fig. 7.19), and even the commander of the French troops occupying Vienna in 1809 (see fig. 1.6). Characteristic of his work is this view of the Altausseer See with the Dachstein (1827). Oil on paper and canvas. [ÖG]

18. The Prater is a large park area east of the old city of Vienna where today sports complexes and a convention center are located. Ferdinand Georg Waldmüller's *Large Prater Landscape* (1849) shows how it looked in the first half of the nineteenth century. Oil on wood. [ÖG]

19. Johann Baptist Drechsler, one of the leading flower painters and teachers of that special art, was greatly influenced by seventeenth- and eighteenth-century Dutch floral painting, many examples of which were to be seen in Viennese art collections. Here is a small flower painting by Drechsler from 1805. Oil on canvas. [ÖG]

20. Josef Nigg was a prize-winning student of J. B. Drechsler who spent the first forty-three years of the nineteenth century working at the imperial porcelain factory, one of the main places of employment of flower painters. His paintings of floral bouquets, such as this of 1838, exemplify his great skill in the genre. Oil on canvas. [ÖG]

21. Ferdinand Raimund was, in the last several years of Schubert's life, the leading figure of the
Viennese popular theater. Playwright as well as actor, he made his mark with a kind of serious
comedy that mixed the supernatural and the everyday and sought to portray the self-betterment of
human characters. Oil painting by Christoph Frank. [HM]

22. Interior of the Burgtheater, 1815. In 1812 it was decreed that the Burgtheater, in which theater, opera, and ballet had been performed, was to be Vienna's official theater for spoken drama, with the Kärntnertortheater becoming the official imperial opera house. Of course, music still continued to be composed and performed for spoken drama, and the Burgtheater was also occasionally used for concerts (see figs. 5.2 and 5.3). Colored engraving published by Maria Geisler. [HM]

23. George Emanuel Opiz's watercolor and sepia *At a Morning Concert in the Augarten* (see also fig. 7.8) suggests the casualness with which the Viennese accepted music in their lives. The scene represents one example of the Viennese tradition of *Musik und Menu*. [HM]

PART TWO

Musical Life

• 4 •

"Classic" and "Romantic," Beethoven and Schubert

LEON PLANTINGA

How does Schubert fit into history? Should we think of him in the company of the older composers active in Vienna, notably Haydn, Mozart, and Beethoven, who have by tradition been called classical? Or does he really belong with the next generation of musicians—with, say, Schumann or Chopin, whom we have got in the habit of calling romantic? Some wish to single out Schubert as the first of the true romantics in music. The author of a 1987 book entitled *Romantic Music,* for example, pointedly begins his discussion with Schubert.[1] But others have seen the matter differently, referring to Schubert as a "Classicist" or "the Romantic Classic."[2] And depending upon which of this composer's compositions one has in mind, a reasonable case can be made for any of these positions. There is much in Schubert's music that seems to lean very heavily on the practice of Mozart. As a single example we might think of Schubert's sunny, distinctly classical Fifth Symphony in B-flat Major, D.485. Although the work's date of composition (1816) places it between Beethoven's Eighth and Ninth, the opening theme of the first movement is quintessentially Mozartian; in fact, it has exactly the distinctive harmonic, textural, and registral configuration of the second theme of the finale of Mozart's beloved Symphony No. 40, in G Minor, K.550. On the other hand, we have the wrenching emotionalism of, say, the Adagio of Schubert's String Quintet in C, D.956, and the songs "Der Atlas" and "Der Doppelgänger."[3]

Of course, in the traditional view, one that seems to have gathered new strength in recent decades, classic and romantic in music present a distinct dichotomy, a palpable contrast in aesthetic stance and musical style. But this opposed pair has always been an odd entry in the grand parade of historical periods, that imaginary procession we envision to mark off successive changes in practice and thought in European music. We have been taught to think of the Middle Ages as ending sometime in the later fifteenth century; the Renaissance carries on thereafter for close to a century and a half, until about 1600; then comes the baroque, another convenient hundred and fifty years. But next is the classical period: traditionally less than a half century long because of a hesitancy to include its earlier phases—which get names like galant and *Empfindsam*—and because of a wish to get romanticism started properly near the beginning of the nineteenth century.

Such historical divisions in music, as we know, were designed to approximate periodizations already established in other disciplines, especially those in literature and art history. Still, it is pleasing how nicely events in music sometimes fall in with the larger scheme. Something different really did happen in European music around 1600 (the beginnings of opera, for one thing); Bach and Handel both conveniently died at about the middle of the eighteenth century; the careers of Haydn and Mozart fit rather neatly into the last third of that century. But we have somehow to deal with the recalcitrant Beethoven, Schubert's elder fellow citizen of Vienna, sprawled awkwardly across the turn of the nineteenth century. Earlier a younger colleague of Mozart and Haydn and of Goethe in his most classic phase (and of the outspokenly neoclassical artists of the French Revolution), Beethoven, like Schubert, worked far into what literary historians call the full flower of romanticism, indeed into a time when that flower seemed distinctly faded. Beethoven and Schubert outlived the English romantic poets Shelley, Keats, and Byron by about a decade. In Germany the literary movement that called itself romantic is said to have begun just before 1800, with the poetry of Novalis (who died in 1801) and the novels of Tieck and Wackenroder. The Schlegel brothers enunciated its theoretical program at just about this time.[4] But Beethoven kept composing for another thirty years, these three decades corresponding roughly with Schubert's entire lifetime.

If we are to think that the music Beethoven and Schubert wrote in the nineteenth century bears no relation to contemporaneous styles and ideals of romanticism but adopts the aesthetic posture of an earlier, classical practice, we must presumably make one of the following assumptions. The first is that these musicians were curiously old-fashioned and ill-attuned to the intellectual and aesthetic issues of their time. Put more concretely, we could assume that when August Wilhelm Schlegel sought to administer the coup de grâce to the hegemony of neoclassical doctrine in his famous lectures on drama at the University of Vienna in 1808, Beethoven, living just down the street in the Mölker Bastei, and Schubert, growing up in the suburb of Lichtental, were unaf-

4.1 The German literary scholar and poet August Wilhelm
Schlegel, opponent of literary neoclassicism and translator and
champion of Shakespeare, lived for several years in Vienna, where
in 1808 he gave an important series of lectures on poetic and dramatic art. Schubert was to set seven of his poems as well as sixteen
by his brother Friedrich. Engraving by John Sartain. [NYPL:Print]

fected by any such newer strains of thought and continued to be so for another two
decades (fig. 4.1). Or, second, we might think that this was a time when developments
in the arts and ideas diverged chronologically: perhaps in German-speaking lands romanticism came later to music than to literature, just as in literature it appeared rather
later in France than in Germany. Thus Beethoven the musician might have been as
avant-garde as his contemporaries thought, but representative nonetheless of an artistic temper that preceded romanticism. Or—a third, more radical alternative—we
might claim that there is no responsible way to draw such expansive parallels between
phenomena as unlike as music and literature. What is described as romantic in literature is for the most part specifically literary in nature; the poems and novels in question
embody ideas and attitudes for which there is no equivalent in music. So there is no
way to tell whether Beethoven and Schubert were allied with, or at variance with, the
the tenets and practice of literary romanticism.

Any pursuit of this vexed question ought to begin with a recognition that descriptions of romanticism in literature are probably still as various these days as they were when Arthur O. Lovejoy wrote a famously skeptical article "On the Discrimination of Romanticisms" in 1924.[5] Having been asked to give a talk on romanticism, he devotes the first part of the resulting disquisition to an entertaining explanation as to why this is impossible. First, who were the founders of such a movement? There ensues a list (chronologically receding) of those for whom a claim to priority has been made: Rousseau, Kant, Francis Bacon, the authors of the pastoral poems of the sixteenth and seventeenth centuries, the writers of the eleventh-century Anglo-Norman Renaissance, St. Paul in the Agora at Athens, and the Serpent in the Garden; some, he says, have difficulty distinguishing the first member of this list from the last.

And what, then, are the principal beliefs participants in this movement espouse? One writer selects "reminiscence" as a distinguishing feature: the romantic sensibility looks toward the past. But another writes, "The classic temper studies the past, the romantic temper neglects it. . . . It leads us forward and creates new precedents." One commentator claims those of a romantic turn of mind find meaning in the actual things we perceive; another quotes Friedrich Schlegel: "Everything visible has truth only as allegory." A detractor notes glumly, "Romanticism spells anarchy in every domain: a systematic hostility to every one invested with any particle of social authority." Another makes the opposite charge: that the climax of political and social thought in the romantic movement sought "to vindicate the sanctity of established social authority embodied in the family and State." And so on. So, finally, Lovejoy concludes, "The word 'Romantic' has come to mean so many things that, by itself, it means nothing. It has ceased to perform the function of a verbal sign." He recommends a two-pronged remedy. First, in analogy to certain practices in psychotherapy, it may be useful to make ourselves aware of the genesis of the disorder. And second, "we should learn to use the word Romanticism in the plural."[6]

One may suspect that Lovejoy's amiable estimate of this confusion was at least partly pretended. But the original formulators of German romantic doctrine, at least, probably would not have had much of a quarrel with him. The first purveyors of romantic literary theory cast the distinction between classicism (or neoclassicism) and romanticism as a particular opposition between "the ancients and the moderns," or, more specifically, between a tradition that claimed to stand in the hereditary line of ancient Greek and Roman art and literature as opposed to a largely independent, typically modern, artistic practice. In his first lecture in Vienna, A. W. Schlegel described thus the formation of the neoclassical position:

It is well known that, three centuries and a half ago, the study of ancient literature, by the diffusion of the Grecian language (for the Latin was never extinct) received a new life: the classical authors were sought after with avidity, and made accessible by means of the press; and the monuments of ancient art were carefully dug up and preserved. . . . But the study of the ancients was immediately carried to a most pernicious extent. The learned, who were chiefly in the possession of this knowledge, and who were incapable of distinguishing themselves by their own productions, yielded an unlimited deference to the ancients, and with great appearance of reason, as they are models in their kind. They maintained that nothing could be hoped for the human mind but in the imitation of the ancients; and they only esteemed in the works of the moderns whatever resembled, or seemed to bear a resemblance to, those of antiquity. Everything else was rejected by them as barbarous and unnatural.[7]

So from about the mid-fifteenth century, Schlegel says, the adulation of ancient letters, by which he means above all the Greek tragedies, carried to excess, grew into a rigid tyranny of taste and practice. The main culprits among more recent enforcers of this rigidity, it is clear, were French literateurs of the later seventeenth and the eighteenth centuries. Some were dramatists, but more particularly they were theorists of drama and art who followed Nicolas Boileau's *L'art poétique* (1674) in their emphasis on correctness and decorum, their exacting prescriptions (including verse forms) for the various genres, and their insistence on the famous three unities of time, place, and action in drama.[8] Schlegel's central thrust in these lectures is an attempt to undermine the authority of this neoclassical apparatus of prescriptions and proscriptions for drama. In the ninth lecture, for example, he levels his attack on the unities, declaring that they derive much less from practice of dramatists than from theories of drama, mainly the *Poetics* and *Rhetoric* of Aristotle, where, he adds, these matters are far from clear. In this spirited attack Schlegel saves his harshest words for foreign, particularly German, adherents of the French doctrine. Prominent among these was the influential Johann Christoph Gottsched of Leipzig, whose *Versuch einer kritischen Dichtkunst für die Deutschen* (1730) sought quite consciously to import French neoclassical standards into German letters, drama in particular. Schlegel, speaking of the sorry state of current German drama, declared: "We have a standard for this wretchedness, when we consider that Gottsched could pass for the restorer of our literature: Gottsched, whose writings resemble a watery beverage, such as was then usually recommended to patients in a state of convalescence, from an idea that they could bear nothing stronger, by which means their stomach became still more enfeebled."[9] The established standards for literature and drama among the French and their imitators, Schlegel maintained, were a tissue of confusion, a system of leaden orthodoxy that misrepresents ancient practice and stifles modern artists.

Was there then nothing better in the intellectual life of the modern world than a rigid, misguided imitation of the ancients? Schlegel, really rather a cheerful critic, recognized a vigorous and very rich alternative: a loosely constructed second tradition— with no clear debt to ancient models—that had for some centuries existed alongside the neoclassical one. This other practice was defined largely by that independence, by its position outside the line of ancient art and its modern imitators. Included in this other tradition was most of medieval literature, for which a strong new appreciation was emerging: the poems on the Arthurian legends, the verses of the troubadours and trouvères, the works of Dante, as well as the Italian epics and pastoral poems of the sixteenth century (for example, Ariosto's *Orlando furioso,* Tasso's *Gerusalemme Liberata* and *Aminta,* and Guarini's *Il pastor fido*). But central among Schlegel's "counter-cultural" figures were the modern dramatists, the Spanish playwrights of the Golden Age (Cervantes, Calderón, and Lope de Vega), and—most central of all—his beloved Shakespeare.

In the eighteenth century Shakespeare's plays were famous for their violations of neoclassical norms, and critics were often known according to their view of Shakespeare. The unities are breached on all sides: action flies from the kingly court to the battlefield and back again; great stretches of time elapse between scenes; an elaborate array of subplots encloses the comic within the serious and the other way around. But perhaps least acceptable to academic sensibilities was Shakespeare's overwhelming richness of language. He fills the mouths of his characters with extravagances of poetic imagination that his French critics found preposterous, that led to easy charges of barbarity. As late as 1822 a traveling troupe of English players performed several plays of Shakespeare to a Parisian audience largely ignorant of his works, and—with the exception of the young Berlioz and a few like-minded companions—not at all inclined to accept them. At the performance of *Othello,* Desdemona was wounded while curtsying, it is said, by a projectile thrown from the audience.[10]

So Schlegel recognized two streams of literary and artistic culture, a classical (and neoclassical) one and a much less unified tradition that departed from it in myriad ways. Schlegel found real value in both, though he did so with difficulty among the modern imitators of the ancients. In his first lecture he said:

The genuine followers of the ancients, those who attempted to rival them, who from a similarity of disposition and cultivation proceeded in their track, and acted in their spirit, were at all times as few as their mechanical spiritless imitators were numerous. The great body of critics, seduced by external appearance, have been always but too indulgent even to these imitators. They held them up as correct modern classics, while those animated poets, who had become the favorites of their respective nations, and to whose sublimity it was impossible to be altogether blind, were at most but tolerated as rude and wild natural geniuses. . . . In this state, nearly, matters continued till a period not far back, when several inquiring minds, chiefly Germans, endeavored to clear up the misconception, and to hold the ancients in proper estimation, without being insensible to the merits of the moderns of a totally different description. . . . The whole play of living motion hinges on harmony and contrast. Why then should not this phenomenon be repeated in the history of man? This idea led, perhaps, to the discovery of the true key to the ancient and modern history of poetry and the fine arts. Those who adopted it gave to the peculiar spirit of *modern* art, as opposed to the *antique* or *classical,* the name of *romantic.*[11]

Leaders among the "inquiring minds, mostly Germans," who now applied the name romantic to the second of these literary traditions, were of course A. W. Schlegel and his younger brother Friedrich (fig. 4.2). (Friedrich later became an acquaintance of Schubert, who set some of his poems to music.) In the mid-1790s Friedrich Schlegel had set himself to working out the distinction between the "essentially ancient" and the "essentially modern" in literature, always praising the former at the expense of the latter. But in about 1798 he seems to have undergone something of a conversion. Among a series of entries in the *Athenaeum,* the journal he founded together with his brother (and whose title points to the erstwhile neoclassical leanings of these spokesmen for romanticism), one, the famous Fragment 116, explains and extols "romantic poetry" (that is, "literature"):

Romantic poetry is a progressive universal poetry. Its disposition is not only to reunite all divided genres of poetry, and to put poetry in touch with philosophy and rhetoric. Rather it tends as well toward, and actually achieves, a mixture, even a fusion, of poetry and prose, genius and criticism, art-poetry and nature-poetry. It makes poetry lively and sociable, and life and society poetic. It poeticizes wit and fills and saturates art-forms with the real and varied stuff of creativity, enlivening them with the pulsation of humor. It embraces all that is poetic, from the grandest systems of art that contain within them yet other systems down to the sigh, the kiss the child-poet breathes out in artless song. . . . Like the epic, it can become a mirror of the whole surrounding world, a portrait of the age.[12]

For Friedrich Schlegel, the essentially ancient was now classic, and the essentially modern—immensely various and inclusive in its grasp—became romantic. Thus when romanticism emerged as a self-conscious movement, it was not (as musicians are often inclined to think) a question of opposing eighteenth-century styles to nineteenth-century ones. *Classic* applied first and foremost to works of the ancient Greeks, and secondarily to their modern-day imitators, most of them undeserving. *Romantic* had its roots in the Middle Ages, but, pressed to name its most characteristic representative, both Schlegels would undoubtedly have singled out not Novalis, Tieck, Wordsworth, or Coleridge but rather Shakespeare. "I am a furious romantic," said Stendahl in 1818; "that is, I favor Shakespeare as opposed to Racine, Lord Byron as opposed to Boileau."[13]

In the course of analysis by such critics as the Schlegels (who were joined by Schiller, among others) there gradually emerged a series of contraries characterizing these two traditions. One tradition urged the normative and exemplary, the other, the original and unique. One favored universal ideas and feelings in literature, the other the particular and individual. On the one hand is a conception of art governed by precept, on the other, art guided by genius, by the artist as a kind of seer or prophet impervious to precept. A finite selection of subjects is opposed to an infinite variety of matter, including the distasteful and bizarre. One tradition exalts measure and restraint, the other, extremes of expressivity and of feeling that must ever remain unsatisfied, as in Chateaubriand's *vague des passions.*[14] One holds to that favorite eighteenth-century aesthetic category, beauty, always understood as implying something like order and de-

4.2 Although Friedrich Schlegel's early freethinking writings
helped establish German romanticism and became influential in
the Schubert circle, he was named Secretary of the Viennese
Court and State Chancellery in 1808, working henceforth on
behalf of the antirevolutionary policies of Emperor Francis and
Metternich and participating in the Congress of Vienna.
Engraving by Joseph Axmann after Augusta von Buttlar. [GSA]

sign; the other favors its antipode, the sublime, with its implications of the mind-
boggling, overpowering, threatening. The first tradition is associated with the blue skies
of the Mediterranean world, the other with the green, misty forests of northern Europe.
At the beginning of the nineteenth century, it was thought, a romantic temperament
was one inclined to favor the second alternative in each of these pairs of contraries.

This list of oppositions always has romanticism coming down on the side of dereg-
ulation, of inclusiveness; it is, after all, expected to embrace whatever of value there is
that stands outside the classical fold. In fact, if it can be said to be governed by any single principle, that principle must be a kind of double negative: romanticism opposes
the exclusion of any subject, any emotion, any authentic flight of the imagination. So
Lovejoy's near-despair (partly feigned, surely) about settling upon a definition of romanticism—and his insistence upon a multiplicity of romanticisms—accorded rather
well with the earliest formulations of the doctrine.

But what does this have to do with Beethoven, just now working at the peak of his powers near the hall where A. W. Schlegel gave his lectures, or with Schubert, a talented youth of eleven just about to become a choirboy in the Imperial Chapel? How does music fit into the disputes about the ancients and the moderns, classicism and romanticism? On the face of it we might answer: with difficulty. Formulators of aesthetic and historical categories in the arts have always had a hard time of it with music. Much about it is devilishly hard to grasp. It has a complex notation, such that only professionals, for the most part, can make much of any but the simplest score. And performances leave listeners, even sensitive ones, unsure as to what has been conveyed or expressed and what sort of verbal response or commentary would be appropriate. At the root of such difficulties is the maddening obscurity of musical reference. Plays and paintings in the period under consideration tended to be *about* something: there might be disagreement about the central theme of *King Lear* (is it a domestic tragedy about old age and distance between the generations, or does it more fundamentally deal with the uses of power and the dangers of self-interest?), but at least one can discuss the matter sensibly. But pursuit of the "subject" of a musical composition—despite recent claims that Beethoven's symphonies tell of the aspirations of the middle classes or that they reenact deeds of male sexual violence—remains in most cases an illusory venture.[15]

Another problem about integrating music into such descriptions of the arts as those the Schlegels devised is that it fits so poorly into their historical categories. How could there be a "classical" or "neoclassical" period or style in music when next to nothing of ancient music survives upon which modern artists might model their work? And what is there, then, for "romantic" music to diverge from? A. W. Schelgel barely mentions music in his Viennese lectures. But in Europe at large in the first decades of the nineteenth century some works of Haydn and Mozart, and many of Beethoven, were a vivid presence that could no longer be ignored by those who pretended to explain the phenomenon of art. In short order music forced itself upon the attention of the literary and philosophical world; by stages it was elevated from a peripheral puzzle to the very center of some writers' thought about the nature of human perception and expression.

A slightly later generation of critics sought to draw music into the discussion not by attempting in any systematic way to integrate its historical and aesthetic categories into those of literature and the other arts but rather by carving for it a special niche, a place of honor all its own—but one unmistakably allied with the romantic side of the larger aesthetic dichotomy. Let us consider the famous statement of E. T. A. Hoffmann from 1813, that music "is the most romantic of the arts—one might say, the only genuinely romantic one—for its sole subject is the infinite. The lyre of Orpheus opened the portals of Orcus—music discloses to man an unknown realm, a world that has nothing in common with the external sensuous world that surrounds him, a world in which he leaves behind him all definite feelings to surrender himself to an inexpressible longing."[16]

In this grandly idealistic view the subject of music is the infinite: what music means is hard to grasp, not because it lacks meaning but because its significance lies on a higher level than that accessible to ordinary rational discourse. To give an adequate account of the workings of music would require, as Friedrich Schlegel put it, an act of "divination." And "it discloses an unknown realm." Music allows us a glimpse of an order of reality otherwise inaccessible to the human mind and spirit. In this characteristically romantic vision, art assumes a transcendental function; it serves as a vehicle for attaining a higher state, as something of a substitute for religion. At the center of this vision is music, and most particularly instrumental music. For unlike his predecessors of the previous century, Hoffman granted pride of place to music without text; words, concepts, and explicit reference to things in this world would only impede its flight and shackle it to the particular and mundane.

Just a bit later, in his *The World as Will and Representation* (Leipzig, 1819), Arthur Schopenhauer installed a view of music fully congruent with Hoffmann's into the very center of his epistemology. Like all philosophers operating in an idealist tradition, Schopenhauer believed that the world exhibits itself to us in varying degrees of "realness." The objects we see, hear, and feel around us are the least real: they are mere phenomena, raw data of sense perception, superficial, unreliable indicators of the true nature of things. At the other extreme, as the most real entity in the universe, he posits a kind of elemental, blind, powerful force he calls Will. This is represented in varying degrees of imperfection in the people, objects, and events that we encounter in this world. The most adequate representation of the Will is the traditional Platonic Idea— that primal pattern or mold that in the idealist tradition is thought to underlie all the phenomena of our experience. But for Schopenhauer (as for Plato), the Idea is not at all easily accessible. The only avenue of access, for Schopenhauer, is through art, which allows us to see beyond the particulars of existence and perceive something of this more fundamental level, only one step removed from the very center of reality. But one of the arts, music, skips this entire intermediate step. For music, Schopenhauer proposes, "is by no means like the other arts, namely a copy of the Ideas, but a copy of the Will itself."[17] It is a direct reflection of this most basic and real of things. Music has no need to refer to other entities in this world, to identifiable objects, ideas, or events, such as those with which language and the other arts concern themselves. In this formulation, art, and most particularly music, offers us a glimpse of the most fundamental nature of the universe, unknowable in any other way. So it is to be expected that language and the ordinary processes of rationality will falter in any attempt to capture the meaning of music, the art that in this remarkable way does duty in a sense for both religion and science.

It may surprise some that Schopenhauer's favorite composer, evidently, was the Italian Rossini, who took Vienna by storm during Beethoven's and Schubert's time.[18] But among other writers in the first decades of the nineteenth century, transcendental views about art and artists attached increasingly to the singular figure of Beethoven. A kind of mythology grew up around this composer in which his manner and habits were seen as a representative illustration of the life of the artist. He appeared to live mainly outside the mainstream of society and its conventions. Reports of his peculiar habits and the disorder of his living quarters abounded. He was perceived as misanthropic, and increasingly singular in appearance and behavior, as evidenced in Gerhard von Breuning's Balzac-like portrayal of the composer walking in the streets of Vienna with his unbuttoned coat flapping about his arms in the wind, one pocket burdened down with his sketchbook, the other with his ear trumpet or his conversation book. And after composing for a time, Breuning reported further, Beethoven would cool his head by pouring water over it in such quantities that the liquid would "go all over the floor and even go through the ceiling to the floor below."[19] He seemed to provide a living illustration of current theories (advanced by Schopenhauer among others) of the affinity of genius and madness.

And both in the generation of Hoffmann and in the 1830s, it is clear, writers of a romantic cast of mind who had anything to say about Beethoven counted him as one of their own. Contemporaneous critics in general, whatever their affinities, routinely ascribed to his music the traits associated with romanticism. We read again and again about originality and individuality carried to sometimes unwelcome extremes, about an abandonment of that prized neoclassical value, decorum. Critics spoke of an unprecedented intensity, even violence of expression, a willingness to forgo the ideal of beauty in the interest of novelty and particularity. And Beethoven himself, as early as the Heiligenstadt Testament of 1802, that remarkable literary outpouring putatively addressed to his brothers but evidently intended more for the world at large, projected an intensely romantic view of the artist as a Promethean figure, a kind of fire-bringer whose responsibility to society overrides the accidents of his own existence. But however his contemporaries saw him, and however novel and individual Beethoven's music written in the early nineteenth century looks to us, it is also clear that it issued, especially in its earlier stages, directly from a tradition, or rather several traditions: from the instrumental music of Haydn, the keyboard writing of Muzio Clementi, the big-band sound of French Revolutionary music.

ORIGINS OF THE CLASSIC-ROMANTIC DICHOTOMY FOR MUSIC

So, to return to the question with which we began, on which side of the classic-romantic divide in music does Schubert fall? As has already been suggested in a number of ways, the problem that bedevils this question is its presupposition that there *was* such a divide. The more closely one looks at any such categorization, of course, the shakier it must appear: human affairs, and especially artistic ones, don't often lend themselves to such easy distinctions. In music there are always myriad variables: some styles follow national lines, some seem to adhere to particular genres, and of course individual composers are always following their own lights in ways that preclude easy classification. But special problems attend the notion of a classic-romantic dichotomy in European music at the turn of the nineteenth century (or, as some would have it, about fifteen years later). The idea was first floated in the mid-1830s by conservative opponents of the current crop of romantic composers (Schumann, Chopin, Berlioz, Liszt), by critics who longed for a return to a time when things seemed clearer and easier. The first to posit a classical period followed by this unfortunate romantic aberration was evidently Amadeus Wendt of Leipzig in his essay "Concerning the Present Condition of Music, Especially in Germany, and How It Got That Way" (fig. 4.3).[20] Wendt held up the work of Haydn, Mozart, and Beethoven as models for the sort of reasonable and balanced music he approved while denigrating "irregular and lawless" composers like Chopin and Berlioz (figs. 4.4, 4.5, 4.6). For the music of the three Viennese composers he borrowed the handy term of approbation *classical* from the literary debates that had raged in Germany since the turn of the century. And that there should be exactly three classical composers surely had more to do with Wendt's general philosophical orientation than with his grasp of music history. For Wendt was an ardent Hegelian, and Hegelians tended to see things in threes in accord with the stages of the dialectic; he provides some assessment of the trinity of classical composers along

4.3 Amadeus Wendt's influential essay "Concerning the Present Condition of Music, Especially in Germany, and How It Got That Way" (1836) helped to establish the notion that Haydn, Mozart, and Beethoven represent a classical style of composition. [NYPL:Music]

4.4 In 1799, Josef Haydn was world famous and honored as Vienna's most venerable musical statesman. Portrait by J. C. Roesler. [Ox]

specifically Hegelian lines.[21] But however specialized in its outlook, Wendt's formulation caught on, and in one version or another has persisted until the present day.

Of course Wendt's use of the term *classical* has a strong component of value judgment that hearkens back to the word's old meaning—of the highest class, the best of its kind, something normative of exemplary. This notion has been subtly mixed with *classical* as a stylistic designation during the entire troubled history of the word's use in a musical context. This was certainly the case with the Viennese music historians of the early twentieth century, Guido Adler and his student Wilhelm Fischer, who more than any others fixed the usual modern understanding of the name and notion of a classical period.[22] Once more there was a conservative agenda at work: the glorification of a previous period in Viennese music at the expense of a new modernism, now that of Schoenberg and his disciples. And, once again, *classical* is a term of approbation, a kind of club with which to attack alarming contemporary developments. This very frank cargo of value judgment led to a severe narrowing of what might be included under the rubric *classical:* Adler and Fischer were loath to admit any lesser composers, such as forerunners of Haydn and Mozart, into the Pantheon, and, indeed, the less mature works of these masters themselves hardly seemed quite fit either. Thus arose the habit—perpetuated by Charles Rosen in our day—of beginning the classical period (or school) in music around 1780, a date that coincided nicely with Haydn's Quartets, Opus 33 with the promotional tag attached to the first edition, "composed in an altogether new and different manner."

So we are left with a style designation that is about twenty (or at most thirty-five years) in length, consisting of the mature works of two (or possibly three) composers, all working in the same city. This is a classicism, moreover, that shows no dependence

4.5 *The Apotheosis of Mozart,* engraved by E. Schuler after a line drawing of Josef Führich, demonstrates the worshipful attitude that developed toward the composer after his death in 1791. Schubert himself wrote in his diary (1816) of "the magic notes of Mozart's music. . . . O Mozart, immortal Mozart, how many, oh how endlessly many such comforting perceptions of a brighter and better life you have brought to our souls!" Appropriately, then, the Mozart *Requiem* was performed at the first memorial Mass for Schubert. The artist Führich, personally known to several friends of Schubert and possibly by the composer himself, developed, along with Leopold Kupelwieser, into one of Vienna's most important religious painters of the nineteenth century. [NYPL:Print]

4.6 This chalk drawing by Johann Stepen Decker portrays Ludwig van Beethoven in 1824, about the time that Schubert began to compose works that likely aspired to emulate the achievement of the older master, whose presence had dominated Viennese musical life in the younger composer's formative years. It is likely that the last music Schubert heard during his final illness was Beethoven's late String Quartet in C-sharp Minor, Op. 131, an experience that reportedly brought him to a state of ecstatic exhaustion. [HM]

whatever upon classical antiquity (it is apparently largely for this reason that both Hoffmann and Hegel designated music as "essentially romantic"—that is, postclassical, modern), nor does it have any visible connection with French neoclassicism. And it first appeared at a time when classicisms and neoclassicisms were clearly falling into disrepute. Is there any way we can regard such a phenomenon, then, as a "period" in Western musical history, a category commensurate with a long-lived and international Renaissance or baroque? Or is the classical period in music analogous to that other misnamed entity wherein it supposedly flourished, the Holy Roman Empire: is it, perhaps, neither classical nor a period?

Perhaps we can yet save the day with an appeal to those aesthetic categories distilled from classical traditions, properties like clarity, balance, order, restraint, universality of expression, and the like. If we exclude for a moment the troublesome Beethoven, can we not credit the mature works of Haydn and Mozart—even in isolation from other classicisms—with these admirable qualities, and thus salvage some vestige of a classical period or school in Viennese music of their time? Such traits, after all, are recognizable in the sonatas and symphonies of these composers. In fact, much of twentieth-century analysis of this music, especially that of a more formalist persuasion, is designed to demonstrate its congruities, symmetries, and balance. But it must surely give us pause that the contemporaries of Haydn and Mozart did not usually see the matter that way; it is not at all common in the literature of their time to find classical qualities attributed to the works of either composer. The mature Mozart was regularly seen as an individualistic, difficult composer, a purveyor of powerful, even excessive emotion in music. One prominent critic said, "He finds his true home in the domain of the overpowering, the shocking."[23] Yet it was precisely those works that Adler and Fischer hailed as achieving a classical status—compositions from the middle 1780s, like the Quartets dedicated to Haydn—that had sowed the seeds of the Viennese disenchantment with Mozart as a kind of unbridled emotionalist. What struck contemporary observers most strongly about Haydn's music was its unorthodoxies, its wit, surprise, and what these days we call irony. Neither of the characterizations fits very well with anybody's definition of classicism. Surely we risk serious distortion if we posit historical periods or schools on the strength of characterizations that have little demonstrable connection with ideas or impressions of their own time.

CLASSIC VERSUS ROMANTIC MUSIC: TWENTIETH-CENTURY VIEWS

More than thirty years ago, the prominent German scholar Friedrich Blume pointed out severe problems with the old classic-romantic paradigm in music history and urged a startling revision: "Classicism and Romanticism, then, form a unity in music history. They are two aspects of the same musical phenomenon just as they are two aspects of one and the same historical period. Within this musical phenomenon as within this period—and, indeed, from their beginnings to their gradual termination in the 20th century—there ran currents that were now more classicizing, now more romanticizing."[24]

This great block of European history, with all its rich intellectual and artistic diversity, Blume contended, saw a certain unity in the dominant stylistic norms of music, including an implied periodization, dominance of a homophonic texture, admission of thematic contrast, and the routine construction of compositions or movements with more than one ruling tonality. He accordingly proposed that we think of a "classic-romantic" period in European music, extending from the later eighteenth century to the end of the nineteenth (giving us another of those 150-year installments). The stylistic and expressive fluctuations within that period, occurring in complex geographical and chronological patterns, would allow us to agree with Beethoven's contemporaries that his music and temperament were allied with certain strains of romanticism and yet not submit to confusion at the apparent antithesis—already recognized in Beethoven's time—between him and that other most dominant of composers, Rossini. Nor need there be any embarrassment about the historical position of Mendelssohn, whom Schumann called "the great classicist of a romantic age," or about the outbursts of passion in the symphonies and sonatas of Haydn in the 1770s. In this light, the disparate facets of Schubert's art, from the transparent and innocent to the profound and anguished, may seem less incongruous from a historical point of view.[25] Both poles of expression would fall easily within the broad embrace of Blume's classic-romantic categorization, a concept that, though it may trouble us with its lack of specificity, nonetheless gives a much more accurate picture of what went on in European music than the old classic-romantic dichotomy, no matter where we draw the line.

But Blume's idea apparently has not caught on. Charles Rosen's *The Classical Style* (1971) and Leonard Ratner's *Classic Music* (1980) have perpetuated, especially in the United States, both the idea of a distinct classical period (or school), and the old historical dichotomy with romantic music. (Both writers have subsequently published books on the latter phenomenon.) But there have also been new stirrings of discontent with the old formulation. Enthusiasts for the Italian opera of the later eighteenth century have objected to its marginal status—in the face of its overwhelming centrality in its own time—in traditional overviews of the period that are mainly German in origin. And, in a recent book, James Webster presents a balanced and informed analysis of the ideas and prejudices that went into our received notion of a classical style, together with a tentative new name, "first Viennese-European modern style."[26] It is not entirely clear just what his new designation is intended to include, but in any case this is surely intended as a more circumscribed effort than Blume's bold attempt to describe an era in Western music commensurate in scope with the Renaissance and the baroque.

Whatever we say or think, we will probably not get rid of those words *classic* and *romantic,* with all the ideological baggage and ambiguity they bring to any discussion of music in the late eighteenth and nineteenth centuries. Nor, probably, are we all likely to follow Blume's suggestion and conjoin them. But a simple recognition of the problems attending their use is itself a considerable gain. If we can only look with a healthy skepticism upon that old dichotomy—the idea of a high point of Apollonian balance and serenity in the late 1700s followed by a turn toward subjective emotion at the turn of the century—our vision will be clarified. Then perhaps we can recognize the intensity of expression in early Haydn and late Mozart without resorting to notions like "protoromanticism"; we may be able to assess the expressive heights of Beethoven's music together with its stylistic patrimony without fearing self-contradiction; and we will feel free to appreciate the elegance and balance in instrumental music of Mendelssohn, Hummel, and—not least—Schubert without mental reservations about "backwardness" or "regression."

NOTES

1. Arnold Whittall, *Romantic Music* (London: Thames and Hudson, 1987).

2. "Classicist": Walter Vetter, *Der Klassiker Schubert* (Leipzig: C. F. Peters, 1953); Alfred Einstein, *Music in the Romantic Era* (New York: W. W. Norton, 1947), has a chapter entitled "Schubert: The Romantic Classic."

3. Just as the "D" numbers for Schubert correspond to the catalog of Otto Erich Deutsch (see Chapter 1, note 10), so the "K" numbers for Mozart represent the attempt at a chronological ordering of that composer's works by Ludwig Köchel.

4. An important reexamination of these early romantics is Frederick C. Beiser, *Enlightenment, Revolution, and Romanticism: The Genesis of Modern Political Thought, 1790–1800* (Cambridge: Harvard University Press, 1992), especially chapters 9 and 10. The latter deals with Friedrich Schlegel,

whose ideas—expressed in the late 1790s, that is, before his subsequent move to Vienna, conversion to Catholicism, and service to the government of Francis I and Metternich—found resonance among members of Schubert's inner circle in the early 1820s. On this last point see John M. Gingerich, "Schubert's Beethoven Project: The Chamber Music, 1824–1828" (Ph.D. diss., Yale University, 1996), prologue, especially 66–75.

5. Arthur O. Lovejoy, "On the Discrimination of Romanticisms," *PMLA* 39 (1924), 229–53. Rpt. in Arthur O. Lovejoy, *Essays in the History of Ideas* (Baltimore: Johns Hopkins University Press, 1948; rpt. New York: Capricorn, 1960), 228–53.

6. Ibid.

7. August Wilhelm Schlegel, *A Course of Lectures on Dramatic Art and Literature,* trans. J. Black (Philadelphia, 1833), 3.

8. Unity of action requires that there be a single plot, without subplots; unity of time that the action be completed in a single day; and unity of place that the action unfold in one location. Renaissance and later theorists of the drama attributed these principles to Aristotle (principally in the *Poetics*), but in fact he discusses only unity of action.

9. A. W. Schlegel, *A Course of Lectures,* 4–5.

10. For Shakespeare on the Viennese stage, see Chapter 10.

11. A. W. Schlegel, *A Course of Lectures,* 423.

12. My translation. The complete "Fragments" published in the Schlegels' journal *Athenaeum,* as well as Friedrich Schlegel's novel *Lucinde,* which had influence in the Schubert circle, are translated by Peter Firchow in *Friedrich Schlegel's "Lucinde" and the Fragments* (Minneapolis: University of Minnesota Press, 1971).

13. *Correspondance de Stendhal* (Paris: Charles Bosse, 1908), 2: 85.

14. Chateaubriand described *le vague des passions* ("vagueness of passions") as a state of strong feeling that has no particular object, one in which "our faculties . . . are focussed only upon themselves, without goal or object." *Génie du Christianisme* (Paris: Garnier-Flammarion, 1966 [1st ed. 1801]), 1: 309.

15. Both explanations have been urged on us by Susan McClary, the first (for example) in "A Musical Dialectic from the Enlightenment: Mozart's Piano Concerto in G Major, K.453," *Cultural Critique* 4 (1986): 129–69, and the second in *Feminine Endings: Music, Gender, and Sexuality* (Minneapolis: University of Minnesota Press, 1991), especially 123–30.

16. As translated in Oliver Strunk, *Source Readings in Music History* (New York: W. W. Norton, 1950), 775. In Roman religion Orcus was the kingdom of the dead.

17. Arthur Schopenhauer, *The World as Will and Representation,* trans. E. F. J. Payne (New York: Dover, 1969), 1: 257.

18. In Schubert's "Overtures in the Italian Style" of 1817, D.590 and 591, he paid tribute to the vastly more famous Rossini.

19. Gerhard von Breuning, *Memories of Beethoven: From the House of the Black-Robed Spaniards,* ed. Maynard Solomon, trans. Henry Mins and Maynard Solomon (Cambridge: Cambridge University Press, 1992), 68.

20. Amadeus Wendt, *Über den gegenwärtigen Zustand der Musik, besonders in Deutschland, und wie er geworden: Eine beurtheilende Schilderung* (Göttingen: Dietrich, 1836).

21. The stages of the dialectic are usually summarized as thesis, antithesis, and synthesis.

22. Charles Rosen has adopted this formulation nearly unaltered in his influential book *The Classical Style: Haydn, Mozart, and Beethoven* (New York: W. W. Norton, 1971).

23. Friedrich Rochlitz, as cited in Leo Schrade, *W. A. Mozart* (Bern: Francke Verlag, 1964), 15.

24. In his articles "Klassik" and "Romantik" in the German musical encyclopedia *Die Musik in Geschichte und Gegenwart*. English versions of these articles are found in Friedrich Blume, *Classic and Romantic Music: A Comprehensive Survey,* trans. M. D. Herter Norton (New York: W. W. Norton, 1970). The passage quoted is on page 124 of the latter publication.

25. In his single extended remark about Beethoven's music, in a diary entry of 1816, Schubert sounded distinctly neoclassical in outlook—much like Beethoven's most conservative critics. Without naming him he attributed to Beethoven "that eccentricity which joins and confuses heroism with howling and the holiest with harlequinades, without distinction, so as to goad people to madness instead of dissolving them in love, to incite them to laughter instead of lifting them up to God"; O. E. Deutsch, ed. *The Schubert Reader,* trans. Eric Blom (New York: W. W. Norton, 1947), 64.

26. James Webster, *Haydn's "Farewell" Symphony and the Idea of Classical Style* (Cambridge: Cambridge University Press, 1991), 335–66. Webster's main focus is on Haydn's earlier works; he offers a corrective to their usual characterization—from a distinct evolutionary bias—as preparatory or immature.

FOR FURTHER READING

In addition to Blume's exposition cited in the text and notes, surveys of nineteenth-century music that consider the issues discussed here include Carl Dahlhaus, *Nineteenth-Century Music,* trans. J. Branford Robinson (Berkeley: University of California Press, 1989), esp. 1–51; John Daverio, *Nineteenth-Century Music and the German Romantic Ideology* (New York: Schirmer, 1993), chapter 1; and Leon Plantinga, *Romantic Music: A History of Musical Style in Nineteenth Century Europe* (New York: W. W. Norton, 1984), 1–22, 107–26.

On Schubert see also Maurice J. E. Brown, *Schubert: A Critical Biography* (London: Macmillan, 1961); William Kinderman, "Schubert's Tragic Perspective," in Walter Frisch, ed., *Schubert: Critical and Analytical Studies* (Lincoln: University of Nebraska Press, 1986), 65–83; and the special issue of *Nineteenth-Century Music* devoted to "Schubert: Music, Sexuality, Culture," summer 1993.

• 5 •

Vienna, City of Music

ALICE M. HANSON

Throughout the nineteenth century, when the still-observed traditions and much of the core repertory of modern concertgoing were gradually established, visitors to Vienna were astonished by the number of opportunities to hear music and by the virtuosity of the performers at every level, from court singer to itinerant harpist. Even before Schubert's day, Vienna sparkled especially brilliantly in the firmament of European musical cities, especially in the realm of instrumental music. But virtually every sort of music was heard in Vienna, from Italian opera to songs sung with guitar accompaniment, from the most profoundly abstract and serious string quartets to gimmicky pieces featuring violinists who played their instruments upside down. Moreover, virtually all traveling virtuosi made Vienna a stop on their tours. It is thus hardly surprising that the German composer Carl Maria von Weber, upon arriving in Vienna in 1822, could exclaim: "And so it came that Vienna was established as the Areopagus where musical art was alone to be judged, where artists were to stand before the judgment-seat, where laurels were to be given or withheld, where verdicts were to be delivered and reputations made."[1] Vienna was thus already then what it still is today: *Musikstadt Wien*—Vienna, City of Music—yet the venues, conditions, and content of musical performances were in many ways different from those of our time.

In the early part of the nineteenth century, when Beethoven and Schubert lived in Vienna, public classical music concerts of the sort we enjoy were still a novelty. Nonetheless, just as today we attend Christmas concerts, so too in Schubert's Vienna many public concerts were tied to special annual holidays or celebrations. Some, like those on May Day or Brigittenkirchtag (a folk festival in July), were performed outdoors or in special settings (fig. 5.1). Other concerts commemorated special events like the birthdays and name days of the royal family, the death anniversaries of important musical figures like Mozart, and the festive openings of theaters or new buildings. The scheduling of these concerts during the regular "season," which began in the fall and continued through spring, was affected by the official observation of the liturgical calendar of the Catholic Church, government regulation, and Vienna's limited number of concert spaces. For example, on national and religious holidays (called *Normentagen*), when the performance of drama was forbidden, theaters were free to present concerts. Hence, concerts were common on Sundays and during the penitential season of Lent, and others preceded or were sandwiched between acts of featured dramas or ballets.

In an age without insurance and adequate pension funds, the purpose of most public concerts was to raise money (fig. 5.2). Indeed, benefit concerts for the Tonkünstler

5.1 Brigittenkirchtag was a popular two-day festival in July that took its name from the church of St. Bridget, located in the meadows outside the city and north of the Danube. The festival lasted until 1847 but was captured for posterity in watercolors and pen by Josef Scheurer von Waldheim, and also in Franz Grillparzer's story "Der arme Spielmann" ("The Poor Minstrel"). Watercolor, c. 1820. [HM]

5.2 Handbill for benefit concerts December 22–23, 1813, in the Burgtheater to benefit widows and orphans of Viennese musicians, a regular feature of Vienna's concert life at that time. The programs featured a cantata entitled "The Battle of Leipzig" (see also fig. 1.9) and Haydn's oratorio *The Seasons*. [ÖNb-Mus]

Society (for widows and orphans of musicians) or for Bürgerspital (housing for the poor) were gala annual social events. Some concerts were in response to local disasters. For example, in March 1830, when a flooding of the Danube caused over seventy deaths and left hundreds of people homeless, a number of professional musicians and aristocrats immediately organized large benefit concerts to pay for relief work. Among the most curious was a concert that featured sixteen pianists (members of the Austrian nobility) playing Carl Czerny's version of the overture to Rossini's opera *Semiramide*. Other benefit concerts were given by individual performers to defray the cost of touring abroad or going into retirement.

For traveling virtuosi and local Viennese performers, public recitals called academies constituted a vital part of their regular income. For some members of theater orchestras, permission to give an annual recital for their own benefit was written into their contracts. In such cases the performer's challenge was to attract a large enough audience to offset the concert costs and make a profit. But in Schubert's day that was a big undertaking, for without modern concert managers and agents, performers themselves had to secure a hall, assemble and rehearse their obligatory accompanying orchestra, arrange for the seating and instrument tunings, and provide their own publicity, not to mention comply with all police and censorship regulations.

A concert's location, date and time, ticket price, and musical offerings were all factors that had to be taken into account if the event were to be a financial success. That is perhaps why midday concerts were so common, for they avoided the expense of candles and heat. Moreover, performance facilities at restaurants—common venues for concerts in this period—usually were far cheaper than court buildings. On the other hand, theaters had better acoustics, and some offered the services of their standing orchestras in return for a percentage of the concert profits. Beethoven hated the whole process; in a letter responding to his friend Johann Tomaschek's complaints about the nuisance of arranging a concert, he wrote: "You are certainly right. So many blunders are made that one cannot get on with things. And the money one has to spend! . . . The devil take it."[2]

Until Vienna built its first official concert hall in 1831, the best locations for large, public concerts were the two court theaters. The Burgtheater, Viennese home of German drama, had good acoustics, notoriously poor ventilation, and a capacity of about one thousand persons (fig. 5.3). The nearby Kärntnertortheater, which specialized in opera and ballet, had the better orchestra and about the same capacity, though, as the

5.3 The Burgtheater (or Theater nächst dem Burg or Hofburgtheater), was so-called because of its proximity to the imperial residence, the Hofburg. In addition to being the official home of serious German spoken drama in Vienna (see Chapter 10), it was used for major concerts. See also plate 22. In the late nineteenth century, it was torn down and replaced, at another location, with the present Burgtheater. Colored engraving by Vinzenz Reim. [HM]

5.4 The Kärntnertortheater, the imperial opera house in Schubert's time, was the venue for most of Schubert's operatic and theater music, as well as for the premiere of Beethoven's Ninth Symphony (1824). Colored aquatint by Eduard Gurk, c. 1826. [HM]

visiting dramatist Helmine von Chezy complained in 1823, the heat within the theater was "truly tropical" (fig. 5.4).[3] Nevertheless, it was there that Beethoven premiered his Ninth Symphony and that the sensational violin virtuoso Paganini presented most of his lucrative concerts. The court theaters were difficult to secure, however, because of their busy dramatic schedules and the vagaries of court theater politics, not to mention their high rents.

As the next best choice, one could rent either the large or small hall of the court ballrooms (*Redoutensäle,* or Redouten Halls) on the Josefsplatz. These ballrooms, able to accommodate more than a thousand people, were favorite spots for benefit concerts, but their large, echoing halls created acoustical problems, and the rooms were difficult to light and heat. Other options included the Aula of the University, the Theater in der Josefstadt, and the Theater an der Wien (fig. 5.5). The capacity of the last was more than two thousand persons, making it the largest of the suburban theaters; moreover, its orchestra rivaled that of the court.

Having secured a concert hall, the concert giver was responsible for informing the police of the date and time of the concert, paying the required Music Impost taxes, and submitting all printed materials—such as the program, libretto, and concert posters—to the censorship office for approval. The latter hurdle was not always easy to clear because, as composer Louis Spohr learned in 1812, just before the premiere of his orato-

5.5 The grand Theater an der Wien (1801), built by Emanuel Schikaneder, Mozart's collaborator on *The Magic Flute* (see Chapter 10), is still one of Europe's great theaters. It was here that Beethoven's *Fidelio* was premiered during the first French occupation of Vienna (1805; see fig. 1.5), as well as *Rosamunde,* a play for which Schubert wrote ballet and incidental music (1823). Colored engraving of 1826. (See also fig. 7.24.) [HM]

rio *Das Jüngste Gericht (The Last Judgment),* censors forbade the names Jesus and Mary from appearing in print in either the program or in the published libretto of the oratorio. In 1824 the censors required Beethoven to list the sections of his *Missa Solemnis* that were on his concert program as hymns because they were presented in a secular setting. Such politically provocative works as a Freedom Symphony were banned altogether around 1800.

Throughout the period, the programs of public concerts and solo academies followed predictable patterns. It was customary to open with some rousing symphonic work, usually an opera overture, and to end with a bang—often an accompanied choral work or set of brilliant variations. Even during instrumental recitals, fashionable Italian arias were a fixture. The featured soloist appeared only two or three times per concert, opening with an obligatory concerto and ending with a virtuosic crowd pleaser such as a polonaise, a set of variations on a popular opera or national tune, or some other kind of musical novelty or improvisation. The other selections always provided contrast and were performed by friends, spouses, or siblings of the concert giver. Two examples taken from surviving concert programs illustrate the norm. On May 2, 1822, at the Theater an der Wien, visiting violinist Alexander Boucher and his wife (unnamed) presented the following program, scheduled just before a ballet:

Overture to *Villanella Rapita* by Mozart ("not a known opera here")

Introduction, Adagio and Rondo for Pedal Harp (Mrs. Boucher)

Violin Concerto (music by "different masters")

Aria from *Ermione* by Rossini

Duet Concertante for Harp and Pianoforte ("composed by Mrs. Boucher and played by her on both instruments at the same time—her own invention")

Polonaise for Violin ("interrupted by a musical storm") by Boucher

At the Kärntnertortheater on November 10 and 18, 1826, pianist Franz Schoberlechner gave an academy to mark his return from St. Petersburg with this program, also presented before a ballet:

Overture to *Euryanthe* by Weber

New Great Concerto in F# Minor by Schoberlechner

Aria, sung by Mademoiselle Schnitt

Piano Variations on a Theme from Rossini's *La Cenerentola*

Polonaise for Violin by Max Mayseder

Free Fantasia for Piano by Schoberlechner

Beyond their predictable shows of brilliant technical skill, public concerts also provided a forum for all manner of musical machines, including such uncommon instruments as the czakan and noseflute and technical improvements like the keyed trumpet and pedal harp (figs. 5.6, 5.7). Ingenious new methods to play traditional instruments were sometimes also advertised, like the playing of a piece entirely on one violin string (by Jacques Fereol-Mazas and Paganini) or playing the guitar with only the left hand (by Carl von Gaertner). Child prodigies and large families performing musical novelties seldom failed to pull at Viennese heartstrings—and to sell tickets (fig. 5.8).

MUSICAL SOCIETIES

Another kind of concert experience, one intended to educate and to uplift musical tastes, was provided by relatively new music societies, founded and led by educated members of the upper middle class. The most important of these was the Society of the Friends of Music *(Gesellschaft der Musikfreunde);* founded in 1818, it established a conservatory and organized for its members a sizable number of well-rehearsed concerts of serious art music. Each year it sponsored four large Society concerts (usually on Sunday afternoons at the Redouten Halls), which featured the talents of its members as composers, conductors, and musicians. The Society's orchestra of about 70 strings and winds and its chorus of 120–140 singers brought together professional musicians, students, and talented amateurs. Although the Society's concerts were technically private, they became little more than subscription concerts for which music lovers paid a set "membership" fee, which then made them eligible to buy a series ticket. Tickets were not sold at the door.

5.6

5.8

5.7

5.6 The czakan (from the Hungarian *csákány*, cane-flute) was an early-nineteenth-century recorderlike wind instrument. The Viennese oboeist Ernst Krähmer, who is known to have also been a member of a male vocal ensemble that sang a Schubert quartet in concert (1821), was the sole virtuoso exponent of the czakan. He also composed for it and wrote a treatise about the instrument. [MMA, Gift of Mr. A. C. Glassgold, 1975]

5.7 The lyra-guitarre was tuned like a six-stringed guitar and had a burst of popularity c. 1785–1810. This one, made by Jacques-Pierre Michelot of Paris, was owned by Schubert's friend the singer Johann Michael Vogl. [GdMf]

5.8 This guitar, made in Vienna by Barnard Enzensperger, is a reminder that Schubert's songs for voice and piano, including "Erlkönig," were sometimes published simultaneously with guitar accompaniments. Schubert himself is known to have played the guitar. [HM]

Although the outward organization of the Society's concerts resembled that of commercial academies, they differed in important ways. First, the Society presented whole symphonies and overtures by such classical masters as Mozart, Cherubini, Spontini, and Beethoven. Vocalists still sang Italian arias by Rossini and his contemporaries, but they also offered selections from oratorios, cantatas, and hymns by local Viennese composers and court musicians. Finally, the Society avoided programming sentimental favorites and virtuosic potboilers, and it actively discouraged applause at the performance: concerts had more "serious" goals.

Eventually made a member of the Society, Franz Schubert presented only a few works at its concerts. The following program of March 3, 1822, illustrates the context of a rare public performance of Schubert's music, as well as the Society's conservative musical tastes:

Great Symphony in C [the Jupiter] by Mozart
Vocal Quartet "Geist der Liebe" by Schubert
Concerto for Violin (I) by Mayseder
Overture to *Egmont* by Beethoven
Finale from *Silvana* by C. M. Weber

Beginning in 1818, the Society also offered an annual subscription series of Thursday Evening Entertainments *(Abendunterhaltungen),* comprising about fifteen musical soirées of chamber music that cost only about three florins a month for three concerts.[4] At first held in various inns and in the County Hall, by 1822 they eventually settled in the rooms of the Red Hedgehog Inn *(Zum roten Igl)* in the Tuchlauben. Like musical salons held in private homes, these concerts featured string quartets, instrumental solos and duets with piano accompaniment, and lieder. Most of Schubert's music that was performed semipublicly during his lifetime was presented in this setting. A sample program from November 10, 1825, again confirms the diversity of medium and genres:

Quartet by Mayseder
Variations on *Molinara*
Polonaise by Mayseder
Duet from *Elisa und Claudio* by Mercadante
Potpourri for Cello by Romberg
Vocal Quartet "Geist der Liebe" by Schubert
Trio with Choir from *Der Freischütz* by C. M. Weber

In the same spirit and setting as these Evening Entertainments, Schubert's only academy—the one formal concert devoted solely to his music during his lifetime—took place on Wednesday evening, March 26, 1828. As a member of the Society, he petitioned and received free use of its rented rooms on the Tuchlauben. The concert performers, who also had Society affiliations, were friends of Schubert's who probably donated their services to increase his profits. Because it was advertised as a "private Academy," Schubert's concert program was not scrutinized by the police, but tickets had to be purchased in advance. Like the Society's musicales, the program began with a movement from a quartet and ended with a substantial choral work:

Quartet [in A], first movement
Songs: "Der Kreuzzug," "Die Sterne," "Fischerweise," "Fragment aus Aeschylus," "Serenade"
Trio for Piano, Violin and Cello [in E-flat]
Songs: "Auf der Strom," "Die Allmacht"
"Schlachtgesang" for double male choir

If Otto Erich Deutsch is correct that Schubert netted eight hundred florins from the concert, then at least 267 persons must have attended, for each ticket cost three florins.[5]

Another amateur music society that presented concerts on a regular basis was that of the Concerts Spirituels, founded in 1819 by the choir director at St. Augustine's, Franz Gebauer (fig. 5.9). Modeled after the organization of the same name in France, this society offered eighteen bimonthly performances on Friday afternoons that featured in their entirety a few, decidedly serious symphonies and sacred choral works as well, while carefully eschewing all demonstrations of bravura. Concertos and Italian arias were banned (until 1830), and Austro-German compositions were favored. The following two programs from 1820 exemplify the concert fare offered:

Series Concert #2: Symphony in E-flat by Mozart and a Mass by Cherubini
Series Concert #11: Symphony No. 8 by Beethoven, three Hymns by Mosel, and sacred
    choruses by Eybler, C. P. E. Bach, and Mozart

The reputed quality of these performances, however, was low, for amateur musicians performed the entire concert at sight or with only a single run-through just before the performance.

In the same vein were the rare subscription concerts of chamber music offered by the court violinist Ignaz Schuppanzigh and three other professional musicians (fig. 5.10). During the 1820s, each of their concerts presented three complete string quartets and quintets of Haydn, Mozart, Beethoven, and Schubert. In a sense, they offered the Viennese middle classes what aristocrats had heard in their private salons during the previous generation.

Increasingly, the educated middle classes became the guardians of Austro-German art music. Through their concerts, conservatory, and writings, they began to define high art in music. Their generally conservative tastes sought to enshrine the music of the "classical" masters (see Chapter 4) and to promote vocal music in German. They insisted that the performances be well-rehearsed and complete. Consequently, they shaped what we consider today to be standard concert repertory and laid the groundwork and biases for the new field of music criticism.

5.9 Diagram of the disposition of the chorus and orchestra of the Concerts Spirituels at the Land-haussaal in the Herrengasse, Vienna, c. 1825–30. The concerts of this organization provided opportunities for Schubert to become acquainted with the oratorios of Handel, who, according to Schubert's friend Anselm Hüttenbrenner, was greatly admired by Schubert for his "mighty spirit." *Messiah,* in fact, was one of Schubert's favorite works. [GdMf]

In sharp contrast to these musical connoisseurs were the growing audiences demanding the new virtuosic styles of Rossini and Paganini (fig. 5.11). Capacity concert crowds, made up of all classes paying inflated prices, rocked the theaters with their applause and stamping feet. The music was entertaining, not edifying, and it was fashionable. By the mid-1820s, the battle lines between the two musical camps were drawn.

MUSIC AND VIENNESE SALONS

Almost every visitor had something to say about the omnipresence of music in Viennese salons (see also Chapter 2). Home concerts for family and friends easily outnumbered those given in public halls during the 1820s. From the nobility down through the ranks of the middle class, Viennese boys and girls began music lessons at four or five years old as a normal part of their education. As they progressed, they were expected to perform prepared pieces upon demand. Many became proficient, even outstanding musicians who could perform difficult works alone or provide accompaniment for others. Because middle- and upper-class women were thwarted from mu-

5.10 The violinist Ignaz Schuppanzigh was the founder of what can be called the first professional string quartet; he championed serious chamber music, especially that of Beethoven, but he also programmed works of Schubert on his concerts. Schubert's String Quartet in A minor, Op. 29 (1824), was dedicated to him. (See fig. A.2.) [HM]

sical professions by social taboos and well-connected men were expected to follow the careers of their fathers, some of Vienna's best musicians may well have been amateurs who played only in salons.

Music was only a part of salon activity. Concentrated during the social season (from fall through late spring), social calls and salon gatherings usually began with tea about four o'clock in the afternoon or in the early evening from about six o'clock. Guests were expected to join in the polite conversation, card and parlor games, reading and writing of literature or poetry, and music making and dance that followed. Of course, social etiquette and the interests of a particular salon's host and hostess determined who was present and what activities they pursued.

For the middle class, a piano in the parlor was a symbol of bon ton as well as a focal point of family entertainment. Many eyewitnesses suggest that the ability to perform music improved one's chances of finding a wealthy mate or of securing new business clients. In 1820 Professor Wilhelm Christian Müller wrote back to his friends in Bremen: "It is unbelievable how far-reaching are the love of music and especially the facility on the piano. In every house is a good instrument. At the home of banker Geymüller we found five by different makers. Women especially play a lot."[6]

For the well-educated bureaucrats, whose work was often tedious and whose public conduct was scrutinized by the secret police, salon concerts were an important outlet and, for some, an avocation. The Schubertiades provides a good example. Sponsored by high-ranking Austrian civil servants who eventually earned titles for their work, Schubertiades combined music with camaraderie between hosts, their business associates, their children, and their guests. Each party began with the performance of

5.11 Although Nicolò Paganini's seemingly superhuman virtuosity caused him to be labeled the "diabolical" violinist, Schubert wrote to a friend after hearing Paganini in 1828: "I have heard an angel sing in the Adagio." Unfortunately, the enormous hubbub over the great Italian virtuoso caused Schubert's only benefit concert to go virtually unnoticed by the press. Lithograph of 1828 by Schubert's acquaintance Josef Kriehuber. [HM]

songs by Schubert, often accompanied by the composer. Then Schubert and his friends played piano duets or sang jocular quartets. After a big meal, the guests played parlor games and danced. Although these musicales no doubt had memorable performances, they still were not deemed the proper setting for Schubert's more serious chamber music, like his string quartets or piano sonatas (see also Chapter 1 and Afterword).

Other middle-class salons, however, did specialize in such music. Schubert's father was a part of a string quartet that met regularly to play serious music. Josef Hochenadel, an official in the Ministry of War, organized Sunday afternoon concerts (1820–25) from November through Easter at which his children and friends presented symphonies and large choral works. Likewise, the law professor Ignaz Sonnleithner sponsored home concerts twice weekly during the winter, bringing together amateur and professional musicians (fig. 5.12). He was responsible for the first publication of Schubert's "Gretchen am Spinnrade," Opus 2, and possibly for introducing the composer to his nephew Franz Grillparzer.

Other salons helped to revive interest in "old" music. Raphael Kiesewetter, chairman of the Imperial War Council and vice president of the Friends of Music (1821–26), was also an avid collector of music manuscripts and prints from the seventeenth and eighteenth centuries. Exploiting his connections with the court archivers and with the members of the Friends of Music, he presented five home concerts of mostly sacred choral music ranging from Palestrina to J. S. Bach. According to his letters, Kiesewetter's choir was an informal and ad hoc group, members of which sang the music from sight without rehearsal. Among the participants were Michael Vogl, Ludwig Tietze, Karl Schoberlechner, and all four of the Fröhlich sisters—all friends of Schubert's and members of the Friends of Music.

Like Kiesewetter, Simon Molitor also used his home to pursue his antiquarian pas-

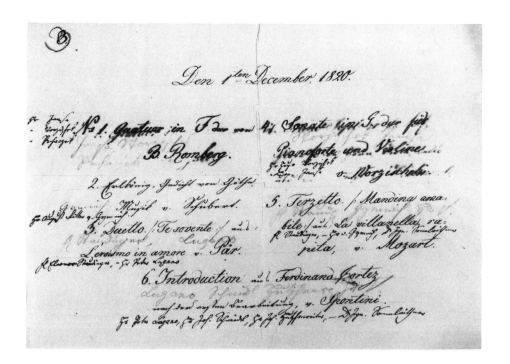

5.12 Law professor and Schubert supporter Ignaz Sonnleithner regularly hosted musical salons at his home; the program for one on December 1, 1820, appears on this hand-written announcement. Listed is a potpourri of instrumental and vocal music, typical of the time, including Schubert's song "Erlkönig." [GdMf]

sion for early music. He and members of the court chapel presented bimonthly performances of instrumental music of the sixteenth and seventeenth centuries in his home from 1832 through 1848. The activities of Kiesewetter and Molitor represent larger currents in the nineteenth century, for their research into early music eventually led to the creation of societies for that purpose, like the Bach revivals of the 1830s and the Cecilian Movement, which sought to restore the ethereal sound of Renaissance vocal polyphony to Roman Catholic worship. Their work also provided the foundation for the more systematic study of historical music, which Guido Adler called musicology in Vienna at the end of the century.

MUSIC IN RELIGIOUS LIFE

The Viennese passion for drama and music also carried over into religious observances. Though not strictly concerts, liturgies with music performed in the city's churches and synagogue constituted a musical attraction for many tourists. Roman Catholic observances of Holy Week, Corpus Christi, and the funerals of dignitaries were always marked with rich ceremony, lavish processions, and special music (see plate 7).

5.13 As a boy, Franz Schubert performed as an imperial choirboy in the Court Chapel, here represented by Johann Hieronymus Löschenkohl on the occasion of a Te Deum for the new emperor Leopold II, father of Francis I, in 1792. [HM]

Austria's showcase for sacred music was the Court Chapel, which employed the best musicians and composers in the Empire (fig. 5.13). In 1825 their number included ten adult male choristers (who also sang at the opera), ten handpicked, well-trained choirboys (Schubert among them from 1808 to 1812), two female soloists, two organists, and an orchestra of about twenty-five musicians. On Sunday mornings at eleven o'clock in the small chapel attached to the imperial palace, they performed sinfonias and fully orchestrated masses by their own choirmasters and native Austrian composers including Josef and Michael Haydn, Mozart, Salieri (fig. 5.14), Eybler, Preindl, and Seyfried.

Large, concerted masses with orchestra were presented at St. Stephen's cathedral, also at eleven o'clock on Sunday mornings. But eyewitness accounts disagree about the quality of the performances there, citing the distractions of the constant motion and talking of the worshipers at the various chapels within the sanctuary, the "earsplitting" and constant pealing of the cathedral bells, and the operatic style of the sacred music. Instead, they praised the music at St. Augustine's, which had a small string orchestra and a choir of about fifteen to twenty singers directed by Salieri and Peter Winter during the 1820s. In addition, the churches of St. Anne, St. Peter, St. Michael, and St. Charles (the Karlskirche) were sometimes mentioned by travelers for their organs and choral music.

5.14 Antonio Salieri was head of Vienna's imperial music establishment. The boy Schubert's musical precosity prompted his father to bring him in 1807 to Salieri, who subsequently recommended him for the imperial choir. Schubert had private lessons from Salieri beginning in 1812 and continued this study after leaving the choir school in 1813. In 1814 his teacher was present at Schubert's childhood parish church in Lichtental to hear the Mass in F, D.105, the first public performance of any of Schubert's works. Afterward Salieri allegedly embraced the teenage composer with the words "Franz, you are my pupil, and you are going to bring me much further honor." [HM]

For Schubert, the church was an important patron. Throughout his career he wrote about twenty-five liturgical works, including six masses and a number of offertories, special antiphons, Salve Reginas, and Stabat Maters. These were composed mostly for suburban Viennese churches with which he had a personal connection, usually to its choir director, like Michael Holzer at the parish church in Liechtental or Schubert's brother Ferdinand, who served as choir director at the church in Alt-Lerchenfeld.

In addition, Schubert composed about twenty-five nonliturgical sacred songs, most of them on commission. For example, his setting of the Twenty-third Psalm in 1822 was composed expressly for his friend Anna Fröhlich's female voice students at the conservatory. The young women performed it at their annual public jury concerts as well as at a number of Evening Entertainments sponsored by the Society of the Friends of Music. Schubert also composed the vocal quartet called "Prayer" at the request of the Countess Esterhazy while spending a second summer in Zseliz (1826) as the Esterhazys' musician-teacher in residence. Although today his most popular sacred song is "Ave Maria," it was first called "Ellen's Song" and was originally intended as part of his musical settings of poems from The Lady of the Lake by Sir Walter Scott.

Vienna's new synagogue on the Seitenstettengasse had an excellent choir and cantor, Salomon Sulzer (see plate 10). A gifted baritone who performed in the theater and later taught at the conservatory, Sulzer urged modernization in setting traditional Hebrew melodies and the commission of new music for Jewish services. Along with Beethoven, Drechsler, Seyfried, and Fischhof, Schubert was asked to compose for the temple. He responded in July 1828 with a setting of the Ninety-second Psalm for baritone and unaccompanied choir. The beauty and novelty of the a cappella singing deeply affected those who heard it. Frances Trollope, the inveterate English travelogue writer, expressed her amazement in 1836: "There is, in truth, so wild and strange an harmony in the songs of the children of Israel as performed in the synagogue in this city, that it would be difficult to render full justice to the splendid excellence of the performances, without falling into the language of enthusiasm."[7]

MILITARY MUSIC

Writing his famous travel guide to Vienna in 1828, Charles Sealsfield (the nom de plume of Karl Postl) pointed out to the tourist that "the musical bands of all these regiments and troops are the best of their kind. Their playing is plainly electrifying."[8] From about 1820 to 1845 newly re-formed Austrian military bands vied with those of England for their smart appearance and musical prowess. The bands' primary duty was to provide music for regimental parades and reviews, but they also took part in city ceremonies like the Corpus Christi processions, the celebration of the emperor's birthday, and the formal reception of foreign dignitaries. They also performed every afternoon at one o'clock near the Neue Burgtor for the changing of the guard.

The bands of the 1820s contained about thirty well-drilled, uniformed musicians who could play difficult music. Improvements of valved and keyed brass instruments about the same time also changed the ensembles' composition and sound, from mostly reeds to a more modern trumpet-dominated corps. The directors of the new bands, who were not necessarily drawn from the military, were often first rate. Thus, Johann Strauss Sr. and Josef Lanner, two men best known to us for their waltzes, directed the First and Second Viennese Citizens' Regimental Bands, respectively (fig. 5.15).

A surviving program from a military band concert in 1836 celebrating the new emperor's coronation in Bohemia suggests what such concerts might have been like. Beginning with a cannonade, three regimental bands alternately played marches and waltzes in the Volksgarten near the palace. Around 9 P.M. Josef Lanner directed the merged ensembles in a march, a "Jubilate," and coronation anthems. Fireworks then followed.

The popularity of military march music carried over into the salon piano repertory as well. Schubert's well-known piano duet "Marche militaire" was only one of three in Opus 51 (c. 1822). He also composed three "Marches heroiques," Opus 27, and three "Grandes marches," Opus 40 (both published 1824). In addition he commemorated the death of Tsar Alexander I and the coronation of Tsar Nicholas I with piano duet marches (published 1826). These marches were transcribed for band soon after Schubert's death.

POPULAR MUSIC

The English organist and music critic Edward Holmes recalled his visit to Vienna around 1828: "No place of refreshment, from the highest to the lowest, is without

5.15 Two leading proponents of the waltz were the orchestra leaders Johann Strauss Sr., in a water-color by Heinrich Wilhelm Schlesinger, left, and Josef Lanner, in an anonymous watercolor. During their careers, the waltz, at first often associated with ecstatic, youthful excess, evolved into a tamer dance associated with polite society and luxurious dance halls. [HM]

music; bassoonists and clarionets are as 'plentiful as blackberries,' and in the suburbs at every turn one alights upon fresh carousing, fresh fiddling, fresh illuminations."9

Vienna's classic popular music was launched from the city's glittering ballrooms, smoky beer and wine halls, and crowded parks and courtyards. Originally venues for lower-class entertainment, these places produced dances and songs so distinctive and irresistible that by the middle of the nineteenth century they were embraced by all of Europe as "art."

Dancing flourished in Vienna, even though it was banned on all religious holidays, national days of mourning, Sundays until about 6 P.M., among other times. During carnival, from January 7 through the eve of Ash Wednesday, dancing reigned supreme. Alongside dressmakers and pastry chefs, Viennese music publishers feverishly prepared for the lucrative carnival season by creating souvenir dance anthologies that one could play at home. Schubert also took advantage of the opportunity by contributing dance pieces to these publications every season from 1822 through 1828 (see Chapter 6).

Carnival also offered good employment to dance musicians, usually men from the lower classes who worked at other occupations. Orchestras that played for the court Redouten Halls numbered from fifteen to twenty members, but the elegant, large, sub-urban dance halls like the Apollo Hall boasted an orchestra of sixty musicians (see figs. 6.3, 6.4). Most balls began with a promenade, accompanied by a slow march or polon-aise. Then followed a series of quadrille dance sets and faster dances like the galop. After 1815 the waltz began to dominate, and by 1829 visitors claimed that it permeated every corner of the city. Guardians of moral rectitude were shocked by the dance's suggestive, circular motion and the close body positions, while others vigorously condemned it as unhealthful, asserting that some dancers collapsed from the exertion and harmed their lungs with the dust clouds that swirling skirts raised.

Because demand for dance music was high in Vienna, there also was keen competition between orchestras and dance halls for the newest and most distinctive music. Beginning in the 1820s, the first generation of "waltz kings" arose out of these suburban ballrooms. Among these, Franz Morelli, Josef Lanner, and Johann Strauss Sr. were the most successful. Soon "ball-fests" were as fruitful as regular concerts for raising money. For example, on August 25, 1830, in the suburban Sperl ballroom, Johann Strauss Sr. gave a benefit concert with an orchestra of forty-five members, amplified by the trumpet corps of a local regimental band. From 7 P.M. to 5 A.M. Strauss presented many of his already popular waltzes and galops, as well as new dances composed for the event.

Even more live music was available where one ate and drank (fig. 5.16). Some neighborhood eateries hired small bands to play popular opera tunes, dances, and songs. Wine and beer halls featured zither music and folksingers. Zithers played all the latest tunes, but they also preserved the old Ländler and folk songs, which were sung in Viennese dialect. Some players were so proficient they performed zither concerti. Johann Strauss Jr. recalled the atmosphere of those earlier places and times by inserting a zither solo at the beginning and end of his waltz "Tales of the Vienna Woods."

5.16 The harp was a much more important and pervasive instrument in Schubert's day than is usually recognized. It was played by professional virtuosi in concerts, by amateurs aspiring to a cultured life at home, and by poor, often itinerant, minstrels eking out a living in taverns (as in this watercolor) and on street corners. [HM]

The same establishments also presented *Bänkelsänger*. These were part-time musicians who sang, yodeled, and told stories to the accompaniment of harps or guitars (both popular instruments at all levels of society). They were especially famous for their ballads recalling the stories of natural disasters and sensational murders, and for sentimental stories in rhymed verse. Beginning in the 1820s, some of these balladeers or folksingers joined together to form companies that presented costumed scenes and folk cantatas. From one such company emerged J. B. Moser, who today is credited with the reform of Viennese folk music because he worked to improve the living and working conditions of these musicians.

Itinerant harpists improvised and performed satirical, irreverent, and off-color songs in Vienna's parks and apartment courtyards. Their notorious wit and provocative gestures helped them to become stock figures in the folk comedies of Raimund and Nestroy. Deemed a harmless nuisance by the police, the harpists had the greatest freedom of speech of any of Vienna's artists to comment on the foibles of their leaders and society's "betters." Their spirit lives on in the improvised, spoken clown roles for civil servants (like Frosch in *Fledermaus*) and raving fiacre drivers found toward the end of the century in Johann Strauss Jr.'s operettas.

Less-skilled itinerant musicians cranked barrel organs or played fiddles, bagpipes, accordions, or other modest instruments to accompany the innumerable medicine men, traveling menageries, marionette theaters, and sideshows that worked the city. By 1821 their numbers grew so rapidly that the police decided to grant city music permits only to war veterans and those musicians who were blind or infirm, because they feared that the others constituted a criminal element. The piteous sight and sound of beggar-musicians thus also became a part of the Viennese landscape. Schubert captured their essence in his song "Der Leiermann," the barefoot, cold, hurdy-gurdy man with his empty money plate endlessly turning his wheel at the conclusion of the song cycle *Winterreise*.

Today, historians argue about the real impact and influence of Viennese music during this period, contrasting the conservative nature of Vienna's musical institutions with the innovations taking place elsewhere in Europe. Others criticize the Viennese for their perceived frivolous musical tastes and their nonintellectual, improvisational theatrical traditions. But such arguments usually reflect more about their writers and our times than the subject. Certainly, the development of the German art song or Lied and the Viennese waltz were major nineteenth-century achievements that all Europe recognized and eventually applauded. But also important were the organization of music societies, conservatories, and concert halls, the establishment of concert repertoires, the research into earlier music, the re-formation of military bands, and the boom in folk music that occurred during the Biedermeier era, for they laid the foundation for the next great flowering of Viennese music at the end of the nineteenth century.

NOTES

1. Carl Maria von Weber, *The Life of an Artist* (London: Chapman and Halls, 1865), 2: 271.

2. Oscar Sonneck, ed., *Beethoven, Impressions by His Contemporaries* (New York: Dover, 1954), 103–4.

3. Helmine von Chezy, *Unvergessenes, Denkwürdigkeiten aus dem Leben von Helmine von Chezy* (Leipzig: Brockhaus, 1858), 2: 255.

4. Viennese currency is discussed in Alice M. Hanson, *Musical Life in Biedermeier Vienna* (Cambridge: Cambridge University Press, 1985), 14–19. Apartments of three to five rooms in Vienna rented for 250–600 florins per year. One could eat well on one florin a day.

5. Otto Erich Deutsch, "Schubert's Incomes," *Music and Letters* 36 (1955), 166.

6. C. W. Müller, *Briefe an deutsche Freunde von einer Reise* (Altona: I. F. Hammerich, 1824), 130.

7. Frances Trollope, *Vienna and the Austrians* (London: Richard Bentley, 1838), 1: 286. The term *enthusiasm* here is used in an ironic twist on the archaic sense of a state of ecstasy resulting from being possessed by a god.

8. Charles Sealsfield, *Austria As It Is* (London: Hurst, Chance and Co., 1828), 183.

9. Edward Holmes, *A Ramble Among the Musicians of Germany* (New York: Da Capo, 1969), 138.

FOR FURTHER READING

For information on Viennese concert life and venues see especially Alice M. Hanson, *Musical Life in Biedermeier Vienna* (Cambridge: Cambridge University Press, 1985). Also useful for the late eighteenth century and the first decade of the nineteenth is Mary S. Morrow, *Concert Life in Haydn's Vienna* (Stuyvesant, N.Y.: Pendragon, 1989). Edward Hanslick, *Geschichte des Concertwesens in Wien* (Vienna: W. Braumüller, 1869), was the pathbreaking study of Viennese concert life. Otto Erich Deutsch, *Schubert: A Documentary Biography* (New York: Da Capo, 1977), contains much information about musical life in Vienna, including concert programs involving Schubert.

On venues for concert performance in Schubert's Vienna, see Hermann Ulrich, "Aus vormärzlichen Konzertsälen Wiens," *Jahrbuch des Vereins für Geschichte der Stadt Wien* 28 (1972): 106–30. On Schubert and the Society of the Friends of Music, see Otto Biba, "Franz Schubert und die Gesellschaft der Musikfreunden in Wien," *Schubert Kongress Wien, 1978, Bericht* (Graz: Akademischer Druck und Verlag, 1978), 23–36. On interest in early music in early nineteenth-century Vienna, see Hierfrid Kier, *Raphael Kiesewetter* (Regensburg: Bosse Verlag, 1968) (Studien zur Musikgeschichte des 19ten Jahrhunderts 13). On the imperial musical establishment, see Karl Wisokor-Meytsky, *Die Hofmusikkappelle* (Vienna: Hofmusikkappelle, 1965). On music in Jewish worship in early-nineteenth-century Vienna, see Alexander Ringer, "Joseph Sulzer, Joseph Mainzer, and the Romantic a cappella Movement," *Studia Musicologica* 11 (1969), 355–70. On Austrian military music see Emil Rameis, *Die Österreichishe Militärmusik von ihren Anfängen* (Tutzing: Hans Schneider, 1976). On street musicians and folksingers see Anna Frei, "Die Wiener Strassensängern und Musikanten" (Ph.D. diss., University of Vienna, 1978).

· 6 ·

Social Dancing in Schubert's World

ELIZABETH ALDRICH

Franz Schubert's symphonic and chamber music is standard fare in concert halls; but it is frequently overlooked that he was one of the most prolific composers of exquisite music composed specifically for social dancing—literally hundreds of dance pieces, often in sets of up to thirty-six individual works (fig. 6.1).[1] Program notes for concerts and liner notes for recordings featuring Schubert's dance music tend to refer condescendingly to these "little pieces" as "charming," "musical posies," "surprisingly sophisticated." Yet we know that Schubert delighted in improvising at the piano music for informal dance gatherings, and in fact dance music constituted about 40 percent of the approximately five hundred works of Schubert's published during his lifetime.[2] In such music, Schubert naturally drew on the rhythms and other formal and expressive characteristics of the many social dances found within the borders of the Habsburg Empire in his time.

Schubert's dance music arose in a city that could claim to be a City of Dance as well as the City of Music. Perhaps because so many activities were circumscribed in the reign of Francis I, dance provided a sense of liberation while affording opportunity to display one's social graces and sophistication. This was especially true at carnival time *(Fasching)*, the period after Epiphany (January 6) to midnight of the Tuesday before Ash Wednesday, during which the Viennese danced their hearts out (fig. 6.2).

6.1 Franz Schubert, *Walzer, Ländler und Ecossoisen für das Pianoforte
. . . 18tes Werk* (Vienna: Cappi and Diabelli, 1823), D.145. Schubert
and Anton Diabelli, the head of the publishing firm of Cappi and
Diabelli, had a falling out over Schubert's compensation for this
and other publications that appeared about this time. (See the
Afterword and fig. A.5.) [GdMf]

6.2 *Carneval 1823. Sammlung original deutscher Tänze für das Piano-Forte*
(Vienna: Sauer and Leidesdorf, 1823). This "Collection of Original
German Dances for the Piano"—which includes pieces by Czerny,
Schubert (D.971), and others—typifies a popular type of publication
and is evidence of the close association of dancing with carnival
time—indeed, it is reported that, on one Carnival Sunday (1821),
sixteen hundred balls took place in Vienna. Although Schubert himself apparently did not dance, there are accounts of his improvising at
the piano to accompany the dancing of his friends. [WSLb]

6.3 The two Redouten Halls, the larger of which is shown here in a colored etching by Joseph Schütz, c. 1815, accommodated a great number of dancers. Note the relative absence of masks, though police ordinances permitted them in the Redouten Halls, if only there. [HM]

Among the many venues for dancing in Vienna proper were the two huge ball-rooms, each with its own orchestra playing the latest music, constituting the Redouten Halls next to the imperial palace or Hofburg on one side of the Josefsplatz (fig. 6.3). Originally used only by nobility, the halls were opened to virtually everybody by Joseph II, who wanted to encourage the mixing of the classes. Although the Redouten Halls became so crowded by the end of the eighteenth century that it was sometimes impossible to find room to dance, they played a long and important role in the history of social dancing in Vienna. In 1808 a brand new dance establishment opened, the Apollo Hall (fig. 6.4). This became the most beloved of the dance halls, although entrance tickets cost more than at the Redouten Halls. The Apollo Hall served mainly the upper middle class, but Tuesdays were reserved for nobility. The less well-heeled could seek out any of the dozens of taverns and inns in and around the city of Vienna that had rooms and music appropriate for dancing; indeed, the right to sell alcoholic beverages at such establishments carried with it the right to have music and dancing until the two privileges were separated in 1820—because the dancing, not the alcohol, was considered a threat to public tranquility (fig. 6.5). At that time it also became necessary to register with the police in advance all private as well as public balls. On the other hand, hours for dancing were extended so that enthusiasts could literally dance through the night.

6.4 The Apollo Hall, designed by the Parisien architect Charles von Moreau and opened 1808 in the suburb of Schottenfeld, southwest of the city proper, was a spectacular venue for dancing and other pleasures, as seen in this colored etching. Descriptions of the time mention the plants, waterfalls, and grottos; guests dined on silver plates in an environment whose springlike smells offered comfort against the cold, snowy wintertime. Although the Apollo survived the financial crises of the Napoleonic wars and immediate post-Congress period, it was converted into a candle factory in 1839. [HM]

Dancing was regulated by the government because this form of human expression was viewed as seriously—and sometimes as suspiciously—as any other in late-eighteenth- and early-nineteenth-century Austria. Dancing was forbidden at various times, including Advent and Lent, every Friday, and during special church feasts. Furthermore, the hours the dance halls could be open were determined by the police. In most of Europe carnival involved masks, costumes, and parades, but not in Vienna: parades were forbidden and so were masks, except inside the Redouten Halls; costumes were similarly restricted. In the course of the eighteenth century and into the nineteenth the use of masks declined; a well-known picture of a ball in the Redouten Halls during the time of the Congress of Vienna shows hardly any masks at all. But perhaps all these restrictions had the effect of fueling the Viennese passion for dance.

In any event, social dance was a significant part of early-nineteenth-century social life, including the gatherings of Schubert and his friends. Specifically cited in the diaries of Schubert's circle are dances called *cotillon, galop, Deutscher,* and *Walzer.* Also included among Schubert's compositions are the *ecossaise, polonaise, allemande, Ländler,* and

6.5 The *Briefe eines Eipeldauers* was a popular weekly journal that was published from 1792 to 1821. Enlivened by the use of Viennese dialect and illustrations, it offers a good picture of daily life in Schubert's Vienna. This image in an 1817 issue suggests that dancing in taverns and inns was a popular activity. [HM]

menuet. The rich palette of social dances most likely known to Schubert also included the *contradanse, anglaise, quadrille,* and *mazurka.*

During the late eighteenth and early nineteenth centuries, social dancing underwent a number of technical and social transformations. The mixing of classes and the involvement of the middle classes in what earlier had been a largely aristocratic activity has been mentioned. But there was also a move away from the ball as a preorchestrated sequence of events involving the whole company to a forum in which individual couples could act with independence. There were also new trends, such as very fast dances that necessitated smoother dance floors. Not that dancing surfaces were just like those of our modern ballrooms: the up-to-date Apollo Hall was notable for sprinkling down the floor surface with water after several dances to keep the dust down. Such ballroom dust (and the dancing that raised it) was blamed by one visitor to Vienna during Schubert's lifetime as a leading cause of death in the city: "'Vienna is windy and unhealthy' goes the saying, for weak lungs cannot withstand the commonly-present dust of the gravel floor. Lung infections are not rare here, although not too dangerous, but among the ten to eleven thousand people who die annually, a quarter of them die from lung diseases, the result of too much waltzing."[3]

Social dances performed during the first decades of nineteenth-century Vienna fell roughly into two categories: dances for couples performing in groups and dances for couples dancing independently. In turn, group dances were divided into those that were performed by a line of men facing a line of women, as in ecossaises and other derivatives of English country dances, and those involving four couples facing in squares, such as cotillions and quadrilles. The polonaise was another group dance performed by a line of couples who processed in columns throughout the ballroom, creating geometric paths.

Couple dances (identified by a broad array of confusing terms) included Deutscher, waltz, and galop. All required partners to turn or whirl, often locked in an embrace. To further complicate categories, some of the elements found in couple dances such as the waltz were often performed as sections or figures of group dances. In other words, it was not uncommon to find a quadrille containing a "waltz" or "galop."

THE MENUET: FROM COUPLE DANCE TO GROUP DANCE

Included in the category of solo couple dances is one that did not require partners to turn, the *menuet*. That it reached a pinnacle of popularity during the baroque in the first quarter of the eighteenth century is common knowledge; less recognized is that it continued to enjoy distinction well into the nineteenth century. Although it was originally a French dance associated with the universally emulated court of Louis XIV (r. 1661–1715), the menuet's popularity spread throughout western and eastern Europe. It continued to flourish through the early decades of the nineteenth century, undergoing, however, a metamorphosis as dancing masters in western Europe, by choreographing their own versions suited to teaching deportment to their students, tried to make an old-fashioned dance relevant to the changing times.

In 1805 the Scottish dancing master Francis Peacock noted that the "menuet is necessary . . . [for those] whose education has been neglected, or their manners perverted by bad teachers."[4] And in 1829, nearly a century after the dance's height of popularity, the Leipzig dancing master E. D. Helmke expressed similar sentiments: "To the menuet belong all the beautiful characteristics that go into dance: majesty, noble bearing, grace, dignity, reverence, gallantry, and finesse. . . . It should be noted that he who cannot dance the menuet well is not a great dancer and can seldom dance other dances well either."[5]

Throughout Europe dancing masters attempted to revive the menuet during the early years of the nineteenth century as a dance designed to display good manners. Although the efforts to invigorate or reclaim the dance in France and England waned in the early years of the nineteenth century, the dance continued to be performed well into the 1830s throughout Austria and Germany. The menuet was grasped by a growing middle class—a class of people with no previous history of performing this noble court dance—because it epitomized the elements considered important to one's presentation of self in the social world: strong bearing, proper deportment, control, and faultless manners. Such characteristics were assumed to reflect the performer's morality and place in society.

Danced by one couple at a time (with all other couples attentively watching), the French courtly menuet of the early eighteenth century was essential in all noble ballrooms, where the ability to perform social dances well was extremely important. This type of menuet contained six "figures."[6] The opening figure placed partners in opposite corners to begin the signature figure known as the Z or reversed S. Tracing a Z pattern on the floor, the figure would be danced as many times as the gentleman desired. At the conclusion of the figure, the gentleman would offer his right hand to his partner and they would dance, each holding right hands, the figure called 'giving of right hands." Upon conclusion, partners would dance the figure called "giving of left hands." The end of this figure placed partners at opposite corners to begin the fifth figure, another series of Z or reversed S patterns. The dance concluded with a figure called "presenting of both arms."

In 1772 the Brunswick dancing master C. J. von Feldenstein published a manual that reflected major changes in the dance's performance throughout Germany.[7] These changes influenced menuet dancing during Schubert's time. Feldenstein describes two types of menuets: one mirthful and quicker—which he unfortunately does not describe—and another, described as slow and serious, for which he provides an excellent description. Furthermore, he reports a major change in the manner of performance—modifications that had important social ramifications. No longer a solo couple dance, designed to show off the dancing abilities of one couple at a time, the menuet had become a group dance.

Feldenstein's suggestions for performance included having couples dance the menuet in rows or in columns. Other possibilities included a circle of couples performing the dance's figures while moving counterclockwise, a circle of men facing a circle of women, and a menuet performed for two or four couples, as in a quadrille.

Social dances all over the Western world began to reflect major style changes by the late 1760s. Dances that featured the solo couple, embodying the traditions of court and aristocracy, were replaced by the more egalitarian simplicity of group dances. It is also precisely at this time that the popularity of English country dances, cotillions, and contredanses began to rise. Thus, with the performance of the menuet by groups of dancers, the menuet's essential nature—that of an aristocratic social dance wherein a critical viewing audience could assess the performance of couples, judged one at a time—was changed to embody a more democratic essence in a period characterized politically by democratic movements in France and North America. Now the menuet had less to do with noble bearing than with community spirit—and community spirit was what dancing at Schubertiades was all about.

Curiously, though performed in group formation, Feldenstein's figures remain essentially the same as those of the baroque menuet just described. Feldenstein notates a Z and the giving of right, left, and both hands (fig. 6.6). In keeping with the slow, se-

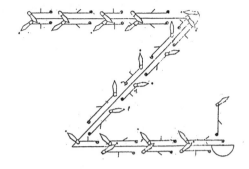

6.6 This diagram from Katzfuss's *Choreographie* (1800) demonstrates the longevity of the **Z** outlined on the floor by dancers of the baroque menuet. However, whereas earlier dancers gazed at each other while moving sideways, here, as symbols for the feet on the diagram show, the partners look straight ahead along the direction of movement. Also to be noted is that by the late eighteenth century there were two distinct types of menuet, differing in tempo and character, a fact not known to most musicians today. [NYPL:Dance]

rious nature of his slow and serious dance, he suggests the use of step rhythm easily adapted to the slower tempo.

A great influence on these slower late-eighteenth-century and early-nineteenth-century menuets was the growing popularity during the 1780s of a processional dance, the *polonaise*.[8] Likewise in triple meter, the polonaise was characterized by the following rhythm: ♩♫♫♩♩♩. It is not uncommon to find examples of menuets replete with Polish-influenced sixteenth notes.

The menuet continued to evolve and, in fact, even developed regional characteristics. For example, Josef Haydn reported in 1791 that "menuets in London are more Polish than in our or the Italian manner."[9] Various comments reveal the existence of Polish, German, English, French, Italian, and Viennese menuets, each apparently reflecting local color. Johann Philipp Kirnberger, a writer on music and student of J. S. Bach, wrote that "a trained ear will easily distinguish a Viennese menuet from one of Prague or Dresden."[10]

The two types of menuets, the slower/serious and the faster/gayer, seemed to have coexisted. As the eighteenth century waned, however, there is no question that the slow, serious tempo began to be increasingly used by dancing masters to transmit a dance that represented ideals of proper deportment, conservatism, and a harking back to an imagined time when people presumably behaved and danced more properly.

The Erfurt dancing master Charles Madel's 1805 treatise provides a good example of the major changes that had transformed the baroque menuet.[11] Madel's dance is performed by couples standing in columns, as in English country dances. He notes that at balls menuet music is played for hours without pause, that a dancer could walk on and off the ballroom floor at will, and that each couple could decide for itself how long to dance. In his wonderful narrative, Madel describes a menuet step similar to eighteenth-century modes and also accentuates the Z figure, but he also adds material found in popular contemporary social dances.

During the 1820s and 1830s the menuet was rarely performed anywhere in western Europe, and then only as a novelty dance. Schubert, however, who lived well into the 1820s, continued to write menuets. That the menuet was still a part of the ballroom scene in German-speaking nations is also evident from the large number of German-language dance manuals that contained extensive discourses on the benefits of performing the menuet.

Throughout the first quarter of the nineteenth century, numerous dance authors, such as Madel, described a constantly evolving menuet, and in 1830 Helmke published yet another argument in defense of the menuet: "The young know the menuet only by name and no longer pay it heed. Things have gone so far that is considered worthless. Why? It doesn't fit the spirit of our time. Old fashioned and stiff, it is not able to be impressive. The menuet in its old form reaps only laughs. How can it be otherwise when one views its extravagant gravity as an old, stiff custom, as a fashionless curiosity? Therefore, I have given the menuet a new form, one which is keeping with today's spirit."[12]

How did Helmke give the menuet a new form? First, he provided a new method of performing its step that could be executed on both the right and left legs. This was a major departure from the original menuet step, as described beginning with Pierre Rameau in 1725 and continuing through other early-nineteenth-century writers.[13] His second departure was the inclusion of many specialized steps found in other popular social dances, including quadrilles. For example, performance of Helmke's menuet required knowledge not only of his special menuet step but of more technically complicated steps used in group dances. Helmke's menuet contained eighteen figures, far more than Rameau's six, but, for reasons we will never know, he did not embrace the dance's signature Z or reversed S figure.

Given the variety of music written for the menuet, it is likely that the dance was performed to a wide range of tempi at this time. Of the many menuets published in Vienna during the last quarter of the eighteenth century, some are characterized by an upbeat. They were probably influenced by music written for the Deutsche turning dances and are meant to be danced to faster tempi, a fact that modern performers of such menuets and menuet-style compositions by, among others, Haydn and Mozart, often ignore.

English Country Dances: The Anglaise

Many dances besides the menuet were known to Schubert and his friends. First of all, there were English country dances, which were group dances. First published under the aegis of John Playford in London in 1651, English country dances were brought to the French court in 1684 (fig. 6.7). Known generically as the *anglaise,* by 1717 they were popular in Vienna, as Lady Mary Montagu noted: "The ball always concludes with English Country Dances to the number of 30 or 40 couples and so ill danced that there is little pleasure in them."[14]

In fact, any number of people could dance the anglaise, a progressive dance that took the form of a line of men facing a line of women. The top couple would begin the figure and dance it with each couple all the way down the line. As the first couple worked its way down, other couples who had moved up the line would, at appropriate times, begin to dance the figure down the line, creating a format described by one mid-nineteenth-century American author as "those still beginning never ending performances."[15]

By the nineteenth century the Viennese anglaise had evolved a singular style. It was performed in suite form, often with numerous meter changes. For example, a typical anglaise might begin with eight bars of menuet in triple meter, followed by eight bars of duple-meter music, and conclude with eight bars for a waltz or other turning figure in triple meter. Choreographically, the anglaise involved two distinct figures: one was for dancing progressively down the line, and the other was a waltz figure, nearly always in 3/8 meter, to conclude.

The anglaise corresponded with the new democratic tendencies moving through the Western Hemisphere in the late eighteenth and early nineteenth centuries. It could be danced by large groups of people or by a smaller gathering of intimate friends and family. As the performers danced up or down the line, everyone eventually danced with each available partner. It was this unselective nature of the dance that eventually pushed it out of favor in countries where class systems were more strict. For in the anglaise one might dance, even if only in passing, with the undesirables defined by each nation's middle class.

Cotillon

A frustrating aspect of studying European dance at this time is that the name of a given dance in the German-speaking world may refer to a quite different dance elsewhere in Europe. On the other hand, a dance in a given area might have several names, as in the case of the group dance cotillion, which was also called contredanse or quadrille.

In Vienna, *cotillon* referred to a (normally) triple-meter dance of any unspecified number of couples usually arranged in a circle.[16] Individual figures from quadrilles or

6.7 The anglaise or country dance, so called because of its English origin, involves a progressive series of figures that moves couples down the line so that by the end everyone has danced with every available partner. The informal ambience rather than the formality of performing figures is particularly characteristic of this dance, as can be seen in the illustration. [NYPL:Dance]

contredanses were danced by a few couples; these alternated with figures performed by the whole group. The figures performed by everyone consisted, for the most part, of general waltzing (that is, turning). At small gatherings, the alternate figures danced by just one or a few couples evolved into a series of party games; then all would join in the figures of general waltzing. The popular children's game of musical chairs, for example, was a popular cotillion figure.

Quadrille

The quadrille, though traditionally performed by eight people (four couples) standing in a square formation, could also be performed by four people (two couples), making it the smallest of the group dances (fig. 6.8). The word *quadrille* was first applied to equestrian ("four-footed"?) ballets popular at large outdoor events during the eighteenth century. Later the term came to signify a group dance performed by people wearing special costumes. By the early nineteenth century quadrille referred, throughout Europe, to a series of individual figures strung together, usually five in number. The figures were borrowed from English country dances (anglaise in Vienna). In Ger-

6.8 The quadrille was a popular nineteenth-century social dance for four couples facing in a square position. *L'eté* is the name of the second of five figures of a popular quadrille called the quadrille française (or, in England and America, the plain quadrille). [NYPL:Dance]

man-speaking lands the quadrille was similar to the cotillion, a series of figures performed by eight people, interspersed with waltzing. The most popular of the group dances in Europe, the quadrille was usually in 2/4 or 6/8 meter; however, in order to accommodate the waltz figures that did not normally appear in western European quadrilles, a Viennese or German quadrille was composed in 3/8.

Contredanse

The contredanse was the most popular type of group dance in France, where it originated, for most of the eighteenth century. Known as *contredanse* in Germany and *quadrille française* in Vienna, it was, like the quadrille, a dance for eight people standing in a square formation, although massive contredanses for up to thirty-two people were not uncommon. Execution of the dance involved performing a specific sequence of figures, called changes, usually twelve in number; performance of the changes alternated with the main figure of the dance, and the dance finished when all the changes had been performed. Contredanses were often performed with technically difficult step combinations that were universal throughout Europe. Marie Antoinette's arrival from Vienna brought to France yet another species of this dance type. Although similar in most respects to other contredanses, this new dance, known as *contredanse alle-*

mande, contained at least one figure which required partners to turn while changing arm positions.

Turning figures, as part of group dances, were well known throughout Germany and Austria, but they were relatively unknown elsewhere in Europe. The contredanse allemande was always performed to allemande music in duple meter.[17] The other, older form became known as the *contredanse française* and was performed to music written in 6/8 or in duple meter, with the half-measure upbeat pattern of *gavotte* tunes. Contredanse allemande and contredanse française existed side by side until the end of the eighteenth century.

Ecossaise

At the end of the eighteenth century Scottish music had become increasingly popular in Vienna. Performed only in Germany and Austria in the line formation of the anglaise, the duple-meter *ecossaise* tempo was much faster and, according to some reports, no one utilized proper steps but danced as they pleased.[18] Although the ecossaise occasionally had a reel or weaving figure, it usually had a figure where one couple would *chassé* down the entire set and back.

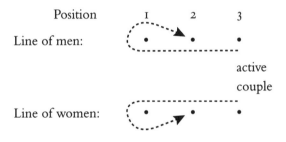

Polonaise

The polonaise was a triple-meter processional, danced by couples in a line, used to open a ball.[19] Although it is rarely cited in dance treatises after 1772, its performance may have been so universal that authors of dance manuals did not feel obliged to mention it. Lines or columns of couples moved around the room, using either the *pas de basque* or simple walking steps, creating various columns and circles.[20] Imported to western Europe from Poland, the processional opened many balls as the "grand march."

THE WALZER AND RELATED DANCES

The vision is universal: turning, whirling, the music of Johann Strauss, elegantly attired women in long sweeping skirts, romance. These are some of the notions commonly associated with the *waltz* (*Walzer* in German). And in fact, a major revolution in nineteenth-century social dance centered around the acceptance of a new form of couple dance performed by partners who held each other in an embrace.

The verb *walzen* means simply "to turn," but that can be interpreted choreographically in many different ways. Compounding the difficulties, many dances within Germany and Austria, either in duple or triple meter, included turning figures. Thus the dance that became simply known as the waltz is, in many respects, an amalgam of many dances.

One other duple-meter dance that involved turning was the *Kehraus,* apparently characterized by a rapid tempo and careless leaping. Also risky to perform was the *galop,* performed with a turning chassé step. The allemande in the later eighteenth century has already been described as a duple-meter dance popular in France; in Germany, however, the word *allemande* was used interchangeably with the three other terms—*Deutscher, Strassburger,* and *Walzer*—and referred not to a duple-meter dance but to one in triple meter (fig. 6.9).[21]

Because there are many different triple-meter dances characterized by turning—*Ländler, Deutscher, Dreher,* and *Walzer,* for example—tempo is a more important criterion than the manner of turning for distinguishing one dance type from another.

Ländler

Related to the waltz, yet distinct from it, the Ländler was a figure dance involving some hand-clapping figures and some turning figures.[22] It was slow, deliberate, and calm. The Ländler also was known for its characteristic bass line accent on the second and third beats, which certainly influenced the 1840s waltz. Its meter was always 3/4 and it was a dance in which couples progressed around the room in circles.

Another frequently encountered term is the *Schwäbische Tanz* (Swabian dance).[23] In 1772 the dancing master Feldenstein wrote that this dance was the same the same as the Deutscher, but performed in duple meter. An 1802 source, however, states that it is the same as the waltz or the *Schleifer* (a German word that suggests sliding or gliding). Like the Ländler, the Schwäbische appeared to have a rhythmic peculiarity. Within a three-count measure, the dancer would hold count one slightly longer and dance counts two and three almost as a dotted-rhythm. The Schwäbische was described as slow with an accent on count one. This variety of slow waltz was, in fact, listed as a separate entry in the 1785–87 Breitkopf catalog, along with Ländler and Deutsche.

Adding to the semantic confusion are the overlapping terms used to describe the triple-meter dances: Deutscher (or Teutscher), Walzer, and Dreher.

Deutscher

The Deutscher (plural: Deutsche) was usually equated with the Walzer, and in fact the terms were used interchangeably in Vienna during the late 1780s.[24] Additionally, *Deutscher* was sometimes used interchangeably with *allemande.* To compound the confusion, sometimes Teutsche, such as Mozart's K.536 and K.600, were published in London under the heading "Waltzes." Some Deutsche were written in 3/8; others, including the Deutsche of Haydn, Mozart, Beethoven, and Schubert, were in 3/4. It was not

6.9 The allemande or contredanse allemande, otherwise known as the Strassburger, is depicted in this pair of illustrations from *Viertes Toiletten-Geschenck für Damen* (Leipzig, 1808). [HM]

uncommon for composers to use a term such as Deutscher in the title and also a tempo marking (allegro, for example). When the word *waltz* was used by French and English composers through the 1820s, the meter signature was almost always 3/8.

Dreher

Found most often in German-language dance manuals, the Dreher was a figure utilized in the anglaise. It was the Dreher that may have directly influenced the step for the dance that eventually became known as the waltz. It was a sequence consisting of six steps performed to six counts of music. Additionally, it was a turning figure that did not progress in space (the verb *drehen* means "to turn" or "to rotate"). In actuality, the

Dreher was constructed of a turning *pas de bourrée* and was considered, in German-language dance manuals, to be an English step.[25] In 1805 Madel used the word interchangeably with *Deutscher* and described a six-step dance sequence identical to the dance destined to be the waltz. In 1830 yet another German manual utilized the word *Dreher* interchangeably with *Walzer*.[26]

Walzer

The word *Walzer* itself appeared in a song—coincidentally, in 3/8 meter—composed already in 1756 (fig. 6.10). Dance manual instructions and tunes for a turning dance with that name, using a six-count, six-step turn, begin to be seen in dance manuals at the beginning of the nineteenth century. In these cases the dance required couples to progress around the room in a counterclockwise circle, performing a six-step sequence to six counts of music. Waltz tunes in England and France were usually composed in 3/8; in Germany and Austria they are found in both 3/4 and 3/8.[27] Although various arm positions could be used by couples as they danced, the most notable characteristic of the late-eighteenth-century and early-nineteenth-century dance called waltz was the emphasis on turning while moving in a prescribed pattern around the room. As noted above, a number of turning dances were identified by a perplexing array of terms, all of which involved turning in place, as in some group dances, or pro-

6.10 Capturing both the unbridled spirit and the variety of positions in early-nineteenth-century waltzing, this caricature nonetheless also provides evidence—as seen, for example, in the placement of arms and feet—for the considerable training in dance possessed by those who enjoyed social dancing. This earlier style of waltzing was more technically difficult than the waltz style of a later time, when dance instruction played a somewhat lesser role in the education of young men and women. [MMA, Irene Lewisohn Costume Reference Library]

gressing around the room. However, the only dance in Europe characterized by turning and dancing counterclockwise around a room was called the waltz.

The key to understanding the waltz in Germany and Austria is the step unit that required six steps to complete one turn and the pattern of revolution without stopping for clapping figures, as in the Ländler. Additionally, while dancers might use arm changes, they would continue to travel counterclockwise, turning clockwise with partners and dancing to a tempo faster than that required for the Ländler.

J. H. Kattfuß wrote in 1800 that the waltz "has now become such a general favorite and is so fashionable that no one can any longer be reconciled to the English [anglaise] dance without it, for practically all English dances are usually mixed with two turns of the waltz."[28] Large dance halls, such as the Sperl, which opened in 1807, and the Apollo Hall, with space for six thousand dancers, helped give Vienna its reputation for creating the waltz—and, of course, for the report that emanated from the Congress of Vienna in 1815: "Le Congrès ne marche pas—il danse."

Many of the dances in Schubert's *16 Deutsche und zwei Ecossaisen für Klavier,* Op. 33 (1825), D.783 are paired, and some have a decidedly marchlike quality. New evidence is surfacing that, in fact, the waltz was preceded by simple, marching steps, a maneuver designed to place the dancing couple into position. In 1816 the Englishman Thomas Wilson wrote a treatise in which he describes "march steps."[29] A recently discovered manuscript of an early-nineteenth-century English dancing master provides us with the only complete waltz choreography from this time. Discovered in New Zealand and dated 1826, this particular choreography likely dates from a decade earlier. Of the eighteen figures described, the first clearly shows the couple moving down the hall with march steps.[30]

DANCE AND DRESS

No survey of social dancing is complete without some consideration of dress, for dance and dress influence one another while reflecting their times.

During the waning years of the eighteenth century, England replaced France as the authority on fashionable dress. Now the ideal became the idyllic, genteel existence of country life, as represented, for example, in Gainborough's portraits of English gentry: the men in their sporting costumes and the women wearing lightweight dresses trimmed with ribbons and wide-brimmed hats. Throughout Europe, the powdered wig and heavy, ornate brocades of the early eighteenth century gave way to simple, untrimmed, lighter fabrics.

The fashion taste of the eighteenth-century English gentry led the way into the nineteenth century, but now France reasserted itself as the dominant arbiter of haute couture. The basis for the shape of women's dress early in the century was a shirtlike dress, high waisted, with a drawstring; the dress was worn with flat slippers. This was known as the Empire style (fig. 6.11).

6.11 This painting of c. 1803, in the style of Napoleon's official painter, Jacques-Louis David, shows a woman in an Empire-style dress, with its high-waisted, shirtlike cut. The style conjured up the ideals of Greek and Roman antiquity that the Revolution and Napoleon alleged to emulate. [MMA, Gift of Julia A. Berwind, 1953]

During the 1820s the waistline of women's dresses began to drop, thus shifting emphasis to the waist itself and leading to the tightly laced corsets that dominated the remainder of the century. While waists were tiny, dresses were augmented by large, whimsical sleeves, and hairstyles were amplified by hairpieces, bows, and feathers.

During the period between 1780 and 1820, Viennese women closely followed the changing styles of European fashion. In the early years of the nineteenth century, for example, the Empire style was zealously adopted by the Viennese, who were kept au courant by the French fashion journals published in Vienna. Nonetheless, Viennese dress often incorporated aspects of the ethnic costumes worn in the many Habsburg-ruled states. People from these areas, looking for even low-paying jobs, flooded Vienna; and although they were not immediately assimilated into city life, their colorful costumes often influenced the more fashionably dressed.

As ladies and gentlemen from all corners of Europe gathered in 1815 for the Con-

6.12

6.13

6.14

6.12 This fashion plate of 1817 shows a woman in a ball dress as if about to curtsy to her partner. Characteristic of early-nineteenth-century costume is the elaborate ornamentation on the dress and the soft, flat shoes (see also fig. 6.14). The turnout of the feet indicates a polished dancer. [MMA, Thomas J. Watson Library]

6.13 These dresses of the later 1820s show the use of the corset to emphasize a tiny waist, which is counterbalanced by the fullness and elaborate design on the skirt. The sleeves have now become puffy and hairdos are very fancy, employing false hair, feathers, and other ornaments. [MMA, Thomas J. Watson Library]

6.14 Women's dance shoes of the early nineteenth century, unlike those of the eighteenth, were soft and without heels. This style, and complementary dress designs, gave dancers greater freedom of movement in their footwork. With dancing shoes and dress of the previous century, the virtuosity and abandon that came to be expressed through waltzing was simply not possible. [HM] gress of Vienna, the city's dressmakers were occupied producing uniforms and ball gowns for those unable to afford a direct order from Paris. Organized by Prince Metternich, the Congress occasioned innumerable dinners, receptions, and balls—transforming at least part of the Congress into a fashion parade. And although women's fashions had changed very little during the beginning of the nineteenth century, ladies coming to Vienna because of the Congress now danced in dresses with newly fashionable gored skirts held out by rows of ribbons, artificial flowers, and puffs of tulle, with hems shortened to display the ankle. One nonpolitical result of the Congress was, in fact, the debut of Hieronymous Löschenkohl's fashion journal in 1816.

Just as the menuet was seen to have evolved from a formal expression of the aristocratic milieu to a livelier, more democratic group dance of Helmke's epoch, so, too, were the stiff paniers worn by women replaced during this period by shorter, softer skirts that lent themselves naturally to different possibilities for movement, such as faster turns, while heeled shoes gave way to the soft shoes appropriate to articulated footwork (figs. 6.12, 6.13, 6.14). Therefore, even if dancing masters of the early nineteenth century wished to preserve a romanticized memory of the old menuet's qualities, new step and spatial patterns—and new clothing styles—became identified with the new, exhilarating, dizzying experience of waltzing around the perimeter of the dance hall in Schubert's Vienna.

NOTES

1. See Chapter 1, note 10, for an explanation of the cataloging system for Schubert's works. The "D" numbers for works of Schubert with dance titles will be given as the dances are discussed; the reader should be aware, however, that a single "D" number can embrace a collection of dance pieces. For example, D.365 comprises thirty-six waltzes.

2. On the latter point see Otto Erich Deutsch, *The Schubert Reader,* trans. Eric Blom (New York: W. W. Norton, 1947), 946.

3. J. Gerning, *Reise durch Österreich und Italien* (Frankfurt am Main, 1802), 1: 30. This quotation and much of the general information concerning the regulation of social dance is found in Reingard Witzmann, *Der Ländler in Wien: Ein Beitrag zur Entwicklungsgeschichte des Wiener Walzers bis in die Zeit des Wiener Kongresses* (Vienna: Arbeitsstelle für die Volkskundeatlas in Österreich, 1976), chapter 1.

4. Francis Peacock, *Sketches Relative to the History and Theory, but More Especially to the Practice of Dancing* (Aberdeen: J. Chalmers, 1805; rpt. Leipzig: Zentralantiquariat der Deutschen Demokratischen Republik, 1982), 73–74.

5. E. D. Helmke, *Neue Tanz- und Bildungsschule* (Leipzig, 1829; rpt. Leipzig: Zentralantiquariat der Deutschen Demokratischen Republik, 1982), 109–10.

6. A figure is a sequence of steps (either special steps as in the menuet or walking as in the mid-nineteenth-century quadrille) that traces a design on the floor. It is performed with a partner and matches an accompanying phrase of music. The basic menuet step is a sequence of movements that requires two bars of triple-meter music, whereas menuet figures usually require six to eight bars to execute.

7. E. J. von Feldenstein, *Erweiterung der Kunst nach der Choreographie zum Tanzen* (Brunswick, 1772).

8. See Sarah Reichart, "The Influence of Eighteenth-Century Social Dance on the Viennese Classical Style" (Ph.D. diss., City University of New York, 1984), 142–52.

9. H. C. Robbins Landon, *Haydn: Chronicle and Works,* 5 vols. (London: Indiana University Press, 1976–1980), 3: 106; cited ibid., p. 133.

10. Quoted in Newman W. Powell, "Kirnberger on Dance Rhythms, Fugues, and Characterization" in *Festschrift Theodore Hoelty-Nickel,* ed. Newman W. Powell (Valparaiso, Ind.: Valparaiso University Press, 1967), 67.

11. E. C. Madel, *Die Tanzkunst für die Elegante Welt* (Erfurt, 1805).

12. E. D. Helmke, *Neue Tanz- und Bildungsschule,* 110.

13. Pierre Rameau, *Le Maître à Danser* (Paris, 1725).

14. Mary Wortley Montagu, *The Complete Letters of Lady Mary Wortley Montagu,* ed. Robert Halsband, 3 vols. (Oxford: Clarendon, 1965–67), 1: 291–92.

15. Eliza Leslie, *The Behaviour Book: A Manual for Ladies,* 3d ed. (Philadelphia: Willis P. Hazard, 1853; rpt. New York: Arno, 1972), 322.

16. There is only one piece by Schubert entitled "Cotillon": D.976.

17. This allemande has nothing to do with the duple-meter allemande of the baroque dance suite.

18. For Schubert's ecossaises, see D.145, 158, 299, 421, 511, 529, 643/2, 697, 734f., 781–3, 816, 977, Anh. 1: 16.

19. D.580, 599, 618a, and 824.

20. The pas de basque was performed as follows:

3/4   ♩   ♩   ♩

    1. Leap onto left foot   3. Step forward onto left foot
      2. Step forward onto right foot
   Repeat, beginning on other foot.

21. Although the French allemande was a duple-meter dance, three dance treatises published in Paris during the 1760s give directions for performing the allemande step to both duple- and triple-meter music. Schubert's two preserved allemandes, D.366/17 and 783/8, are in triple meter.

22. D.98bc, 145, 354f., 366, 370, 374, 378, 618, 681, 734, 814, and 970.

23. Swabia is an area of today's southwestern Germany.

24. Works by Schubert with the title "Deutscher" are D.89, 128, 135, 139, 420, 618, 722, 769, 783, 790, 820, 841, 944a, 971–75, and Anh. 1: 13.

25. The pas de bourrée consists of two three-beat units. On each beat there is a forward step with a change of weight (right and left alternating), but on beats two and three of each unit there is also a quarter turn. Thus, a complete six-beat pas de bourrée effects a 360-degree turn.

26. *Neue Vollständige Tanzschule für die Elegante Welt* (Ilmenau, 1830).

27. All of Schubert's waltzes are in 3/4 meter: D.145–46, 193, 365, 779, 844, 924, 969, 978–80, 980d, and Anh. I:14.

28. Johann Heinrich Kattfuß, *Choreographie, oder vollständige und leicht faßliche Anweisung zu den verschiedenen Arten der heut zu Tage beliebtesten gesellschaftlichen Tänze,* Erstertheil (Leipzig: Heinrich Gräff, 1800), 154.

29. Thomas Wilson, *A Description of the Correct Method of Waltzing* (London, 1816), 63–65. In this treatise, Wilson assigns the performance of "The Four March Steps" to what he calls French waltzing as opposed to German waltzing.

30. The title page of this manuscript (in a collection in New Zealand) reads *Dance Book T. B. 1826.* Its contents suggest that the book is the work of a Scottish or English dancing master. The manuscript contains sixty-five pages of text and includes some diagrams of dance figures and music notations. It was clearly a teaching aid and is important for its choreographies of "fancy dances," dances used for special occasions. Contrary to the date on the title page, many of the dances hail from a later period, perhaps as late as the 1850s.

FOR FURTHER READING

Dance history is a new (if growing) discipline, and basic research into the late eighteenth and early nineteenth centuries is only beginning. The basic modern treatment of the French noble style of dance that includes the early-eighteenth-century minuet is Wendy Hilton, *Dance of Court and Theatre: The French Noble Style, 1690–1725,* ed. Caroline Gaynor, with labanotation by Mireille Backer (Princeton, N.J.: Princeton Book, 1981). Aspects of the later menuet are the concern of "The Menuet Alive and Well in 1800: Four German Dance Manuals," *Proceedings of the Seventh Annual Conference of the Society of Dance History Scholars* (1984), 53–62. A study of the late-eighteenth-century and early-nineteenth-century contradanse is Herbert Lager and Hilde Seidl, *Kontratanz in Wien: Geschichtliches und Nachvollziehbares aus der theresianisch-josephinischen Zeit* (Vienna: Österreichischer Bundesverlag, 1983). For a view of nineteenth-century dance and manners in the United States (not without some relevance to the topic here), see Elizabeth Aldrich, *From the Ballroom to Hell: Grace and Folly in Nineteenth-Century Dance* (Evanston: Northwestern University Press, 1991).

PART THREE

The Other Arts

Architecture and Sculpture

THOMAS DACOSTA KAUFMANN

The visual arts of Schubert's Vienna clearly cannot claim the same fame as its music. Except for some statuary by the Italian sculptor Antonio Canova, most of the artists and the works made by them during Schubert's lifetime remain little known. Even the organizers of a commemorative exhibition of sculpture and architecture of that time held in Vienna for the Schubert Year of 1978 referred to this period as a *Zwischenzeit,* or transition period, in the history of the visual arts, an interval between the glorious Viennese baroque of the late seventeenth and early eighteenth century and the period in which the famous Ringstraße encircling the old city of Vienna and the impressive buildings on the Ring were constructed.[1]

This negative assessment coincides with a long-standing view of building in Schubert's Vienna. For already in the composer's lifetime his contemporary Maximilian de Traux, author of an architectural treatise, remarked that without doubt big buildings were being built, but no palaces with great and sublime ornaments.[2]

These opinions also suggest, however, that the evaluation of the visual aspects of Schubert's Vienna have been based on a standard of comparison with the longer history of art in the city. Thus any adequate treatment of the urban fabric of Schubert's Vienna needs to take into account the longer historical context, before dealing with is-sues of the Vienna that Schubert knew. Music (and, for that matter, literature) is created in a physical setting that antedates the music itself; in Schubert's case, much of the architectural environment in which he lived was built long before he was born. Moreover, the conditions for sculptural and architectural activity in the period around 1800 were established to a large extent before architects and sculptors contemporary with Schubert came on the scene.

To obtain an idea of the monumental architecture and sculpture of Vienna that Schubert would have seen, it is necessary to look back at designs or buildings of previous times. A brief overview of what was standing circa 1800 may thus help to set the stage for a consideration of what was done in Schubert's own Vienna.

VIENNA CIRCA 1800: THE LEGACY OF THE PAST

Vienna is an ancient city, the site of the Roman fort Vindobona, which was located near the present Graben of the city. Nothing above ground remains from this time, but there are several major medieval churches still extant in the city. Most important of these, because Vienna was the seat of a bishopric, is the cathedral church of St. Stephen (around which many of Schubert's favorite coffeehouses and taverns were later located; fig. 7.1). St. Stephen's has parts from many centuries, with an imposing late-fourteenth-century tower that still dominates the inner city. Several other impressive Gothic churches also exist in Vienna, including that of Maria am Gestade, and the Minorites (Franciscan) church (fig. 7.2).

7.1 St. Stephen's cathedral, which dominated (and still dominates) the old city of Vienna, was very familiar to Schubert, although he had no official connection with it. During his years as an imperial choirboy at the Stadtkonvikt (1808–13) he lived practically adjacent to the edifice, and later in life he is known to have visited friends and inns in the immediate area. Schubert's funeral was not at St. Stephen's, but the music was nonetheless directed by the choirmaster of the cathedral, an indication of Schubert's status at the end of his short life. Watercolor by Rudolf von Alt (1834). [HM]

7.2 The church of the Minorite Order, dating from medieval times, was made the official church of Vienna's Italian community by Joseph II with the mandate that, in accord with Josephinistic principles, it be purged of all excess in its decoration. Accordingly, the interior was structurally modified and restyled by the architect Ferdinand Hetzendorf von Hohenberg (1784–86); the result has been called an outstanding monument to the confrontation of romanticism with medieval Gothic. Watercolor and pen by Jacob Alt (1814). [HM]

From the late fifteenth century the city's fate and status was associated with the rise to preeminence of the Habsburg dynasty, members of which with one exception held the position of Holy Roman Emperor until the dissolution of that Empire in 1806. During the course of the sixteenth century the Habsburgs also became kings of Hungary and Bohemia. Surviving from this period of the Renaissance are constructions in and near the Hofburg, the imperial palace, where the arcaded Schweizerhof (1550s) and Stallburg (1560s), and the Amalienburg (1570s) still stand as evidence of the lively activity at this time.

The succeeding period of the early seventeenth century brought a wave of church construction in the flood of Catholic spiritual movements. These new churches parallel the offensives of the Thirty Years' War, the conflict that otherwise largely halted construction by the court or aristocratic patrons in the city. Yet aside from these churches, little of note remains in Vienna from before the late seventeenth century.

Then the Leopoldine tract of the Hofburg, a long drawn-out wing with giant pilasters started in the 1660s, acted as an overture to the glorious Austrian artistic achievement of baroque ecclesiastical and especially palatial architecture (and sculpture). This period, starting around 1690, set the standard both for Schubert's contemporaries like de Traux and for later historians who disparage the art of Schubert's era.

A little more than a century before Schubert's birth, in 1683, the last Turkish siege of Vienna was broken, and the Osmanli threat to central Europe (the Europe of the Christian and classical traditions) ended. The Habsburgs in turn pushed the Turks back. Vienna, prime residence of the head of the Habsburg dynasty, now became the capital of a great power, not only in protocol (because of the claim to imperial and royal dignity) but also in actuality.

The renewed self-assertion of the Habsburgs—and the increasing wealth and power of the aristocrats (and religious orders) who gained lands—now found expression, especially in and near Vienna, in patronage of building and the other arts. A score of important architects came to Vienna to work, including such figures as Johann Bernhard Fischer von Erlach and Johann Lucas von Hildebrandt, as well as Domenico Martinelli. They designed a host of churches, palaces, and other utilitarian structures in a boom that lasted until about 1740. Residences were built in and just around the Vienna city walls not only for the Habsburg emperor but also for the Liechtenstein, Lobkowicz, and Schwarzenberg families, Prince Eugene, and many, many others.

From designs such as the imperial palace at Schönbrunn or the Belvedere for Prince Eugene or the Palais Trautson, to name but a few among the many structures designed by Fischer von Erlach and Hildebrandt, sprang a grand architecture that other architects, both Italian and Austrian, carried out in Vienna and surroundings for the emperor, for other aristocrats, and for the Church (fig. 7.3). In order to express and retain their prestige, aristocrats had designs made for city palaces, suitably splendid to represent their dignity. Moreover, decorum required that in the summer months they also have summer garden palaces in the suburbs that were now freed from external dangers. The result was noted by the widely traveled letter writer, essayist, and poet Lady Mary Wortley Montagu in 1716: "I must own I never saw a place so perfectly delightful as the faubourg of Vienna. It is very large and almost wholly composed of delicious palaces."[3] Father Ignaz Reiffenstüel said further that all the city's "gardens and places of recreation—whether because of their immense vastness, or from their varied and superb buildings, or from the wonderful flowers and fruits, or from other reasons, from the covering trees, whole little woods, statues, pictures, and other pleasant garden delights—procure for the city of Vienna no less glory than they bring to its souls genuine delight and pleasure."[4]

Similarly, the great monasteries constructed at this time, such as that at Melk and Klosterneuburg on the Danube west of Vienna, all had external residences in the city. Thus Vienna possesses a Melker Hof and a Klosterneuburger Hof, in addition to all the earlier-established monasteries of the capital. And much of the notion of the glorious baroque of Vienna also applies to church architecture as well. For the orders and the parish churches also engaged in extensive building in and near Vienna. The most famous example of this development is that of the Karlskirche, built outside of the old

7.3 The Belvedere, which now houses the Austrian national museum of art, the Österreichische Galerie, was built around 1720 for the Paris-born Prince Eugene of Savoy, who, in the service of the Holy Roman emperors, helped first to save Vienna from capture by the Turks and later to defeat the armies of Louis XIV. [HM]

city (fig. 7.4). It consists of a conglomeration of many different formal architectural elements that suggest various references, all culminating in an expression of the glory of the Habsburgs.

The glorious tradition associated with the early eighteenth century and its expansion of architecture and the related arts could not be continued in the next period. Either because of a reaction against the period 1690–1740 as excessive, or because many opportunities had largely already been realized, or because wars with Prussia in 1740–48 and 1756–63 gave a check to Austria, the pendulum of style and taste swung in a direction away from this ideal of glory. In any instance the next period, associated with the reigns and impact of Maria Theresa (r. 1740–80) and Joseph II (r. 1780–90), gave rise to much different sorts of possibilities and designs.

In the main this meant turning away from the great claims to power and the universal-imperial vision of the baroque period. Official taste shifted from the grander Italian to a more refined French style, with consequences that lasted into Schubert's time. The Habsburg rulers, for example, consciously ignored and turned away from architecture of the era of Hildebrandt and Fischer: when asked once about Hildebrandt, Maria Theresa's spouse, Francis Stephen, said he did not know the name.[5]

The new architecture from the 1750s involved less the introduction of an exuber-

7.4 This nineteenth-century Artaria engraving depicts the early-eighteenth-century Karlskirche
(Church of St. Charles), designed for Emperor Charles VI by the great Fischer von Erlach the Elder
Its religious and political claims of universality are symbolized by an eclectic baroque architectural
style, incorporating elements that recall Turkish minarets and possibly even Asian pagodas. Next to
the Karlskirche is the early-nineteenth-century Polytechnic Institute (see also figs. 2.1 and 7.23).
During 1825–26, Schubert lived practically next door to the Karlskirche. [NYPL:Print]

ant rococo than a transformation of symbolic and meaningful architectural elements. Furthermore, many of the projects of late-eighteenth- and early-nineteenth-century architecture that result from direct patronage of the monarch are alterations of or additions to previously existing plans or buildings rather than completely new creations: one good example is Schönbrunn Palace (fig. 7.5). The redecoration and alteration of Schönbrunn represents a major development in the eighteenth century, namely the turn by architects and designers to more intimate interior spaces.

By the end of the eighteenth century, when Schubert was born, greater Vienna had moreover experienced a population boom; a huge growth in building construction accompanied this growth in the number of inhabitants to more than 200,000. Thus the areas that appear as open green fields in Bernardo Bellotto's paintings of midcentury, which showed the major buildings of the city, had been filled in by this time. Only the districts outside, beyond the city walls that existed until 1848, offered spaces for construction. These are some of the topographic areas with which Schubert is associated.

7.5 This interior of Schönbrunn Palace shows how official taste shifted in the mid–eighteenth century to favor the lighter, yet elegant French rococo over the more monumental Italianate style. [HM]

NEOCLASSICISM IN ARCHITECTURE AND
SCULPTURE: THE PALAIS FRIES

It is instructive therefore to consider what sorts of buildings were actually built, particularly in the period immediately before Schubert's birth. Perhaps the most significant edifice in the inner city at this time is the Palais Fries (now the Palais Fries-Pallavicini; fig. 7.6). This new town palace of the 1780s closes off the square that had been begun by the early-eighteenth-century Imperial Library of J. B. Fischer von Erlach; his son Joseph Emanuel had added structures at the sides, including the Redouten Halls, now home to the Spanish Riding School. This palace was built by the court architect J. Hetzendorf von Hohenberg, designer of the Gloriette in the gardens of Schönbrunn Palace. It was constructed in 1783, not for a member of the court but as a residence for the Swiss-born banker, contractor, and maker of cotton and brass goods, Johann Fries, who had been recently ennobled (fig. 7.7).[6]

The passing of major patronage from Emperor Joseph II and the imperial court to bourgeois patrons hints that this is the brink of a new era. There is even some suggestion of revolutionary change here. The Palais Fries was built directly, almost symbolically, on the site of one of the monasteries that Joseph II had suppressed in the course of his ecclesiastical reforms.[7] This fact may suggest one cultural element that may, better than some other notions, capture some of the change that was involved in the arts

7.6 The Palais Fries (today Palais Fries-Pallavicini), built by the Swiss Protestant banker Johann Fries, is a paradigm of late-eighteenth-century architecture in Vienna and a symbol of the status that Vienna's successful entrepreneurs might achieve. Nonetheless, the original design—lacking a piano nobile and classical orders on the facade—created an uproar, being regarded by some as not impressive enough for a building facing the Hofburg. The present entrance portal with caryatids (themselves important examples of neoclassical sculpture) and broken pediment, more dramatic than the main entrance originally planned, ultimately was built in response to such criticism. [Photo BDA]

7.7 Johann Josef von Fries, by Johann Baptist Lampi the Elder, c. 1783–85. Although one of the richest men in Austria, Fries commited suicide in 1785, shortly after his palace was built. His son Moritz, the richest man in Austria c. 1800 and dedicatee of Schubert's "Gretchen am Spinnrade," lost and spent most of his fortune in the next two decades; he was allegedly the inspiration for Ferdinand Raimund's play *Der Verschwender (The Spendthrift)*. For Raimund, see Chapter 10. [GNM]

of Schubert's time and his milieu. Schubert's Vienna, unlike the earlier city, was dominated not by grand aristocratic patronage, nor the church, nor for that matter the consistent trumpeting of an imperial message. Instead, bourgeois patrons and consumers came to preside over the arts.

Fries also chose for his palace the simplified new architectural style associated with Joseph II. This style was evinced in such public buildings as the Josephinum, a school building where the language of baroque architecture had been dressed down. In Josephine architecture the amount of ornament is reduced, and the grand effects of the previous baroque era are eschewed in favor of a "noble simplicity," to echo the influential critic and historian Johann Joachim Winckelmann, in *Thoughts on the Imitation of Works of the Greeks* (1755); this is a direction often associated with neoclassicism.[8] In its most radical appearance this simplification of forms is found in such constructions as the chapel of the Allgemeines Krankenhaus (general hospital) in Vienna. These notions are encapsulated by the mid-eighteenth-century Saxon architect and critic F. A. Krubsacius, who in his *Thoughts on the Origin, Growth, and Decline of Decoration in the Fine Arts* suggested that "buildings can be made much more noble if one refrains altogether or at least as much as possible from decorating them. They have their essential beauty and need no extraneous assistance. . . . The only purpose is to indicate to passers-by the use of a building or the status and dignity of its owner and so to make them view its true beauty with attention."[9] These features may be found in the comparative lack of ornament in the Palais Fries.

Simplicity is also found in unprepossessing buildings constructed for the monarch himself, such as the so-called Josephsstöckl in the Augarten, the park north of the Danube (fig. 7.8). In the Palais Fries a comparably modest move may be found in the elevation of the palace, and its disposition of interior spaces. A mezzanine has been substituted for the conventional *piano nobile,* the main reception floor above ground in Renaissance and baroque palaces.

The Palais Fries also evinces a kind of "quiet grandeur," to pick up another of Winckelmann's terms. The building is as noteworthy for its architecture as for the sculpture that it contained, both within and on its exterior. This ornament serves well as an introduction to the sculpture done during Schubert's own lifetime, just as the style of the architecture is characteristic of a building of the 1780s. A more thorough consideration of sculpture may suggest another insight into the evaluation of art in Schubert's time. Histories of the visual arts of the late eighteenth and early nineteenth century outside France have put too much emphasis on architecture or painting. It may well be that sculpture is in fact the premier art of the time in central Europe.

In any event, although the exterior decoration includes some rather typical and undistinguished allegorical Attic figures by Franz Anton Zauner that are similar to what could be found on many a building of the early eighteenth century, the portal displays the mark of the new style that was to flourish especially from the 1790s. Caryatids by Zauner hold up the lintel. These figures wear garments, have facial types, and assume

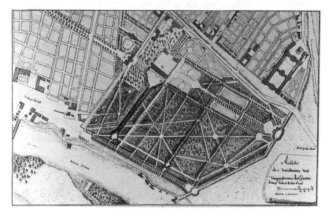

7.8 The *Josephsstöckl* (1781–83), essentially unchanged today and
located north of the old city across the Danube in the Viennese park
called the Augarten (see plate 23), was built as a pleasure house for
Emperor Joseph II. The lack of grandiose ornament is typical for the
Josephine style, but from the upper floor it had wonderful views of
the Augarten, the city, the Danube, and the Prater. [HM]

poses that are modeled after the antique. More significantly, they specifically recall ancient works in function and type as well as in style: they are obviously related to the
caryatids of the Erectheum on the Acropolis in Athens. Unification of classical form
and classical content was deemed by the twentieth-century theorist Erwin Panofsky to
be characteristic of the Renaissance.[10] But something more is present here: there is also
a matter of function, in that these female figures are also used to support a doorway.

These figures were drawn from, if not inspired by, the archaeological discoveries and
the handbooks of the time, including such newly published works as James Stuart and
Nicholas Revett's *The Antiquities of Athens* (1762), which contained many views of the
Acropolis. In this regard they can justifiably be called examples not only of the neoclassical but even of the neo-Grec. They are done in a spirit of archaeological exact-

ness that stems from a veneration for the antique. This was a form of the antico-mania that gripped Europe from the time of Winckelmann's effusive praise of the Greek. Winckelmann wrote, in fact, that the only way to become great is by imitating the works of the Greeks. Winckelmann was very much in vogue in Vienna from the late 1760s; the first complete edition of his writings was published in Vienna.

In this palace there is an aesthetic attitude that will continue throughout Schubert's period. The Germans even adapted a Greek word, using *Plastik* to describe sculpture around this time. The turn to the Greek, to the archaeologically correct as opposed to the imagined in eighteenth-century art and criticism, even goes a step beyond Winck-elmann, who had relied on later Hellenistic or Roman works in formulating his opin-ions and teachings about ancient Greek art. Emulation of the newly discovered Greek works of art from Hellas itself or southern Italy is a mark of the neoclassical in its stricter or "advanced" form.

Another sign of this move is also seen within the building. For the Palais Fries once contained the first work to reach the lands north of the Alps that was done by the most important neoclassical sculptor of the time, Antonio Canova. Canova's *Theseus and the Minotaur,* commissioned in 1781 by the Venetian ambassador Zulian in Rome and com-pleted in 1783, came eventually to Vienna, where it was set up on the ground floor in a cupola inside the Palais Fries (fig. 7.9).[11] This work, a harbinger of a new era, was the first work by Canova to be sold outside of Italy. It presents a classical Greek subject, a hero. Theseus and the Minotaur may even be interpreted as representing Reason (for Theseus is a specifically Attic hero, from the Athenian home of philosophy) overcom-ing Unreason and Bestiality (the Minotaur). It may not be too much to suggest that

7.9 In 1783 the Italian Antonio Canova, the leading neoclassical sculptor of the age, de-picted the myth of the Athenian hero Theseus killing the Minotaur, a monster with the head of a bull and the body of a man, in the labyrinth on the island of Crete. Count Johann von Fries brought the sculpture from Rome to Vienna, where it was inherited by his son Moritz and placed in his palace. It is now in the Victoria and Albert Museum in London. [HM]

this might be an apt image for the "heroism" of the Enlightenment, the ideals of which correspond to some of Joseph II's motivation.

ARCHITECTURE AND SCULPTURE IN THE REIGN OF FRANCIS I

The major public monument of the Vienna of Schubert's time faces the Palais Fries. This is an equestrian monument to Joseph II himself, a work that was begun somewhat later than the Palais, during the reign of Francis I in 1795–96 (figs. 7.10, 7.11). Finished in 1806, it is set up in the middle of the Josefsplatz, the square closed off by the Palais Fries. Appropriately, the monument is by the same artist, Zauner, who executed the sculpture on the palace facade.

The monument to Joseph depicts the ruler in a classical guise: it closely resembles the statue of Marcus Aurelius on the Capitoline Hill in Rome. The choice of material, bronze—somewhat unusual in Vienna, where lead and lead-related material had most often been used for public monuments since the activity of Georg

154
Kaufmann

7.10 What became designated as the Josefsplatz in Schubert's day was an open area bounded on three sides by eighteenth-century additions by Fischer von Erlach and his son Joseph Emanuel Fischer von Erlach to the imperial residence or Hofburg. Counterclockwise from the north, these were the imperial riding school, the imperial library, and an extension into which the medieval Augustiner church and seventeenth-century parts of the palace were embedded. On the fourth side, opposite the library but across the Augustinerstrasse, the Palais Fries (see fig. 7.6) was built in the 1780s. [HM]

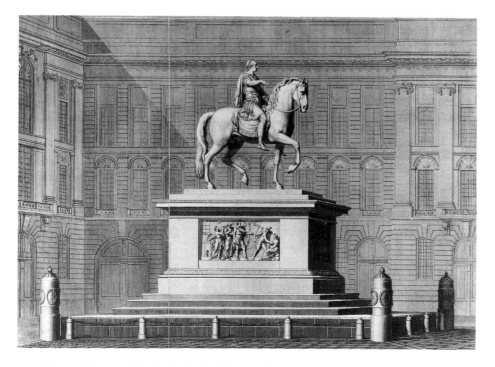

7.11 A central feature of the Josefsplatz in Vienna is the equestrian statue of Joseph II (1795–1806)
by Anton Zauner, erected during the Napoleonic wars in part to stir up patriotism and support
for the Habsburg monarchy. The statue has much in common with the ancient Roman equestrian
statue of Marcus Aurelius, and serves as a symbol of a philosopher king. Zauner also created the caryatids holding up the portal of the Palais Fries that faces the Josefsplatz (see fig. 7.6). [HM]

Raphael Donner—as well as the form of the statue reveal its emulation of the ancient model.

The statue of Joseph II also belongs to a long postantique tradition of freestanding
equestrian monuments (many of them in bronze) for rulers, popular from the stone
Magdeburg Rider of the mid-thirteenth century; the tradition is exemplified in such
famed fifteenth-century works as Donatello's *Gattamelata* in Padua and Verrocchio's
Colleoni in Venice, seventeenth-century examples such as the works of Bernini or
Mocchi in Rome or Pavia, and eighteenth-century statues like those by Andreas
Schlüter in Berlin and Falconet in Russia. Yet no such work was to be seen in Vienna;
in fact, a Habsburg public monument of this nature was unprecedented in the city (in
contrast to paintings, which, because of their disposition in an interior, would not have
been seen by a large public). There is a distinct difference between the monument to
Joseph II, which focuses on the ruler, depicting him without any religious trappings,
and another one put up by a predecessor: the nearby baroque plague column on the
Vienna Graben, where the sculptural portrait of Emperor Leopold I at prayer is subsumed into a larger, allegorical, and religious composition.

Zauner's return and close adherence to the Roman source of the iconographic tradition of ruler monuments exemplifies something of the archaeological exactness of the neoclassical. Joseph is not merely shown in the garb of an ancient ruler: his pose and that of his horse are similar to those of Marcus Aurelius. The horse is not courbetting, or otherwise showing off the ruler's equestrian skills, as in many paintings and sculptures of the seventeenth and eighteenth centuries, but striding forward, like that of the Roman emperor.

The reliance of the monument to Joseph on that of Marcus Aurelius, a philosopher-emperor who died, coincidentally, in Vindobona (Vienna) in 180 A.D., also offers a meaningful prototype for Joseph II in another way. The parallel to the philosopher suggests that Joseph is to also to be regarded as an "enlightened" monarch. Much as the close parallel to Marcus Aurelius is significant, so also the variation from type significantly brings home this point. Most derivations from the type show the ruler holding a baton, leading troops into battle; the statue of Joseph II does not. Marcus Aurelius is shown as a commander, making a gesture in which he seems to be addressing troops. Joseph's hand gesture in contrast is conceived not as beckoning or commanding, but, as was said at the time, as protecting the population: he spreads his hand over the heads of the people. The reliefs on the sides of the base of the monument are not allegories of conquest but portrayals of Joseph as a protector of commerce and agriculture. These provide a different image of the ruler and reinforce the meaning of the central statue and its gesture.

The construction of this work belonged to an effort by Francis I to create a new public national propaganda for the Habsburg dynasty in a time of conflict and trouble. The later 1790s, as recounted in Chapter 1, represented a period of defeats and loss of territory in northern Italy; the Habsburgs had to meet the challenge of a national movement in France; the Holy Roman Empire was dissolved in 1806, two years after the establishment of a strictly Austrian empire. The completion of the statue in the same year as the end of the old Empire seems more than mere coincidence. The statue provides a more effective, direct, and immediate form of imagery than spending on buildings—with its more generalized expression of grandeur—would have created.

This motivation may explain the proliferation of sculpture at this time. At the end of the eighteenth century and in the early nineteenth were produced not only portraits of the ruler and his family, for which there is of course an older tradition of imagery, but also several fountains, many put up by the city of Vienna. In 1804–5, for example, the fountains on the Graben and Hoher Markt were renewed. The results, which incorporated images of the Austrian patron saints Joseph and Leopold, would seem to be more than a manifestation of the religious spirit of Austria; the imagery may also be read as recognition by Vienna of the Habsburg dynasty's dedication to its lands, where St. Leopold Babenberg had reigned from 1095 to 1136, and where recent Habsburgs had borne the names Leopold and Joseph (fig. 7.12).[12]

The allegorical fountains by Johann Martin Fischer in the square called Am Hof

7.12 The Graben, now a pedestrian thoroughfare in
the old city of Vienna (see also plate 7), is the site for
this votive monument commemorating relief from the
plague. This view celebrates the Austrian piety of the
Habsburgs, showing Emperor Leopold I (r. 1658–1705)
at prayer. The name Leopold was also common in the
medieval ruling house of Austria, the Babenbergs, who
preceded the Habsburgs. Schubert's first publisher,
Cappi and Diabelli, was located in the Graben. [HM]

were even more direct in their message. These depicted the "Loyalty of the Austrian
Nation Toward its Emperor and Fatherland" and the "Zeal of the Austrian Nation for
Science and Art," the latter suggesting as well that agriculture was flourishing under
the Habsburgs (fig. 7.13). The political point of these works, made in 1812, during the
period of *Befreiungskrieg,* the so-called war of liberation against Napoleon, should be obvious. Again, the abstract style of sculpture associated with neoclassicism—including
classically attired and idealized figures—is to be related to the abstract design and elevated message.

Canova's great monument for Maria Christina in Vienna's Augustinerkirche can be
placed in this context (fig. 7.14). Habsburg enthusiasm was strong for Canova, who
had visited Vienna in 1798, when he was granted a pension and ennobled. Albert of
Sachsen-Teschen commissioned him, from about 1795, to create a large tomb monument for his lost wife, a daughter of Maria Theresa and sister of Joseph II. But the
monument was more than a private sign of love. It employs ancient figures and such
ancient motifs as the *imago clipeata*—the presentation of a portrait in a medallionlike
form—and the personification of fame or genius with a palm, and it employs a pyramidal form for the tomb. It also has allegorical elements (invented by Albert) that
bring home its message: Piety and Beneficence enter the tomb, as Mourning and For-

7.13 Figures that were originally part of Johann Martin Fischer's fountain in the plaza Am Hof depict the loyalty of the Austrian nation to emperor and fatherland. It was erected in 1812, in the midst of the upheavals of the Napoleonic wars. [HM]

titude lament the lost wife. The tomb has several possible levels of meaning, among them references to the three ages of man and the universal mystery of death.

This tomb was the largest of the Vienna public tomb monuments at this time. Its inscription and the portrait of the deceased make the identification of the figure clear and thus make dynastic associations inescapable: it might be thought that the virtues of the archduchess are those of the Habsburgs more generally, stressed to all who will see them in the church.

The choice of the form of imagery also seems deliberate. In keeping with the Winckelmannian demand to create a new form of allegory, an arcane language of personification is not entirely needed, and ambiguity is rejected. Thus complicated baroque forms of allegory (as seen in the layers of reference in the Vienna Karlskirche or Fischer von Erlach's design for Schönbrunn) are avoided in favor of the presentation of a clearer message. This change can be related to the transformation of allegorical imagery, as it was demanded by many figures beside Winckelmann in the later eighteenth century, when, for example, the Italian critic Francesco Milizia argued that "a monument should demonstrate in its simplicity the character of the person commemorated and bear no symbols that are not immediately intelligible."[13]

That, of course, does not mean that monuments cannot be read according to their

7.14 Installed in Vienna's Augustinian Church is Canova's monument to Maria Christina, wife of Albert of Sachsen-Teschen, who
established the collection of the Albertina (see fig. 7.19). The
sculpture, embodying an original conception of death and
immorality, is one of the artist's—and Vienna's—most notable
neoclassical works. Engraving by Artaria, 1808. [HM]

context; witness another important work by Canova bought by the Habsburgs that
made its way to Vienna, where it is now found in the Kunsthistorisches Museum. This
is *Theseus Fighting the Centaur* (fig. 7.15). The centaur is a mixed being, like the Minotaur, and thus an example of disorder and bestiality—indeed, the centaurs had dis-
rupted the feast of the Lapiths in mythology. Canova's work also reflected a debate
over how this subject should be represented: in contrast to the Minotaur group, the
centaur group shows Theseus in combat. At first it might seem that this work could be
easily related to the conflicts with Napoleon. The trouble is that this work was actually
commissioned by Napoleon himself; after the Napoleonic wars, it was brought to Vienna in 1819. Only then was it read as a symbol of victory over the *Unmensch*
Napoleon.

The statue was set up in the Temple of Theseus, or Theseon, in the Volksgarten, a
new public garden near the Hofburg palace (fig. 7.16). And this brings up the question of the close relation of sculpture and architecture at this time. The Theseus temple and its circumstances of construction suggest something of the contemporary his-

7.15 Canova's *Theseus Fighting the Centaur* depicts the Athenian hero struggling against a centaur, a creature that was half man, half horse. The subject, originally deriving from the centaurs' offensive behavior at the wedding feast of Theseus's friend Pirithous, here represents the triumph of order over irrationality. The sculpture group is now dramatically placed in Vienna's Kunsthistorisches Museum. [KHM]

7.16 The Theseon, a classically correct building employing the severe Doric order, was designed by Peter von Nobile after an ancient temple in Athens honoring that city's mythological hero Theseus. It was erected in 1819–23 in Vienna's Volksgarten, a public park opened in 1823. Built to house Canova's *Theseus Fighting the Centaur,* the Theseon was dedicated in 1824. [HM]

torical situation and thus reinforce the meaning of the work. The Theseus group was to be placed in a neoclassical temple, a building that in fact was modeled after a severe Doric structure, the Theseus temple in Athens. The Doric order was the most ancient and severe, fit for the most ancient Athenian hero, Theseus, whose archaeologically exact sanctuary was constructed in 1819–23, when memories of the Napoleonic wars were still fresh. This building, with its sculpture within, became an emblem of victory over hostile forces.

The Theseus temple was built as part of a programmatic imperial square or Burgforum. The Neue Burgtor, or new castle gateway, also was a part of this plan (fig. 7.17). This building was again modeled on a Greek original, a propylaon, or gateway, exemplified at Athens by the Propylaon on the Acropolis. The severe Doric style was again employed as the appropriate order for virile, martial subjects. The Neue Burgtor and the Theseus temple were in fact both erected by soldiers; the gateway was also dedicated to soldiers, and to the people of Austria, by the emperor.

The Neue Burgtor was erected on the site of the Burgglacis, the defensive circumference where Napoleon's soldiers had deliberately destroyed part of the city walls in 1809 in order to neutralize the fortifications of Vienna. It thus made a virtue out of necessity. The dedication of the Neue Burgtor in 1823 occurred on the tenth anniversary of the Battle of Leipzig, when Napoleon's power was broken by the power

7.17 The Neue Burgtor, which arose on the former site of city fortifications leveled by Napoleon in 1809, was, along with the Theseon, part of an ambitious architectural and city-planning program to erase the defeats of the past and honor Austria's ultimate military victory over Napoleon. Colored engraving by Eduard Gurk, 1823. [NYPL:Print]

of allied forces under the command of the Austrian field marshal Schwarzenberg. Its forms are Greek, but its proximity to the Hofburg raises imperial associations: it thus also suggests that the idea behind them may also be related to the evocation of an imperial Roman forum, such as that of Trajan.

It has been suggested that the severe neoclassical style was appropriate to reactionary politics. That apt assessment should be tempered, though: there may be other grounds for the choice of style. It might be better to see this choice as a direct reaction to Napoleon, who also used the style. In any instance, the style was that adopted by the Habsburg court just at a time of threats from Napoleon; a major change in the interior design of the Hofburg, namely, the decoration of the Ceremonial Hall of 1804–7 (fig. 7.18), occurred just at the time of Napoleon's rise to imperial status (he crowned himself emperor in 1805). The design of this room by Louis Montoyer, a Frenchman, again points in any instance to the French impact on neoclassicism. This room represented one of several plans for the decoration and extension of the Hofburg, most of them unrealized.

This space is consistent with the generalization that three major types of rooms were the focus of interior design during the period of neoclassicism, and in general during Schubert's period: large salons or hall-like spaces, hallways, and stairways. Neoclassical style favors interior columns and pilasters; there is an emphasis on the wall and a reduction of decoration to architectural elements; not playful forms, but classicizing elements provide a basis for designs.

The new style is connected with the members of the court and its close servitors. Albert of Sachsen-Teschen, who had commissioned the tomb to Maria Christina, also

7.18 The decoration of the Ceremonial Hall in the Hofburg by the architect Louis-Joseph Montoyer, a Paris-trained Walloon, in 1804–7 is one of the few renovation projects undertaken in the Hofburg at the time. It shows the continuing influence of the French neoclassical style of decoration—even during the wars against Napoleon. [HM]

had the Palais Tarouca near the Hofburg rebuilt as his residence in Vienna (fig. 7.19). This building—well known to students of drawings because it is still the seat of the present Albertina, the largest collection of drawings and prints in the world—was rebuilt for the prince in 1801–4. In 1821–23, the major architect of the next period, Joseph Kornhäusel, carried through the redesign of the interior, which includes a forehall with sphinxes, pilasters, modified Doric columns, and a neo-Grec ceiling (resembling the designs of the Scottish architects and decorators Robert and James Adams), a stairway, and a Fest Hall with statues of the muses, added to the ceremonial room in 1823 (fig. 7.20).

On the whole, however, new palace architecture was limited at this time. The most important early-nineteenth-century example is perhaps the Palais Rasumofsky of 1805–11, by Montoyer (fig. 7.21). This was built for the Russian ambassador to the imperial court. Its patronage echoes the character of what was to be the Holy Alliance of 1815 (see Chapter 3). This palace was more opulent than other designs of the time, perhaps suggesting something of the pretensions of the Russian court. It uses compos-

7.19 Sebastian Warmuth depicted the departure of the Archduke Karl and his daughter Maria Theresa from the Albertina. This palace was rebuilt as the residence of Albert of Sachsen-Teschen, who began the Albertina's collection of graphic art, now the largest in the world and still housed there. [GSA]

ite half-columns and pilasters, the most elaborate and decorative of the architectural orders, to express grandeur. Panels with reliefs also embellish the interiors.

This building and its patronage reflect the relation of the fine arts to music. Rasumofsky was the patron of Beethoven's famed string quartets, Opus 59 (composed 1805–6); and in a certain sense this architecture and design can be related to Beethoven's music, even beyond patronage. But Beethoven responded to the political events of his time: at first an admirer of Napoleon, he wrote the *Eroica* symphony in his honor. Beethoven also reacted to the struggles against Napoleon, writing "Wellington's Victory" as a paean to the foe of the French. Like others, he was caught in the ambiguities of the time: much as Canova renamed or rededicated his *Theseus Fighting the Centaur,* Beethoven rededicated the *Eroica.*

But all this is Beethoven's Vienna, not Schubert's. Although Schubert wrote some little-known music related to contemporary events, he was not connected with the court, nor with all the splendor, pretension, and grandeur around it. Although he set some songs with classical themes, his work is not a product of the social milieu in which the neoclassical style flourished.

7.20 An interior space of the Albertina showing neoclassical decor: classical orders, classicistic sculptures and decorative motifs, and avoidance of complex decoration. Architect for the palace was
Joseph Kornhäusel, the leading Austrian architect of Biedermeier Vienna. [Photo BDA]

THE ARCHITECTURE OF SCHUBERT'S MILIEU

It is in another part of Vienna where one should look for Schubert, in another
realm also anticipated by the period of Joseph II—the period of the 1780s, but not the
neoclassical aspects alone of that time. Rather, one should recall that when Joseph II
reduced grandeur, he also had buildings built for public good and public interest; the
neoclassic of the succeeding era can thus be seen as a response to Joseph's realm, when
a demand returned for a more expensive, splendid style for aristocrats and the court.
But in style and substance this does not correspond to much of what was done in late
eighteenth and early nineteenth century. Perhaps for this reason it has not attracted as
much attention from art historians.

The broadest current of architecture at this time, like that of the period of Joseph II,
can be compared to another aspect of what happened to the city bastions, which were
turned into public promenades in 1817 (fig. 7.22). In Joseph II's time public, utilitarian building provided one of the major sources for projects. This trend continued into
the next period, when theaters, coffeehouses, cloisters, dance halls, school buildings, a
polytechnical academy, and a veterinary school were constructed. Whereas Joseph II

7.21 The palace of Count (later Prince) Andreas Rasumofsky, Russian ambassador to Vienna, was designed by Montoyer, Vienna's leading architect at the turn of the nineteenth century, who also left his mark with work at the Hofburg (fig. 7.18). Until the palace was destroyed in a fire on December 31, 1814, Rasumofsky was an important patron of Beethoven. [HM]

had built the Josephinum, now a Technische Hochschule (Polytechnic Institute) and a veterinary Hochschule were built, in a rather subdued, unornamented style (fig. 7.23). If the early eighteenth century was characterized by palaces, the emblems of the early nineteenth were coffeehouses and bathing establishments. The Theater an der Wien, with its Papageno portal inspired by the character in Mozart's opera *Die Zauberflöte,* stands for the popular character of this age (fig. 7.24).

In what might be considered another continuation of the Josephine period of religious tolerance, a variety of religious structures were now built. Whereas only Catholic houses of worship had been erected before, now Protestant churches and a synagogue were built. Worthy of particular note is Kornhäusel's synagogue of 1825–26 (for which Schubert set Psalm 92 [D.953]—in Hebrew—in 1828, the year of his death), a combination of baroque and revolutionary classicism (not neoclassicism). Also introduced at some churches of the time was the neo-Gothic, a sign of the plurality of styles.

The leading genre in terms of the amount of work done, however, was the public residence. Here another heritage of the Josephine period is evident. The huge increase of population from the last quarter of the eighteenth century, when the city grew to a metropolis, occasioned much building. In particular, new forms of architectural development emerged: factories and *Miethäuser* (tenements), not palaces. The new apart-

7.22 The former site of city fortifications was transformed into a promenade and location of the first of the famous Biedermeier coffeehouses, established in 1819 by Pietro Corti. By the mid-1830s, there were about eighty coffeehouses in the city, ranging from the high-toned (as was Corti's) to the plain and simple. Drawing and watercolor by Jacob Schufried, 1825. [HM]

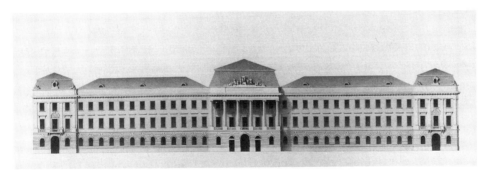

7.23 The early-nineteenth-century Polytechnic Institute (see also fig. 7.4), built around the time of the Congress of Vienna, continued the tradition of architectural austerity established in the reign of Joseph II for utilitarian public works, as seen in this architectural drawing. [GSA]

7.24 The Theater an der Wien, shown in this watercolor, was opened in 1801 by Emanuel Schikaneder. A sculpture of the bird-man character Papageno from Mozart's *The Magic Flute* ornamenting one of the entrances celebrates Schikaneder's authorship of the libretto. When Schubert was in his early teens, he was taken by his older friend Josef von Spaun to see *The Magic Flute*. (See also figs. 5.5, 10.3, and 10.4.) [GSA]

ment blocks are characterized by interior courtyards and stairways. They may be related to palaces in their presentation of a facade on the street, but their style is closer to tendencies of the late eighteenth century, such as the formation of the so-called *Plattenstil* (flat or plain style, characterized by shallow decorative elements and the absence of freestanding columns), as seen on the *Schuhbladkastenhaus* ("chest of drawers house") on the Freyung place. As in the radical classicism of thr Anstaltkapelle (the hospital chapel) or the Josephsstöckl, in these buildings the *Baublock* cubic form was used, atop a square ground plan. These details suggest a relation to revolutionary classicism, the architecture of the Frenchmen Ledoux, Lequeu, and Boullée of the previous period.

A building from the end of Schubert's lifetime, the Schottenhof of 1827, provides a characteristic example of the Biedermeier *Wohnhaus,* or apartment block (fig. 7.25). It lacks the usual application of the classical orders of architecture on its exterior and possesses little more than a relief as part of its minimal ornament. This work stands for a whole host of buildings on which no great classic figural decoration is to be found. Simple interior wall spaces and structures and cubic blocks for houses abound, particularly in the outer districts of Vienna. Often the interior courtyard of these structures has balconies leading to the individual dwellings, a form designated by the term *Pawlatschenhof* (derived from the Czech word for balcony). This sort of building is by

7.25 The Schottenhof (1827–35) by Josef Kornhäusel, built on the site of a cloister that had been converted to a school and apartments during the 1770s, faces the Freyung and represents a common type of Biedermeier structure: the apartment house. Before Kornhäusel's renovation, Franz Schubert heard some of his music, including the symphonies No. 5 and 1 (in that order), performed at the residence of one of his friends there, and Franz Grillparzer wrote his *Sappho* during the time he lived in the same building. Oil painting by Fr. Ludovicus Schütz, 1835. [HM]

no means a grand palatial structure but one in which the interiors are all split up for individual families (fig. 7.26).

An infrequently used alternative building design can also be seen in Pötzleindorf, a suburb of Vienna, at the Geymüller Schlössl—where the neo-Gothic was employed (fig. 7.27). This last structure reminds us that this is also the period of the expansion of the villa, of the development of Grinzing, of the outer districts. This suggests something of the relation of building to the purposes of pleasure.

It is with these sorts of construction that we can talk with some meaning about the bourgeoisification of the city at this time, a turn away from the splendor of the baroque that accompanied the assumption of a radical, reduced style of new forms, along with the growth of an increasingly middle-class urban population. And it was in this milieu, and for this population, that much of Schubert's music arose. This was not the locus for grand opera or court performances or oratorios. Rather, here music sounded in coffeehouses, taverns, restaurants, smaller theaters, apartments, and in other like locales, settings found not only in the inner, older center, but especially in the

7.26 Reinhard Völkel's watercolor depicts the courtyard of a *Pawlatschenhaus* on the Ulrichsplatz. This type of apartment house was characterized by balconies in the interior courtyard. [HM]

7.27 Outside the central city of Vienna, the Geymüller Schlössl
(built between 1808 and 1820), a modest mansion owned by a rich
banking family, adumbrates the later fashion of historicist design in
its neo-Gothic elements. Although there is no known direct connection between Schubert and the Geymüller family, a number of
his friends did frequent the Geymüller home in the city. [MAK]

outer districts of Vienna. These more modest locales were where Biedermeier musical life was centered, where new dwellings had their pianoforte, their sheet music, and
their violins, and where people sang Schubert's lieder as they enjoyed an evening of
Hausmusik. In this way Schubert's music is in consonance with some aspects of the architecture of his time.

NOTES

1. Géza Hajós, "Klassizismus und Historismus: Epochen oder Gesinnungen? Gedanken an-
läßlich einer Ausstellung." *Österreichische Zeitschrift für Kunst und Denkmalpflege* 32, no. 3/4 (1978).

2. Maximilian de Traux, *Kurzer Abriß der bürgerlichen Baukunst . . .* (Wiener Neustadt, 1813), as
paraphrased by Renate Wagner-Rieger, *Wiens Architektur im 19. Jahrhundert* (Vienna: Brüder
Hollinek, 1970).

3. Mary Wortley Montagu, *The Complete Letters of Lady Mary Wortley Montagu,* ed. Robert
Halsband, 3 vols. (Oxford: Clarendon, 1965–67), 1: 261.

4. Ignaz Reiffenstüel, *Germania Austriaca* (Vienna, 1701).

5. Cited in Eberhard Hempel, *Baroque Art and Architecture in Central Europe,* trans. Elisabeth
Hempel and Marguerite Kay (Baltimore: Penguin, 1965), 291 n. 31.

6. Johann von Fries was the father of Moritz von Fries, one of Vienna's most notable patrons
of the arts, to whom Beethoven dedicated his Seventh Symphony and Schubert his famous song
"Gretchen am Spinnrade," Op. 2 [Ed.].

7. Joseph II's reforms, a product of Enlightenment thinking and collectively referred to as

Josephinism, included bringing ecclesiastical institutions (but not religious doctrine) under the control of the state. Believing that the Church's human and material resources were not being properly used, Joseph went beyond the reforms initiated by his mother, Maria Theresa. He closed monasteries whose members practiced a contemplative life rather than providing pastoral care to the faithful, terminated many religious practices he felt were superstitious or unnecessary, brought the training of the clergy under state control, and reorganized the parish system to permit a more equitable distribution of priests. To implement and enforce these policies, against which there was a backlash that lasted into the reign of Francis I, an extensive bureaucracy was created, which carried the spirit of Josephinism well into the nineteenth century. It is known that Schubert had admiration for, and contact with, some leading Josephinists in the 1820s [Ed.].

8. J. J. Winckelmann, *Gedanken über die Nachahmung der griechischen Werke in der Malerei und Bildhauerkunst* (Dresden, 1755), in *Winckelmanns Werke* (Berlin: Aufbau-Verlag, 1982), 17.

9. F. A. Krubsacius, *Gedanken von den Ursprung, Wachstum und Verfall der Verzierungen in den Schönen Künsten* (Leipzig, 1759).

10. In his book *Renaissance and Renascences in Western Art* (Stockholm: Almqvist and Wiksell, 1960) and elsewhere.

11. The work is now in the Victoria and Albert Museum, London.

12. The Babenbergs were the first Austrian dynasty, ruling as margraves and dukes from at least the late tenth through the mid-thirteenth centuries. Leopold was the most common name of those rulers. The Habsburgs gained control of the former Babenberg territories later in the thirteenth century.

13. Francesco Milizia, *Principi di Architettura Civile* (Finale, 1781), quoted in Hugh Honour, *Neoclassicism* (Harmondsworth: Penguin, 1968), 150. Cf. also the reprint (Milan: Gabriele Mazzotta, 1972) of the second Milanese edition of Milizia's treatise (1847), 361.

FOR FURTHER READING

English-language treatments of Viennese architecture and sculpture of Vienna of the late-eighteenth and early-nineteenth centuries are regrettably few and are often included in broader surveys, such as Hugh Honour, *Neoclassicism* (Harmondsworth: Penguin, 1968); Thomas DaCosta Kaufmann, *Court, Cloister, and City: The Art and Culture of Central Europe, 1450–1800* (Chicago and London: University of Chicago Press and Weidenfeld and Nicolsen, 1995); and Fritz Novotny, *Painting and Sculpture in Europe, 1780–1880* (Harmondsworth: Penguin, 1978). Robert Waissenberger, ed., *Vienna in the Biedermeier Era, 1815–1848* (New York: Rizzoli, 1986), contains chapters on architecture by Renata Kassal-Mikula and on sculpture by Selma Krasa.

Recommended German-language sources include *Die Ära Metternich*, exhibition catalog (Vienna: Historisches Museum der Stadt Wien, 1984); *Biedermeier in Wien, 1815–1848: Sein und Schein einer Burgeridylle* (Mainz: Von Zabern, 1990; Hermann Burg, *Der Bildhauer Franz Anton Zauner und seine Zeit: Ein Beitrag zur Geschichte des Klassizismus in Österreich* (Vienna: A. Schroll, 1915); Rupert Feuchtmüller and Wilhelm Mrazek, *Biedermeier in Österreich* (Vienna: Forum, 1963); Angelika Gause-Reinhold, *Das Christinen-Denkmal von Antonio Canova und der Wandel in der Todesauffassung um 1800* (Frankfurt am Main: R. Lang, 1990); Géza Hajós, "Klassizismus und Historismus: Epochen oder Gesinnungen? Gedanken anlässlich einer Ausstellung," *Österreichische Zeitschrift für Kunst und Denkmalpflege* 32, no. 3/4 (1978): 98–109; *Klassizismus in Wien: Architektur und Plastik*, exhibition catalog (Vienna: Historisches Museum der Stadt Wien, 1978); Margarethe Poch-

Kalous, *Johann Martin Fischer: Wiens bildhauerischer Repräsentant des Josefinismismus* (Vienna: E. Müller, 1950); Wilhelm Georg Rizzi and Mario Schwarz, "Die Architektur zur Zeit Josephs II," in *Österreich zur Zeit Kaiser Josephs II,* exhibition catalog (Vienna: Amt der Niederösterreichischen Landesregierung, 1980), 200–210; and Renate Wagner-Rieger, *Wiens Architektur im 19. Jahrhundert* (Vienna: Brüder Hollinek, 1970) and *Das Wiener Bürgerhaus des Barock und Klassizismus* (Vienna: Österreichischer Bundesverlag für Unterricht, Wissenschaft und Kunst, 1957).

· 8 ·

Viennese Biedermeier Painting

GERBERT FRODL

When Franz Schubert died in 1828, those trends in painting that were later generally designated Biedermeier had recently become established. In the first two decades of the nineteenth century a classicistic emphasis had dominated, promoted above all in the Academy of Fine Arts and by its professors, most notably Friedrich Heinrich Füger; this style was characterized by monumentality, allegory and symbolism, mythology, and the depiction of great deeds. Only from about 1810 did a movement away from classicistic principles of form emerge, and this first of all in portraiture. As one of the consequences of the French Revolution and also as a reaction against the representational and ostentatious art of the baroque, European painters turned away from the glorified representation of individuals toward a greater realism. As a result, in Vienna the less pretentious, more down-to-earth Biedermeier portrait arose, followed some years later by a parallel development toward realism in landscape painting. The decades before 1820 were therefore a time not only of great political and social upheavals but also of important changes in the fine arts that prepared the way for the Biedermeier style.

Biedermeier is an attitude toward life—a lifestyle rather than an artistic style like classicism or baroque.[1] This attitude—induced by external circumstances, to be sure—found expression in the fine arts, in crafts, and in architecture through works closely related to real life and to the needs of real people—hence the term *Biedermeier realism*. The variety and vitality of the paintings created by many artists is such that, even when viewers possess no specialized knowledge of the time, the works communicate a good idea not only of the art but also of life and customs in the Vienna of that era.

The Biedermeier period may be said to span the years of peace between the Congress of Vienna of 1814–15 and the revolutionary year of 1848. It is understandable that, after two decades of war, the Austrian people yearned for tranquility, stability, and the joys of domestic happiness and security, an impulse that influenced Viennese Biedermeier painting. In spite of the tendency to realism, therefore, many negative aspects of life—social injustice, poverty, exploitation—found little expression in art. Then, too, the artist faced strict censorship and a generally inhospitable atmosphere toward representation of the less favorable aspects of Austrian society in the Metternich era.

In Biedermeier life the family was central to all aspirations (see Chapter 2). It was a primary social element in both the private and governmental sectors. Consequently, the Biedermeier period produced especially lively and intimate pictures of families and children. These paintings arose in both middle-class and aristocratic milieux—indeed, even at the imperial court—usually the work of artists specializing in this métier. That Emperor Francis I of Austria was the patriarch of a large family furthered the emphasis on middle-class family values and also enabled him to be represented and accepted as father of all the peoples of the Habsburg realm. Government policies of that time, under the tight leadership of the state chancellor, Prince Clemens Metternich, corresponded to this general attitude. Moreover, Metternich was from 1810 to 1840 the president of the Vienna Academy of Fine Arts, then the only official art institution in the country. Even though Metternich did not directly meddle in artistic matters, he was the guarantor that works of art would not embody criticism of Austrian society. Pictures had to be approved by the censor before they could be exhibited, travels (even mere painting trips into the mountains) had to be approved, and so on. The revolutionary ideas emanating from France were to be kept from the people and hence also from art by these and other means, while the policies of the post-Napoleonic restoration were to be supported.

Biedermeier painting was, above all, an expression of the life and aspirations of the middle class. Since the late eighteenth century the bourgeoisie or the so-called Third Estate, as this broad stratum of society is also designated, had been in a steady social, economic, and political ascent all over Europe (see Chapter 2).[2] This development necessarily had an enormous impact on all the arts everywhere, for the new culture was centered on the home. Furniture, glass, porcelain, and other household products, which still to this day have lost neither their charm nor their usefulness, document the self-consciousness of the middle classes.

The great goal of painting in this epoch was the rendering of visible reality. The new realism, which entered into painting around 1820 and reached an early high point in Vienna ten years later, expressed itself strongly in certain themes for paintings; these were, above all, the common events of daily life, people themselves, and the natural world surrounding these. Thus landscapes, portraits, and genre pictures (including family scenes) are characteristic of Biedermeier art. Painting quickly became the ideal medium for depicting the wishes, needs, and yearnings of society and for satisfying the growing desire to be pictured (as the photograph serves us today). The family portrait therefore experienced a particular blossoming. The central figure of the father in the midst of his wife and a flock of children was repeatedly stressed as the foundation of the state (see fig. 1.12, plates 11, 12). Also striking is the strong interest in children. Such pictures provided an underpinning for the new self-awareness of the middle class. Also enjoying great popularity with the public were pictures that depicted the life of farmers and small craftsmen, the poor, and people victimized by fate. Certain Viennese painters specialized in such themes and, in fact, specialization played a large role: most Viennese painters of the Biedermeier period focused on a specific type of painting, and they ventured seldom or not at all into other genres. (The portraitist Friedrich von Amerling produced, for example, only one or two landscapes.) Only Ferdinand Georg Waldmüller was an exception: he turned out paintings in virtually every thematic category.

GENRE PAINTING

In the biennial expositions of the Vienna Academy during the 1830s and 1840s, life-like genre paintings were especially numerous. The development began with simple one- or two-figure scenes in small format, such as those of Peter Fendi; they struck a bittersweet note, but not seldom also a humorous one. About 1835 artists like F. G. Waldmüller and Josef Danhauser began to populate the canvasses, now larger in format, with more figures, arranged as if on a theater stage. Convincing and realistic representation demanded an old master–like painting technique. The buyers of the bourgeoisie and aristocracy, among them some collectors in the modern sense of the term, regarded these paintings not only as works of high artistic and technical quality but also as exemplars of moralizing admonition. (The emperor also bought art, both for himself and for the imperial gallery.) To be sure, this attitude also corresponded to the romantic tendency to idealize the life of simple country and suburban people, who were presumably close to nature and uncorrupted.

Among subjects of pictures, the picnic excursion played a special role, for it expressed the longing of the city dwellers for nature. Two such representations, both of which arose as recollections of Sunday pleasures and of friendship, are the watercolors *Outing to Atzenbrugg* and *Social Games of the Schubertians* (see figs. 1.15, 1.16) by Leopold Kupelwieser. The artist transmits a lively view of the stimulating atmosphere of friendship, creativity, and lust for life in the circle around Franz Schubert. In their directness and authenticity as representations of Schubert's life, however, these two sheets are the exception. Schubert's other trusted painter friend, Moritz von Schwind, produced his many works relating to Schubert many years later in Munich, memorializing the youth they experienced together (see figs. 1.14, 10.17, A.6). There is, for example, the so-called *Lachner-Rolle* (1862), which preserves a series of scenes drawn from the life of Schubert. It is important to remember that most Schubert portraits, and even most scenes from his life, were produced posthumously and tend to idealize their subject.

Biedermeier artists sounded moralizing tones, reflecting the literary origin of some themes—for example, in the works of Danhauser—and forfeiting the immediacy and freshness of the earlier, smaller genre pictures that captured real life. Also typical for the Viennese Biedermeier were representations that portray the universal piety of the time, but as a part of daily life: baptisms, pilgrimages, processions, marriages (see plate 7). On the other hand, pictorial images of great social and political events are the exception. Only Johann Peter Krafft painted scenes from the life of Emperor Francis I (see plate 1). These authentic, eyewitness accounts, although they date from around 1830, are based on French models from the Napoleonic era yet also clearly show local color with an immediacy and vividness not otherwise encountered in Viennese painting.

One painter who became famous for his seemingly effortless, virtuosic, lifelike scenes featuring children, painted mostly in watercolor, was Peter Fendi. His touching family scenes in middle-class homes and at the bourgeoislike imperial court convey the Biedermeier preoccupation with and love of children, who are always depicted as radiant and full of life.

In these years Vienna experienced a blooming of watercolor painting. Fendi was one of its chief masters, and Karl Schindler and Friedrich Treml also created lively genre scenes in this medium. But the greatest watercolorist was Rudolf Alt, whose landscapes and views of different regions of the monarchy and of Italy are among the timeless artworks of the nineteenth century (see fig. 7.1).

The master of the theatrical-literary genre painting of this period was Josef Danhauser, who worked for many years as a theater painter and married a singer who became a prima donna at the court opera. Many of Danhauser's paintings are rather like large scenes on the stage, dramaturgically through-composed, descriptive and aspiring to be both entertaining and moralizing (see plate 13). Sumptuous color and the handling of light are also in the service of this directorial, auteurlike approach. Danhauser's name—as well as that of his father, Josef Ulrich—is also inseparable from Viennese furniture of the Biedermeier period, for the Danhauser furniture factory (1804–38) was renowned for its excellence and originality. (In 1830, a year after his father's death, the painter took over the direction of the firm for a while.)

Danhauser, like many of his Viennese painter colleagues, emulated again and again the Dutch masters of the seventeenth century, not only in painting technique but also in picture content; Viennese painters could study the Dutch Golden Age in various collections of the royal painting gallery, among them Count Lamberg's Gallery in the Academy.

Viennese genre painting did not spontaneously appear: seventeenth-century painting, local, French, and English traditions from the eighteenth century, and the Viennese environment of the moment all played a role in producing a unique style. This style draws its essential charm and distinctive quality from a conflict—the dualism of ideal and actual experience, of glorification and realism. Moreover, this holds not only for genre paintings but also for landscape painting, for the portrait, and especially for the floral still life adapted from seventeenth-century Dutch works.

PORTRAIT PAINTING

The self-awareness of the rising bourgeoisie (see Chapter 2) expresses itself most clearly in portraits. Even as realistic representations moved the personal and the unique into the foreground, however, the traditional official portrait continued to exist. The postbaroque tradition was still vital (see fig. 4.4), especially because of the presence of some famous older painters, like Friedrich Heinrich Füger and Johann Baptist Lampi (father and son); furthermore, there was a constant demand for portraits of persons in high office.

But about 1820 Waldmüller began an entirely new chapter in Viennese portrait painting. The object was to represent people as they were, not as they would like to be. These early paintings, which date largely from between 1819 and 1830, are witnesses of a nearly fanatical striving toward truth, of a merciless, often exaggerated realism that perhaps also is to be understood as a reaction to the idealism of the preceding decades, which was clearly tempered already by 1830. Peter Fendi, Franz Eybl (see plate 14), and other painters also had a part in this development. In his mature period, Waldmüller produced portraits characterized by strong attention to detail and to people by means of perfect painterly form, handling of light, and strikingly confident composition that signaled the high point of portrait art in this decade. He avoided the exaggerations of his earlier years and achieved the expression of a becalmed, heartfelt humanity that still enchants the viewer.

To the same period, however, belongs the most famous and sought after portraitist of Vienna, Friedrich von Amerling (see plate 15). This artist was influenced by the great English tradition of portrait painting and especially by Thomas Lawrence, the most famous of English portraitists of the time (see figs. 3.4, 3.5). In 1828 Amerling worked in the London atelier of Lawrence, who came to Vienna at the time of the great Congress. Amerling impressed the public with his virtuosic painting, and for two decades he dominated the field in Vienna. In his work the pendulum swings back and forth between ideal and realistic, with opposites happily united in several pictures. In general, however, Amerling tended more to the idealizing representational picture, which clearly coincided with the wishes of his rich bourgeois and aristocratic patrons. Moreover, in small, spontaneous, and quickly painted studies in oil, he demonstrated his many artistic facets, notably his masterly ability to capture the essence of a particular moment.

The family portrait, as already explained, was a special expression of the Biedermeier period. Works by Waldmüller and Amerling are the most beautiful, most impressive and artistically valuable examples. They are also extremely valuable as contemporary documents. Amerling's 1837 painting of the family of the Viennese industrialist Rudolf von Arthaber is a masterpiece of the period (see plate 11); another is his family portrait of Count Breunner (1834). A third central work of this type, and perhaps the most important, is the family portrait of the Viennese notary Josef August Eltz, painted by Waldmüller in 1835 (see plate 12). This work is characterized by the artist's dualism of ideal and reality. Very typical of Waldmüller is the attempt here to establish the union of human activity and nature, while nonetheless resorting to very conservative models of composition. In most family and group pictures of the time, individuals interact with each other through movement and gesture, or simply by eye contact.

LANDSCAPE PAINTING

Viennese landscape painting at the beginning of the nineteenth century was realized in several styles, as was true in other European countries. The realistic approach was compositionally rooted in the traditional seventeenth-century Dutch paintings; the conservative approach maintained the theatrical ethos of baroque painting; and the religious-patriotic approach incorporated nature symbolically, as a pantheistic unity.[3] This third category includes in particular the works of several German and Austrian painters who began to associate in 1809 in Vienna. Later some of them resettled in Rome, where Schubert's close friend Leopold Kupelwieser got to know them in 1823. Their long hair, suggestive of depictions of Jesus, led to their being called Nazarenes.

With the new interest in nature came a preference for certain locations: for example, the charming and relatively untouched area around Vienna was discovered as a subject of painting. Somewhat later, between 1815 and 1820, it became popular to travel through the city of Salzburg—at first from Germany on the way to Rome, and later also from Vienna en route to the Salzkammergut and the Berchtesgaden region. During the next fifty years, almost innumerable landscape painters found their treasured subject matter here in this romantic setting of mountains and lakes. Friedrich Loos (see plate 16) and Friedrich Gauermann (see plate 17) from 1825 and Ferdinand Georg Waldmüller from 1831 painted small-scale landscapes in the Salzkammergut that today are valued as quintessential examples of Biedermeier realism and are among the most important Viennese achievements in nineteenth-century painting. Artists sought to depict nature not only through truth of detail but also by capturing the atmosphere. The relation of this development to the objectives of the Barbizon School of French painting is apparent, even if the pictures from Austria and France are in other respects quite different from one another.[4]

It must be remembered that a great difference existed between the studies and sketches produced outside in nature and the larger paintings subsequently executed inside the studio. Only the paintings were regarded as autonomous artworks, not the studies. The general appreciation of the sketch as artistic expression of spontaneously experienced nature became established only in the second half of the century. Again, Waldmüller was the exception: he displayed, in the exhibitions of the Academy, his small, emotionless pictures of the Salzkammergut and of the Prater (a lush area on the Danube near Vienna; see plate 18) as studies from nature, seen by himself—but only by him—as independent works. This first high point of realistic landscape painting, produced by only a few painters, has nothing to do with Biedermeier narrowness or even parochialism. Quite the opposite: here is an incomparable, independent artistic achievement, free from political and societal associations. Even Franz Steinfeld, who through his long teaching career and his advanced teaching methods at the Vienna Academy achieved a special place in the realm of landscape painting, sought, in spite of all trueness to nature in the detail, to maintain a glorified portrayal of the landscape. We also find here the bipolarity of ideal and actual, of glorification and reality, that underlies many realms of Biedermeier art. In literature this theme finds its best expression in the plays of Ferdinand Raimund (see Chapter 10).

Waldmüller's small nature studies draw their artistic value not from the specialness of the subject but rather from the rendering of the light, which breaks up into the most multifarious gradations of color. As no other, this painter illuminates the objects, trees, and mountain slopes. He is the preeminent painter of light among the Viennese; only the great watercolorist Rudolf Alt approaches and, in the late works, surpasses him; but these works already stand under the influence of impressionism.

How to render light, especially the sparkling sunlight of a bright day, became increasingly the most important challenge for the landscape painters of the nineteenth century. The key to how the problem could be convincingly solved was found by the French impressionists fewer than ten years after Waldmüller's death.

FLOWER PAINTING

Finally, we must consider flower painting which became a Viennese specialty in the late eighteenth century and then especially in the Biedermeier period. The preference of the Viennese public for the representation of more or less lavishly assembled bouquets of flowers, the disproportionately large number of flower painters, the mass of pictures—all these were directly connected with the existence of the Imperial-Royal

Viennese Porcelain Factory, which since 1772 had developed into an exceedingly successful enterprise. One art school associated with the factory trained one hundred thirty painters between 1785 and 1805, fifty of them flower specialists, whose task was to paint porcelain products of various kinds. In 1812 the Vienna Academy of Fine Arts established a professorship in flower painting, further reflecting the demand for well-trained artists in this specialty.

Most flower and still life painters were occupied variously: as porcelain painters they decorated precious display vases, ornamental plates, and large-format porcelain tables partly embellished with lavish compositions; and as easel painters they created the oil paintings that were then as beloved (and expensive) as today. Yet this had nothing to do with a period-bound painting, as was the case with other types of Biedermeier painting; rather, it was an art for a public with spending power. For decades this public wanted to see paintings that adhered to the established compositional schemes, which allowed no kind of experiment. To this capacity for constancy a rigorous technical schooling contributed much, producing art of such quality that viewing the pictures is still a constantly new experience. The broadly based Viennese love of nature liked to express itself in these paintings as well, even though the representation was of an artificial nature. These decades in Vienna were also a time of amateur gardening, carried on with great understanding, as well as of professionally operated gardens and hothouses. The work of the famous Dutch botanist Nikolaus von Jacquin, called to Vienna in 1752 by Maria Theresa, thus had great impact.

The most famous Viennese flower painters were Johann Baptist Drechsler (see plate 19), Sebastian Wegmayer, Johann Knapp, Franz Xaver Petter, and Josef Nigg (see plate 20). Drechsler's contribution was to build up the teaching activity at the Academy on the basis of the study of old Dutch flower painting. Exemplars from the Dutch seventeenth century were available for study in the various Viennese art collections. The painters also created a stock of patterns with the help of botanically exact detail studies, which permitted, independent of the time of seasonal blooming and maturity, the assembling and painting of favorite flower bouquets and still life fruits. In viewing several such pictures, we soon notice a preference for certain flowers and fruits. Next to well-known and ordinary kinds we find exotic rarities and fashionable flowers. The limitations of the traditional compositional vocabulary are redeemed by the virtuosic, old master–like painting technique and by the charm of the painting surface exhibited by these works.

Viennese flower painting died with the painters; after 1850 this specialty was no longer taught at the Academy. The other favorite forms of Biedermeier painting—above all, genre painting—had a similar fate. Only landscape painting, the most innovative genre of painting, survived. By coming to grips with new developments, it maintained a lively continuity after midcentury at the hand of a new generation of artists.

1. On the term *Biedermeier,* see Chapter 1, note 17.

2. This term derives from the threefold classification of feudal social orders into clergy, nobility, and commoners, respectively. See also Chapter 2.

3. It has been argued that Schubert was a pantheist, that he felt that God was to be found in, or was identical with, nature. These sentiments are embodied in the song "Die Allmacht," the text of which was written by Ladislaus von Pyrker, the patriarch (archbishop) of Venice, who was a friend and patron of Schubert's. It is noteworthy that Schubert included this song in the only public concert devoted solely to his music during his lifetime. Pyrker was also in the 1820s a prime patron of the painter Josef Danhauser, who depicted several events in Pyrker's heroic *Rudolphias* (1825) as well as many religious works commissioned by Pyrker. Cf. John Michael Gingerich, "Schubert's Beethoven Project: The Chamber Music, 1824–1828" (Ph.D. diss., Yale University, 1996), 30–47 [Ed.].

4. Barbizon is a village in the forest of Fontainebleau near Paris where various painters, among them Camille Corot, initiated their nature studies.

FOR FURTHER READING

There is little on Austrian painting available in English. The Biedermeier style in the German-speaking world, including Austria, is surveyed in Fritz Novotny, *Painting and Sculpture in Europe, 1780 to 1880* (Harmondsworth: Penguin, 1960); and Geraldine Norman, *Biedermeier Painting, 1815–1848: Reality Observed in Genre, Portrait, and Landscape* (New York: Thames and Hudson, 1987). The principal survey of specifically Viennese Biedermeier painting is Gerbert Frodl, *Wiener Malerei der Biedermeierzeit* (Rosenheim: Rosenheimer Verlagshaus, 1987), which contains approximately two hundred illustrations. The Biedermeier painters are also represented in Heinrich Fuchs, *Die österreichischen Maler des 19. Jahrhunderts,* 4 vols. (Vienna: privately printed, 1972–74) and its two supplementary volumes (1978–79), which consist of thumbnail sketches of the artists preceding black and white illustrations of representative paintings.

There are also beautifully illustrated volumes devoted to individual artists, such as Klaus Albrecht Schröder, *Ferdinand Georg Waldmüller* (Munich: Prestel, 1990).

· 9 ·

The Poetry of Schubert's Songs

JANE K. BROWN

Romanticism evokes many different ideas—love, *Weltschmerz,* demons, madness, simplicity, folktale and folk song, primitivism, attacks on classicism, Greek revival, Gothic revival, enthusiasm for the French Revolution, reaction against the French Revolution, organicism, irony—so many that the term can be defined in many different ways. Let us begin instead by dividing and naming. Because romanticism in its broadest European sense corresponds roughly with the lifetime of Goethe (1749–1832), it is often referred to in Germany as the Age of Goethe. Literary historians often divide it into ages of sensibility (1750–80), German classicism (Goethe, Schiller) and romanticism (all the others, both about 1790–1815), and Biedermeier (1815–48). The distinction between classicism and romanticism in this context derives from the self-definitions of two "schools," which in turn derive mainly from accidents of geography and personality. But all these constitute romanticism in the larger sense.

The introduction to August Wilhelm Schlegel's "Lectures on Dramatic Poetry," the so-called Vienna lectures of 1808, contains one of the most famous and influential definitions of the concerns of this period in Germany (see also Chapter 4). Romantics, according to Schlegel, are mediators trying to achieve universality in a historical world structured by oppositions. The most important of these is between the "classic" (represented by the ancient Greeks) and the "romantic" (represented by northern European literature from the Middle Ages on, but especially by Schlegel's Germany). To the classical Greeks Schlegel attributes harmony, objective presence, and finitude, and to the romantic Germans individuality, subjective longing, and infinity. Because the modern romantic self has the German qualities but seeks the Greek ones, it always suffers from consciousness of division within itself. The struggle to achieve unity in the face of dichotomy characterizes virtually all aspects of political, philosophical, and psychological life in European culture from the mid-eighteenth century into the 1830s.

We can understand Biedermeier, the late phase of European romanticism in German-speaking lands, as a shift in attitude toward the synthesis of dichotomies. Before 1805 romantics envisioned some glorious synthesis arising from the power of their longing, but after 1815 the culture became extremely pessimistic, for obvious reasons: political oppression and censorship, disappointment that the Napoleonic wars had led to no democratic and united German state, widespread poverty in the German-speaking countries, the religious crisis that accompanied the advent of materialist thinking.[1] This anxious age perceived the same dichotomies as the romantics, but it could neither synthesize nor transcend them. With the onset of this *Weltschmerz*, as such specifically romantic pessimism is called, we speak of a Biedermeier rather than a romantic sensibility; they are opposite sides of the same coin.

These tensions and developments are reflected in the poetry of the period, even when it seems most innocent, as in Goethe's ballad "Der Fischer" of 1778, set by Schubert in 1815 (ex. 9.1).[2] A fisherman is tempted into the water by a mermaid and, as the text laconically puts it, "was never seen again." But beneath this simple facade lurk typically romantic complexities. As the poem proceeds, the apparently antithetical worlds of air and water become more alike; their differences come to depend more on the differing points of view of the fisherman and the mermaid, and the fisherman loses his confidence in their difference. By showing him how sky and water, then his own face and water come together in the reflection he sees as he looks down from his boat, the mermaid awakens in him intense longing that is romantic in both the philosophical and conventional sense ("as when the loved one calls"). Just as in August Wilhelm Schlegel's lecture, polar oppositions are overcome by the power of romantic longing for unity—perhaps.

Human and natural worlds are momentarily synthesized when the fisherman sees his face reflected in the water, but when he destroys that image by plunging into it, does he die or transcend to a higher level of self-knowledge? Does he disappear into the world or into himself? No one can know, for humans exist in only one of the worlds, and synthesis must combine both. If he did remain visible to us, the fisherman would certainly look different; he would look, perhaps, like Schubert's apparently mad traveler at the end of the song-cycle *Winterreise*. Ending in a passionate embrace or ending in madness are the two sides of the romantic–Biedermeier version of the attempt to unify opposing worlds.

Example 9.1

Der Fischer

(Johann Wolfgang von Goethe)

Das Wasser rauscht', das Wasser schwoll,	*The Fisherman*

Das Wasser rauscht', das Wasser schwoll,
Ein Fischer saß daran,
Sah nach dem Angel ruhevoll,
Kühl bis ans Herz hinan.
Und wie er sitzt und wie er lauscht,
Theilt sich die Flut empor;
Aus dem bewegten Wasser rauscht
Ein feuchtes Weib hervor.

Sie sang zu ihm, sie sprach zu ihm:
Was lockst du meine Brut
Mit Menschenwitz und Menschenlist,
Hinauf in Todesgluth?
Ach! wüßtest du, wie's Fischlein ist
So wohlig auf dem Grund,
Du stiegst herunter wie du bist,
Und würdest erst gesund.

Labt sich die liebe Sonne nicht,
Der Mond sich nicht im Meer?
Kehrt wellenatmend ihr Gesicht
Nicht doppelt schöner her?
Lockt dich der tiefe Himmel nicht?
Das feuchtverklärte Blau?
Lockt dich dein eigen Angesicht
Nicht her in ew'gen Thau?

Das Wasser rauscht', da Wasser schwoll,
Netzt' ihm den nackten Fuß;
Sein Herz wuchs ihm so sehnsuchtsvoll,
Wie bey der Liebsten Gruß.
Sie sprach zu ihm, sie sang zu ihm,
Da war's um ihn geschehn:
Halb zog sie ihn, halb sank er hin,
Und ward nicht mehr gesehn.

The Fisherman

The water swirled, the water rose,
An angler sat nearby,
Gazed calmly at his fishing rod,
Cool to his very heart.
And as he sits and as he looks,
The rising flood divides;
Forth from the troubled water swirls
A woman dripping wet.

She sang to him, she spoke to him:
Why do you lure my brood
With human wit and human guile
Up into the deadly heat?
If only you knew how the fishes live
So cozy in the depths,
You'd climb on down, just as you are,
And would then feel well for once.

Does not the sun refresh herself,
The moon himself, in the sea?
Does not her face, wave-breathing,
Return doubly beautiful?
Does not the deep heaven lure you,
The moist transfigured blue?
Does not your own countenance
Lure you to eternal dew?

The water swirled, the water rose,
Dampened his naked foot;
His heart swelled with yearning,
As when the loved one calls.
She spoke to him, she sang to him,
Soon his fate was sealed:
Half she pulled him, half he sank,
And was never seen again.

• • •

"Der Fischer" thus embodies the qualities of romantic poetry important for understanding Schubert's attraction to it. It is typical in its simple form, ambiguous resolution, pervasive use of nature, concern for an inner and not fully conscious self, and above all in its dualities. Translated into song, such dualities can be further extended in the dialogue between piano and voice. There are places in Schubert, for example, where the piano evokes feelings of which the voice only later, if ever, becomes conscious, and other places where piano and voice, sometimes even the two hands in the piano, articulate opposing stances. Or other places, in "Der Fischer," for example, where piano postludes and interludes offer an opposing point of view to the accompanied voice.

We are now in a position to understand the larger framework within which Schubert's common themes of yearning, isolation, wandering, and death operate. Since fairy-tale figures and extremes of sentimentality are the language in which the age addressed its basic concerns with identity and opposition, texts that might seem trivial to us could evoke the powerful response they clearly did from Schubert. Because of the importance poems like this typically attributed to feeling over judgment, to image over explicit plot, to—in a word—subjectivity—lyric poetry became the primary genre for the romantics, as did the *Lied* ("song") for romantic composers.

SCHUBERT'S POETS

Goethe was Schubert's favorite poet.[3] By examining Schubert's selection of Goethe's poems in the context of what else he set, we can refine our sense of how Schubert and his contemporaries related to the world. It is therefore useful to look at the relative frequency with which Schubert set different poets, and on that basis to characterize the Goethe who appealed to Schubert and understand that profile in the larger context.

Who, then, were Schubert's other favorite poets (to judge by the frequency with which he set their poems)?[4] Goethe is far and away the favorite, with seventy settings. Second is Schubert's close friend and one-time roommate Johann Mayrhofer, with forty-seven; Schiller and Wilhelm Müller, author of the texts for *Die schöne Müllerin* and *Winterreise,* are next, with forty-five each. This grouping is already typical for Schubert's selection of poets. About half of them are still famous—Goethe and Schiller are the two great heroes of German literature—and the other half are known chiefly from Schubert's songs. The age distribution is also typical: Goethe and Schiller came to their first maturity in the 1770s and 1780s, Mayrhofer and Müller after 1815. Strikingly absent from Schubert's preferred poets are those of the main romantic generation, which came to intellectual maturity between 1795 and 1810.

The same pattern holds as we continue down the list. A substantial gap separates the first four poets from the next most frequently set ones, Friedrich von Matthisson and Ludwig Hölty, at twenty-nine and twenty-six, respectively. Matthisson began writing poems in the late seventies and was at his most prolific and popular in the eighties and nineties. The later poems show no significant aesthetic advances over the early ones, thus demonstrating the persistent popularity of the poetic style established in the seventies and associated with admirers of Friedrich Gottlieb Klopstock, the founding father of modern German poetry. Hölty was born within a year of Goethe but died very young in 1776. These two thus locate Schubert's preference in the poetry of the seventies and eighties, the age of sensibility.

Thirteen poets follow by whom Schubert set between ten and twenty poems. Seven of these are contemporaries of Schubert: Walter Scott and six German and Austrian poets (Körner, Leitner, Rellstab, Schober, Schultze, Seidl), some close friends of the composer, none with a substantial independent reputation. Four are famous eighteenth-century poets: Claudius and Klopstock (again with high points in the seventies and eighties), Metastasio (the famed opera-seria librettist and Habsburg imperial court poet for a half century), and the supposed Irish bard Ossian, later revealed as a forgery, but a major influence on the generation writing in the seventies. A fifth figure related to this group is Johann Gaudenz Freiherr von Salis-Seewis, who wrote a lot in the nineties, but in the style of the seventies; he is never considered a high romantic. The last figure in this larger group, Friedrich Schlegel, is considered today the most important theoretician of German romanticism. But he was never considered an important poet; furthermore, the poems by him that Schubert set date from *after* he moved to Vienna and converted to Catholicism—that is, after the generative period of high romanticism.

In fact, with sixteen poems, Schlegel is the most frequently set of the high romantic group. Next most frequently set is his brother August Wilhelm, with seven. August Wilhelm, too, is valued less for his poetry than for his theoretical writings and his superb translations. Of the major, representative poets of the German romantic school, only Novalis and Tieck are represented, with six and one, respectively. The only other poet whom we sometimes call romantic to be significantly represented is Heinrich Heine, whose poems all date from after 1820. Of all the settings of poets in this group, only those of Heine are well known. Thus, none of the texts of what is known as German romanticism resulted in a major Schubert song. Evidently Schubert's real enthusiasm lay rather with the groups that are considered to be romantic in European terms but that in German literary history are distinguished from the romantics. The later generation of Schubert's contemporaries is called, as we have already seen, Biedermeier; Goethe and Schiller are placed in the category of German classicism, and the generation of the seventies and eighties, starting with Klopstock, are considered preromantic, or poets of sensibility. It is now well established that the Biedermeier generation (and succeeding generations until the late nineteenth century in Germany) felt a stronger affinity with the age of sensibility than with the age of high romanticism.[5] In this regard Schubert is absolutely typical.

Consider Schubert's Goethe against this background (fig. 9.1). Goethe unquestion-
ably evoked some of Schubert's greatest musical responses—Gretchen's songs from
Faust, the songs of Mignon and the harper from *Wilhelm Meisters Lehrjahre,* "Erlkönig,"
"Heidenröslein" are only the most obvious examples. Any number of the Goethe texts
set by Schubert capture quintessential romantic moments—not only "Der Fischer"
but equally well the two *Wanderers Nachtlieder,* "Erlkönig," "An den Mond," or "Auf
dem See." The Goethe who struggled with the fundamental dichotomies of romanticism is certainly represented in Schubert's selection. How does this fact relate to the
generalizations derived from our general survey? In terms of European literary history,
Goethe is as central and typical a romantic as, say, Wordsworth or Coleridge; in terms
of German literary history he embodies German classicism, the parallel movement to
the romantic school. In a sense, then, it fits in with Schubert's avoidance of the central
romantic generation.

But in fact, Schubert showed a marked preference for Goethe's early poetry. He set
twenty-five of Goethe's poems from the 1770s, fourteen from the eighties, only seven
from the nineties, nine from the first decade of the nineteenth century, and only five
from the next decade. This distribution does not correspond to the relative quantity or
quality of Goethe's lyric output. The nineties, for example, represent the high point
both of his ballad output and of his poems in classical meters. An even more striking
example: in February and March 1821, Schubert set four poems from Goethe's collection *West-östlicher Divan,* published in 1819. The entire collection runs to a few hundred poems; of the four set, two were actually not by Goethe at all but by his friend
Marianne von Willemer (Goethe included three of her poems in the collection). Apparently, Schubert had distinctly less taste for Goethe's poetry after his first major creative period. In this respect Schubert is typical of his generation—the adulation of the
classical Goethe is a phenomenon of the late nineteenth century, and admiration for
the work of his old age has come largely in the last fifty years.

Schubert's Goethe is thus the young Goethe of the age of sensibility. What does this
statement mean? These poems can be grouped by genre and theme. First come settings of four pieces from *Faust,* all involving not Faust but Gretchen and the sentimental story of her love, guilt, and abandonment. The second group consists of the
great free-verse hymns "Prometheus," "Ganymed," and "An Schwager Kronos." In
each a titanic figure dynamically imposes himself on nature. Free-verse hymns, known
as Pindarics in the period, are associated with the first generation to value the sublime
over the beautiful, an important aspect of romantic views on art. The bond with nature seems an important part of what appealed to Schubert in these poems. The
smaller lyric poems Schubert set from the same period confirm this thesis, for essentially all deal with nature. About half of them involve an enthusiastic bond to nature
with an intensity bordering on the tragic. Such texts include "Willkommen und Ab-

9.1 Angelika Kaufmann's portrait of Goethe (1787), painted in Rome during the poet's Italian journey, captures the still youthful poet of sensibility to whose early work Schubert was so attracted. Schubert set more texts of Goethe than any other poet. [SWK (Photo by Sigrid Geske)]

schied," whose boisterous hero abandons his beloved at the end; "Der Musensohn," who seems condemned to dance eternally through nature at the expense of all human contacts; or even "Heidenröslein," in which a rose is plucked and the last word is "leiden" ("suffer"). The other half describe reflective immersions in nature, often with some touch of melancholy. Examples include "Jägers Abendlied," "An den Mond," and above all the two *Wanderers Nachtlieder*. Two texts span, or rather synthesize, this dichotomy: "Der Fischer," of course, and "Auf dem See." They address and dramatize extreme emotional states, they are concerned with loss, they explore the bond between self and nature over and over again, often in connection with the love bond between individuals. Anyone who has read *The Sorrows of Young Werther* (1774) will recognize in this summary a fair description of the novel that became a European best-seller overnight, grounded Goethe's fame for the rest of his long life, and has remained the most typical and famous work of the age of sensibility. The nature enthusiast Werther falls in love with a woman he cannot marry. He idealizes her, then comes to see in her inaccessibility his complete alienation from nature. He commits suicide. Sensibility in a nutshell.

Let us now consider why Schubert did not respond to the full range of Goethe's lyric output. With regard to *Faust,* Schubert confined himself to the tragedy of Gretchen and ignored both Faust and Mephistopheles. The absence of Faust is not so surprising; his role does not seem to have inspired any nineteenth-century composers to great songs. But Mephistopheles—how could Schubert ignore the possibilities of the great flea song from *Faust,* Part I? Beethoven's earlier presence on the turf did not deter Schubert from setting the Mignon songs from *Wilhelm Meister,* nor from several other texts. The absence of *Faust* signals a respect in which the older Beethoven still had something in common with Goethe that Schubert did not. Schubert had no eye, for lack of a better word, for evil. Regardless of how he would have understood it (and this is a controversial question with regard to Goethe), Schubert just did not set texts where evil is an issue; instead what ought to be evil somehow dissolves into pathos— as in "Der Zwerg" (by Matthäus von Collin), in which an "evil" dwarf murders his beloved queen out of frustrated love for her and condemns himself to eternal misery in expiation. He is not evil after all, but a sufferer at the hands of a heedless nature that created him a dwarf and not a king. One might better say Schubert had plenty of sense for suffering evil, but none for generating it. Like his Biedermeier contemporaries, Schubert had immense awareness of Weltschmerz, the generalized suffering of living in an apparently indifferent world. Goethe got over *Werther,* the great novel of Weltschmerz, as he got over many of his enthusiasms of the 1770s. Indeed, he came to find his youthful hero quite tiresome; Schubert's generation found him newly sympathetic.

It is striking that Schubert did not set any of the parts of *Faust* written in the 1790s, for the tragedy of Gretchen belongs to the part of the play written in the early 1770s. Yet almost half of *Faust,* Part I, was written between about 1797 and 1803; these sections tend to philosophical complexity, irony, and irreverent humor. Similarly, Schubert set none of Goethe's substantial body of openly philosophical poetry. Much of it is quite cynical, but much of it is not. Apparently neither the cynicism nor the philosophical aspect interested him. But Goethe's playful moments, with rare exceptions, seem also not to have appealed to Schubert, even within the context of the 1770s. Although Schubert set three of Goethe's great Pindaric hymns, he did not set the grandest of these, "Wanderers Sturmlied." In this remarkable text the speaker, traveling through rain and wind, first challenges Jupiter and also prays to Pindar and various other spirits for inspiration. He finally lands on Bacchus, god of wine, as perhaps the best source of inspiration under the circumstances; in the openly comic ending this bold spirit must slog home in the mud, worse off than the peasant he sees passing. Such broad self-parody was Goethe's antidote to the Weltschmerz he was simultaneously popularizing in *Werther;* but the antidote had less appeal than the malady to Schubert and his generation.

The most important aspect of Goethe's poetry that is entirely ignored by Schubert is what we call the classical Goethe. Apart from the Pindaric hymns, Schubert simply does not set Goethe's poems on classical themes. The omission seems at first mystifying: how could a reader with Schubert's devotion to Goethe fail to sympathize with the central importance of the classical world for him? Goethe's *Roman Elegies* are the greatest love poems in the German language. They were considered indecent when they were first published in 1795 (though hardly so by current standards); perhaps Schubert's avoidance of them is related to the rigid public orthodoxy of the age of Metternich. But there is nothing remotely indecent about Goethe's other elegies of the 1790s: some are laments for the dead, some are innocent love elegies, some are veritable idylls. Perhaps Schubert just preferred not to set texts written in classical meters, though he did set some by Klopstock. But Goethe also wrote poems on classical themes and materials not in classical meters—he wrote ballads, and the extraordinary song of the fates in the play *Iphigenia in Tauris*. These, too, Schubert ignored. Nor did he generally avoid classical themes. Indeed, there is a recording of Schubert Lieder entitled *Songs of Greek Antiquity*, with texts mostly by Schubert's friend Johann Mayrhofer.[6] Schubert also set any number of Schiller texts on classical themes. Evidently there is something special about Goethe's classicism; the problem is best explored by brief comparisons between Goethe's classicism and some of the classical poems that Schubert did set.

It would be hard to confuse any of the poems in the recorded collection of Schubert's classical settings just cited with poems by Goethe, for several reasons. First, these poems are reflected and self-conscious in a way that Goethe's never are. The most typical in this regard is "An die Leier," adapted from the Greek of Anacreon by Franz von Bruchmann, a one-time friend of Schubert's. The poem dramatizes the struggle between the poet's desire to sing about Greek heroes and his lyre's refusal to play anything but songs of love. The lyre wins, and the speaker must renounce his claim to epic poetry. Or in "Aus Heliopolis," by Mayrhofer, the poet seeks a city of warmth and light from his place in the cold, gray north (read: Germany); a sunflower tells him to follow the sun, presumably forever. Goethe is often self-conscious about his status as a modern intruder on classical territory, but he always takes it with a chuckle, and he is never driven away, given advice by flowers, or, in his classical period, eternally under way. (The eternal deferral of heaven comes only at the end of *Faust,* II, written after Schubert's death; it belongs to what we ought to call the Biedermeier Goethe.) Goethe's capacity to adopt easily the role and voice of the ancients was precisely what amazed his contemporaries about his classicism.

At the thematic level the classical texts set by Schubert express a strong need for warmth ("Aus Heliopolis") and safety ("Lied eines Schiffers an die Dioskuren"). They involve repeated prayers and celebrate piety and virtue ("Orpheus" by Jacobi). Their speakers usually suffer from some painful separation from the Other ("Aus Heliopolis") or rejoice in momentary union in the instant of death ("Der zürnenden Diana"). Like Schiller's classicism it is nostalgically focused on a lost past or seeking a never-to-be-realized future. It is domesticated, private, internal. And it is all utterly contrary to Goethe's classicism at its height in the 1790s. Goethe's *Roman Elegies* focus entirely on fulfillment in love; that is why they were considered indecent. Goethe's antiquity is present, sensual beauty, not a lost or hoped-for ideal; to the considerable extent that it is ideal, the ideal is present and visible in the objects and images antiquity places before us (remember the importance of the reflected image in "Der Fischer"). In this respect Goethe's classicism is unrealistic, even naïve. Schubert's avoidance of Goethe's classicism shows how much he and his contemporaries preferred pathos to naïveté.

The most stunning example of Schubert's avoidance of the classical Goethe is *Die schöne Müllerin*. Verbal and structural echoes demonstrate that Wilhelm Müller's famous cycle is actually based on a group of four poems by Goethe first published in 1799—"Der Edelknabe und die Müllerin," "Der Junggeselle und der Bach," "Der Müllerin Verrat," and "Der Müllerin Reue." But Goethe's cycle is rather less sentimental than Müller's: the coquettish miller's daughter betrays her aristocratic lover not for another man but by arranging for her family to discover her in bed with him so that he will have to marry her. When he escapes through the window with only a cloak to cover him, she repents and becomes his mistress. The texts were intended to be set; Goethe even considered expanding them into an operetta. And they were set right away by Zumsteeg and Reichardt, who are hardly likely to have frightened Schubert off. But for Schubert and his generation Goethe's unabashedly sensual poems were acceptable for domestic consumption only in Müller's sentimental and sanitized elaboration.

SCHUBERT AND SCHILLER

This hypothesis can be tested and extended by examining Schubert's Schiller (fig. 9.2). Goethe and Schiller are so closely associated in German literary history that comparison of Schubert's response to the two poets is particularly informative. Schubert set some forty-five songs to Schiller texts, compared with seventy to Goethe texts. Nevertheless, he set a larger proportion of Schiller's total oeuvre. The relative decline in numbers of Schiller texts among Schubert's settings from the eighties to the nineties to the first decade of the nineteenth century is much less precipitous than was the case with the Goethe texts. Evidently Schiller's classicism affected the composer differently than did Goethe's. In fact, Schiller already was writing poems on classical themes in the 1780s, and Schubert set them happily. And he set those from the nineties and beyond as well. The reason for Schubert's response becomes clear from the topics of the poems, which basically fall into only three types: pathetic laments, pathetic love poems, and moral narratives (or situations) with unhappy endings. The pattern holds for Schiller's poems on classical topics as for all the others and remains constant over the whole span of his career, from the early eighties to his death in 1805. Although similar topics can be found in Goethe's poems of the seventies and eighties, they become rare with the advent of his classical style in the nineties. Schubert does not, then, lose interest in all poetry written in the nineties or during the height of German classicism: he loses interest only in works that are significantly different from the sentimental style that had taken form in the seventies and early eighties. We need to distinguish Goethe and Schiller, as Schubert clearly did.

Schiller drew the distinction between himself and Goethe as clearly as it has ever been drawn in one of the most important theoretical essays of the period, "On Naive and Sentimental Poetry" (1795–96). Like August Wilhelm Schlegel in his introduction to the Vienna lectures, Schiller establishes the classical and modern, northern Euro-

9.2 Friedrich Schiller, arguably Germany's greatest dramatist, was, after Goethe, Schubert's favorite poet. The mature Goethe and Schiller together came to embody the spirit and highest achievement of German literary classicism, often referred to as Weimar classicism. John Sartain after Antoine Graff. [NYPL:Print]

pean culture as the opposing poles of a dialectic—indeed, this essay was a major influence on Schlegel's thinking. For Schiller the self-consciousness of the moderns separates them from the ancients, with their more attractive naïveté. He explains at length why modern writers can no longer be naïve. But he is willing to attribute naïveté to one modern writer, Goethe. Naïveté here does not carry its usual deprecatory connotations; rather, it refers to the ability to accept the presence of the image without nostalgia, to take possession of the past without insecurity; it refers to a style in which pathos attaches only to the object itself, never to the relation of self to object. In calling Goethe a naïve poet, Schiller meant the same thing that August Wilhelm Schlegel would have had he called him a romantic poet—he synthesizes the opposing possibilities of classical and modern culture.

Schubert's Goethe is thus not the "naïve" Goethe admired by Schiller and the German romantics in the late 1790s, but rather the "preromantic" Goethe, the Goethe who established the greatest monuments of the age of sensibility in German culture—the Goethe of the previous generation whose famous novel of love and whose daring poems enabled them all (and himself also) to articulate Kant's philosophical program in literary form two decades later.

GOETHE, WILHELM MÜLLER, AND SCHUBERT

The real importance of the early Goethe for Schubert and his generation emerges most clearly if we pursue his influence on the texts of *Die schöne Müllerin* and *Winterreise,* Schubert's two major song cycles. These texts, of course, are not by Goethe but by Wilhelm Müller. Nevertheless, both of Müller's cycles are so profoundly influenced by Goethe's first novel that much of the appeal of the cycles must have been their similarity to the Goethe texts to which Schubert was so attracted. The plot of the *Schöne Müllerin* is virtually identical to that of *Werther*. Each begins with its hero putting his past behind him and entering a new world. Werther's opening words, "How happy I am to be away," could well be those of Schubert's miller, who takes such pleasure in wandering. Each enters an idyllic springtime world inhabited by a lovely young woman with whom the hero falls in love. In each case it develops that the young woman actually belongs to someone else—to an earlier betrothed in the case of Werther's Charlotte, to the hunter in Schubert. It is, by the way, not explicit that the girl was ever so in love with the miller as he with her, or that she did not have some earlier relationship with the hunter, for everything is seen so narrowly through the eyes of the miller. About halfway through each work the surrounding world begins to seem hostile to the hero, and his alienation grows apace. Both end with suicide. *Winterreise* repeats the second half of this plot, for it begins after the lover has lost his beloved, if he ever really had her. ("Das Mädchen sprach von Liebe, die Mutter gar von Eh'," "the girl mentioned love, the mother even marriage," implies less commitment than the traveler thought he had.) The famous linden tree in the fifth song ("Der Lindenbaum") alludes to a sentimental episode late in Goethe's novel in which Werther visits his childhood home, a small town with a memory-laden linden tree before the gates. As in *Winterreise,* the tree is associated with journeying and with failure.[7] If Schubert's winter traveler fails to commit suicide, it is surely not for lack of longing for death but only, apparently, for lack of a gun.

Both cycles have in common with *Werther* a generous tendency for the hero to project his emotions onto the landscape. It appears most explicitly in the constant writing activity: *Werther* is a novel in letters, in which the hero writes down his feelings and describes the world around him, especially nature, in terms of his own feelings. In the two Schubert cycles the heroes literally write their emotions into the landscape, by cutting names and dates into trees or into the surface of frozen river: they also read the language of nature, whether the babbling of the brook or the falling of the last isolated leaf from a tree, as personal messages to them alone. "War es also gemeint?"—"Was that what you meant?" the miller keeps asking the brook. Like Werther, the heroes of Müller's cycle are totally self-involved. The only difference is that Goethe's novel critiques Werther's extreme subjectivity, while Müller and Schubert romanticize it. In this respect the Biedermeier embraces and goes beyond sensibility.

SCHUBERT'S BIEDERMEIER POETS

A substantial proportion of the texts set by Schubert, something on the order of 20 percent, are by friends, or friends of friends. These belong to the later, Biedermeier, phase of romanticism.

The pertinent authors here include Bauernfeld, Bruchmann, Collin, Craigher, Hüttenbrenner, Kenner, Körner, Leitner, Mayrhofer, Pyrker (fig. 9.3), Reil, Schlechta, Schober, Seidl, Senn, Spaun, and Stadler. They are either friends of Schubert, acquaintances, or friends of friends. Most of them were not primarily poets but petty officials or teachers.[8] Some were, to be sure, published poets in their own right—Bauernfeld, for example, was a popular playwright—though none is today considered a "major" poet; others were simply amateurs, published only because of their connection to Schubert. But precisely their lack of importance as poets makes them such a dependable index to the taste of the period. Most of the people on this list were school friends of Schubert, or else friends and relations of school friends. This is hardly surprising in a composer who died so young, but other consistencies follow from it. With few exceptions they were born between 1787 and 1804; only the very oldest of them (Pyrker, a friend of Schubert's friend Grillparzer, and Collin, cousin of Schubert's friend Spaun) came of age during the height of the romantic period. Most, like Schubert himself, belonged to the next generation. Almost all came from the bourgeoisie; their fathers were by and large officials or professionals—only Pyrker and Schlechta were the sons of officers and hence from the older aristocracy. The others with "von" in their names belonged to what was known as the *Verdienstadel,* rising members of the bourgeoisie ennobled for cause (service to the state, or perhaps just access to special interest; Goethe's patent of nobility was of this sort).

Johann Mayrhofer, with whom Schubert shared a room from 1819 to 1821, may serve as an example for the group and for the period (fig. 9.4). After a four-year novitiate he left the church to study law, during which time he supported himself as a private tutor. Upon completion of his studies he became an ·official in the imperial *Bücherrevisionsamt*—that is, he became a censor. On the side he wrote poetry and

9.3 Johann Ladislaus Pyrker is shown here as patriarch (archbishop) of Venice, then Austrian territory. He subsequently returned to Austria, where he became friendly with Schubert, who set some of his poems. One of these was "Die Allmacht" ("The Almighty"), which was featured on the single formal concert (1828) devoted to Schubert's music during his lifetime; its pantheistic text, which asserts the presence of God in the beauties of nature, may well encapsulate the core of Schubert's own religious beliefs. Lithograph by Christoph Frank. [NYPL:Print]

9.4 Johann Mayrhofer was one of Schubert's close friends, here represented by Ludwig Michalek after an original by Moritz von Schwind, another Schubert intimate. The poetry of Mayrhofer, who committed suicide, embodies the pessimistic *Weltschmerz* of Biedermeier culture. [HM]

edited literary journals. Like many of his contemporaries he suffered from the discrepancy between his personal liberal political beliefs and the demands of his profession, which he fulfilled conscientiously. He also suffered from melancholy and physical illness; he died in 1836 as a result of his second suicide attempt. Mayrhofer is in all these respects a typical, if somewhat extreme, example of the social and emotional profile of bourgeois intellectuals of the period. If melancholy and death are common topics in Schubert's songs, the phenomenon cannot be attributed exclusively to Schubert's individuality.

Let us consider first "Am Strome" (ex. 9.2). This poem is quintessential Mayrhofer, and indeed quintessential "Schubert's friends." First—and this is by no means a trivial observation—it involves flowing water. Schubert was evidently fascinated with the musical representation of flowing water—one has only to think of *Schöne Müllerin,* but even *Winterreise* devotes generous attention to the frozen brook and memories of its flow in summer. Whatever musical reasons there may be for this fascination, the phenomenon has undeniable literary significance. German romantic poetry abounds in babbling brooks and in rivers that glitter like necklaces in the landscape. Flowing water takes on particular importance for the romantic because it makes noise: brooks are the voice of nature. Wind also serves this function—think of "Erlkönig" or the gentle zephyrs we associate with romantic poetry. In fact, "Am Strome" has wind, too, in the second stanza. But flowing water is more interesting than wind, because you can drown in it and lose your identity to nature. Except in *The Wizard of Oz,* few characters in literature are literally blown away, but one can plunge into the water—a not infrequent occurrence in these texts—or accidentally fall in, or be snatched in by a passing mermaid, as already seen.[9] Water is so important in these texts precisely because it

Example 9.2

Am Strome	*By the River*
(Johann Mayrhofer)	
Ist mir's doch, als sey mein Leben	I feel as if my life
An den schönen Strom gebunden.	Were bound to the lovely river.
Hab' ich Frohes nicht am Ufer,	Have I not expressed joy on its bank,
Und Betrübtes hier empfunden?	And sadness here?
Ja, du gleichest meiner Seele;	Yes, you resemble my soul;
Manchmal grün, und glatt gestaltet,	Often green, and smoothly shaped,
Und zu Zeiten—herrschen Winde—	And sometimes—when the winds blow—
Schäumend, unrohvoll, gefaltet.	Foaming, unquiet, rough.
Fließest fort zum fernen Meere,	You flow on to the distant sea,
Darfst allda nicht heimisch werden.	You may not dwell here too long.
Mich drängt's auch in mildre Lande—	I too am driven to milder climes—
Finde nicht das Glück auf Erden.	I find no happiness on earth.

• • •

images central romantic concerns with the voice of nature and the threat of self-loss; evidently these themes are still central for the Biedermeier generation.

The speaker's ambivalence is also paradigmatic. He has experienced both joy and sorrow by the river. As an image of his soul, the river is both calm and stormy. Notice that the river itself is calm; but the speaker cannot ever let nature, memory, or self be one-sided. Schubert, in fact, emphasizes that the duality lies in the speaker: the first and third stanzas about the river flow peacefully, and only the memories evoked in the second stanza perturb the music. In Goethe's "Fischer" ambivalence was part of a larger and more fluid play of dualities. Here in Mayrhofer it is schematic. This speaker is entirely self-conscious about his relation to nature. Indeed, he does not listen to the voice of the river at all; he explicitly projects onto it his own view of himself—"I feel as if" the poem begins, and "You resemble my soul" the second stanza asserts. What he really means is "I resemble you," as he in fact says in the last stanza ("I too am driven . . . "). He is interested not in the river, but in himself—in the state of his emotions and soul (not very clearly distinguished), with typical Wertherian self-involvement. If high romanticism aspired to harmony between man and nature, the Biedermeier has given up hope; at its calmest, as in this poem, it aspires only toward similarity.

Finally, absolutely typical is the turn at the end of the poem—as the stream flows to the sea, the poet will pass "to a milder land," heaven, for he can never be happy on earth. At the end of "Der Fischer," Goethe, remember, smirks ironically; in Mayrhofer and most of Schubert's friends, the end is routinely earnest. We do not know why the speaker cannot be happy in the world, whereas Goethe outlined specifically the dichotomies that tore his hero apart. The speaker's Weltschmerz is so obvious that it never occurs to Mayrhofer or to us to wonder what his problem is. No sensitive being can be happy in the world, which is "hard" and "alien to ideals"—as specific a complaint as Mayrhofer ever provides.[10] Whether all of Schubert's friends were really such gentle, timid souls in real life is doubtful, but in the pattern of the period they cast themselves as virtuous children, helpless beneath the blows of adversity and hoping only for peace in the next world.

If we generalize from this group of poets, several typical themes and motifs emerge: nature, especially water; death, night, and darkness; children; wanderers; alienation from home, from fellow man, from knowledge, from transcendence; God; mixed emotions ("Wohl und Weh"—"joy and sorrow"—is the standard phrase). There are occasional texts on happier topics, like the coming of spring, but happiness is rarely without a shadow, and often it turns out to be only a memory. To be sure, we are looking at a group of poems selected by Schubert. Nevertheless, we know from wider reading and from studies of the period that poetry written in Germany during the Restoration tended to be about just these themes. Furthermore, the Goethe poems that Schubert set—a smaller number than represented by this group—show a wider range of themes and motifs. We are dealing with the pattern of a specific generation.

BIEDERMEIER AND SENSIBILITY

Much of the same thematic material is evident in the poetry of the 1770s and 1780s. We have already observed the Biedermeier tendency to jump back over high romanticism to the generation of sensibility; now let us see what that really means. With the poets of this group (Claudius, Gerstenberg, Herder, Hölty, Jacobi, Klopstock, Kosegarten, Matthisson, Ossian, Salis-Seewis, Schubart, Stolberg) we are dealing with an even larger body of texts (something over 25 percent of Schubert's settings) than with those by the composer's friends. The poets were the staple of anthologies of German poetry throughout the nineteenth century; thus in Schubert's day they represented the German tradition. Some of the concerns of sensibility emerged from the discussion of Goethe above, but let us summarize. First, nature. These poems, too, are full of lakes, brooks, and fountains, as well as all the other paraphernalia of nature. This is, in fact, the first generation to worship nature in the fashion we associate with romanticism, although the worship is rather less developed and also rather less obvious than it was to become in succeeding generations. Most often nature is the creation of God and still reflects the comforting existence of God. Romantic doubts as to whether transcendence and meaning in nature are just a projection of the human mind occur only occasionally and only to the most far-sighted among this group. The projection of one's own ambivalence onto nature is the exciting discovery of Goethe's *Werther*, the great novel of the decade; only in the course of two succeeding generations would it become routine.

This is not to say, however, that melancholy was foreign to sensibility. Quite the reverse. The second third of the eighteenth century saw a tremendous fascination with death—one thinks of Edward Young's "Night Thoughts," or even earlier of Thomas Gray's "Elegy in a Country Churchyard," or of the popularity of the gothic novel. Along with it goes a fascination with night and darkness. (High romanticism is typically more interested in evening and dawn than deep night.) If any of these poems must take place in the presence of light, the light is typically diffused by fog or moving clouds. Even the moon is typically obscured by clouds or is but a crescent. This world is under considerable pressure of time, and not only because people die young. The poems specialize in delicate, evanescent moods momentarily captured; they are as transient as the light effects they catalog. Indeed, this is a poetry of states much more than of action or mood change. As a result it is static—it describes rather than tells a story—and tends not only to be written in strophes but also to be composed by Schubert in strophes.

A classic example is Friedrich Leopold Graf zu Stolberg's "Auf dem Wasser zu singen" (ex. 9.3). Stolberg was a friend of Goethe's in the 1770s. Lots of nature, water, thoughts of death and the comforting presence of God just behind nature, diffused evening light ("Abendrot," "rötlich" twice)—just what we would expect. In one important respect this poem appears to deny the generalizations above, for it seems to be full of movement: the waves shimmer, the rocking boat glides, the soul glides, the evening red dances on the waves, and, in the last stanza, time seems to rush past. But if we look more carefully, no one actually goes anywhere between the beginning and end of the poem—the gliding is only the slow movement of swans, the shimmering is gentle, the boat is clearly located—almost pinned—beneath the overshadowing trees, and the soul only breathes. In the last stanza time seems to rush past, but it did exactly the same yesterday, and the poet has long to wait before he will glide off with it. This essential stasis is emphasized by the remarkable simplicity of the rhyme scheme, in which the same word rhymes with itself three times in each stanza. Schubert's setting captures admirably the tension between gliding and rocking that pervades the song. We are dealing not with motion and change, but only with reflections on change as the boat rocks gently in the middle of a quiet lake at twilight. Amid the apparent rush of time the self remains securely static, but somewhat divided.

We can pursue the affinities between sensibility and the Biedermeier further and simultaneously identify the uniqueness of Schubert's generation by looking at several pairs of poems set by Schubert. In each pair, the first is by a poet of the earlier generation, the second by a poet from Schubert's circle. That texts can be paired so readily demonstrates the dependence of Schubert's generation on the poets of the 1770s and 1780s; the often subtle differences provide a sharpened sense of the differences between the first and last generations of romanticism.

We may begin with our paradigm, "Auf dem Wasser zu singen," and compare it with "Des Fischers Liebesglück," by Karl Gottfried von Leitner (ex. 9.4). Leitner was

Example 9.3

Auf dem Wasser zu singen
(Friedrich Leopold Graf zu Stolberg)

Mitten im Schimmer der spiegelnden
    Wellen
  Gleitet, wie Schwäne, der wankende
    Kahn;
Ach, auf der Freude sanftschimmernden
    Wellen
  Gleitet die Seele dahin wie der Kahn;
Denn von dem Himmel herab auf die
    Wellen
  Tanzet das Abendroth rund um den
    Kahn.

Über den Wipfeln des westlichen Haines
  Winket uns freundlich der rötliche
    Schein;
Unter den Zweigen des östlichen Haines
  Säuselt der Kalmus im rötlichen Schein;
Freude des Himmels und Ruhe des
    Haines
  Athmet die Seel' im erröthenden
    Schein.

Ach, es entschwindet mit tauigem Flügel
  Mir auf den wiegenden Wellen die
    Zeit.
Morgen entschwinde mit schimmernden
    Flügel
  Wieder wie gestern und heute die Zeit,
Bis ich auf höherem strahlendem Flügel
  Selber entschwinde der wechselnden
    Zeit.

To Sing on the Water

Amid the shimmer of the reflecting waves
  The rocking boat glides like a swan;
Ah, on joy's gently shimmering waves
  My soul glides along like the boat;
For down from the heaven onto the waves
  The sunset dances all around the boat.

Over the treetops of the western grove
  Kindly beckons the reddish gleam,
Beneath the branches of the eastern grove
  The calmus rustles in the reddish
    gleam;
In the reddening gleam my soul breathes in
  Joy of the heavens and peace of the
    grove.

Ah, time vanishes away with dewy wings
  From me on the rocking waves.
Tomorrow let time vanish with
    shimmering wings
  Again as yesterday and today,
Till I, on higher, radiant wings,
  Myself vanish from the changes of time.

• • •

not actually a friend of Schubert's; he was a high school teacher in Graz whose poems were called to Schubert's attention by friends. A striking assortment of motifs connect the two texts: shimmering light on the lake, pale light (from the window of the beloved) and fog, rocking and reflection, constant movement back and forth and up and down, the wide heavens above, ecstatic hovering between worlds, and finally the thought of death and heaven. But the differences are also significant. The most im-

Example 9.4

Des Fischers Liebesglück	The Fisherman's Happiness in Love
(Carl Gottfried Ritter von Leitner)	

Dort blinket   There's twinkling
Durch Weiden,   Through willows,
Und winket   And winking
Ein Schimmer   A shimmer
Blaßstrahlig   Faint gleaming
Von Zimmer   From the room
Der Holden mir zu.   Of the fair one to me.

Es gaukelt   It flutters
Wie Irrlicht   Like a will-o'-the-wisp
Und schaukelt   And
Sich leise   The reflection
Sein Abglanz   Rocks gently
Im Kreise   In circles
Des schwankenden See's.   On the lapping water.

Ich schaue   I gaze
Mit Sehnen   With longing
In's Blaue   Into the blue
Der Wellen,   Of the waves
Und grüße   And greet
Den hellen,   The bright
Gespiegelten Strahl.   Reflected gleam.

Und springe,   And leap
Zum Ruder,   To my oar,
Und schwinge   And swing
Den Nachen   The boat
Dahin auf   Thither on
Dem Flachen,   The level,
Krystallenen Weg.   Crystalline course.

Fein-Liebchen   My sweetheart
Schleicht traulich   Slips secretly
Vom Stübchen   Down from
Herunter,   Her chamber,
Und sputet   And hastens
Sich munter   Merrily
Zu mir in das Boot.   Into my boat.

Example 9.4 (*continued*)

Des Fischers Liebesglück	*The Fisherman's Happiness in Love*
Gelinde	Gently
Dann treiben	Then drive us
Die Winde	The winds
Uns wieder	Once more
See-einwärts	Onto the lake
Vom Flieder	Away from the lilacs
Des Ufers hindann.	On the shore.
Die blassen	The pale
Nachtnebel	Night mists
Umfassen	Embracing
Mit Hüllen	Veil
Vor Spähern	From spies
Den stillen,	Our quiet,
Unschuldigen Scherz.	Innocent play.
Und tauschen	And when we exchange
Wir Küsse,	Kisses,
So rauschen	Then the waves
Die Wellen.	Murmur.
Im Sinken	In sinking
Und Schwellen	And swelling
Den Horchern zum Trotz.	To spite eavesdroppers.
Nur Sterne	Only the stars
Belauschen	Listen
Uns ferne,	From afar,
Und baden	And swim
Tief unter	Far beneath
Den Pfaden	The wake
Des gleitenden Kahn's.	Of our gliding boat.
So schweben	Thus we float
Wir selig,	Blissful,
Umgeben	Surrounded
Vom Dunkel,	By darkness,
Hoch überm	High over
Gefunkel	The shining
Der Stern einher.	Of stars on our way.

Example 9.4 (*continued*)

Des Fischers Liebesglück	*The Fisherman's Happiness in Love*
Und weinen	And weep,
Und lächeln,	And smile,
Und meinen,	And think
Enthoben	We are free
Der Erde,	Of the earth,
Schon oben,	Already above,
Schon drüben zu seyn.	Already arrived.

• • •

portant underlying difference is that Leitner's poem has a plot, while Stolberg's has none. Stolberg's speaker seems to be lazing around alone in the boat at sunset; he dramatizes, in fact, what Rousseau defined as the moment of supreme selfhood in the *Reveries of a Solitary Wanderer* (1782)—lying alone in a gently rocking, drifting boat in the center of a lake. But Leitner's speaker narrates a whole sequence of events: he sees the light from the beloved's window glittering on the surface of the lake, jumps to his oar, fetches the willing girl into the boat, then the two of them drift happily in the privacy of the fog, kissing, crying, and laughing with typical Biedermeier ambivalence, and generally feeling ecstatic. Although it leads to thoughts of heaven, their ecstasy is not Stolberg's quasi-religious enthusiasm evoked by nature. Rather it derives from the rather banal love affair in which nature coyly assists (the sound of the waves covers the sound of their kisses). The speaker is, after all, a professional fisherman, not an upper-class nature enthusiast. Leitner has transformed Stolberg's solitary emotive reflection into a Biedermeier genre piece.

Consider another pair, this time one where the dependence is explicit. "Der Tod und das Mädchen" is perhaps one of Schubert's most famous titles, but his string quartet that uses the melody of the song is not the only allusion to his setting of this poem by Matthias Claudius (ex. 9.5). The other is in Schubert's song "Der Jüngling und der Tod," by his friend Josef von Spaun (ex. 9.6). Spaun's text, the only poem of his that Schubert ever set, is a companion piece to Claudius's poem in direct response to Schubert's setting (they were set a month apart in 1817). The poems are linked by the dialogue structure, by the references to Death as "man of bones," and by the phrases "touch me [not]" and "gently in my arms." Here the similarities end. Spaun's text dramatically alters the proportions allotted to the two speakers, with the result that his poem gains in coherence—though, probably, loses in interest. In Claudius's poem we have no idea why Death has come for the girl; from this incomprehensibility arises the pathos. Spaun's youth, by contrast, hangs his death on the setting sun, and longs, in good Mayrhofer fashion, to be freed from the torments of life on earth to an afterlife in the better world of his dreams. The poems of sensibility are filled with melancholy, but rarely with the longing for freedom from their own Weltschmerz. In Claudius's

Example 9.5

<table>
<tr><td>*Der Tod und das Mädchen*
(Matthias Claudius)</td><td>*Death and the Maiden*</td></tr>
</table>

DAS MÄDCHEN:

Vorüber! Ach, vorüber!
Geh wilder Knochenmann!
Ich bin noch jung, geh Lieber!
Und rühre mich nicht an.

DER TOD:

Gib deine Hand, Du schön und zart
   Gebild!
Bin Freund, und komme nicht, zu strafen.
Sei gutes Muths! ich bin nicht wild,
Sollst sanft in meinen Armen schlafen!

THE MAIDEN:

Pass by! ah, pass by!
You wild man of bones!
I am still young, go, dear sir!
And touch me not.

DEATH:

Give me your hand, you lovely delicate
   thing!
I'm a friend and do not come to punish.
Be of good cheer, I am not wild.
You shall sleep softly in my arms.

• • •

poem, finally, Death's gentleness is unpredictable and hence remarkable; in Spaun's it is in complete harmony with the expectations of the youth—and with ours, formed by the period—that the afterlife is a kinder, gentler place. In effect, then, Spaun has turned Claudius's momentary encounter with death into a little narrative, at least inso-far as he makes room for causality. This slight expansion into narrative is exactly com-parable to the difference between "Des Fischers Liebesglück" and "Auf dem Wasser zu singen." By thus "rationalizing" the situation Spaun also domesticates it: death be-comes part of a predictable pattern brought into action by the speaker's own sensibil-ity, not by the unpredictable otherness of nature. Thus the contrast between the poems illustrates the not uncommon Biedermeier tendency to collapse the romantic dialec-tic of self and other.

As the extreme example of this phenomenon, consider Klopstock's "Die frühen Gräber" (ex. 9.7) in relation to Mayrhofer's "Nachtstück" (ex. 9.8). What do the poems have in common—beyond the theme of death, of course? They are linked by the opening glance in each at the moon struggling with the clouds, and then further with the allusions to the beauties of spring and the personifications of nature. Klop-stock dwells with loving interest on the light effects: the moon fitfully appearing from the clouds receives four lines as the speaker addresses it; the soft reddish light (quintes-sential sensibility) is referred to twice. For Mayrhofer these sensitive light effects are long since givens; hence he can dispose of them all in two brief lines of narration. In exchange, however, he devotes much more space to the speaker's longing for death. For Klopstock the deaths of his friends mean the loss of companions in his enthusiasm for nature; they are real losses, in stark contrast to the beauty of self-renewing nature

Example 9.6

| Der Jüngling und der Tod | The Youth and Death |
| (Josef Freiherr von Spaun) | |

DER JÜNGLING:

Die Sonne sinkt, o könnt' ich mit ihr
   scheiden,
Mit ihrem letzten Strahl entfliehen,
Ach diese namenlosen Qualen meiden,
Und weit in schön're Welten zieh'n!

O komme, Tod, und löse diese Bande!
Ich lächle dir, o Knochenmann,
Entführe mich leicht in geträumte Lande,
O komm und rühre mich doch an!

DER TOD:

Es ruht sich kühl und sanft in meinen
   Armen,
Du rufst, ich will mich deiner Qual erbar
   men!

YOUTH:

The sun is setting, o could I but depart
   with it,
Flee with its last ray,
Ah, escape these nameless torments
And pass far away into fairer worlds!

O come, Death, and loose these bonds!
I smile at you, o man of bones,
Bring me gently forth to lands of dreams!
O come and do please touch me!

DEATH:

Rest in my arms is cool and soft,
You call, I will take pity on your torment.

• • •

personified by the May morning. But for Mayrhofer's speaker death is welcome, and only in death does his true harmony with nature emerge. In Klopstock the loss of self in nature causes pain. In Goethe's "Fischer" the complete loss of self in nature was a dangerous temptation; in Mayrhofer it is bliss.

Nowhere can the differences between the two generations be seen more clearly than in comparisons with poems by Goethe. Partly this has to do with the differences between Goethe and the other poets of the generation of the 1770s; but partly it arises from the fact that Goethe embodies the essence of the period in such intense, concentrated form that the discursiveness of the later generation shows up in particularly strong contrast. In order to catch Goethe in the mood closest to the others we will refer only to water poems, though they are less typical for him.

Let us look first at "Meeres Stille" (ex. 9.9), and compare it with Collin's "Der Zwerg" (ex. 9.10). In eight brief lines Goethe's poem evokes the anxiety of being becalmed at sea—it emphasizes deadly stasis, is full of negatives, refers to fear and death. At first glance one might wonder why this poem should be compared with Collin's twenty-eight-line ballad about the murder of a queen by her frustrated dwarf. Nevertheless, Schubert sensed a relation, for neither the insistent pianissimo markings in "Der Zwerg" nor its tempo, "nicht zu geschwind," is otherwise obvious from the drama narrated. And when we look more closely at the two, the parallels emerge. The pilot in

Example 9.7

Die frühen Gräber	*Early Graves*
(Friedrich Gottlieb Klopstock)	

Wilkommen, o silberner Mond,
Schöner, stiller Gefährt der Nacht!
Du entfliehst? Eile nicht, bleib, Gedanken-
    freund!
Sehet, er bleibt, das Gewölk wallte nur
    hin.

Welcome, o silver moon,
Lovely, silent companion of Night!
You flee? Haste not, stay, friend of
    thought!
Behold, she stays, the clouds only bil-
    lowed.

Des Mayes Erwachen ist nur
Schöner noch, wie die Sommernacht,
Wenn ihm Thau, hell wie Licht, aus der
    Locke träuft,
Und zu dem Hügel herauf röthlich er
    kömt.

Only the awakening of May
Is even lovelier than the summer night,
When dew, bright as light, drops from his
    locks,
And he comes reddish along the hillside.

Ihr Edleren, ach es bewächst
Eure Maale schon ernstes Moos!
O wie war glücklich ich, also ich noch
    mit euch
Sahe sich röthen den Tag, schimmern die
    Nacht!

You nobler ones, alas, now solemn moss
Grows over your markers!
O how happy I was, when with you I still
Saw the day redden, the night shimmer!

• • •

Goethe's poem sees nothing but smooth surface all around him; in Collin the mountains disappear in the murky light of the first line and the ship floats on the smooth swell of the sea. Both sea and boat are conspicuously absent from the rest of Collin's poem—there is no natural motion of any sort. (Human action alone finally commits the queen's body to the water.) Most of the ballad consists of conversation between the protagonists, and its interest lies in whether the dwarf will really murder the queen. Thus anxiety and death are the pervasive themes, as in Goethe's poem, and little more happens than in Goethe. Not that the death of the queen is not a happening, but the murder takes place *between* the eighth and ninth stanzas; it is not actually narrated in the poem. There is a sense, then, in which Collin's poem, like Goethe's, has as its central theme the anxiety of being becalmed on the sea of human life.

    Now we can look at the differences. Most obviously, Collin goes on at greater length, but more important, he turns the evocation of mood into a narrative. The pilot who must be present in Goethe's poem to focus and experience as anxiety the unnatural stillness of nature becomes in Collin the queen, who experiences not only anxiety but also the events that logically generate it. The impersonal brooding power of

Example 9.8

Nachtstück	*Night*
(Johann Mayrhofer)	

Wenn über Berge sich der Nebel breitet,
Und Luna mit Gewölken kämpft,
So nimmt der Alte seine Harf', und schreitet,
Und singt waldeinwärts und gedämpft:

"Du heil'ge Nacht:
"Bald ist's vollbracht.
"Bald schlaf ich ihn
"Den langen Schlummer,
"Der mich erlöst
"Von allem Kummer.

"Die grünen Bäume rauschen dann,
"Schlaf süß du guter alter Mann;
"Die Gräser lispeln wankend fort,
"Wir decken sein in Ruheort;

"Und mancher traute Vogel ruft,
"O laßt ihn ruhn in Rasengruft!"
Der Alte horcht, der Alte schweigt—
Der Tod hat sich zu ihm geneigt.

When the mist spreads over the
  mountains,
And Luna battles with clouds,
Then the old man takes his harp, and
  strides,
And sings into the forest, and quietly:

"You holy night:
"Soon it will be over.
"Soon I shall sleep,
"The long sleep,
"That will free me
"From all sorrow.

"Then will the green trees murmur:
"Sleep well, you good, old man;
"The grasses whisper on as they wave,
"We will cover his place of rest;

"And many a dear bird will call:
"O let him rest in his grassy vault!"
The old man listens, the old man falls
  still—
Death has been gracious to him.

· · ·

Example 9.9

Meeres Stille	*Calm at Sea*
(Johann Wolfgang von Goethe)	

Tiefe Stille herrscht im Wasser,
Ohne Regung ruht das Meer,
Und bekümmert sieht der Schiffer
Glatte Fläche rings umher.
Keine Luft von keiner Seite!
Todesstille fürchterlich!
In der ungeheuern Weite
Reget keine Welle sich.

Profound stillness rules the water,
The sea rests motionless,
And anxiously the pilot sees
Perfect smoothness round about.
Not a breath in any direction!
Dreadful the stillness of death!
In the monstrous expanse
Not a wave stirs.

Example 9.10

| Der Zwerg | The Dwarf |
| (Matthäus von Collin) | |

Im trüben Licht verschwinden schon die
    Berge,
Es schwebt das Schiff auf glatten
    Meereswogen,
Worin die Königin mit ihrem Zwerge.

In the murky light the mountains already
    fade,
On smooth ocean swell there floats the
    boat,
The queen and her dwarf on board.

Sie schaut empor zum hochgewölbten
    Bogen,
Hinauf zur lichtdurchwirkten blauen
    Ferne,
Die mit der Milch des Himmels blaß
    durchzogen.

She gazes up to the high-arched vault,
Up to the blue distance shot through with
    light,
Palely marked with the milk of the
    heavens.

Ihr habt mir nie gelogen noch, ihr Sterne,
So ruft sie aus, bald werd' ich nun
    entschwinden,
Ihr sagt es mir, doch sterb' ich wahrlich
    gerne.

"You have never yet lied to me, you stars,"
Thus she cries out, "and now I'll soon
    vanish,
You tell me so, but I shall indeed die
    willingly."

Da geht der Zwerg zur Königin, mag
    binden
Um ihren Hals die Schnur von rother
    Seide,
Und weint, als wollt' vor Gram er schnell
    erblinden.

The dwarf then goes to the queen, to
    bind
About her neck the red silk cord,
And weeps, as if he would soon go blind
    with grief.

Er spricht: Du selbst bist schuld an diesem
    Leide,
Weil um den König du mich hast
    verlassen,
Jetzt macht dein Sterben einzig mir nur
    Freude.

He speaks: "You alone are to blame for
    this sorrow,
Because you left me for the king,
Now only your death can make me glad.

Mich selber werd' ich ewiglich wohl
    hassen,
Der dir mit dieser Hand den Tod
    gegeben,
Doch mußt zum frühen Grab du nun
    erblassen.

"I shall surely hate myself forever
For giving you death by my own hand,
Still you must now fade to an early grave."

Example 9.10 (*continued*)

Der Zwerg	*The Dwarf*
Sie legt die Hand auf's Herz voll jungem Leben,	She lays her hand upon her heart so full of youth,
Und aus dem Aug' die schweren Thränen rinnen,	And heavy tears flow from her eyes,
Das sie zum Himmel betend will erheben.	As she tries to raise them to heaven in prayer.
O möchtest du nicht Schmerz durch meinen Tod gewinnen!	"O may you not reap pain from my death,"
Sie sagt's, da küßt der Zwerg die bleichen Wangen,	She says it, and the dwarf kisses her pale cheeks,
Und alsobald vergehen ihr die Sinnen.	Whereupon her senses depart.
Der Zwerg schaut an die Frau, vom Tod befangen,	The dwarf gazes at the woman, in the snares of death,
Er senkt sie tief in's Meer mit eignen Handen.	He sinks her into the water with his own hands.
Ihm brennt nach ihr das Herze voll Verlangen,	His heart burns, full of longing for her.
An keiner Küste wird er je mehr landen.	He'll never land on any coast again.

• • •

nature is now personified in the dwarf, who is given if not rational, at least understandable, psychological motivation for his hostility: the queen spurned his love and married the king. In other words, what happens to the queen is what Goethe's pilot fears—death at the hands of some irrational malevolent force. But the fear is presented not in the form of a passing shudder, but as a fully elaborated paranoid fantasy. It is this tendency to literalize, make explicit, and turn into narrative that so distinguishes the style of Schubert's friends from that of the poets they were imitating. It is probably a major component in our feeling that they are not as good poets, for they leave less to the imagination of the reader.

To come full circle, let us look again at Goethe's "Fischer," contrasting it with "Fischerweise," by Franz Xaver von Schlechta (ex. 9.11). As in Goethe a fisherman who is happily going about his business risks being caught by an attractive young woman, this time the roguish shepherdess angling for him from the bridge. Memories of Goethe's poem haunt this one in the references to the fisherman's calm and careless mood at the beginning, and especially in the reference in stanza four to the heavens reflected in the water.

And yet this poem doesn't feel anything like Goethe's. The condensed layers of

Example 9.11

<table>
<tr><td>*Fischerweise*</td><td>*Fisherman's Song*</td></tr>
</table>

(Franz Xaver Freiherr von Schlechta)	
Den Fischer fecten Sorgen	The fisherman is not bothered
Und Gram und Leid nicht an,	By worries, grief or pain,
Er löst am frühen Morgen	Early in the morning he unties
Mit leichtem Sinn den Kahn.	His boat with a light heart.
Da lagert rings noch Friede	Peace still lies round about
Auf Wald und Flur und Bach,	On forest, meadow and brook,
Er ruft mit seinem Leide	With his song he calls
Die gold'ne Sonne wach.	The golden sun to wake.
Und singt zu seinem Werke	He sings to his work
Aus voller frischer Brust,	With vigor and love,
Die Arbeit gibt ihm Stärke,	His work gives him strength,
Die Stärke Lebenslust!	His strength joy in life.
Bald wird ein bunt Gewimmel	Soon a gay crowd can be heard
In allen Tiefen laut,	In all the depths
Und plätschert durch den Himmel	And it paddles through the sky,
Der sich im Wasser baut—	That takes form in the water—
Und schlüpft auf glatten Steinen	And glides on smooth stones
Und badet sich und schnellt	And swims and darts,
Der Große frißt die Kleinen	The big ones eat the small ones
Wie auf der ganzen Welt.	As always in the world.
Doch wer ein Netz will stellen	But to cast a net
Braucht Augen klar und gut,	Takes eyes clear and sharp,
Muß heiter gleich den Wellen	Good cheer like the waves'
Und frey seyn wie die Flut;	And freedom like the flood's.
Dort angelt auf der Brücke	There is the shepherdess fishing
Die Hirtinn—schlauer Wicht,	From the bridge—you sly thing,
Gib auf nur deine Tücke,	Give up your pranks,
Den Fisch betrügst du nicht!	This fish you'll never trick.

• • •

meaning in Goethe's poem are neatly separated out. Human feelings and the force of nature are distinguished, the fisherman's feelings in the first stanza, nature in the second. Since Schlechta never says a word about the water, which in Goethe rushes and swells and awakens the fisherman's latent passions, one could never misunderstand nature as a metaphoric projection of the human subconscious. Similarly, the unity of the world of air and water is demystified and rendered completely safe in the reference to the sky in the water. In Goethe the expression is "the deep heaven"—mysterious, not quite clear, we must supply the explanation. But in Schlechta we understand immediately, "the heaven that forms itself in the water" can only be a reflection. Heaven is also rendered less than dignified and certainly not dangerous by the word *plätschert,* "splashes" (what a small child does in mud puddles). Most telling of all, the shepherdess, clever rogue though she may be, is more Disneyish than demonic. She does not emerge mysteriously from the water, but hangs out on the bridge above it; in no sense does she personify the seductive power of nature. One might say she personifies the letter but not the spirit of the seduction in Goethe's poem. Were she to catch the fisherman, he would not die but end up in a nice little house. The temptation for the self to dissolve into nature has simply evaporated.

Lest this reading seem far-fetched, consider the same pattern in *Die schöne Müllerin*—not, to be sure, by a friend of Schubert's, but by a contemporary with whom he clearly felt a strong affinity. Instead of reading *Die schöne Müllerin* as a version of *Werther,* as we did before, let us consider a different aspect. In the second song, "Wohin?" the wandering miller follows the sound of a little brook, which eventually leads him to the mill of the schöne Müllerin. He is attracted by the rushing sound ("Rauschen"—the same thing the water does in Goethe's "Fischer") but corrects himself: what he hears is not rushing water but the singing of the mermaids. This is the sound he follows "hinunter und immer weiter" ("downward and ever further"); in effect he travels the path of Goethe's fisherman, following the voice of nature into the depths. When he arrives only at a new mill he seems quite confused. "Was this what you meant?" he asks at the end of the third song and repeatedly in the fourth, as he transfers his affections from the mermaids of the brook to the pretty miller's daughter. Soon after, he forgets the brook in his tempestuous passion for the girl, and the brook's music seems to fade from the piano part. Only after the girl abandons him (or whatever it is that happens) for the hunter does he return to the brook, in which he ends up drowned. The spirits of nature have their revenge at the end, albeit under the gentle guise of a lullaby. We know from Goethe that one does not surrender oneself to the mermaids with impunity. Even worse, however, as countless other romantic tales tell us, is to betray the mermaid beloved for a mortal woman.[11] This is what the queen in Collin's "Der Zwerg" dies for. And this, not unrequited love, is surely what the young miller is drowned for.

In "Der Zwerg," finally, oddly enough, the gender roles in the mermaid seduction paradigm of "Der Fischer" have been reversed. Now the beautiful woman appeals to heaven and the air, while the dwarf sinks her body into the water in punishment for her refusal to share his passion. Water at least has the same value here as in Goethe—irrational passion—but it is almost as if the world has forgotten about the existence of it. As a quasi-supernatural figure the dwarf is still subject to the passion embodied in Goethe's mermaid, but the all-too-human queen has apparently forgotten it (what *was* her earlier relationship with the dwarf?). Yet the dwarf does not sink into the water embracing the queen, as Goethe's mermaid does with her fisherman; he is left behind in the upper air to repent and long for death. As the one who still remembers passion but is frustrated and ridden with guilt from his attempts to remind the rest of the world, Collin's dwarf is a perfect figure of the Biedermeier poet. He is an alienated outsider in a world that no longer remembers or desires the emotional intensity and unity that inspired the earlier generations of romantics. Driven to re-create it regardless, he can only, with Biedermeier ambivalence, destroy what he loves most and then repent in endless Weltschmerz. The Biedermeier's cult of sensibility and Weltschmerz is its own punishment for the turn away from the romantic challenge to achieve the unity of self and nature.

NOTES

1. The most influential analysis of the period and concept Biedermeier is in Friedrich Sengle's monumental *Biedermeierzeit* (Stuttgart: Metzler, 1971), 1: 1–82. The description here of the relation of Biedermeier to romanticism derives from Virgil Nemoianu, *The Taming of Romanticism: European Literature and the Age of Biedermeier* (Cambridge: Harvard University Press, 1984), 1–40. [See also Chapter 1, note 17. Ed.]

2. The texts of poems to be discussed are taken from Maximilian and Lilly Schochow, *Franz Schubert: Die Texte seiner einstimmig komponierten Lieder und ihre Dichter*, 2 vols. (Hildesheim: Georg Ohms, 1974) and the original printing of the editions Schubert is known or presumed to have used. The English translations are my own.

3. Well known is the pathetic story of how the young composer sent his settings to the elderly poet and was cruelly ignored, although there is a report by the Weimar actor Anton Genast of Goethe's enthusiastic response to a performance of "Erlkönig" in 1830 by Wilhelmine Schröder-Devrient, cited in Fritz Hug, *Franz Schubert: Leben und Werk eines Frühvollendeten* (Frankfurt am Main: Heinrich Scheffler, 1958), 73–74. This essay, however, focuses not on Goethe's musical limitations but on Schubert's taste in literature and the ways in which it was typical of its time. [For an assessment of Schubert's interpretation of Goethe's poem "Erlkönig" and the reception of both, see Christopher H. Gibbs, "'Komm, geh mit mir': Schubert's Uncanny *Erlkönig*," *Nineteenth-Century Music* 19 (Fall 1995), 115–33. Ed.]

4. The tabulation is based on the catalog of songs in Maurice J. E. Brown with Eric Sams, *The New Grove Schubert* (London: Macmillan, 1982), 125–58. Because it includes more than strictly Lieder for one voice, the numbers sometimes vary from the tally in Schochow and Schochow, *Franz Schubert,* but the exact number here is not the issue.

5. Documented repeatedly by Sengle, *Biedermeierzeit*, e.g., 1: 114–18.

6. Franz Schubert, *Songs of Greek Antiquity,* Dietrich Fischer-Dieskau, baritone, and Jörg Demus, Piano (Heliodor HS25062).

7. Book 2, letter of May 9.

8. Thumbnail biographical sketches are available in German in Schochow and Schochow, *Franz Schubert.*

9. Coleridge's Ancient Mariner is the obvious romantic exception.

10. The quotations are from Mayrhofer's poem "Sehnsucht" ("Yearning"), also set by Schubert.

11. The most famous is "Undine" of 1811 by Friedrich de la Motte Fouqué. Other famous examples involving earth spirits rather than mermaids are Ludwig Tieck's "Der Runenberg" (1804) and "Der blonde Eckbert" (1797).

FOR FURTHER READING

The best current biography of Goethe is Nicholas Boyle, *Goethe: The Poet and the Age* (Oxford: Clarendon, 1991–); only the first volume has appeared to date, but it covers all the literary material Schubert knew. There is a good literary reading of the song cycles by Alan P. Cottrell in *Wilhelm Müller's Lyrical Song Cycles* (Chapel Hill: University of North Carolina Press, 1970). See also Harry Seelig, "The Literary Context: Goethe as Source and Catalyst," in *German Lieder in the Nineteenth Century,* ed. Rufus Hallmark (New York: Schirmer, 1996), 1–30.

The reader interested in Schubert's songs per se can turn to Richard Capell, *Schubert's Songs* (London: Duckworth, 1928; 3d ed., 1973); Dietrich Fischer-Dieskau, *Schubert's Songs: A Biographical Study,* trans. Kenneth Whitton (New York: Knopf, 1977); Lawrence Kramer, "The Schubert Lied: Romantic Form and Romantic Consciousness," in *Schubert: Critical and Analytical Studies,* ed. Walter Frisch (Lincoln: University of Nebraska Press, 1986), 200–236; Richard Wigmore, trans., *Schubert: The Complete Song Texts* (New York: Schirmer, 1988); and several books by Susan Youens: *Retracing a Winter's Journey. Schubert's Winterreise* (Ithaca: Cornell University Press, 1991), *Schubert: Die Schöne Müllerin* (Cambridge: Cambridge University Press, 1992), *Schubert's Poets and the Making of Lieder* (Cambridge: Cambridge University Press, 1996). See also her "Schubert: The Prince of Song," in *German Lieder in the Nineteenth Century,* ed. Rufus Hallmark (New York: Schirmer, 1966), 31–74.

The Viennese Theater

SIMON WILLIAMS

In no European city has theater been so central to social and political life as in Vienna. Theaters in London and Paris have been more numerous, attracted more foreign tourists, and created drama with a broader international appeal, but in neither city has theater been so much part of the fabric of everyday life as in Vienna. Since the early eighteenth century, local and international politics have had less interest for the Viennese than the politics of their theater, while the transactions and rituals of social life have been centered more consistently on the theater in Vienna than in other cities. Accordingly, Viennese drama has both generated and precisely reflected ideals and myths that make life in the city so distinctive.

There are several reasons for the preeminence of theater in Vienna. After the defeat of the Turks in 1683, Vienna, as capital of the Habsburg lands, quickly became a center of international importance so that by the early eighteenth century it was the only German-speaking city large enough to support permanent theater on a year-round basis. Theater, a social art, depends on urban environments for its livelihood, and the unique geniality of life in eighteenth-century Vienna particularly encouraged theatrical activity. Narrow living quarters in the city and its suburbs, combined with a relatively mild and pleasant climate, meant that life was lived more in public—in streets, parks, cafes, and other open places—than in the cities of northern Europe. Travelers testified to the unusually lively street life and social world. If sociability is a prerequisite for vibrant theater, so, too, is love of spectacle, something Vienna offered in abundance. The Habsburgs, eager to sustain and strengthen their hold over the diverse territories that composed their empire, materialized their power through grandiose ceremonies and cultivated especially the elaborate production of opera seria to demonstrate the legitimacy of their rule and magnitude of their wealth.[1] Vienna provided an ideal site for the practice of theater as popular and high art.

JOHANN STRANITZKY, FATHER OF THE VIENNESE POPULAR THEATER

The putative father of Viennese theater worked decisively in a popular mode. Johann Stranitzky, leader of a wandering troupe of players from Salzburg, arrived in Vienna in 1705 after years of supporting himself by dentistry and acting (fig. 10.1). In 1711 he and his company took over the recently built Kärntnertortheater, which had previously been occupied by a company of Italian opera singers. The formidable reputation and enthusiastic following that Stranitzky acquired lasted until his death in 1726, while the manner of performance he promoted established a tradition that was

10.1 The actor Johann Stranitzky, considered the father of the Viennese popular theater, is represented as the Viennese Hanswurst in this painting by Gabriele Gräfin St. Genois Stolberg. [HM]

sustained until the end of the eighteenth century and can be traced vestigially well into the nineteenth. Stranitzky and his company were improvisers who, in a manner not entirely removed from that of the Italian commedia dell'arte, invented extemporaneous dialogue and comic situations to a prearranged scenario. But parallels with the Italians cannot be taken too far, as Stranitzky's comedy was probably more earthy; in fact, it may have been unabashedly obscene. In September 1716, the English traveler and letter writer Lady Mary Wortley Montagu saw Stranitzky's company perform a version of the Amphitryon myth; she claimed she "never laughed so much in [her] life," though she was nonplussed by several lapses in taste: "I could not easily pardon the liberty the playwright has taken of larding his play with not only indecent expressions but such gross words as I don't think [the London] mob would suffer from a mountebank, and . . . two [of the characters] very fairly let down their breeches in the direct view of the boxes, which were full of people of the first rank that seemed very well pleased with their entertainment, and they assured me this was a celebrated piece."[2]

Lady Mary's account is probably accurate, but she erred in calling the creator of the piece a playwright. Built on an improvisational base, the performances of Stranitzky and his company had a volatility and unpredictability that scripted drama can rarely achieve. As improvisation is a humorist's mode, comedy of a broad and farcical nature predominated in the repertory of the Kärntnertortheater, and memorized speeches were confined to the serious characters. This established a tension between the comic and the pathetic or heroic that would characterize Viennese theater for the next hundred years. Several of Stranitzky's performances were drawn from plays that had been the backbone of the repertoire of traveling players in seventeenth-century Germany: the *Haupt- und Staatsaktionen*, bombastic history plays structured in episodes. Stranitzky also introduced a figure that would recur for the next several decades, a clown named Hanswurst—Johnny Sausage—who mocked the pretensions of his master. One of the great figures of the eighteenth-century theater, Hanswurst was a coarse peasant from Salzburg, unscrupulous in his conduct, exceptionally cunning, but a survivor with whom the audience could identify. Over the decades, as this character was perpetuated by different actors, he was naturalized to a Viennese setting and dialect. He was given different names and various occupations, and his harsher features were softened, but his anarchic drollery and vulgarity remained the same. It is in the nature of popular theater that the comic and subversive serves to illuminate the foolishness and pretentiousness of that which presents itself as heroic and morally admirable; parody and farce, therefore, became the characteristic mode of the Viennese theater's early years, and Hanswurst was its most recognizable figure.

THE *MAGIC FLUTE* IN THE CONTEXT OF THE VIENNESE THEATER

Stranitzky's successors, such as Gottfried Prehauser and Josef Felix von Kurz, kept the tradition of improvisation alive, though its survival was threatened by demands from

10.2 Josef Felix von Kurz was famous for his portrayal of the character Bernadon. He was also one of the most gifted improvisers and mimics of his time, but he ultimately ended his life in poverty. Engraving by J. Landerer. [ÖNb:Ba]

the authorities that the practice stop (fig. 10.2). Eventually, despite Hanswurst's widespread popularity, theatrical reforms advocated by the influential professor of politics and imperial adviser Josef von Sonnenfels, in *Briefe über die wienerische Schaubühne* (*Letters on the Viennese Stage*, 1768) led to the expulsion of the popular theater from the city to the suburbs; theatrical performances in the center, at the Kärntnertortheater and the Theater nächst dem Burg, or Burgtheater (founded in 1741), were henceforth confined to the predictable scripted drama or opera. Nevertheless, in its new home, the popular theater continued to flourish.

Because most performances were unscripted, few popular plays from the eighteenth century have survived. Those that have, particularly those of Philipp Hafner, show fertility in invention and a decline in the coarseness characteristic of Stranitzky. There was a Shakespearean quality to the Viennese theater of this time, as it fed from a multitude of sources, in which high and low, elevated and bathetic, tragic and comic, realistic and artificial, coexisted in an unforced and rich relationship. Scholars have attributed the origins of the Viennese theater to sources as varied as baroque opera, Jesuit drama, Haupt- und Staatsaktionen, Austrian peasant comedy, Italian commedia dell'arte, Shakespeare, Calderón, and Molière.

The richness of this versatile theater is apparent in the single work that has won international recognition, Mozart and Schikaneder's comic opera *Die Zauberflöte* (*The Magic Flute*, 1791; figs. 10.3, 10.4). In several ways this opera represents a full flowering of the Viennese theater just before the age of Schubert. In a characteristically Viennese fashion, the comic is skillfully blended with the serious. Papageno's pragmatism, timidity, and appetite serve as foils to Tamino's idealism and heroic strivings, but while Papageno deflates any tendency toward aggrandizement in his princely master, he does not diminish him; indeed, his very humanity guarantees the integrity of Tamino's as-

10.3 *Die Zauberflöte (The Magic Flute)* by Schikaneder and Mozart (1791) represents a culmination of Austrian Enlightenment culture. This engraving by Josef and Peter Schaffer of an early production shows the stage in act I, scene 3, with Tamino, Papageno, and the three Women sent by the Queen of the Night. (See also fig. 7.24.) [HM]

pirations. The magic world of *Die Zauberflöte* is eclectic in the extreme. Not entirely Christian, nor altogether Egyptian, it has been widely interpreted as a representation of Masonic belief.[3] But application of dogma violates appreciation of a stage work that asks us to delight in contrasts and differences, in a world peopled by magic figures, strange animals, and monsters, in the darkly enigmatic but exhilarating Queen of the Night, and in the mysterious cult of sages that inhabits the temples of Reason, Nature, and Wisdom. Most moving is the easy relationship between the human and divine and the benign nature of the pluralistic divinity that presides over the play world. The whole radiates an optimism characteristic of the Enlightenment, in which idealism and the objects of romantic and sexual desire are fused. The philosophical eclecticism of the work was complemented in its first performance at the Theater auf der Wieden by an eclecticism in costume and scenery. The setting for the opening scene combined the disparate elements of a romantic chasm and a classical temple, while the costumes worn by the actors during the trial by fire and water were drawn from the Middle Ages, the eighteenth-century court, the heroic opera seria, and popular drama with an Oriental setting.

Die Zauberflöte represents the supreme achievement of popular theater in eigh-

10.4 *The Magic Flute* enjoyed extraordinary popularity after Mozart's death, and has never gone out of
favor. Schubert himself first saw it in his early teens. Depicted here is a production from about 1818
in the Kärntnertortheater showing the Temple of Wisdom. Engraving by Norbert Bittner after
Antonio de Pian. [HM]

teenth-century Vienna, but it is also a gateway to the greatest period in the life of that
theater. Far from commemorating the past, it embodies a phase when the popular theater was undergoing fundamental transition. This transition had two major aspects, the
first institutional, the second repertorial.

VIENNESE THEATER DURING SCHUBERT'S LIFETIME

After being expelled from the city in the late 1760s, acting troupes settled in its
rapidly growing suburbs, where they quickly established a network of as many as ten
commercial theaters operating at a time. By the end of the century, three theaters prevailed, and these, in terms of popularity, continuity of performance, and quality of
repertoire, ensemble, and production, formed the core of the system. The earliest, the
Theater in der Leopoldstadt, which opened in 1769, was home to a succession of
thriving comic troupes (fig. 10.5). A permanent Theater auf der Wieden was built in

10.5 A scene from Ferdinand Raimund's popular play *Der Bauer als Millionär (The Peasant as Million-aire)* of 1826 in the Theater in der Leopoldstadt, to which Raimund moved in 1817 from the Josef-stadt theater. He soon established himself as the major comic playwright-actor of Schubert's Vienna. Raimund and Schubert were both pallbearers at Beethoven's funeral; they were not, however, artistic collaborators. Engraving by Eduard Gurk. [HM]

1787 in the courtyard of a vast housing project, and it was here that *Die Zauberflöte* was first performed in 1791. Profits from this enormously successful show allowed Schikaneder to build the Theater an der Wien, which opened in 1801 and is still in operation. One of the most splendid theaters in Europe, it accommodated an audience of 2,200, of whom all but 700 stood. Its beautiful auditorium and technologically advanced stage made it a favorite theater of the Viennese, and magnificent spectacles ensured its survival, despite a complex history of bankruptcy, sexual scandal, and bureaucratic intrigue. The still-functioning Theater in der Josefstadt, founded in the eponymous suburb in 1788, was only half the size of the later Theater an der Wien, but in contrast to that theater, where emphasis was on spectacle, and to the Leopoldstadt, which confined itself mainly to comedy, the Josefstadt cultivated a repertoire drawn from most genres of spoken and musical theater.

During the years immediately following *Die Zauberflöte,* Viennese theater developed the dramatic genres that make it unique among European traditions. Improvisation declined and scripted drama became more common, partly because strict laws required prior authorization of all performances by the court-appointed censor.[4] This seems to have had little effect on the productivity of its playwrights, the sheer volume

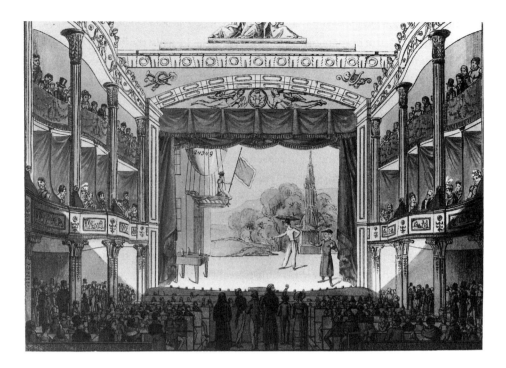

10.6 Viennese popular comedies of the late eighteenth and early nineteenth centuries were not fully scripted and provided opportunities for improvisation, despite censorship regulations. This broad scripting enabled playwrights like Karl Meisl, a scene from whose *1722.1822.1922* of 1822 is depicted by Eduard Gurk in its production by the Theater in der Josefstadt, to create two hundred or more plays. [HM]

of whose work is breathtaking. For example, Karl Friedrich Hensler and Karl Meisl wrote more than two hundred plays each, and Alois Gleich penned between two hundred and three hundred fifty (fig. 10.6). Adolf Bäuerle wrote only seventy-eight plays, but between 1806 and 1850 he was editor of the *Theaterzeitung,* which, as the only newspaper in Europe devoted solely to the theater, testified to the vitality of the art in Vienna.

The Viennese dramatists were extremely prolific partly because the creation of literary masterpieces was not their primary intent. The plays that survive are more than scenarios but are not generally carefully crafted pieces. Rather, they provided actors with a basic script that, despite laws to the contrary, allowed them to improvise. Structured in episodes, these plays include familiar plots, in which situations and dramatic characters recur with considerable frequency. By depending on the habitual, playwrights could complete their work with facility and be assured of a sympathetic reception from the audiences. They worked in a broad range of genres: melodramas, *Ritterstücke* (popular plays about medieval knights), comedies, farces, and various musical pieces. Ultimately, however, one or two of the generic forms of *Volksstücke* (folk plays) prevailed to give the theater a unique stamp.

One was the *Zauberstück,* the magic play of which *Die Zauberflöte* is a noted example. In such works, the human and divine intermingle. Usually the human world is explicitly Viennese, the divine a mixture of figures from Christian, Oriental, and classical mythology, along with Alpine spirits that have their origin in the animistic beliefs of the Austrian peasants. Censors forbade the representation of specific Christian figures on stage, but the divine world was almost invariably benign. The divine characters typically helped reconcile human beings to the limitations of their condition, in the process bringing about their moral betterment. For example, in Gleich's play *Der Berggeist,* the Spirit of the Mountains embodies optimism and trust in people, while the protagonist of the play, Mißmuth (literally "ill humor" or "discontent"), is a vile misanthrope. The Spirit gives Mißmuth three wishes, the fulfillment of each wish taking up one of the three acts. Mißmuth uses these to attain unlimited love, power, and wealth—he strives, in other words, to exist without limitations. In each of the three acts the Spirit of the mountains leads him to realize the self-destructiveness of his desires, and at the end Mißmuth is reconciled to being human. This work, like countless others produced at this time, is essentially a morality play, dressed in the attractive poetry of fairylike divinity and set among spectacular scenery that draws from both theatrical tradition and from the beauty of the local Alps.

Viennese drama was obsessively given to the glorification of its own city. This, no doubt, is a reason why it has not appealed broadly to international audiences. Furthermore, the unquestioning faith in the city's quality of life has struck some as complacent, suggesting that theater was complicit in the repressive Metternich system that limited the freedom of the individual and encouraged social paralysis.[5] There may be some truth to this, but the common values, interests, and communal affections shared by the audience meant that Viennese theater was unusually homogeneous and not unrelievedly sentimental. The *Lokalstück,* the play that praised Vienna, was often touched with irony, even self-parody, through which social criticism, though not expressed openly, can be sensed. For example, Bäuerle's popular comedy *Die Bürger in Wien* (*The Bourgeois of Vienna,* 1813) introduces Staberl, a droll umbrella maker who chatters incessantly and is immensely proud of his position in life, but in any confrontation he is inevitably the victim; thus he emerges as a born loser, a character at whom the audience laughs but with whom they also feel a bond of sympathy. Occasionally this drama can achieve distinction. Bäuerle's *Die falsche Primadonna* (*The False Primadonna,* 1818), a minor classic that centers on the theme of false appearances, satirizes both the Viennese adulation for the opera singer Angelica Catalani, who visited the city in 1818, and small-town politics that had parallels in the narrow municipal world of Vienna.

Parody remained a constant function of the Viennese theater. Consistent with the spirit of Stranitzky, the theater trivialized heroic experience, as in Meisl's famous *Othellerl* (1828), in which Shakespeare's mighty crisis of passion occurs in the house of a sober Viennese citizen, and both the citizenry and Shakespeare are lampooned. Audiences demanded spectacle. The Zauberstück especially depended on the appeal of glorious mountain scapes, which had a moralistic purpose, the idyllic landscape serving as the materialization of an idealized world, an illusory plane of existence lying beyond the realm of human experience.[6]

During Schubert's lifetime, the liveliest of the suburban theaters was the Theater in der Leopoldstadt, from its very beginnings associated with comedy. In the late eighteenth century and early in the nineteenth its company was most noted for the actor Johann Laroche, who created the celebrated role of Kasperl (fig. 10.7). He first appeared as this character in Hensler's *Das Donauweibchen,* and it proved so popular that Kasperl recurred in dozens of later plays, acted first by Laroche, then by others. Kasperl, who has his origins as a clownish figure in folk mythology, was a descendant of Hanswurst. Stocky, vigorous, with angular gestures and strong features close to caricature, Kasperl perpetuated Hanswurst's improvised comic passages and appealed as a low character, noted for drollery, obscenity, and coarse humor. Such humor was the essence of the Leopoldstadt, where performances were decidedly inelegant, though exceptionally funny. After the Congress of Vienna, an event that encouraged a flurry of theatrical activity, the Leopoldstadt became known as the "laugh theater of Europe," a place where comedy reached heights of hilarity, due both to the talents of individual performers and their capacity to work as an ensemble. The performers, not the play, were the main drawing power of the Theater in der Leopoldstadt.

Noted comedians included Anton Hasenhut, creator of the role of Thaddädl. His Thaddädl was described as childish, timid, and stupid but impertinent, with a voice like the "warble of a child's trumpet," which made the most commonplace events absurd.[7]

10.7 As Stranitzky had created the Viennese Hanswurst, so Johann Laroche created another stock character of Viennese low comedy, Kasperl, depicted here in this engraving after Louis-Joseph (?) Watteau. [ÖNb:Th]

10.8 Joseph Korntheuer was a comic virtuoso described by Ignaz Castelli, librettist of one of Schubert's operas, as "bizarre, baroque, grotesque." Here he is shown as the aged lame character Hohes Alter in Ferdinand Raimund's *Der Bauer als Millionär.* Both Korntheuer and Raimund were acquaintances of Schubert's. Lithograph by Joseph Kriehuber after Moritz von Schwind. [HM]

Hasenhut's humor was of the common man, as was the comedy practiced by Ignaz Schuster, creator of the role of Staberl, who satirized the bourgeoisie's pretensions to social grace. Possibly the most successful comic actor of all was Josef Korntheuer, described by Schubert's friend Ignaz Castelli as "bizarre, baroque, grotesque," who could reduce his audience to a "St. Vitus' dance of laughter" (fig. 10.8). Everything about him was long—his body, his legs, his nose, and his fingers; his delivery was slow, and he adopted lazy gestures. A noted scene stealer and improviser, he refused to stick to the script and once achieved the remarkable feat of taking over the role of the mayor in *Die falsche Primadonna* at short notice without having even read the play. Most celebrated of all was Therese Krones, the toast of Vienna, a woman of great beauty who openly played on her sex appeal. The skillful cut of her costumes, the freedom and boldness of her acting, the suggestive allusiveness of her gestures, and her indulgence in titillating double-entendres—all outraged or delighted audiences.

FERDINAND RAIMUND

The greatest member of the Leopoldstadt theater, whose work has survived its time, was Ferdinand Raimund (fig. 10.9, plate 21). He began as an actor, first in the provinces, then in the Theater in der Josefstadt, and finally, from 1817 on, in the Leopoldstadt. An actor of a timbre distinctly different from his colleagues, he was ill-suited for the low comedy that prevailed. Rather, he mixed comedy with pathos. His most famous early role was Adam Kratzerl in Gleich's *Die Musikanten am hohen Markt*

10.9 Johann Christian Schöller's engraving shows two of the most celebrated actors of the Viennese stage during Schubert's lifetime: Ferdinand Raimund and Theresa Krones in *Der Bauer als Millionär.* [HM]

(*The Musicians from the Upper Market,* 1815), an uncommonly realistic play that acknowledged the ills of contemporary Vienna. Kratzerl is a complex character; a hardworking violinist of blunted intelligence and a hopeless alcoholic. But audiences saw him as an Everyman figure. The plot ultimately reinforces the status quo—the one aristocratic figure in the cast bringing plenty and happiness to all—but the figure of Kratzerl challenges the authenticity of that happy ending. Raimund was vivid, even disturbing, in the role: "There was a vehemence in his movements and gestures, a sharpness in the turn of his hands and head, a rolling of his great and lively eyes, a hasty staccato in his words that one had to attribute to a continuous inward anger, except that it was made softer through the deepest good nature."[8] Inner division was the essence of Raimund's acting. The urge to misanthropy collided with that of generosity, a sense of alienation agitated feelings of complacency, and the representation of pathos crossed with that of comedy. Such conflicts are the essence of great acting.

Raimund turned to playwriting because the theater could provide few roles to suit his genius, and he took the drama in unexpected directions. His first play, *Der Barometermacher auf der Zauberinsel* (*The Barometer Maker on the Magic Island,* 1823) stands out from the general run. Here, in contrast to his contemporaries, Raimund showed himself capable of devising a plot that extends easily over the two hours or so of a full-length play. Although his dialogue is relatively simple and plain, he created a moving theater poetry in which the world of magic is represented with a wholeness greater than his contemporaries achieved. The facile morality of the popular drama also gathers complexity when the comic hero, Bartholomäus Quackselber, triumphs at the end and is not punished for his failings. Raimund was aspiring to transcend the customary limitations and moral purpose of the average drama.

His subsequent work developed in two directions. Some plays are refined versions of the traditional Zauberstück, while others are philosophical dramas, in which ideas outweigh incident, character, and plot. These encountered confused, even hostile audiences when first performed at the Leopoldstadt; consequently, Raimund's sense of alienation from the theater grew. Nevertheless, he was to contribute three works that represent the Viennese theater at its finest, *Der Bauer als Millionär* (*The Peasant as Millionaire*, 1826), *Der Alpenkönig und der Menschenfeind* (*The Alpine King and the Misanthrope*, 1828), and *Der Verschwender* (*The Spendthrift*, 1834). The last two are among the greatest German plays of the nineteenth century, for the medium of comedy articulates an action with an unwontedly wide resonance, in which moralistic conclusions are not always as confidently articulated as they were in the popular theater as a whole.

An overwhelming success when first produced, *Der Alpenkönig* has held its status as a classic (fig. 10.10). The protagonist, Rappelkopf, is a brutal misanthrope whose hatred of his family eventually drives him to renounce the world and retreat into a hermit's existence. In so doing, he causes grief to his family and virtually destroys his daughter's engagement to a young painter. In the magic world of Viennese theater, however, benign spirits divert the erring ways of humans to generous ends. In this instance the guardian is Astragalus, King of the Alps, a figure of folklore who inhabits the mountain peaks, attended by a chorus of ghostly huntsmen. Astragalus persuades Rappelkopf to cooperate in a stratagem by which the misanthrope will see himself for what he is and so be cured of his hatred of mankind. The stratagem involves Rappelkopf's being transformed into his brother-in-law, a genial figure much beloved by Rappelkopf's family, while Astragalus takes on the guise of Rappelkopf himself. Rappelkopf as the brother-in-law returns to his family and is received by them with love, which causes him unaccustomed pleasure. He then sees Astragalus, as himself, behave so brutally toward his family that he challenges Astragalus/Rappelkopf to a duel, which is prevented only when Rappelkopf realizes that he will be fighting with himself. The play ends with Rappelkopf acknowledging the evil of his misanthropy, converted toward a charitable view of the human race, while the family, reunited, celebrates its unity in the Temple of Understanding.

The central events of the relatively simple plot are worked through with compelling logic, and at the climax plot and action are in perfect unity. Local allusions are sparse, so the play transcends the limited domain of Vienna and its immediate environs. Characterization in much Viennese drama is rudimentary at best, but the figure of Rappelkopf, possibly an ironic self-portrait by Raimund, provides the actor with a major challenge. His misanthropy, arising partially from setbacks early in life, is raised

10.10 *Der Alpenkönig und der Menschenfeind* (1828), which combines the realms of the imaginary and the real, is considered one of Raimund's masterpieces and holds the stage even today. This scene shows the magical apparition of the Alp King in act I, scene 18, among the human family at the center of the story. Engraving by Zincke after Schöller. [ÖNb:Th]

to the level of psychotic obsession, but Raimund ensures that the character, who shows a latent warmth early in the play, does not entirely lose touch with reality, for he sees personality as changeable and capable of conversion by persuasion. Although no other characters achieve Rappelkopf's psychological complexity, Raimund skillfully portrays theatrical stereotypes—the long-suffering wife (Rappelkopf's fourth); the young lovers blocked by the stupidity of the older generation; and, in particular, two comic servants, with their origins in earlier drama, a maid, Lisa, derived from the commedia dell'arte's Columbina, and a Staberl-like servant Habbakuk, who compares everything to his experience of living two years in Paris. These characters ensure the mixture of comedy and pathos that was the mark of Raimund's drama. The poetry lies in this and in the grace of the dialogue, the ingenuity of the plot, and in the spectacle that invests the play with a romantic allure. Astragalus, the animistic spirit of the Alps, has more than a touch of Dionysus about him; he injects the action with a demonic energy that transcends the pure morality play, allowing us to understand the generosity of the ending as a natural rather than a purely moral phenomenon. *Der Alpenkönig und der Menschenfeind* is among a handful of masterpieces from the European romantic theater.

While the suburban theaters were central institutions in Vienna's social life, adjacent to the Habsburg palace was a theater that played an equally central role in the political life of the Habsburg domains—the Burgtheater. Founded in 1741, the Theater nächst dem Burg (literally, "the theater next to the Hofburg," the imperial palace) provided entertainment for the Empress Maria Theresa's court. In its early years, this entertainment was provided by theater troupes run by various entrepreneurs, and the repertoire was a mix of Italian opera, French neoclassical drama, and some popular drama in German. In 1776, Emperor Joseph II, stimulated by the reformist ideas of Sonnenfels, decided to convert the Burgtheater into a German national theater. Sonnenfels advocated theater as a means to cultivate audiences so they would become productive and tractable citizens. Joseph accordingly conceived of the theater as embodying his own ideas. He was transforming the Habsburg domains from a feudal dispensation, where subjects owed prime loyalty to the landowning aristocracy, to a more modern state, where order was imposed by centralized government operating through a bureaucracy. This state required moderate citizens, people open to reason, in whom the extremes of experience were tempered by a rational personality, people who were free from separatist ambitions and disinclined to place local interests above the national good. The Burgtheater was to be a key institution in the education of this citizenry. The elegant comportment, gracious speech, and fine sentiment of its actors would serve as a model, and in their capacity as servants of the monarch these actors would provide a conduit between government and people. In short, the Burgtheater was the consummate example of the Enlightenment conception of theater as an institution that provides personal, moral, and social education to its audiences.

The quality of Burgtheater performances can best be understood through Joseph's instructions to the actors as to how they should choose the repertoire. Plays should be selected, he insisted, that are in accordance

with the rules of a purified theater. . . . Tragedy should be rich in action, of elevating sentiment, not falling into the monstrous or unnatural; it arouses pity and fear, not disgust and terror; it promotes noble, high speech, but not tangled verbiage, full of fantasy. The sentimental comedy, the action of which resides between the everyday and the exceptional, demonstrates special characteristics, possibly a more moving action than tragedy, without falling into the novelistic; the emotions it arouses should be pleasant without being violent; every character should be instructive, and the work should tend toward instruction in moral philosophy, without being tasteless; language should be more exalted than in comedy, without crossing over into the tragic. . . . The comedy . . . includes characters from common life, yet with interest, and satire, without degenerating into lampoonery. It arouses laughter through wit and decorous nature, not through farcical situations, indecency, or unnatural happenings; it aims to improve through the representation of ridiculous characters, without appearing to be systematic; language is taken from nature, not the mob.[9]

The ideal state of being that Joseph posits in this passage eschews extremes of behavior, severely represses the expression of untrammeled emotion—the plays of the German *Sturm und Drang* were anathema to the emperor—and embodies nature as an ennobling force, not as the transcendent power of the later romantic movement. Balance, poise, control, and harmony among separate parts made up the image of humanity propagated from the Burgtheater stage. Through this theater the common human being could be raised to the level of an aristocrat.

Although Joseph's specific ambition of promoting German-language drama was soon abandoned for lack of suitable material and his intention to create a classically based repertoire was delayed for several decades, his larger ideals have proved durable. In fact, the Burgtheater has carefully nurtured the ideals of its origin in the Enlightenment into the twentieth century. Essential to its mission of cultivating audiences was the creation of an ensemble of actors in which the talents of the individual were subsumed into the whole, so the acting company became the microcosm of a perfect society in which individual differences and self-fulfillment are identical to the good of the larger whole. From 1776 onward, the theater fostered a company of actors that combined naturalistic detail, portraying the emotional life of the character, with gestures borrowed from the aristocratic life of the court. The Burgtheater actor, a substitute courtier, represented the presence of the ruler on stage and served as a model of polite conduct. When Joseph sent an agent on a tour of Germany to hire actors for the Burgtheater, he instructed him to choose those who not only had mimetic skills but who could comport themselves with elegance and grace. In searching for a Young Hero and Lover, one should look for a man "superior in youth and maturity, with easy, noble manners and pure idiom. He must not be too tall, nor have a protruding stomach, his eyes must be expressive, large, round and not far apart, his gait firm and not shuffling. Through the grace of his youthfulness, he must produce the warmth that one seeks in the drama."[10]

Early in its history, the Burgtheater oscillated between naturalistic and more idealistic styles of acting. In the 1780s, Friedrich Ludwig Schröder, the great north German naturalistic actor, dominated the company, but the most favored manner of acting remained that of Johann Brockmann, the central pillar of the ensemble from 1777 to 1812, an actor prized for his graceful and natural stage presence and for the beneficent personality he projected. Mozart's brother-in-law, Josef Lange, active in the company until well into the nineteenth century, was also prized for the elegance of his acting.

Well before the retirement of these two actors, the Burgtheater had fallen on hard times. The court theater had gone into severe decline because of the mechanical quality of ensemble acting, which led to a loss of creative energy among the actors. Furthermore, the draconian censorship that was imposed on all theaters in Vienna after the accession of Emperor Francis in the age of Metternich robbed the plays of much of their power and wit. Indeed, at no period in its history can theater have been so subject to censorship as it was in early-nineteenth-century Vienna. As Heinrich Anschütz records in his memoirs,

No priest could appear on stage, no Austrian uniform placed on view, no political event, no religious or philosophical idea treated on stage. For several years the word "God" was forbidden and "heavens" written instead; in the place of "church" one said "temple"; frivolous and criminal [military] officers were changed to civilians; ill-bred and malicious counts were degraded to the rank of baron and the more unworthy to "Herr von"; presidents became mythical viceroys; privy councillors became trade advisers; Franz Moor and Ferdinand [originally rebellious sons in Schiller's *Die Räuber* and *Kabale und Liebe,* respectively] became the nephews of their fathers; princes and kings had to champion the right to the very end.[11]

Under Francis I, the moderation of Joseph II was reduced to debilitating prudery, and the Burgtheater, always more under the control of the censor than the unruly popular theater, lost its vitality. Its conformist repertoire centered around the unchallenging melodramas and comedies of August von Kotzebue and August Wilhelm Iffland.[12]

In Schubert's youth, however, two crucial events occurred that revived the theater's fortune. First, in November 1812, a royal decree announced that opera and spoken drama should be performed by separate companies; the Burgtheater would continue to perform spoken drama, while opera would be staged by a different company at the Kärntnertortheater. Until this time, actors were expected both to act in spoken drama and to sing in opera, with the predictable result that much acting in spoken drama and singing in opera were mediocre at best. The separation was dictated in part by the increasing technical difficulty of operatic music that required specially trained singers to perform it—Rossini's operas were soon to prevail at the Kärntnertortheater—but it also benefited the Burgtheater, for it allowed the company to establish clearly defined objectives and to cultivate acting in spoken drama as an art to itself.

The other, equally important event was the appointment in 1814 of Josef Schreyvogel to the position of general secretary of the Burgtheater (fig. 10.11). Schreyvogel was a key figure in the artistic life of Schubert's Vienna. He had been educated at the University of Jena, where he had come under the influence of Goethe and Schiller. A regular visitor to the Weimar Court theater, he absorbed values similar to those of the Burgtheater, though articulated in a more consciously neoclassical way. Although Schreyvogel did not fully embrace the tenets of Weimar classicism, he returned to Vienna convinced of its vision of theater as a means of ennobling the individual and improving humanity. Administrative intrigue during his seventeen years at the Burgtheater kept him from assuming the title of artistic director, but he fulfilled all the functions of that position and, in so doing, raised artistic standards to unprecedented levels.

In spite of the stifling influence of the censor, Schreyvogel achieved changes in the repertoire that made it possible for the Burgtheater to become the leading classical theater of central Europe. Public taste for the watery sentimentalism of Iffland and Kotzebue was on the decline, and Schreyvogel moved closer to Joseph II's ambition to

10.11 Josef Schreyvogel's enlightened leadership (1814–32) lifted the Burgtheater, despite the impediments of heavy censorship, to the status of central Europe's leading classical theater. The outstanding company he developed performed dramatic masterpieces of Goethe, Schiller, Kleist, Lessing, and (in translation) Calderón and Shakespeare. Collotype after drawing by J. Mukarowsky, c. 1820. [HM]

create a theater with drama of the highest literary quality. Over the years he introduced major works that previously would have been unthinkable at the Burgtheater: most of the major works of Goethe and Schiller, key plays by Lessing and Kleist, works by such foreign playwrights as the Spanish dramatists Calderón and Moreto, and, most notably, the plays of Shakespeare (fig. 10.12).[13] Until Schreyvogel's appointment, Shakespeare's plays had been seen only fitfully at the Burgtheater and even then only in radically truncated form. Schreyvogel managed to get fairly complete versions of seven of the plays past the censor and onto the stage.[14] That was a significant achievement, for what passed for Shakespeare in the German theater of the early nineteenth century would hardly be recognized today. For example, in Goethe's version of *Romeo and Juliet,* first performed at Weimar in 1812, all violence is eliminated and scenes of street life cut. The nurse is excised for the scatological frankness of her speech; so, for the same reason, is Mercutio. Sexuality is reduced, as is wit; as a result the whole play more closely approximates the moribund sentimentality of operetta than Shakespearean tragedy. When Schreyvogel adapted *Romeo and Juliet* in 1816, he intended to go with Goethe's version, then rejected it as inadequate. He still cut the nurse and Mercutio, toned down sexual allusions, turned Friar Lawrence into a religiously indeterminate hermit, and blunted the sharp personality traits of the original characters—in particular, converting Romeo from a volatile young man to a conventional, responsible hero. Nevertheless, in contrast to Goethe, he maintained the balance between the idyll of private love and the brutality of public conflict that is the essence of Shakespeare's play. His version of *King Lear* is also closer in all ways to the original than earlier German-language revivals of the play. He includes both the character of the fool and the dou-

10.12 Ludwig Devrient as Shylock in the *The Merchant of Venice*. Although Shakespeare's plays were much altered in eighteenth- and nineteenth-century productions, Shakespeare fared better at the Burgtheater under Schreyvogel than elsewhere. Colored lithograph. [HM]

ble plot, thereby sustaining the play's unique blend of tragedy and grotesque parody, though to conclude the play he was forced to follow the dictates of both the censor and contemporary taste, tacking on the so-called "Viennese ending," in which Lear and Cordelia survive. His refusal to prepare for this in terms of the action suggests that such a conclusion was against his better judgment.

Perhaps the main reason why the classics were so well accepted in the Burgtheater was the excellence of Schreyvogel's ensemble. He realized the ambitions Joseph had first articulated. He considered his major function throughout his tenure to be the recruitment and nurture of an acting company from which all types of roles could be satisfactorily cast and whose players were dedicated enough to perform small roles as conscientiously as larger ones. Actors were encouraged to attend to the meaning of the drama as a whole. In accordance with the traditions of the theater, company members were chosen for their capacity to provide audiences with models of eloquent speech and elegant carriage, and the practice of Burgtheater actors setting the fashions of the social world was initiated. At the same time, they were versatile artists, enabling Schreyvogel to challenge effectively the typecasting practices of the German theater, whereby actors had been selected for their skill at playing stereotypes. Instead, he fit the individual qualities of the actor to whatever he saw was individual in the character to be represented. He even cast against type, a technique that can produce exciting and unpredictable theater.

The company he assembled offers a litany of famous names from the early-nineteenth-century theater: Maximilian Korn, a splendid lover, flexible in movement, light in speech; Karl Costenoble, a noted comic actor and a striking cameo player; Sophie Müller, a model of natural grace, who was glorified after her early death; and Karl Fichtner, a master of light comedy, who is said to have raised amiability to a level of virtuosity.

Indeed, amiability provides the key to Schreyvogel's company. The Burgtheater was an intimate space. All facings to the boxes and walls were of wood, so the acoustics were excellent, and the dimensions of the auditorium were comparatively small, so that the audience felt themselves close to the actors—a rare sensation at a time when theaters elsewhere were expanding rapidly to accommodate an expanding audience.[15] Hence, while performance in the Burgtheater was no conversation between actors and audience, as decorum did not allow for active audience response, regular visitors to the theater felt themselves personally attached to the actors. Under these conditions, the extremes of acting associated with popular tragedy, melodrama, or farce would strike one as shrill, exaggerated, and therefore inappropriate.

The most representative actor of Schreyvogel's company was Heinrich Anschütz, who was hired in 1820 and remained with the Burgtheater until his death in 1865 (fig. 10.13). Anschütz was not a great actor, but he embodied to perfection the virtues expected of a Burgtheater performer. Not intimidatingly noble, like the ideal Weimar actor, he personified reliability, exuded warmth, and struck everyone as an ideal father. He concretized what were held to be the virtues of *Bürgertum* (the middle classes). His King Lear was among the most admired performances in the European theater of that time. Adalbert Stifter has the hero of his novel, *Der Nachsommer (Indian Summer),* visit the Burgtheater to see Anschütz as Lear. He refers to the performance as "the highest level that a man in this branch of art could achieve," and his young hero is moved to tears by it.[16] This response would have arisen from Anschütz's focus on pathos rather than on detailed depiction of mental decline. Decline there was, not of a degenerating mind, but of a "beautiful world," which softened the impact of the tragic fall. Furthermore, no attempt was made to touch on the political aspects of the action. Anschütz represented Lear wholly as a deceived father, not as a betrayed king. Tears rather than anger were the essence of his performance, and he extended a strong bond of sympathy to the audience. At the end, his Lear was not a man who has achieved, by dint of suffering, understanding of the world; rather, he was reduced to the dependence of a child, an object of pity, not awe.

FRANZ GRILLPARZER

If Anschütz flourished by substantiating the Burgtheater's dominant ideology, the man who appointed him did not always conform so readily. Indeed, perhaps the ultimate strength of Schreyvogel's tenure at the Burgtheater was his capacity to perceive

10.13 Heinrich Anschütz, a longtime acquaintance of Schubert's, was an archetypal Burgtheater actor of the nineteenth century. Hired by Schreyvogel in 1820 and continuing as a member of the troupe until 1865, he effectively embodied and conveyed to his sympathetic audiences the virtues of middle-class morality that Burgtheater policy sought to propagate. Watercolor on pencil by Moritz Michael Daffinger. [HM]

greatness in those whose work did not adapt easily to social norms. This was apparent above all in his vigorous championing of Austria's greatest tragedian and Schubert's acquaintance, Franz Grillparzer (fig. 10.14). The danger of the Burgtheater ideology is that it can easily become insipid. Theater does not necessarily flourish in an atmosphere of mutual approval and good feeling; it must disturb and question as well. The plays of Grillparzer fulfilled this latter function well. His first success came not at the Burgtheater but at the Theater an der Wien, where his grim tragedy of fate, *Die Ahnfrau* (*The Prophetess,* 1817), caught the public imagination. His first work for the Burgtheater, *Sappho* (1819), is a classical tragedy on the irreconcilability of art and life. From then on, all his plays received their first performances at the Burgtheater. His works represent the most sustained achievement in tragic drama in the Austrian theater. When his experiment in comedy, *Weh dem, der lügt (Woe to Him Who Lies),* failed in 1838, however, he withdrew from the public stage and his final works were given at the Burgtheater only late in his life or after his death.[17]

In contrast to the German classical plays of the previous generation, Grillparzer's drama is subjective and, to a twentieth-century audience, modern. This is most apparent in *Medea,* the final play of his great trilogy *Der goldene Vließ* (*The Golden Fleece,* 1820), one of the few examples in world theater of the rewriting of an ancient play that is as powerful as the original. Grillparzer presents a compelling study of middle-aged marriage, in which the jealousy, passion, and possessiveness of Medea encounter the indifference, moral cowardice, broken ambitions, and midlife crisis of Jason. With its classical setting and verse dialogue, this pitiless study of broken marriage equals anything

10.14 Franz Grillparzer, here portrayed in 1827 by Moritz Michael Daffinger and regarded as Austria's greatest dramatist, gained Schreyvogel's confidence early on: from 1819 all of the playwright's dramas received their premieres at the Burgtheater. [HM]

Ibsen was to produce in the realistic psychological drama two generations later. Indeed, Grillparzer's study is strangely prescient in its anticipation of a recurring relationship in Ibsen: the mature and powerful woman who is fatally attracted to a broken and desexualized man. Not all Grillparzer's works focus on sexuality, but they all require of the actors detailed attention to the psychology of the characters. Ultimately, these plays question rather than affirm the values upon which Habsburg society was founded. Their inclusion on the stage of the Burgtheater represented a major step toward the artistic maturity of the city.

The plays also provided a major vehicle for the one actor of genius produced by the Burgtheater in the first half of the nineteenth century, Sophie Schröder (fig. 10.15). Schröder was neither a striking nor a beautiful person; in fact, being short and tending to obesity, she was far from prepossessing in appearance. The King of Bavaria unkindly observed that her charm resided in her classically beautiful forearms. Nevertheless, her stage presence was compelling. She was a regular member of the company from 1815 to 1829 and paid occasional visits later. Noted for her creation of the title roles of Grillparzer's *Sappho* and *Medea,* she played a wide range of emotions, unlike other members of the company, employing stark contrasts and taking each emotional state to its extreme. Although she acted with acute attention to psychological detail, she moved audiences away from concern with purely individual psychology by giving the illusion that the emotions filling the character were projected on to a plane higher than that of purely individual experience.[18] Hence she struck audiences as a materialization of the emotions of romanticism that were experienced in reading poetry or in listening to music but rarely represented in the performance of spoken drama. In spite of her unpromising appearance, she skillfully represented all aspects of love, from

10.15 The years of Sophie Schröder's acting career at the Burgtheater (1815–29) coincide almost precisely with those of Schubert's creative life. Schröder, creator of the title roles of Grillparzer's *Sappho,* depicted here, right, and *Medea,* was known for inspiring, passionate acting that reached the level of genius. [HM]

total happiness and affection to devastating, murderous jealousy. She also invested characters with heroic dimensions, frequently playing the character type of the "heroic mother" to great effect. But above all, the passions she kindled in her audiences removed her from the ranks of the average Burgtheater actor, for whom the moral admirability of the role was the uppermost concern.

SCHUBERT AND THE VIENNESE THEATER

Given the centrality of theater in Viennese life, it is puzzling that Schubert made so little mark on the theater in his time. This was not because he lacked contacts, nor was it for want of trying. In the close intellectual and artistic life of the city, he was friends with several of the theater's leading figures, including Grillparzer, Anschütz, Eduard von Bauernfeld (the house dramatist of the Burgtheater, who wrote the libretto for his last, uncompleted opera, *Der Graf von Gleichen* [*The Count of Equals,* 1827]; fig. 10.16), and the baritone Johann Michael Vogl, who sang at the Kärntnertortheater after it had

10.16 Eduard von Bauernfeld, Schubert's close friend, eventually became the house dramatist of the Burgtheater and a much honored citizen of Vienna. But he also wrote the daring libretto for Schubert's unfinished opera, *Der Graf von Gleichen*, which was rejected by the censor— the plot involved bigamy. Lithograph by Schubert's acquaintance Joseph Kriehuber. [HM]

become the official Imperial Court Opera in 1812. Vogl arranged the commission for the one opera by Schubert that was produced in his lifetime, *Die Zwillingsbrüder (The Twin Brothers),* of which six performances were given at the Kärntnertortheater in the summer of 1820. Other than a commission for a duet and aria inserted in an opera by Hérold, performed at the Kärntnertortheater in 1821, the remainder of Schubert's theatrical activity was confined to writing incidental and accompanying music for a melodrama, *Die Zauberharfe (The Magic Harp),* and a play, *Rosamunde,* produced at the Theater an der Wien in 1820 and 1823, respectively. The music from this last commission has, of course, survived in a suite that has proved to be one of Schubert's most attractive and durable compositions.

For those who think of Schubert as primarily a composer of Lieder, chamber, and orchestral music, it might come as a shock to know that he was actually as prolific a composer of opera as he was of other musical genres. He completed seven operas, wrote substantial passages for operas that remained incomplete, and produced fragments and initial sketches for seven further musical stage works. Furthermore, as recent performances have indicated, these pieces are far from inept. Indeed, as Schubert progressed in his opera-writing career, he demonstrated an increasing mastery of various contemporary operatic idioms; had circumstances been different, he might have developed into an opera composer of considerable significance.[19] The complete operas are *Des Teufels Lustschloss (The Devil's Pleasure Palace,* 1813–15), a three-act Zauberstück to a libretto by August von Kotzebue; *Der vierjährige Posten (Sentry-duty for Four Years,* 1815), a one-act Singspiel to a libretto by the celebrated young nationalist dramatist Theodor Körner; *Die Freunde von Salamanka (The Friends of Salamanca,* 1816), a two-act Singspiel on a libretto by Johann Mayrhofer; *Die Zwillingsbrüder,* a one-act Singspiel with text by Georg Ernst von Hoffmann and the only one of his operas performed in his lifetime; the full-scale romantic opera *Alfonso und Estrella* (1821), composed to a libretto by Schubert's close friend Franz von Schober (fig. 10.17); *Die Verschworenen oder*

10.17 Moritz von Schwind drew this portrait of Franz von Schober, the librettist of Schubert's romantic opera *Alfonso und Estrella*. Schober was the most powerful personality in the various circles of friends around Schubert, and his loose and reckless living seems to have had a deleterious impact on the composer, whose drinking and sexual adventures (one of which resulted in syphilis) surely hastened his tragically early death at age thirty-one. [HM]

Der häusliche Krieg (*The Conspirators, or Domestic Warfare*, 1823), a one-act Singspiel to a text by Ignaz Franz Castelli based on Aristophanes' *Lysistrata;* and, finally, a grand heroic-romantic opera *Fierrabras* (1823), to a text by Josef Kupelwieser.

Although only two of these operas, *Die Zwillingsbrüder* and *Fierrabras,* were actually written on commission, evidence indicates that Schubert intended all to be performed. Indeed, their failure to find a place on the Viennese stage was due primarily to theatrical intrigue and mismanagement and an inconvenient craze for Rossini when Schubert was at the height of his opera composition.[20] Nevertheless, the operas were well suited for the Viennese stage. The comedy of the Singspiels rarely breaches the decorum of good humor that was so characteristic of the city. Hence, while *Die Verschworenen*—the one operatic work of Schubert's that has been fairly widely performed over the past two centuries—is based on *Lysistrata,* it possesses none of the racy satire or gross sexuality of the original. The ladies' refusal of favors to their knights—the opera having a medieval setting—is delicately posited, a solution is reached by a deft turn of plot, no declaration of affection goes beyond the conventionally romantic, and the music has an elegant Mozartian ring to it.

Schubert and his librettists were skilled at employing landscapes of the popular theater. *Die Freunde von Salamanka,* in a setting that owes something to Shakespeare's Illyria in *Twelfth Night,* celebrates the innocence of country living in contrast to the stress and noise of life in the city. *Alfonso und Estrella* is even structured around this contrast between an idyllic life in the country, where innocence, honesty, and kindness abound, and the city, which is the domain of violence and deceit. While Schober, the librettist, provides no stage directions, the mountain fastness where the usurped King Triola takes refuge bears much similarity to the landscapes of such plays as Gleich's *Der*

Berggeist and Raimund's *Der Diamant der Geisterkönigs*—this highly idealized scenery embodies a value system that carries the rejection of modern urbanism to almost metaphysical limits.

Magic was the one aspect of Viennese theater that Schubert seems constantly to have eschewed in his operas. Although some of his early work was based on Zauberstücke, the texts he chose tended to be satirical of the form, and magic was revealed to be a product of human ingenuity. Schubert as a musician and an opera composer seems otherwise to have shared much with the greatest popular dramatist of his time, Ferdinand Raimund. The two men met only once, at Beethoven's funeral, where both were pallbearers. Their lack of association was regrettable. Music was a major element in Raimund's plays, as it was in the popular theater as a whole. His plays were prefaced by overtures and included several orchestral passages, both as interludes and as accompaniment to melodrama; the action was also interrupted by formal arias and ensembles. *Der Alpenkönig* even has a celebrated score by Wenzel Müller, the most prolific theater composer of his time (fig. 10.18). As is apparent from the scores for *Die Zauberharfe* and especially *Rosamunde,* Schubert had little difficulty in tempering his music to the ingratiating idiom of the theater; had he worked with Raimund, he might have found a collaborator whose work was compatible with his own musical genius.[21] Certainly the melodious, pastoral atmosphere of his music and his tendency, apparent particularly in *Die Zwillingsbrüder,* to color comic situations with a penetrating tincture of melancholy, parallels the mixture of comedy and pathos that so distinguished Raimund's plays and often confused his audiences.

Like Raimund's plays, Schubert's operas end with harmony restored, amid hymns of praise to love and friendship—forces that can overcome all obstacles, even the most

10.18 Precocious and prolific, Wenzel Müller was the leading composer of music for the popular theater during Schubert's time. For more than forty years he was Kapellmeister at the Theater in der Leopoldstadt and composed the music for some of Ferdinand Raimund's greatest plays. He was especially noted for his theater songs for solo voice. It has been proposed that tunes by Müller were used by Schubert in the *Wanderer Fantasie* for piano and the song cycle *Die schöne Müllerin*. Lithograph by Wolf after Georg Decker. [HM]

brutal tyrannies of military oppression and egotistical greed. In the comic operas, the general well-being of the world is hardly threatened and there is never any doubt that the interests of the lovers will prevail. Mishaps, when they occur, are slight. The action of the first of Schubert's two grand operas, *Alfonso und Estrella,* is, in contrast, highly romantic and melodramatic, but never does one sense that the fate of the eponymous hero and heroine are in any way threatened. This congenial tale is informed throughout by the clearest moral sense: a young prince, raised in a mountain idyll, sets out to avenge the usurpation of his father by quelling military rebellion in the usurper's kingdom, and then marries the enemy's daughter. Alfonso and Estrella embody the virtues of innocence, courage, and filial loyalty; Alfonso's father, Troila, is a sage of the utmost benignancy; and the rebel Adolfo is that universal commonplace of nineteenth-century melodrama, a lustful, ranting villain. Only Estrella's father, Mauregato, displays any internal conflict, as circumstances activate his remorse at having usurped Troila. Although this unremarkable dramatic text allowed Schubert to compose much music in his most agreeable pastoral idiom and at times to achieve moments of dramatic intensity—the duet of reconciliation between Troila and Mauregato being particularly fine and moving—it did not enable him to put to dramatic use his most distinctive musical skills, the representation of *Innigkeit*—inwardness—of emotions that both motivate and subvert the calmly ordered moral world of the opera. We understand nothing of the characters beyond their status as ciphers in the action. Consequently, for most of the time we feel distant from them, a distance that is magnified by the lack of concrete detail and causally linked dramatic episodes in Schober's libretto. With the exception of the duet of reconciliation, the most moving passages are dramatically static ones. The haunting "Song of the Cloud Maiden" sung by Troila, for example, an allegory on the destruction caused by desire for worldly power and sex, is in the form of a stanzaic Lied rather than an operatic aria in which the action is impelled forward. Schubert excelled as a lyrical and descriptive composer, not a dramatic one, in *Alfonso und Estrella.*

That things might have been different is borne out by his last complete opera, *Fierrabras,* which was completed in October 1823 to a commission by the Kärntnertortheater. *Fierrabras* is the least Viennese of Schubert's stage works, modeled as it was on the heroic-romantic form that had reached its first stage of generic development in the operas of the German composers E. T. A. Hoffmann and Carl Maria von Weber. Nevertheless, it has a similar standing in the world of Viennese music theater to that of Grillparzer's plays in the spoken theater. Based on *The Bridge of Mantible* by Calderón, *Fierrabras* dramatizes the conflict between the Christian court of Charlemagne and the Moors of northern Spain, ending with the defeat of the Moors and their conversion to Christianity. Artistically, the opera is not wholly successful. The epic action lacks dramatic compulsion, the dramaturgy is often awkward in the extreme, and, despite some serene lyrical passages that create an intriguingly bucolic aura to surround the action, the music, as in other of Schubert's operas, is often derivative, Rossini and Beethoven's *Fidelio* being the most insistently mined sources. Nevertheless, *Fierrabras* demonstrates a powerful sense of theater through music that depicts war and dynastic conflict with a breadth and power that had so far been unequaled in Schubert's output.

Above all, in Fierrabras himself Schubert found a dramatically complex hero who was not a participant in the moral conflict that was the stuff of the action but was instead violated by it. Fierrabras, the son of the Moorish king, has been captured and is held prisoner in Charlemagne's court; he loves the king's daughter, who does not return his feelings. He is alienated from all aspects of his world. He fights not to be a hero or to defend his land, but as one possessed: in a striking monologue Charlemagne's general, Roland, describes his manic conduct on the battlefield. That these torments characterize the figure in other contexts of life as well is clear from the single aria he is given, one strongly reminiscent of Beethoven's opening aria for Florestan in *Fidelio,* in which his whole personality is disclosed to be a compound of suffering, frustration, and confused romantic longings. Schubert's music realizes these wasting emotions with a devastating directness that strangely prefigures the tormented characters at the center of Wagner's operas, which were still some twenty years in the future. Schubert did not, unfortunately, have the opportunity to explore Fierrabras's existential crisis further, for the action, in accordance with contemporary expectations of large-scale romantic opera, becomes embroiled in political conflict and romantic intrigue. Fierrabras's concerns become secondary and subservient to the moral pattern of the action. Nevertheless, Schubert was able briefly to go beneath the bland surface of accepted social value and explore the uncertain world of impulse and feeling that ultimately belies that value. This was a purpose he could fulfill more systematically in his late song cycles, *Winterreise* and *Schwanengesang,* and a purpose for which the stage of his time was particularly ill-suited. Nevertheless, Fierrabras's fate casts a cold light over the otherwise confident action of the opera. Schubert, like Grillparzer, practiced a theater that recalled past heroism, but he managed, too, to undermine faith in that heroism and so lead one toward insights into a more disturbing world.

AFTER SCHUBERT AND RAIMUND

Soon after Schubert died in 1828, that more disturbing world started to encroach markedly on Vienna and its theater. Early in 1832, Schreyvogel was brusquely dismissed from the Burgtheater due to a petty argument with the court-appointed director of the theater. Not even allowed back into the office to collect his umbrella, he walked home in a downpour. He caught a cold, severely weakening his constitution, and two months later he died in an outbreak of cholera. Four years after this, Ferdinand Raimund died under equally distressing circumstances. His final play, *Der Verschwender,* had been a great success at the Theater in der Josefstadt in 1834, and there was no sign of a diminution in his powers; indeed, he seemed to be moving into the genre of the drama of ideas. But two years later, while staying in the country, he was

10.19 The principal figure of the Viennese popular theater of
the post-Raimund, post-Schubert generation was Johann
Nestroy, who had been one of Schubert's classmates at the
Stadtkonvikt. He is depicted here as Hanswurst in an 1841
performance of a 1777 play, testimony to the long popularity
of the most famous character in the Viennese comic tradition.
Andreas Geiger after J. C. Schöller. [HM]

bitten by a dog; fearing he might have contracted rabies, he shot himself and died a few
hours later in hospital. Popular myth, often too quick to attribute symbolic reasons to
personal catastrophes, has suggested that Raimund was distressed by the rise of Johann
Nepomuk Nestroy as a potential rival (fig. 10.19). His place in the theater was secure,
however, and his powers still whole, so it is probable he committed suicide for emotional reasons; his private life had been disturbed, and he never found the personal happiness or fulfillment that he had always suggested in his plays was within grasp of each
human being. All the same, his death heralded a time when, in the words of Grillparzer, "the popular theater in the best sense of the word" was unrecallable.[22]

A year before the premiere of *Der Verschwender*, Vienna had seen the first performance of Nestroy's *Der böse Geist Lumpazivagabundus (The Evil Spirit Lumpacivagabundus)*, an immensely popular comedy. Raimund saw it and deplored what he sensed to

be a new comic spirit. This was not the comedy of assent that his generation had prized, nor was it tempered by the ironic mix of humor and melancholy characteristic of his own work. *Lumpacivagabundus* was a satire that, viewing the world with little sympathy, asked for little sympathy in exchange. The dialogue was witty and full of puns. Nestroy's humor was more complex than Raimund's, something Raimund himself recognized when he said he could never give a play such a title.[23] Nestroy, a brilliant virtuoso with words, an extraordinary mime, a resourceful improviser (for which he was threatened with jail), and a relentless critic, became the mouthpiece for a less cohesive society in which art was confrontational and overtly utilitarian, a society with less respect for the past.

In 1832, the year before *Lumpacivagabundus,* a theater revolutionary of the future, the nineteen-year-old Richard Wagner, visited Vienna and its theater. He later recalled, "Vienna remained for a long time my idea of creativity rooted in the originality of a people." His next visit was in 1848 when, as the embattled *Kapellmeister* of the Dresden opera house, he traveled to Vienna in the hopes of reforming the five major theaters in the city by uniting them "under a kind of federal administration, to be composed of the active members of these theaters and the literary talents employed by them."[24] He did not succeed, as his own revolutionary plans were canceled by the outbreak of revolution itself.

The Revolution of 1848 threatened the values upon which Viennese society and its theater had previously been founded. The result was the destruction of Metternich's regime and the institution of a more bureaucratic government that aspired to regulate an industrial and commercial world. The rulers of the city's theater changed, too. Nestroy, however, maintained his preeminence and popularity until his death in 1862. The Theater in der Leopoldstadt was demolished in 1847. In its place was erected the Carltheater, managed by the actor Karl Carl who, though popular early in the century, later became symbolic of a new aggressively materialistic society by openly exploiting the theater to make his fortune. As for the Burgtheater, after some years of indecisive direction, it was taken over in 1849 by Heinrich Laube, a radical of the 1830s who had since become more comfortable with prevailing social norms. Through the mid-1860s he carefully crafted a company that used the old models of elegant ensemble to articulate values of the new middle class. Accordingly, the flow within the conduit by which the emperor had communicated to his people via the actors was reversed—a reversal made apparent as the Emperor Franz Joseph adopted an increasingly middle-class way of life due to changes in the political and social environment of which the Burgtheater was a part. As for the popular theater, nineteenth-century stages were increasingly occupied by extended runs of the operettas of Johann Strauss and his associates. A more recognizably modern world was at hand.

1. Opera seria was a highly stylized type of eighteenth-century Italian opera with serious, often historical subjects, characterized by elaborate arias and virtuoso singing. It was considered the appropriate musical genre to grace important state and dynastic celebrations, including those of the Habsburgs.

2. *The Selected Letters of Lady Mary Wortley Montagu,* ed. Robert Halsband (New York: St. Martin's, 1970), 83.

3. On the Masonic interpretation see Jacques Chailley, *The Magic Flute: Masonic Opera,* trans. Herbert Weinstock (New York: Knopf, 1971).

4. Johann Hüttner, "Theater Censorship in Metternich's Vienna," *Theater Quarterly* 10, no. 37 (Spring 1980), 62. It should be noted that Hüttner considers censorship to have been so ubiquitous and the number of regular theaters in Vienna—five in all—so small, that he questions whether designation of this period as a "golden age" of Viennese theater is justified at all.

5. For a polemical treatment of this theme with a historical perspective, see Erich Joachim May, *Wiener Volkskomödie und Vormärz* (Berlin: Henschel, 1975), 17–43.

6. On the idealization of landscape by painters, see Chapter 8.

7. Ignaz Franz Castelli, *Memoiren meines Lebens* (Munich: Winkler, 1969), 79. Most of the information on the actors of the Theater in der Leopoldstadt is taken from this source.

8. Castelli, *Memoiren meines Lebens,* 85.

9. Quoted in Heinrich Laube, *Das Burgtheater* (Leipzig: Haessel, 1891), 37–38.

10. J. H. F. Müller, *Abschied von der k.k. Hof- und National-Schaubühne* (Vienna: Wallishausser, 1802), 100. Quoted in Simon Williams, *German Actors of the Eighteenth and Nineteenth Centuries* (Westport, Conn.: Greenwood, 1985), 114–15.

11. Heinrich Anschütz, *Erinnerungen aus dessen Leben und Werken* (Leipzig: Reclam, 1900), 177.

12. Kotzebue and Iffland were the most popular German playwrights of the time, who also acquired an international audience.

13. Among the plays that Schreyvogel brought to the Burgtheater were Goethe's *Iphigenie auf Tauris* (1815), *Torquato Tasso* (1816), and *Goetz von Berlichingen* (1830); Schiller's *Wallenstein* (1814), *Maria Stuart* (1814), *Die Jungfrau von Orleans* (1820), *Wilhelm Tell* (1827), and *Fiesko* (1828); Kleist's *Prinz Friedrich von Homburg* (under the title *Die Schlacht von Fehrbellin*) and *Das Käthchen von Heilbronn* (both 1821); Lessing's *Nathan der Weise* (1819) and *Emilia Galotti* (1824); and Calderón's *The Surgeon of His Honor* (1818) and *Life Is a Dream* (1822). All performance statistics are taken from *Burgtheater, 1776–1976,* ed. Österreichischen Bundestheaterverband (Vienna: Ueberreuter, n.d.).

14. *Romeo and Juliet* (1816), *Macbeth* (in Schiller's version, 1821), *King Lear* (1822), *Othello* (1823), *Hamlet* (1825), *The Merchant of Venice* (1827), and *All's Well That Ends Well* and *Henry IV Parts 1 and 2* (1828).

15. Although the auditorium held 1,125 people, it measured only 12 meters high by 22 meters long by 13.5 meters wide (approximately 39 feet by 71 feet by 44 feet); Verena Keil-Budichowsky, *Die Theater Wiens,* (Vienna: Zsolnay, 1983), 105–6.

16. Adalbert Stifter, *Der Nachsommer,* ed. Max Stefl (Augsburg: Kraft, 1954), 188.

17. *Libussa* in 1861, the fragment *Esther* in 1868, *Ein Bruderzwist in Habsburg* (*Family Strife in Habsburg,* 1872), and *Die Jüdin von Toledo* (*The Jewess of Toledo,* 1873).

18. Rudolph Lothar, *Das Wiener Burgtheater: Ein Wahrzeichen österreichischer Kunst und Kultur* (Vienna: Augartenverlag Stephan Szabo, 1934), 84–85.

19. Schubert's operas are described in detail in Elizabeth Norman McKay, *Franz Schubert's Music for the Theater* (Tutzing: Hans Schneider, 1991).

20. For a thorough exploration of these factors, see Maurice J. E. Brown, "Schubert and the Kärntnertor Theater," *Essays on Schubert* (New York: St. Martin's, 1966), 126–38.

21. In 1898, Felix Mottl adapted Schubert's incidental music for the melodrama *Die Zauberharfe* for a production of Raimund's *Die gefesselte Phantasie,* apparently with great success. The combination has since been tried elsewhere in Austria. See McKay, *Franz Schubert's Music for the Theater,* 182–83.

22. Quoted by Gunther Erken in "Ferdinand Raimund," in *Deutsche Dichter des 19. Jahrhunderts,* ed. Benno von Wiese (Berlin: Schmidt, 1969), 323.

23. Renate Wagner, *Ferdinand Raimund: Eine Biographie* (Vienna: Kremayr and Scheriau, 1985), 296.

24. Richard Wagner, *My Life,* trans. Andrew Gray, ed. Mary Whitall (Cambridge: Cambridge University Press, 1983), 368.

FOR FURTHER READING

The major study of the Viennese comedy is Otto Rommel, *Die Alt-Wiener Volkskomödie* (Vienna: Schroll, 1952). A general history of Viennese theater is Joseph Gregor, *Geschichte des österreichischen Theaters* (Vienna: Donau, 1948). On Ferdinand Raimund, see Renate Wagner, *Ferdinand Raimund: Eine Biographie* (Vienna: Kremayr and Scheriau, 1985), and Dorothy Prohaska, *Raimund and Vienna: A Critical Study of Raimund's Plays in Their Viennese Setting* (Cambridge: Cambridge University Press, 1970). For Nestroy, see W. E. Yales, *Nestroy: Satire and Parody in Viennese Popular Comedy* (Cambridge: Cambridge University Press, 1972).

Vienna's Schubert

ERNST HILMAR

There is an enormous and enthusiastic literature depicting Vienna, City of Music, the Biedermeier period, and the Viennese love of vocal and chamber music making. But rare, especially in the popular literature, are descriptions of the darker side of an epoch that, for all the nostalgia, was scarcely the "good old days."

In Schubert's day Vienna was for many musicians, greater and lesser, the city of which they dreamed and to which they made regular pilgrimages. But what really awaited them there as musicians, composers, performers? In fact, to be a musician in Vienna meant to stand on a low step of the social ladder, without special privileges, without real social importance—and with an income commensurate with such lowly status.

Furthermore, as several essays in this volume attest, the political situation of this City of Music during the first third of the nineteenth century was anything but inviting. First, the Napoleonic wars bled the country dry; then, financial collapse and staggering price increases followed a brief period of euphoria during the Congress of Vienna. It was the Viennese, after all, who in a particularly cruel way were presented with the bill for the extravagances of the imperial court and for the festivities during the Congress (fig. A.1). No wonder that afterward the Viennese viewed the "success" of the

A.1 This coin, with the text on one side reading "Give me bread, I am starving *[mich hungert]*" and on the other "Despair not of God, live on," is stark evidence of the real hardships faced by the Viennese in the period following the Napoleonic wars and the Congress of Vienna. [HM]

Congress with jaundiced eye. Indeed, a bitter saying circulated around the city aptly characterizing the participating monarchs:

Alexander [of Russia] makes love for all,
Friedrich Wilhelm [of Prussia] thinks for all,
Frederick of Denmark speaks for all,
Maximilian of Bavaria drinks for all,
Friedrich of Württemberg eats for all, and
Emperor Francis pays for all.

Meanwhile, intellectual development stagnated because of state-controlled surveillance and censorship. Even if these were somewhat mitigated by Austrian inefficiency, they nevertheless drove the intellect indoors, away from public spaces, and fear of informers impeded open discussion. Schubert's friend the poet-dramatist Eduard von Bauernfeld wrote in his *Aus Alt- und Neu-Wien (From Vienna, Old and New)* that the "highly touted Austrian system" was a "pure negative: fear of intellect, negation of intellect, absolute stasis, lethargy, stultification."[1]

But to be sure, Vienna always has had a sense of "tradition" embedded in its consciousness, although no one has thoroughly investigated what this really means. It seems related to the typically bohemian indifference the Viennese have had toward all artistic achievements. To quote Gustav Mahler, who had gotten to know the Viennese ambience but didn't particularly treasure it, "Tradition is just so much *Schlamperei!*"[2]

It was no different in Schubert's day: people were attracted to the big names. The critics, then as now the more (or less) qualified mouthpieces of public opinion, outdid each other in praising famous virtuosi. If a composer were unknown, he would seldom be performed, if at all, and then badly; and if he were also unpublished, he would not be noticed at all. This was the situation with which Schubert had to live for a long time. Of course, this does not apply only to Vienna, but it is especially characteristic of the place.

The Viennese also have an easy relationship with genius. By definition, a genius can achieve something with little effort, whereas others have to labor at it. The easygoing flair for living practiced by the Viennese is doubtless an art—but it manifested itself in Schubert's day also in an easygoing attitude toward art. For in this city there developed a tendency, aptly characterized with the phrase *Musik und Menu* ("music with food"), to treat music as merely music; one saw therein no artistic manifestation so serious that, for example, one could not also loudly converse and eat heartily during a musical performance. Indeed, singing and playing were so deeply integrated into daily life that pretentious seriousness had no place. This was reflected even in the way performances were organized: boredom was banned and pleasure was the highest priority.

Concerts offered variety in the widest sense of the term, and this also applied to the so-called serious institutions, including occasionally even the Gesellschaft der Musikfreunde, of which Schubert was an elected member. Declamations or popular arias followed upon symphony movements, songs by third-rank composers upon vocal quartets. Solo pieces were supposed to "delight" the listener, and if a hymnic composition did not form the conclusion, an overture might serve. Schubert's music found itself in such potpourris, whether he liked it or not, for he could not escape the conventions of the time.

Nonetheless, we should recognize that the Viennese public was to a considerable extent a *knowledgeable* public. The song composer Schubert excited the public's notice with his "new sounds," especially harmonies, with often unconventional, difficult accompaniments. Furthermore, the elite Schuppanzigh Quartet introduced not only (and especially) Beethoven but also Schubert into its programs and had among its adherents also many Schubertians (fig. A.2). Still, the public knew virtually nothing about Schubert's chamber music—as little as of the symphonies, none of which was publicly performed or published in Schubert's lifetime.

Opera figured importantly in the musical life of Schubert's Vienna. Of course, there were star composers then as today, and Rossini was at the top of the list. Schubert himself, who loved the theater, devoted considerable efforts to the genre of opera, and the reviews were not especially negative, notwithstanding today's generally unappreciative scholarly and popular treatments of his operas (but see Chapter 10). A considerable part of the opera audience preferred the ballet even more, but Schubert did not contribute anything notable in this area.

As a creative artist Schubert never catered to the taste of the public, save occasionally to favor requests of his circle of friends, and he compromised only grudgingly. His friend Josef von Spaun later recalled Schubert's comment concerning his song accompaniments, especially that of "Erlkönig": "When his publisher told him that people found the accompaniment of his songs too heavy and the keys often too difficult, and that he should, for his own interest, take this into account, he always replied that he could not compose in any other way: whoever could not play his compositions should leave them alone and whoever found the keys unsatisfactory was simply not musical" (fig. A.3).[3]

A.2 Program for the subscription concert of the Schuppanzigh
Quartet on April 16, 1827. The works performed included Schubert's Octet for Strings and Winds, D.803, and two works by
Beethoven: the song cycle *An die ferne Geliebte* and the Piano Concerto in E-flat (the "Emperor") arranged for two pianos and string
quartet. [GdMf]

Regarding all this, however, the question repeatedly arises: what was Schubert's reputation in his own time? How was he seen by his contemporaries and by his friends,
who established through their reminiscences that image of the composer transmitted
up to our day?

In fact, the image of the composer portrayed in most monographs is oversimplified
and simply false or at least very one-sided. Schubert is presented as a chubby, shy, with-
drawn genius, unappreciated and unsupported by society, who dashed off masterworks
without any effort. There is some truth in this image, but precisely what is false? From
the historical perspective, it is still an extraordinarily difficult undertaking to characterize Schubert the man. Furthermore, the investigation of personality reaches into intimate, undocumentable realms, and so the researcher is well advised to retreat at a certain point. But it is an entirely different matter to correct some patently false aspects
of the picture of Schubert carried into our time.

To begin with, the pictorial representations of Schubert made during his lifetime

A.3 Title page of Schubert's setting of Goethe's ballade "Erlkönig" (Vienna: Cappi and Diabelli, 1821). Although Goethe did not appreciate Schubert's astounding achievement in this early work, composed in 1815, it was one of the pieces that early on established the composer's reputation as an extraordinary composer of songs. [GdMf]

are to a certain degree unsatisfactory. The few depictions that survive come mostly from his circle of friends. These are innocuous attempts, without psychological depth, and do not aspire to characterize his personality. Nonetheless, from these the remarkable conclusion has been drawn that Schubert can hardly have been known to the Viennese public beyond his circle of friends.

Recent research, especially that of Rita Steblin, based on materials of the International Schubert Society in Tübingen, has given cause—for the first time, it appears—to rethink this notion. It has been determined that the portrait long attributed to Schubert's friend Josef Teltscher in fact is by another artist, namely Friedrich Lieder, a painter of high repute in his own time, who traveled and worked in aristocratic circles (fig. A.4).[4]

That has far-reaching implications. How does a painter employed by the imperial house and by the aristocracy come to Schubert, or vice versa? What kind of relationship existed between Schubert and Lieder, who was much in demand in his time? Was there something unusual about the person of the composer, about his place in the public, that could also have appealed to an "important" painter of the time? So it would seem.

Schubert was portrayed by Lieder in a way that contradicts the common image of the composer as shy and of delicate constitution. On the contrary, the Schubert in the portrait looks energetic and self-possessed. Could this be the *real* Schubert? Lieder presumably had no reason to paint him other than he was. And if the portrait was commissioned by the Esterhazy family, who were among Schubert's patrons, then Lieder

A.4 This portrait of Schubert from 1825, now attributed to the eminent society painter of the time Friedrich Lieder, is evidence that Schubert enjoyed a greater status during his lifetime than is often suggested. [MS]

has transmitted this self-confident bearing through the common portrait type of the musical servant. This painted image suggests a person who knew his worth, in spite of the divergent statements of his friends.

The next question concerns the composer: how long did it take the public to notice him?

Today a musician becomes known through a variety of means, including performances, reviews, and printed works. That was the case in Schubert's Vienna, too. But if we begin to measure Schubert's impact by the availability of his printed works, we are again confronted with absurdities found in historical accounts. Were publishers actually uninterested in publishing the songs, especially the famous "Erlkönig," which was much performed in private circles and was well known early on? Schubert's friends bragged about finally publishing his work at their own expense, but were real efforts made to attract the interest of Anton Diabelli or some other publisher?

Schubert seems to have shied away from promoting his interests with any of the major publishers of the time, perhaps assuming that he would be rejected. It is thus no wonder that his circle of friends became more engaged, each member later magnifying his own importance in this matter; it does appear that the matter developed independently of Schubert's involvement. The composer likely saw his primary task to be composing, not bargaining with publishers.

But contrary to the statements of friends is the conduct of Schubert's first publisher Diabelli, of Cappi and Diabelli: although he took advantage of Schubert's lack of business acumen, Diabelli immediately propagandized for him with unusual energy, touting in advertisements the genius evident in the composer's songs (fig. A.5). Either Diabelli quickly realized Schubert's worth or the composer's friends grossly exaggerated when they sought to denigrate that publisher's association with Schubert. Parallels to this debate can be found today, for the business relationships between publishers and composers are rarely prized. Composers typically tend to feel themselves manipulated by their publishers, and that is precisely what happened between Schubert and Diabelli.

Nonetheless, upon the publication of his music, the name Schubert—especially the song composer Schubert—soon developed a good reputation with the Viennese public. Considering his age—he was twenty-four when "Erlkönig," "Gretchen am Spinnrade," "Heidenröslein," and others of his most famous songs were published—his renown was astonishing. So much to the contrary, unsupported by evidence, is found in writings about Schubert because many authors have not made the effort to study the relevant documents. Ample documentary evidence exists to lay to rest the claims that Schubert was little recognized in his own time, that he could not claim the usual sort of "popularity."

Nevertheless, many questions remain concerning Schubert's position in the musical life of Vienna and his relationship with the public.

A.5 Although Anton Diabelli and Schubert had a falling out early on, Diabelli later became one of the most important publishers of his music. Joseph Kriehuber, 1841. (See fig. 6.1.) [HM]

From the perspective of the social history of music, Schubert must be considered among the first "freelancers." His brother Ignaz congratulated him: "You happy man! Your lot is so enviable! You live in sweet, golden freedom. You can give your musical genius full rein. You can let your thoughts pour out freely. You are loved, admired, and idolized."[5]

The calculated freedom was, in fact, not so "golden," for life was daunting for any artist of the time who lacked the financial security guaranteed by some generous patron. Not surprisingly, then, how Schubert managed to survive financially in Vienna has been the subject of many and often dubious hypotheses. Often one reads that his friends bore the brunt of this support, that they paid his bills, fed him, and guaranteed him housing. That, in turn, led to an image of the artist as a societal freeloader.[6]

But those writings that transmit the touching image of a destitute composer overlook the fact that Schubert, at least after his works began to be published, had an income. For example, the dedications of first editions to respected personages of the aristocracy were acknowledged with substantial gifts of money equivalent to the annual income of a civil servant. Moreover, while there were at that time no official royalties for authors or composers, there were commensurate payments. (Schubert's disagreement with his first publisher Diabelli was most likely over the amount of such an honorarium.)

To understand better Schubert's place in Viennese life, we must return again to Schubert's specific public. No notion of a musical entertainment or a gathering for the purpose of general music making has become more popular than that of the Schubertiade. Indeed, some have complained that the Schubertiade is better known than the

A.6 Moritz von Schwind's famous *A Schubert-Evening at Spaun's* is a late (1868) pictorial depiction
of a Schubertiade at the home of Schubert's friend Josef von Spaun. The painting artificially
and nostalgically assembles in one scene a composite audience of persons attending
various Schubertiades. [HM]

music of the composer (fig. A.6). The origin of the term is obscure, but the word
denotes something very specific: an evening devoted to Schubert's music. Furthermore, the Schubertiade is one of the few explicit notions of the Viennese Biedermeier
period preserved into our time, finding today worldwide acceptance in musical life.

The Schubertiades stand in the tradition of musical soirées, of musical tryouts. They
took place first in the Schubert family home and subsequently in a larger circle; finally,
they evolved into rehearsals and concerts of an orchestral society. They were an important forum for Schubert, even if occasionally he would rather have absented himself from these events.

From the points of view of dance and hospitality—both belong to the notion of
"music with food"—these social evenings named for Schubert were the occasion of
many first performances. Schubert otherwise had little opportunity to present his latest works and to test their impact. His only other regular venue was the continuing series of "evening musical entertainments" of the Gesellschaft der Musikfreunde, which
offered him the possibility to appear as a song composer before an exclusive audience
and, most important, before the *paying* members of the Society.[7]

Most commentators emphasize the entertainment value of the Schubertiade as the
Biedermeier institution par excellence within a milieu under surveillance by the Austrian police. Its function, nonetheless, must be seen somewhat differently, for the typical Schubertiade was not presented to a closed circle; on the contrary, it was open to

literati, painters, and other artists, as well as to a public drawn from the upper classes. That same refined public also participated in public musical life, and thus it is logical to conclude that an appreciation of Schubert's art was spread among a broader public by those who attended the Schubertiades.

That the composer developed contacts with the public was one positive side of the Schubertiade. Another was that Schubertiades likely provided impetus for the revision of works performed there. We must recognize, however, that Schubert frequently improvised in these social settings; much of the music he played there was never put on paper.

This leads to a final point, which explains even better the attitude of the Viennese public toward Schubert's achievements as a composer.

Schubert's contemporaries formed the legend about Schubert's "divine inspiration." The skilled author and conversationalist Caroline von Pichler, who saw Schubert in her salon, depicted Schubert as a naïve composer for whom songs and other works simply flowed from the pen.[8] Generations of Schubert commentators have followed her lead.

The legend spawned another notion as well, shared even today by many musical scholars, that Beethoven's instrumental compositions, particularly the symphonies, haunted Schubert like a nightmare and had a constricting effect on Schubert's own development. The two-movement relic that is the *Unfinished* Symphony is offered as the prime piece of evidence.

To be sure, Schubert's contemporaries were dazzled by Beethoven's instrumental music, including Schubert's. The comparisons made only reveal the stylistic insecurity of the critics of the time, but readers took their statements literally and therefore—and this is the critical point—the view of Schubert's independent development as a composer of instrumental music was skewed for decades.

It is astonishing to consider that, in spite of the enormous literature that now exists about the *Unfinished* Symphony (composed 1822), nothing of the work was known by any contemporary of the composer except a few friends—the brothers Anselm and Josef Hüttenbrenner and possibly Johann Baptist Jenger. Thus there is no evidence by which to judge whether Schubert was stopped in his tracks after two movements because of the comparisons with Beethoven that might be made.

And so much of what is casually said about Schubert and Vienna—but even more how this has been interpreted—must therefore be revised. The same may apply to the significance of Schubert's circle of friends. Traditions are protectively cherished by everyone, and tradition includes the endearing image of Schubert as *Schwammerl,* because of which the chubby composer has won such sympathy and has become especially dear.[9] But the spirit of the late piano sonatas and the chamber music—the last of the string quartets is difficult to understand even today—testifies against this image and gives us a different, richer portrait of Schubert. And finally, it must be recognized that Vienna did not let Schubert's genius go as unrecognized as popular opinion would have it.

NOTES

1. Eduard von Bauernfeld, *Gesammelte Werke von Bauernfeld* (Vienna: Wilhelm Braumüller, 1873), 11: 205.

2. *Schlamperei* is one of those difficult-to-translate words: literally it means "dirtiness," "laziness," or "slovenliness." The intended meaning here is that the Viennese do things simply out of inertia, because they have always been done that way. Change and innovation, therefore, are resisted. [Ed.]

3. *Schubert: Memoires by His Friends,* coll. and ed. Otto Erich Deutsch (New York: Macmillan, New York, 1958), 140.

4. Rita Steblin, "Friedrich Lieders Schubert-Porträt von 1827," *Schubert durch die Brille* 12 (1994), 92–100.

5. Letter of October 12, 1818, *The Schubert Reader,* ed. Otto Erich Deutsch, trans. Eric Blom (New York: W. W. Norton, 1947), 103–5.

6. This theme was once publicly and shamefully expounded, beginning in the late 1920s with Robert Lach, professor of musicology at the University of Vienna.

7. The *Abendunterhaltungen* are discussed in Chapter 4.

8. For more on Caroline Pichler as author and *salonnière,* see Chapter 2.

9. On *Schwammerl,* see Chapter 2, note 7.

ELIZABETH ALDRICH, former president of the Society of Dance History Scholars, is the author of *From the Ballroom to Hell: Grace and Folly in Nineteenth-Century Dance.*

JANE K. BROWN is professor of German and comparative literature at the University of Washington and former president of the Goethe Society of North America. Her books include *Goethe's Cyclical Narratives, Goethe's "Faust": The German Tragedy,* and *Goethe's "Faust": Theater of the World.*

RAYMOND ERICKSON is Dean of Arts and Humanities, Queens College, CUNY, and professor of music at Queens College and the Graduate School, CUNY. He has been the director of the Aston Magna Academy program since its inception in 1978.

GERBERT FRODL is the director of the Österreichische Galerie in the Belvedere, Vienna, and the author of *Wiener Malerei der Biedermeierzeit.*

ALICE M. HANSON is associate professor of music, St. Olaf's College, and author of *Musical Life in Biedermeier Vienna,* which has also appeared in German and Japanese translations.

WALTRAUD HEINDL is associate director of the Austrian East and Southeast European Institute in Vienna and the author of *Gehorsame Rebellen: Bürokratie und Beamte in Österreich, 1780–1848.*

ERNST HILMAR is the director of the International Franz Schubert Institute in Vienna, editor of *Schubert durch die Brille,* the journal of the Institute, and author of *Schubert in His Time* in German and English editions.

THOMAS DACOSTA KAUFMANN is professor of the history of art, Princeton University, a winner of the Mitchell Prize for best art history book in English, and author of *Court, Cloister and City: The Art and Culture of Central Europe, 1450–1800.*

ENNO KRAEHE is William W. Corcoran Professor of History emeritus, University of Virginia, and the author of the multivolume, award-winning *Metternich's German Policy.*

LEON PLANTINGA is professor of the history of music, Yale University, and author of *Romantic Music: A History of Musical Style in Nineteenth-Century Europe,* which won the ASCAP Deems Taylor Award, 1985.

SIMON WILLIAMS is professor of dramatic art, University of California, Santa Barbara, and author of *Shakespeare on the German Stage, 1587–1914,* and *German Actors of the Eighteenth and Nineteenth Centuries: Idealism, Romanticism, and Realism.*

• INDEX •

Editor's note: References to captions for the illustrations are given in bold. Non-English titles are alphabetized according to the first word, but English titles are found under the first substantive word in the title—e.g., *Die Zauberflöte* but *Magic Flute, The.*

abdication, **8,** 14, 17, 19, 20, 70
Abendunterhaltungen, 106, 113, 254, 256
academies (concerts), 100, 103, 104, 106, 107
Academy of Fine Arts, 10, 16, 29, 32, 33, 174–76, 178, 180, 181, **pl.17**
Academy of Sciences, 28
a cappella, 113, 118
Acropolis, 152, 161
Adam and Eve, **30**
Adams, Robert (1728–92) and James (1732–94), 163

Adler, Guido (1855–1941), 91, 93, 111
Adriatic Sea, 11, 17
Advent, 122, 184, 192
agriculture, 156, 157
Albert (Albrecht), duke of Sachsen-Teschen (1738–1822), 157, **159,** 162, **164, pl.17**
Albertina, **159,** 163, **164, 165**
Alexander I, tsar of Russia (1777–1825, r. 1801–25), 19, 56, 61, **62, 63,** 63–67, 72–74, **73,** 114
Alfonso und Estrella, 237, 238, **238,** 240
alienation, 189, 194, 198, 225, 226
allegory, 82, 151, 155–58, 174, 240
allemande, 122, 130–32, **133,** 139
Allgemeines Krankenhaus, 151
Alps, 11, 153, 222, 226, 227
Alt, Jakob (1789–1872), **145, pl.8**
Alt, Rudolf von (1812–1905), **144,** 177, 180
Althausseer See, **pl.17**

Alt-Lerchenfeld, 113

Amalienburg, 145

amateurs, 26, 104, 107, 109, 110, **116,** 181, 195

Amerling, Friedrich von (1803–87), 176, 178, 179, **pl.11, pl.15**

Am Hof, 156, **158**

Aminta, 84

Amphitryon myth, 216

"Am Strom," 196

Anacreon (d. c. 495 B.C.), 191

ancient art and literature. *See* art and literature, ancient

ancients and moderns, 82–84, 87, 191, 193

An die ferne Gebliebte, 249

anglaise, 123, 128, 129, **129,** 131, 133

Anglo-Norman Renaissance, 82

Anschütz, Heinrich (1785–1865), **31,** 229, 233, 236, 244

Anstaltkapelle, 168

anthems, 10, **10,** 114

Antibes, **68**

anticlericalism, 11

antiquities, 10, 152

Antiquities of Athens, The, 152

antiquity, 82, 83, 85, 93, **136,** 151, 153, 161, 162, 184, 190, 191, 192, 212. *See also* art and literature, ancient; classicism

anti-Semitism, 47

apartments, 38, 117, 118, 166, 168, 169, **169, 170**

Apollo Hall, 115, 121, **122,** 123, 135

archbishops, 11, 182, **195**

archdukes, 5, 6, **7, 8,** 14–16, **164, pl.4**

architects, 67, **122, 145,** 149, 151, 163, **163, 165, 166**

architecture, 143–49, **150,** 151, 159, 162–66, 168, 171, 172, 175

Arcole, Battle of, 36

arias, 103, 106, 107, 237, 239, 240, 241, 244, 248

Ariosto, Ludovico (1474–1533), 84

aristocracy, 17, 38, 39, 41–47, 49, 53, 55, 69, 75, 100, 107, 123, 125, 138, 145, 146, 151, 165, 175, 176, 179, 191, 195, 225, 228, 229, 250, 253

Aristophanes, 238

Aristotle (384–322 B.C.), 83, 96

Arnstein, Fanny, Freifrau von (1758–1818), 47, 48, **48,** 50, 54

Arnstein, Nathan Adam, Freiherr von (1748–1838), 47

art and literature, ancient, 82–85, 87, 152, 153, 155–57, **155,** 161, **161,** 184, 234. *See also* antiquity; classicism

Artaria (publisher), **21, 148, 159**

Arthaber, Rudolf von (1795–1867), **39,** 179, **pl.11, pl.13**

art history, 80, 143, 151

Arthurian legends, 84

artists: collectively, 16, 41, 47, 52–54, 80, 83, 85, 87, 89, 98, 117, 143, 175–77, 180–82, 232, 255; individuals, 24, 49, 58, **92,** 118, 154, **159,** 175–79, 248, 250. *See also* specific names

art song, 117. See also *Lieder;* songs

Ash Wednesday, 115, 119

At a Morning Concert in the Augarten, **pl.23**

Athenaeum, 85, 96

Athens, 82, 152, 153, 161, **161**

Attic, 151, 153

Atzenbrugg, **28–30,** 29, 177

"Auf dem See," 188, 189, 199, 204

"Auf den Sieg der Deutschen," 19

"Auf der Strom," 107

Augarten, 151, **152, pl.23**

Augustinerkirche, **154,** 157

Aula, 102, **pl.6**

Aumühl, **29**

Aus Alt- und Neu-Wien, 33, 247

"Aus Heliopolis," 191

Austerlitz, Battle of, 14

Austria, 6, 8, 9, 11, 14–21, 25, 33, 34, 36–38, 41, 47, 61, 62, 65, 66, 71, 72, 74, 112, 118, 122, 124, 131, 132, 134, 135, 147, 156, 161, 175, 180, 182, 234, 245; army, 9, 11, 15–17, 68, 71

Austrian court, 16, 24, 29, 48, 50, 53, 58, 69, **86,** 98, 101, 102, 106, 107, 110–12, **112,** 115, 124, 145, 149, 162, 164, 165, 169, 175, 177, 187, 218, 220, 228–29, 237, 241, 246

Austrian Empire, 14, 20, 72, 74, 156

Austrian National Library, 5

Austrian patron saints, 156

Austrian ruling families. *See* Babenbergs; Habsburg

"Austrian system," 24, 30, 33, 37, 247. *See also* censorship; police

Austrian territories, 6, 7, 9, 11, 14, 75

Axmann, Josef (1793–1873), **86**

Baader, Franz von (1765–1841), 73

Babenbergs, 156, **157,** 172

Bach, Carl Phillip Emmanuel (1714–88), 107

Bach, Johann Sebastian (1685–1750), 80, 110, 111, 126

Bacon, Francis (1561–1626), 82

bagpipes, 117

balconies, 168, **170**

Balkans, 61, 66

ballads, 117, 184, 188, 190, 205, 206

ballet, 26, 99, 101, 103, **103,** 104, 129, 248, **pl.22**

ballrooms, 65, 102, 115, 116, 121, 123, 124, 125, 127, 140

balls, 47, 52, 55, **58,** 59, 115, 116, **120,** 121, 122, 123, 124, 127, 128, 131, 138, 140

Balzac, Honoré de (1799–1850), 89

bands, 114, 116, 117

Bänkelsänger, 117

Barbizon School, 180, 182

barrel organs, 52, 117

Bartsch, Rudolf Hans (1873–1952), 54

Bassano, Battle of, 36

bassoonists, 115

bath houses, 166

Battle of Leipzig, The, **21, 100.** *See also* Leipzig, Battle of

Baublock, 168

Bäuerle, Adolf (1786–1859), 221, 222

Bauernfeld, Eduard von (1802–90), 24, 28, 30, 31, 33, 194, 195, 236, **237,** 247, 256

Bavaria, 14, 56, 235, 247

beauty, 32, 85, 89, 113, 151, 191, 204, 222, 224

beer halls, 116

Beethoven, Ludwig van (1770–1827), 8, 9,

14, 18, **20,** 21, 22, 26, 27, **31,** 32–34, 36, 41, 44, 53, **57,** 59, 79–81, 87–90, **90, 93,** 93–97, 99, 101–3, **102, 103,** 106, 107, **109,** 113, 118, 132, 164, **166,** 171, 182, 189, **220,** 239–41, 248, **249,** 255, **pl.3**

Befreiungskrieg. See Wars of Liberation

beggar-musicians, 117

Belgium, 6, 71, 72

Bellotto, Bernardo (1720–80), 148, **pl.9**

Belvedere, 146, **147, pl.9**

Berchtesgaden, 179

Berlin, 47, **48,** 57, 65, 72, 155, 172, 244, 245, **pl.15**

Berlioz, Hector (1803–69), 84, 90

"Bernadon." *See* Kurz, Josef Felix von

Bernini, Gianlorenzo (1598–1680), 155

Biedermeier, 25, **25,** 26, **27,** 33, 34, 41, 42, **42,** 44, **45,** 49–54, 117, 118, **165, 167,** 168, **169,** 171, 172, 174–77, 179–84, 187, 189, 191, 194, **196,** 197–99, 203, 204, 212, 246, 254; Biedermeier realism, 175, 179

bigamy, 31, **237**

birthdays, 10, 99, 114

birth houses, 38

bishops, 39, **64**

Bittner, Norbert (1786–1851), **219**

Blücher von Wahlstatt, Gebhardt Leberecht, Prince (1742–1819), 66, 68, 70

Blume, Friedrich (1893–1975), 94, 95, 97

Bohemia, 6, 52, 68, 114, 145, 245, 247

Boileau-Despréaux, Nicolas (1636–1711), 83, 85

Bollmann, Justus Erich (1769–1821), 58

bombardment of Vienna, 17, **17**

Bonaparte. *See* Napoleon Bonaparte

bon goût, 46

Boucher, Alexander (1778–1861), 103, 104

Boullée, Etienne Louis (1728–99), 168

Bourbons, 63, **64,** 67, 71. *See also* Louis XIV; Louis XVI; Louis XVIII

bourgeoisie, 25, 27, 39, 40, 41, 42, 43, 45, 49, 50, 52, 53, 149, 151, 169, 175–79, 195, 196, 222, 224. *See also* burghers; middle class

Breitkopf, Johann Gottlob Immanuel (1719–94), publisher, 132

Bremen, 56, 109

Brentano, Clemens (1778–1842), 26

Breuning, Gerhard von (1813–92), 89, 96

Breunner-Enkevoirth, August Graf, 179

Bridge of Mantible, The, 240

Briefe eines Eipeldauers, **123**

Briefe über die wienerische Schaubühne, 217

Brigittenkirchtag, 99, **99**

Britain, 9, 19, **56,** 60, **61, 62,** 65, 67, 68, 74, 75

Brockmann, Johann Franz Hieronymus (1745–1812), 229

Bruchmann, Franz Seraph, Ritter von (1798–1867), 30, 191, 194

Brunswick, 125, 139

Bücherrevisionsamt, 195. *See also* censorship

bureaucracy, 31, 40, 172, 220, 228, 243

bureaucrats, 9, 31, 32, **40,** 41, 54, 109

Bürgerspital, 100

Bürgertum, 233

Burgforum, 161

Burgglacis, 161

burghers, 39–41. *See also* bourgeoisie; middle class

Burgtheater, 26, **100,** 101, **101,** 217, 228–36, **231, 232, 234–37,** 241, 243, 244, **pl.22**

Burke, Edmund (1729–97), 33

Buttlar, Augusta von (b. 1857), **86**

Byron, George Gordon Noel Lord (1788–1824), 80, 85

cafes, 52, 215. *See also* coffeehouses

Calderón de la Barca, Pedro (1600–1681), 57, 84, 217, 231, 240, 244

Campo Formio, 11

Canaletto (Antonio Canal, 1697–1768), **pl.9**

Canova, Antonio (1757–1822), 143, 153, **153,** 157, 159, **159–61,** 164, 172

cantor, 113

Cape of Good Hope, 71

Cappi, Pietro (fl. c. 1790–1830), 252

Cappi and Diabelli, **120, 127, 250,** 252

Carème, Marie Antonin (1784–1833), 60

Carl, Karl (1787–1854), 243

Carltheater, 243

Carneval 1923. Sammlung original deutscher Tänze für das Pianoforte, **120**

carnival, 66, 115, 119, **120,** 122

Carnot, Lazare (1753–1823), 9

carousel, **58**

caryatids, **150,** 151, 152, **155**

Castelli, Ignaz Franz (1781–1862), 24, 224, **224,** 238, 244

Castiglione, Battle of, 36

Castlereagh, Viscount. *See* Stewart, Robert Vane

Catalani, Angelica (1780–1849), 222

cathedral, **37,** 112, 144, **144, pl.9**

Catholic Church. *See* Roman Catholic Church

Cecilian Movement, 111

censorship, 6, 22, 31, 36, 37, 40, 50, 52, 53, 101–3, 175, 184, 195, 220, **221,** 222, 229–32, **231, 237,** 244, 247

centaur, 159, **160, 161,** 164

Ceremonial Hall (Hofburg), 162, **163**

Cervantes Saavedra, Miguel de (1547–1616), 84

Ceylon, 71

chamber music, 26, 34, 55, 96, 106, 107, **109,** 110, 119, 182, 246, 248, 255

Charlemagne, 240, 241

Charles VI, Holy Roman Emperor (1685–1740, r. 1711–40), 53, **148**

chassé, 131, 132

Chateaubriand, François René, Vicomte de (1768–1848), 85, 96

Cherubini, Luigi (1760–1842), 106, 107

Chezy, Helmine Christiane von (1783–1856), 102, 118

child labor, 38

children, 38, 40, 43, 44, 85, 104, 109, 110, 114, 129, 175–77, 198, 211, 223, 233, **pl.11, pl.12**

choir, **17,** 44, 106, 107, 110, 112, 113, **113**

choirboys, 87, 112, **112, 144**

choir director, 107, 112, 113, **144**

Chopin, Frédéric (1810–49), 79, 90

choral music, 103, 107, 110, 112. *See also* Mass; oratorio

choristers (adult), 112

chorus, 59, 104, **108**, 226

churches, 29, **99**, 111–13, **113**, 144–46, **145, 148, 154,** 158, **159,** 166, 230, **pl.8**

circle (dance pattern), 125, 128, 131, 132

circle(s), social: of Schubert's friends, 26, **27–30,** 28–31, 34, 36, 41, 44–45, 50, 52, **86,** 96, 122, 177, 199, 248, 250, 252, 254, 255, **pl.13;** others, 28, 46. *See also* salons

city walls, **37,** 146, 148, 161

Clancarty, Richard LePoer Trench, Lord (1767–1837), 69

clarionets, 115

classical culture, 146, 183, 184, 188, 193, 222

Classical Style, The, 95, 97

classical style in music, 91, 93–95, 99, 106, 107, 139

classicism: in architecture, **150,** 151–53, 159, 161–63, **161–63,** 165, **165–67,** 166, 168; in painting and sculpture, 153–56, **155,** 156–59, **159, 160,** 161–64, **165,** 174; versus romanticism, see Chapters 4 and 9, *passim. See also* neoclassicism

Clarot, Alexander (1796–1842), **5**

Claudius, Matthias (1740–1815), 187, 198, 203, 204

Clementi, Muzio (1752–1832), 89

clergy, 39, 172, 182

cloisters, 165, **169,** 172

coalitions, 9, 11, 14, 74

coffeehouses, 52, 144, 165, 166, **167,** 169. *See also* cafes

Coleridge, Samuel Taylor (1772–1834), 85, 188, 213

Colleoni, Bartolomeo (1400–1476), 155

Collin, Heinrich Joseph von (1771–1811), 26

Collin, Matthäus (1779–1824), 26, 190, 194, 195, 205, 206, 211, 212

columns, 124, 125, 127, 131, 155, 162, 163, 168

comedy, 26, 117, 216, 217, 220–28, **221, 223,** 230, 233, 234, 238, 239, 242, 243, 245, **pl.21**

commedia dell' arte, 216, 217, 227

Committee of Eight, 63, 64, 69, **70**

commoners, 182

compensation, 71, 72, **120**

Concerning the Present Condition of Music, 90, **90**

concerti, 96, 103, 104, 106, 107, 116, **249**

Concert of Europe, **61,** 74

concerts, 26, **31,** 45, 47, 52, **57,** 59, 74, 99–104, **100, 101, 105,** 106–11, **108–110,** 113, 114, **116,** 116–19, 182, **195,** 248, **249,** 254, **pl.22, pl.23**

Confederation of the Rhine (Confédération Germanique), 14, 16, 17

Congress of Vienna, 3, 19, 26, 33, 34, 36, 40, 41, 48, **48,** 55, **56–59, 57–67, 61–64, 68,** 69, 70, **70,** 72, 74–76, **86,** 122, **122,** 135, 136, 138, **167,** 175, 178, 223, 246, 247, **247, pl.5**

Consalvi, Cardinal Ercole (1757–1824), 56

conservatories, 104, 107, 113, 117

contemplative life, 172

Continental system, 15

contredanse, 125, 128–30, 131, **133**

convention, 9

coronation anthems, 114

Corot, Jean-Baptiste-Camille (1796–1875), 182

Corpus Christi, 111, 114, **pl.7**

Corsica, 9, 18

Corti, **167**

Costenoble, Karl Ludwig (1769–1837), 233

costumes, 16, 122, 129, 135, 136, **137,** 218, 224; ethnic, 136. *See also* fashion

cotillion *(cotillon),* 139

country dances, 124, 125, 127–29, **129**

country life, 42, 135

couple dances, 124, 125, 131

court. *See* Austrian court; France, court; Russia, court

court chapel, 111, 112, **112, pl.6**

courtyards, 115, 117, 168, **170,** 220

Cracow, 64, 65

crafts, 38, 54, 175, 176

Craigher, Jachelutta Jakob Nikolaus, Reichs-freiherr von (1797–1855), 194

Creation, The, 47, 111, 198, 221, 229, **pl.6**

critics, 33, 66, 83–85, 87, 89, 90, 93, 97, 114,
    151, 158, 243, 247, 255
Croatia, 6, 53
currency, 18, 118
czakan, 104, **105**
Czech Republic, 6
Czerny, Carl (1791–1857), 100, **120**

Dachstein, **pl.17**
Daffinger, Moritz-Michael (1790–1849),
    234, 235
Dalmatia, 6, 11
dance anthologies, 115
dance halls, 115, **115,** 116, 121–23, **122,** 135,
    165
dance manuals, 127, 131, 133, 134, 139, 140
dance music, 116, 119
dancing masters, 124–27, 132, 135, 138, 140
dancing shoes, **137,** 138
Danhauser, Josef (1805–45), 42, **45,** 176–78,
    182, **pl.13**
Danhauser, Josef Ulrich (1780–1829), 42, 177
Danhauser furniture, 42, 177
Dante Alighieri (1265–1321), 84
Danube, **99,** 100, 146, 151, **152,** 180
Das Donauweibchen, 223
Das Jüngste Gericht, 103
David, Jacques-Louis (1748–1825), **136, pl.3**
Decker, George (1818/19–94), **239**
Decker, Johann Stephan (1784–1844), **93**
decoration, **145,** 151, 162, **163, 165,** 168
Deffands, Marie de Vichy-Chamrond, Mar-
    quise du (1697–1780), 46
deism, 31. See also religion
Denmark, 56, 72, 247
Der Alpenkönig und der Menschenfeind, 226,
    227, 239
"Der Atlas," 79
Der Barometermacher auf der Zauberinsel, 225
Der Bauer als Millionär, **220, 224, 225,** 226
Der Berggeist, 222
"Der blonde Eckbert," 213
Der böse Geist Lumpazivagabundus, 242, 243
Der Diamant des Geisterkönigs, 32
"Der Doppelgänger," 79

"Der Edelknabe und die Müllerin," 192
"Der Fischer," 184, 186, 188, 191, 211
Der Freischütz, 106
Der goldene Vließ, 234
Der Graf von Gleichen, 31, 236, **237**
"Der Junggeselle und der Bach," 192
"Der Kreuzzug," 107
"Der Leiermann," 117
"Der Lindenbaum," 194
"Der Müllerin Reue," 192
"Der Müllerin Verrat," 192
Der Musensohn, 189
Der Nachsommer, 233, 244
"Der Runenberg," 213
"Der Tod und das Mädchen," 203
Der Verschwender, **150,** 226, 241, 242
Der vierjährige Posten, 237
"Der zürnenden Diana," 191
"Der Zwerg," 190, 205
Des Teufels Luftschloss, 237
Deutsch, Otto Erich (1883–1967), 32, 33, 54,
    95, 97, 107, 118, 138, 256
Deutscher (dance), **120,** 122, 124, 147,
    132–35, 139
Devrient, Wilhelmine. See Schröder-
    Devrient, Wilhelmine
Diabelli, Antonio (1781–1858), **120, 157,
    250,** 252, 253, **253.** See also Cappi and
    Diabelli
dialect, 4, 116, **123,** 216
dialectic, 90, 96, 193, 204
Die Ahnfrau, 234
"Die Allmacht," 31, 107, 182
"Die Befreier Europas in Paris," 19
"Die Bürger in Wien," 222
Die falsche Primadonna, 222, 224
Die Freunde von Salamanka, 237, 238
"Die frühen Gräber," 204
Die gefesselte Phantasie, 245
"die gute alte Zeit," 25, 33, 246
Die Musikanten am hohen Markt, 224
Die Räuber, 230
Die schöne Müllerin, 186, 192, 193, 194, 196,
    211, 213
Die Schöpfung. See Creation, The

"Die Sterne," 107

Diet, 39, 71, 72

Die Verschworenen, 237, 238

Die Zauberflöte, 26, **103,** 166, **168,** 217, 218, **218, 219,** 220, 222

Die Zauberharfe, 26, 216, 217, 237, 239, 244, 245

Die Zwillingsbrüder, 237

Dionysus, 227

Directory, 9

division of labor, 20, 21, 42–44, 184, 225

Donatello (Donato di Niccolo di Betto Bardi, 1386–1466), 155

Donner, Georg Raphaël (1693–1741), 155

Doric order, 161, **161,** 163

drama, 24, 26, 52, 80, 83, 96, 99, 101, **101,** 111, 205, 214, 216–18, 220, 222, 225–32, 234, 235, **235,** 241, **pl.22.** *See also* comedy; tragedy

Drechsler, Johann Baptist (1756–1811), 181

Drechsler, Joseph (1782–1852), 113, **pl. 19, pl.20**

drehen, 133

Dreher, 132–34

Dresden, 126, 172, 243

duchy, 64, 72

Duet Concertante for Harp and Pianoforte, 104

duets, 104, 106, 110, 114, 237, 240

dukes, 4, 6, 11, 48, 56, 66, 172

duple-meter, 128, 131, 132, 139

Dutch, 20, 68, 71, 75, 178, 179, 181, **pl.19**

early music, 110, 111, 117, 118

East Prussia, 64, 72

ecclesiastical reforms, 37, 149, 172

economy, 8, 36, 40, 49, 52, 58, 175

ecossaise, 122, 124, 131, 139

Edict of Tolerance, 47

education, 4, 16, 22, 32, 34, 44, **45,** 47, 52, 54, 108, 124, **134,** 228

Egmont, 106

Egypt, 11, 18, 218

Eight Powers. *See* Committee of Eight

Einstein, Alfred (1880–1952), 95

Elba, 19, 67

electors, 14

elegies, 190, 191, 199

Elisa und Claudio, 106

"Ellen's Song," 113

Eltz, Josef August (1788–1860), 179, **pl.12**

emperor, 3–6, **7, 8,** 9, 10, **10,** 14–16, 19, **19,** 22, 32, 34, 36–38, **43,** 47, 49, 50, 55, 66, 67, **68,** 70, **86, 112,** 114, 145, 146, **148,** 149, **152,** 155, 156, 157, **157, 158,** 161, 162, 175–77, 228, 229, 243, 247, **249, pl.1, pl.3, pl.4, pl.15.** *See also* specific names

"Emperor" Quartet, **10**

Empfindsamkeit, 80

empire, 3, 6, **8,** 11, 14, 16, 18, 20, 33, 36, 37, 39, 41, 42, **42,** 60, 64, 71, 72, 74, 93, 112, 119, 135, 136, **136,** 145, 156, 215

Empire style, 41, 42, 135, 136

England, 11, 14, 15, 52, **56,** 58, 65, 71, 74, 114, 124, **130,** 134, 135; army, 20; art, literature, and culture, **59,** 80, 84, 135, 178; dance, 124–29, **129,** 133–35, 140

English travelers, 113, 114, 216

enlightened monarchs, 4, 38, **62, 73,** 156

Enlightenment, 4, 9, 33, 36–38, 47, 50, 54, 95, 96, 154, 171, 218, **218,** 228, 229

ennoblements, 41

entertainment(s), 25, 52, 69, 106, 109, 113, 115, 216, 228, 253, 254

"enthusiasm," 114, 118

Enzensperger, Bernard (1788–c. 1855), **105**

epics, 84, 85, 190, 240

Epinay, Mme. Louise Florence Pétronille de la Live d' (1726–83), 46

Epiphany, 119

epitaph, 29, **31**

equestrian ballets and exhibitions, **58,** 129

equestrian statues, 16, 154–56, **154, 155**

Erectheum, 152

Erfurt, 127, 139

"Erlkönig," 32, 188, 196, 212, 240, 252

Ermione, 104

Eskeles, Henriette, 49, **53**

Essling-Aspern, Battle of, 17

estates, 38–40, 56, 72, 175

Esterhazy family, 113, 250

Esterhazy residence: Vienna, 38; Zseliz, 41, 113

Esterhazy von Galanta, Karoline Countess (1805–51), 113

Eugene, prince of Savoy (1663–1736), 146, **147**

eulogy, **31**

Euryanthe, 104

Evening Entertainments. See *Abendunterhaltungen*

evil, 189, 226, 242

exile, 19, **23, 68–70**

Eybl, Franz (1806–80), 178, **pl.14**

Eybler, Joseph von (1764–1846), 107, 112

facade, **150,** 154, 168, 184

factories, 38, **39,** 40, 42, 43, 44, **45,** 66, **122,** 166, 177, 181, **pl.11, pl.13, pl.20.** *See also* industrialization; silk

Falconet, Etienne-Maurice (1716–91), 155

family, 3, 25, **25,** 26, 33, 38, 39, **39,** 41, 43–45, **45,** 47, 49, 54, 56, 82, 99, 104, 108, 109, 128, 146, 156, 169, 175–77, 179, 191, 226, **227,** 244, 250, 254, **pl.5, pl.12, pl.14**

fantasia, 104

farce, 216, 221, 228, 233

Fasching, 119. *See also* carnival

fashion, 135, 136, **136, 137,** 138

Faust, 188, 190, 191

Feldenstein, C. J. von (fl. late 18th c.), 125, 132, 139

Fendi, Peter (1796–1842), 176–78

Ferdinand I, King of the Two Sicilies (1751–1825, r. 1816–25), 63, 71

Fereol-Mazas, Jacques (1782–1849), 104

Fertbauer, Leopold (1802–75), **25**

Fichtner, Karl (1805–73), 233

Fidelio, 14, 19, **20,** 44, **103,** 240, 241

Fierrabras, 238, 240, 241

figures (dance), 124, 125, **126,** 127–32, **129, 130,** 135, 138, 140

fine arts, 10, 16, 29, 32, 33, 84, 164, 174, 175, 181. *See also* decoration; painters

Finland, 72

"first Viennese-European modern style," 95

Fischer, Johann Martin (1741–1820), 156, **158,** 173

Fischer, Wilhelm (1886–1962), 91, 93

Fischer von Erlach, Johann Bernhard (1656–1723), 146, 147, **148,** 149, **154,** 158

Fischer von Erlach, Joseph Emanuel (1693–1742), 149

"Fischerweise," 107, 209

Fischhof, Josef (1804–57), 113

Flanders, 68, 70

Fledermaus, 117

Fliegende Blätter, 34

Florence, 4, **7**

florin, 106, 107, 118

flowers, 80, 138, 146, 178, 180, 181, 191, **pl.19, pl.20**

folk music, 10, 116, 117, 183

folk plays, 221

folksingers, 116–18

Fontainebleau, 182

France, 4, 6, 8, 9, 11, 14, 15, 18, 22, 33, 36, 41, 46, 52, **56,** 57, 60, 61, **62,** 63–68, **64,** 70–72, 74, 75, 81, 107, 124, 125, 130, 132, 134, 135, 151, 156, 175, 180; architecture, fine arts, and decoration 147, 162, 168, 177, 178, 180; army, 9, 11, 14, **15,** 16, **17,** 18, 22, 62, **68, 103, pl.17;** court, 58, 124, 125, 128, 140; culture and taste, 42, 44, 46, 49, 83, 84, 89, 93, 124, **149, 163;** dance, 124–26, 128, 133, 139, 140; drama, 228; fashion, 136, **136;** language, 4, 49, 52

Francis I, emperor of Austria (1768–1835, r. 1804–35; Holy Roman Emperor as Francis II, r. 1792–1806), Chapter 1, *passim;* **5, 8, 19, 23, 25,** 36, 41, **43,** 49, 50, 55, 56, **64,** 67, 69, 96, **73, 86, 112,** 119, 154, 156, 172, 175, 229, 230, 247, **pl.1, pl.15**

Franciscan, 144

Francis Stephen (1708–65; duke of Lorraine, r. 1729–35; grand duke of Tuscany, r. 1737–65; Holy Roman Emperor as Francis I, r. 1745–65), 147

Francis Stephen I, Holy Roman Emperor, 147

Frank, Christoph (1787–1822), **195, pl.21**

Franz Joseph, emperor of Austria (1830–1916, r. 1848–1916), 243

"Franzl," 32, **pl.1**

Frederick VI, king of Denmark (1768–1839, r. 1808–39), 56, 247

Frederick the Great. *See* Friedrich II, king of Prussia

French allemande, 139

French Revolution, 3, 8, 9, 36, 37, 40, 53, **64,** 80, 89, 166, 174, 183

French Revolutionary Wars, 8, 9, 21

Freyung, 168, **169**

Friedrich II ("The Great"), king of Prussia (1712–86, r. 1740–86), 47, 65

Friedrich Augustus, duke of Saxony (1750–1827, r. 1768–1827; king of Saxony as Friedrich August I, r. 1806–27), 63

Friedrich Wilhelm III, king of Prussia (1770–1840, r. 1797–1840), 61, 63, **63, 73,** 247

Friedrich Wilhelm Karl, king of Württemberg (1754–1816, r. 1806–16), 65, 247

Friends of Music. *See* Gesellschaft der Musikfreunde

Fries, Johann Reichsgraf (1719–85), 149, **150,** 151, **153,** 171

Fries, Moritz Reichsgraf von (1777–1826), **153,** 171, **pl.17**

Fries Palace, Fries-Pallavicini Palace, 38, 149, **150,** 153, **153–55,** 154

Fröhlich sisters, **27,** 110, 113

Füger, Friedrich Heinrich (1751–1818), 10, 33, 174, 178

Führich, Josef von (1800–1876), 92

funerals, **31,** 111, **144, 220,** 239

furniture, 25, 41, 42, **42,** 176, 177, **pl.13**

Gaertner, Carl von, 104

Gainsborough, Thomas (1727–88), 135

galant, 80

Galicia, 6, 39

gallery, 176, 178

galop, 115, 116, 122, 124, 132

gardens, 75, 82, 146, 149, 159, 181

Gattamelata, (equestrian statue of Erasmo da Narni), 155

Gauermann, Friedrich (1807–62), 179, **pl.17**

gavotte, 131

Gebauer, Franz Xaver (1784–1822), 107

Geiger, Andreas (1765–1856), **242**

Geisler, Maria, **pl.22**

"Geist der Liebe," 106

Gemütlichkeit, 41

gender, 44, 54, 96, 211

genius, 49, 85, 89, 157, 225, 235, **236,** 239, 247, 249, 252, 253, 256

Genoa, 71

genre, 166, 176–78, 181, 182, 186, 188, 203, 241, 244, 248

Gentz, Friedrich (1764–1832), 14, 16, 33, 48, **56,** 57, 76

Geoffrin, Mme. Marie-Thérèse (1699–1777), 46

Gérard, François-Pascal-Simon (1770–1837), **pl.3**

Gerasch, Franz (b. 1826), **17**

German classicism, 83, 183, 187, 188, 192

German dance, **120,** 126–34, 139

German drama and theater, 83, 101, **101, 193,** 226, 228, 229, 231, 232, 234, 244

German federations, 65, 67, **70,** 71, 74. *See also* Confederation of the Rhine

German language, 4, 6, 11, 15, 17, 33, 34, 49, 52, 54, 81, 107, 117, 127–29, 132–34, 182, 184, 190, 214, 229, 231, 232, 234

German music, 95, 97, 98, 107, 117, 240

German national anthem, 10, **10**

German nobility, 14, 16, 63, 68

German painting, 179, 182

German religious mystics, 73

German romanticism, 16, 30, **81,** 82, **86,** 97, 187, 193, 196

German states, 52, 65, 66, 71, 72, 184

Germany, 6, 11, 14, 16, 23, 34, 36, 56, 57, 61, 62, 65, 66, 68, 72, 80, 81, 90, **90,** 118, 124, 125, 130–32, 134, 135, 139, 179, 183, 184, 187, 191, **193,** 198, 216, 229

Gerstenberg, Georg Friedrich von (1780–1838), 198

Gerusalemme Liberata, 84

Gesellschaft der Musikfreunde, 59, 104, 106–8, 110, 113, 118, 248, 254

Geymüller, Johann Heinrich the Elder (1754–1824), Geymüller Schlößl, 109, 169, **171**

Ghent, 6

Gleich, Joseph Alois (1772–1841), 221, 222, 224, 238

Gloriette, 149

Gneisenau, August Wilhelm Anton Graf Neihardt von (1760–1831), 66

Godefroy, Jean (1771–1839), **56**

Goethe, Johann Wolfgang von (1749–1832), 27, 32, 80, 183, 184, 186–95, **189, 193,** 197–99, 205, 206, 209, 211–13, 230, 231, **231,** 244, **250**

"good old days." *See* "die gute alte Zeit"

Gothic, 42, **42,** 144, **144, 145,** 166, 169, **171,** 183, 199

gothic novel, 199

"Gott erhalte." See *Kaiserhymne*

Gottsched, Johann Christoph (1700–1766), 83

Graben, 144, 155, 156, **157, pl.7**

Graff, Antoine (1736–1813), **193**

grand duke, 4, 11

"Grandes marches," 114

grand march, 131

Gray, Thomas (1716–71), 199

Graz, 36, 118, 200

Greek antiquity. *See* antiquity

Greek revival, 183

Greiner, Franz Sales von (1732–98), 47, 49

"Gretchen am Spinnrade," 32, 110, **150,** 171, 188, 189, 252

Gries, Johann Michael (1772–1827), 57

Grillparzer, Franz (1791–1872), 24, 26, 29, 30, **31,** 32, 36, 50, 52, 53, **99,** 110, **169,** 195, 233–36, **235, 236,** 240–42

Grimm, Jakob (1785–1863), 57

Grinzing, 169

Grob, Theresa (1798–1875), **39**

group dances, 124, 125, 127–31, **129, 130,** 134, 138

Guarini, Battista (1538–1612), 84

guitar, 98, 104, **105,** 117

Gurk, Eduard (1801–41), **102, 162, 220, 221**

"gute alte Zeit." *See* "die gute alte Zeit"

Habsburg: House of, 3–6, 10, 11, 14, 16–18, 21, **25,** 32, 33, 36, 37, 39, 50, 54, 71, 119, 136, 145–47, **155,** 155–57, 162, 175, 187, 214, 228, 235, 244; rulers, 14, 53, 145–47, 156–59, **157,** 172, 215, 244, **pl.1, pl.4, pl.15**

Hafner, Philipp (1731–64), 217

Hamburg, 56, 57

Handel, Georg Friedrich (1685–1759), 80, **157**

Hanover, 66, 71

"Hanswurst," **215,** 216, 217, 223, **223, 242**

Hardenberg, Karl August Prince von, 48, **56,** 62, 65, 71

harp, 104, 117, 237

harpists, 52, 98, **116,** 117

Haschka, Lorenz Leopold (1749–1827), 10, **10**

Hasenhut, Anton (1766–1841), 223, 224

Haupt- und Staatsaktionen, 216, 217

Hausmusik, 25, **27,** 52, 171

Haydn, Josef (1732–1809), **10,** 10, 17, 21, 26, 36, 47, 79, 80, 87, 89–91, **90, 91,** 93–95, 97, **100,** 107, 112, 118, 126, 127, 132, 139, **pl.6**

Haydn, Michael (1737–1806), 112

Hegel, Georg Wilhelm Friedrich (1770–1831), 90, 91, 93

Heidelberg, 36, 70

"Heidenröslein," **188, 189, 252**

Heiligenstadt Testament, 89

Heine, Heinrich (1797–1856), 187

Heinrich, Thugut (fl. 19th c.), **31**

Heligoland, 71

Hellas. *See* antiquity

Hellenistic, 153

Helmke, Eduard David (1794–1879), 124, 127, 138, 139

Hensler, Karl Friedrich (1759–1825), 221, 223

Herder, Johann Gottfried von (1744–1803), 198

Herrengasse, **108**

Hesse-Cassel, 57, 66, 71

Hetzendorf von Hohenberg, Johann Ferdinand (1732–1816), **145,** 149

Hickel, Joseph (1736–1807), **7**

high romanticism, 187, 197–99. *See also* romanticism

Hildebrandt, Johann Lukas von (1668–1745), 146, 147

Himmelpfortgrund, 38

historicist, 41, 42, **42, 43, 171**

Hochenadel, Josef, 110

Hoechle, Johann Nepomuk (1790–1835), **17, 19,** 24, 58, **58**

Hofburg, 4, 16, 26, 38, **58,** 66, **101,** 121, 145, **150, 154,** 159, 162, **163, 166,** 228

Hofburgtheater. *See* Burgtheater

Höfel, Blasius (1792–1863), **61**

Hoffmann, E. T. A. (1776–1822), 87–89, 93, 240

Hofmann, Georg Ernst von (1771–1845), 237

Hohensalzburg Fortress, **pl.16**

Hohenzollern, 66

Hoher Markt, 156

holidays, 99, 115

Holland, 9

Holmes, Edward (1797–1859), 114, 118

Hölty, Ludwig Christoph Heinrich (1748–76), 186, 187, 198

Holy Alliance, 72, **73,** 74, 163

Holy Roman Empire, 6, **8,** 11, 14, 33, 36, 71, 72, 93, 156

Holy Week, 111

Holzer, Michael (1772–1826), 113

Hormayr, Joseph Freiherr von (1781–1848), 16, 26

house music. See *Hausmusik*

House of Austria, 6, 14, 71, 96, **157,** 222. *See also* Habsburg

Humboldt, Wilhelm Freiherr von (1767–1835), 48, 50, **56,** 57, 64

Hummel, Johann Nepomuk (1778–1837), 95

"Hundred Days," 20, 70

Hungary, 6, 39, 41, 53, 72, **105,** 145, **pl.4**

hurdy-gurdy, 117

Hüttenbrenner, Anselm (1794–1868), 194, 255

Hüttenbrenner, Heinrich (1799–1830), 194

Hüttenbrenner, Josef (1796–1822), 255

hymns, **10,** 103, 106, 107, 188, 190, 239

Hyrtl, Jakob (1799–1868), **37**

Ibsen, Henrik (1828–1906), 235

Idea, 9, 83, 84, 88, 90, 95, 97, 144, 162, 175, 203, 230, 243

idealism, 61, 178, 217, 218

idealist, 88

idealization, 25, 28, 44, 157, 176, 177, 223, 239, 244

Iffland, August Wilhelm (1759–1814), 230, 244

illegitimacy rate, 38

Il pastor fido, 84

imago clipeata, 157

imperial art collection, 17, 176

imperial cities, 12

imperial court, 69, 163, 175, 177, 246

imperial court music, **17,** 24, 44, 59, 87

Imperial Court Opera, 237. *See also* Kärntnertortheater; opera

imperial legislature, 11

Imperial Library, 149

imperial patronage, 149, 250

imperial residences, 4, 26, 38, 112, 121, 145, 156, 228

imperial Rome, 162

Imperial-Royal Viennese Porcelain Factory, 180

imperial title, 6, **8,** 14, 145, 162

Imperial War Council, 110

impressionists, 180

improvisation, 26, 103, 117, 119, **215,** 216, **217,** 220, **221,** 223, 224, 243, 255

incidental music, **103,** 245

industrialization, **37,** 37–39, **39,** 42, 43, 66, 243

inns, 24, 50, 52, 106, **116,** 121, **123, 144**

instrumental music, 88, 89, 95, 98, 111, 255.
   See also bands; quartets, string; symphonies; etc.
intellectual life, 30, 46–51, 80–85, 236, 247
intellectuals, 9, 22, 24, 40, 41, 47–49, 52, 57, 75, 196
intermarriage, 41
International Schubert Society, 250
Introduction, Adagio and Rondo for Pedal Harp, 104
Ionian Islands, 71
Iphigenia in Tauris, 191
irony, 94, 183, 190, 222
Isabey, Jean-Baptiste (1767–1855), **56,** 58
Ischl, **pl.12**
Istria, 11
Italian church in Vienna. *See* Minorites
Italian comedy. *See* commedia dell' arte
Italian origins of salons, 46
Italian states, 67, 72, 75
Italy, 6, 9, 11, 14–16, 20, 21, 36, 46, 56, 61, 67, 68, 71, 72, 74, **149,** 153, 156, 177, 192;
   architecture, 146, 147, 158; dance, 126;
   epics, 84; language, 4, 49, 52; music, 88, 95, 96, 98, 103, 106, 107, **110,** 215, 228, 244.
   See also arias; concerti; opera
Itzig family, 47

Jacobi, Johann Georg (1740–1814), 191, 198
Jacobins, 9, 22, 40, 47
Jacquin, Nikolaus Joseph Freiherr von (1727–1817), 181
"Jägers Abendlied," 189
Jena, 230
Jenger, Johann Baptist (1792–1856), 255
Jerusalem, 6
Jesuit drama, 217
Jesus, 103, 179
jeu d'esprit, 46
Jews, 47, **48,** 56, 113, 118, **pl.10**
Johann Baptiste Joseph Fabian Sebastian, archduke of Austria (1782–1859), 15, 16
Josefsplatz, 16, 102, 121, 154, **154, 155**
Josefsstöckl, 151, **152,** 168

Josefstadt, 26, 102, 220, **220, 221,** 224, 241
Joseph I, Holy Roman Emperor (1678–1711, r. 1705–11), 53
Joseph II, Holy Roman Emperor (1741–90, r. 1765–90), 4–6, **7,** 16, 22, 36–39, 47, **48,** 50, 54, 121, **145,** 147, 149, 151, **152,** 154–57, **155,** 165, **167,** 171, 228, 230, **pl.4, pl.10**
Josephinism, **27,** 37, **145,** 151, **152,** 166, 172, **pl.4, pl.10**
Josephinum, 151, 166
journals, 34, 36, 85, 96, **123,** 136, 138, 196

Kabale und Liebe, 230
Kaiser, 6, 173. *See also* emperor
Kaiserhymne, 10, **10**
Kant, Immanuel (1724–1804), 82, 193
Karl Ludwig, archduke of Austria (1771–1847), 15
Karlskirche, **37,** 112, 146, **148,** 158, **pl.8, pl.9**
Kärntnertortheater, 26, 101, 104, 215–17, 230, 236, 237, 240, 245
Karolina Augusta, empress of Austria (1792–1873), **pl.15**
"Kasperl," 223, **223**
Kattfuß, Johann Heinrich (fl. c. 1800), 135, 139
Kaufmann, Angelika (1740–1807), **189**
Kaunitz, Wenzel Anton Fürst von (1711–94), 14, 47, 54
Keats, John (1795–1821), 80
Kehraus, 132
Kenner, Josef (1794–1868), 195
keyed trumpet, 104
Kiesewetter, Raphael Georg (1773–1850), 110, 111, 118
Kingdom of the Netherlands, 71
Kingdom of the Two Sicilies, 71, 74
King Lear, 87, 231–33, 244
King of Rome. *See* Napoleon, Franz Joseph Karl
kings, 5, 6, 8, 9, 14, 18, 33, 60, 61, 63–67, 71, 74, 87, **155,** 189, 209, 226, **227,** 231, 233, 235, 238, 241, 244. *See also* specific names
Kininger, Vincenz Georg (1767–1851), **48**

Kinsky Palace, 38

Kirnberger, Johann Philipp (1721–83), 126, 139

Klein, Johann Adam (1792–1875), **21**

Kleist, Heinrich von (1777–1811), 231, **231,** 244

Klopstock, Friedrich Gottlieb (1724–1803), 187, 191, 198, 204, 205

Klosterneuburg, **28,** 146

Klosterneuburger Hof, 146

Knapp, Johann (1778–1833), 181

Köchel, Ludwig Alois Ferdinand Ritter von (1800–1877), 95

Korn, Maximilian (1782–1854), 233

Körner, Karl Theodor (1791–1813), 26, 28, 31, **181, 195, 237**

Kornhäusel, Josef (1782–1860), 163, 166

Korntheuer, Friedrich Josef (1779–1829), 224, **224**

Kosegarten, Ludwig Theobul (1758–1818), 198

Kotzebue, August von (1761–1819), 23, 24, 230, 237, 244

Krafft, Johann Peter (1780–1856), 177, **pl.1, pl.14**

Kratzerl, 224, 225

"Kriegslied der Österreicher," 9

Kriehuber, Joseph (1800–1876), **110, 224, 237, 253, pl.14**

Krones, Therese (1801–30), 224, **225**

Krubsacius, F. A. (1718–90), 151, 172

Krüdener, Juliane Freifrau von (1764–1824), 73

Krüger, Franz (1797–1857), **63**

Kunsthistorisches Museum, 159, **160**

Kupelwieser, Josef (1791–1866), 24, 238

Kupelwieser, Leopold (1796–1862), 24, **29,** 29–33, **30, 92,** 179

Kurz, Josef Felix von (1715–84), 216, **217**

Kussmaul, Adolf, 33, 34

La Cenerentola, 104

Lach, Robert (1874–1958), 256

Lachner-Rolle, 177

Lady of the Lake, The, 46, 47, 113

Lamberg, Franz Philipp Graf von (1791–1848), 178

Lambert, Anne Thérèse de Marguerat de Courcelles, Marquise de (1647–1733), 46

Lami, Eugène Louis (1800–1890), **62**

Lampi the Elder, Johann Baptist (1751–1830), **150,** 178

Lampi the Younger, Johann Baptist (1775–1837), 178

Landhaussaal, **108**

Ländler, 116, 122, 132, 135, 138

landscape(s), 117, 174, 176–82, 194, 196, 223, 238, 244, **pl.16–18**

Landwehr, 15

Lange, Joseph (1751–1831), 229

languages, 4, 47, 49, 52

Lanner, Josef (1801–43), 52, 114, **115,** 116

Lapiths, 159

Laroche, Johann Joseph (1745–1806), 223, **223**

Lászny, Katherine von (c. 1789–1828), 31

Laube, Heinrich (1806–84), 243, 244

Lauenburg, Duchy of, 72

Lawrence, Thomas (1769–1830), 58, **59, 61,** 178, 213, 231

LeBeau, Pierre Adrien (1748–early 19th c.), **15**

"Lectures on Dramatic Poetry," 80, **81,** 83, 87, 96, 183, 192

Ledoux, Claude-Nicolas (1736–1806), 168

legitimacy, 63, 65, 215

Leipzig, 83, 90, 124

Leipzig, Battle of, 18, 19, **21, 100,** 161

Leitner, Karl Gottfried Ritter von (1800–1890), 187, 195, 199, 203

Lent, 99, 122, 138

Leonore, **20**

Leopold I, Holy Roman Emperor (1640–1705, r. 1658–1705), 53, 155, **157**

Leopold II, Holy Roman Emperor (1747–92, r. 1790–92), 4, 6, 8, **8,** 10, **12,** 22, 29, 33, 54, 156

Leopold Babenberg, St. *See* St. Leopold Babenberg

Leopoldine tract of the Hofburg, 145

Leopoldstadt, 26, 219, 220, **220,** 223, 224, 226, **239,** 243, 244
Lequeu, Jean-Jacques (1757–1825), 168
Leslie, Eliza (1787–1858), 139
Lespinasse, Julie-Jeanne-Eléonore de (1732–76), 46
Lessing, Gotthold Ephraim (1729–81), 231, **231,** 244
Letters on the Viennese Stage. See *Briefe über die wienerische Schaubühne*
levée en masse, 9
librettists, librettos, 28, 31, 102, 103, **168,** 187, **224,** 236–38, **237, 238,** 240
Liechtenstein, 146
Liechtental, 38, 80, **113**
"Lied eines Schiffers an die Dioskuren," 191
Lieder, 106, 117, 171, 186, 190, 191, 212, 213, 237, 240
Lieder, Friedrich Johann (1780–1859), 58, 250, **251**
Liszt, Franz von (1811–86), 28, 90
literary circles, reading circles, 46, 47, 50, 87
literary publications, journals, 44, 196
literary tea table, 50
literary theory, **81,** 82–86, 90, 184–86
literature, 16, 24, 30, 46, 50, 53, 80–83, 85, 87, 93, 96, 109, 143, 180, 184, 186, **193,** 196, 212, 246, 255
liturgical calendar, 99
liturgical music, 113
Livorno, 67
Lobkowitz Palace, 26, 38
Lodomeria, 6
Lokalstück, 222
Lombardy, 71, 74
London, 33, 34, 36, 38, 60, 75, 76, 95, 97, 118, 126, 128, 132, 139, **153,** 172, 178, 212–14
Loos, Friedrich (1797–1890), 179, **pl.16**
Löschenkohl, Johann Hieronymus (fl. c. 1779–1807), **112,** 138
lottery, 31
Louis XIV (1638–1715, r. 1643–1715), 124, **147**
Louis XVI (1754–93, r. 1774–92), 8, 9
Louis XVIII (1755–1824, r. 1814–24), 56, **64,** 67, 70

Lovejoy, Arthur O. (1873–1962), 82, 86, 96
lower classes, 38, 39, 42, 44, 53, 115
loyalty, 157, **158,** 228, 240, **pl.1**
Lucinde, 96
Ludlamshöhle, 24, 33
Lunéville, Treaty of, 11
Lysistrata, 238

Madel, Charles (fl. early 19th c.), 127, 134, 139
Magdeburg Rider, 155
magic, 26, **92, 103, 168,** 216–18, **218, 219,** 222, 225, 226, 237, 239, 244
Magic Flute, The. See *Die Zauberflöte*
magic plays. See *Zauberstück*
Mahler, Gustav (1860–1911), 247
Malta, 71
Mansfield (Mansfeld), Johann Ernst (1739–96), **23**
Mantua, 6
march, 4, 11, 18, 19, **19,** 22, 33, 61, 67, **68,** 69, 100, 106, 114, 115, 131, 135, 139, 188
"Marche militaire," 114
marches, 114
"Marches heroiques," 114
Marcus Aurelius Antoninus, emperor of Rome (121–80, r. 161–80), 154, **155,** 156
Marengo, Battle of, 11
Maria am Gestade, 144
Maria Christina, archduchess of Austria (1714–98), 157, **159,** 162
Maria Ludovica, empress of Austria (1787–1816), 16, 55
Maria Theresa, archduchess of Austria (1717–80, r. 1740–80), 47, 54, 147, 157, 172, 181, 228, **pl.4**
Maria Theresa, archduchess of Austria (1816–67), **164**
Marie Antoinette, queen of France (1755–93, r. 1774–92), 4, 8, 9, 130
Marie-Louise, archduchess of Austria (1791–1847; empress of France, r. 1810–15; duchess of Parma, Piacenza, and Guastalla, r. 1816–47), 18, **19,** 47
marriage, 6, 18, **19,** 31, 38, 41, 43, 44, 46–48, 50, 54, **64,** 177, 189, 191, 194, 209, 234

Martinelli, Domenico (1650–1718), 146

masks, **121,** 122

Masonic, 218, 244

Mass, 31, 32, **92,** 107, 112, 113, **113,** 180

Matthisson, Friedrich von (1761–1831), 186, 198

Maximilian, king of Bavaria (1756–1825, r. 1806–25), 235, 247

May Day, 99

Mayer (Meyer?), Ludwig (fl. 1813–24), **63**

Mayrhofer, Johann (1787–1836), 27, 31, 186, 191, 195–98, **196,** 203–5, 213, 237

mazurka, 123

McClary, Susan, 96

Medea, 234, 235, **236**

medieval. *See* Middle Ages

Mediterranean, 71, 86

"Meeres Stille," 205

Meisl, Karl (1775–1853), 221, **221,** 222

melancholy, 52, 189, 196, 199, 203, 239, 243

Melk, 146

Melker Hof, 146

melodrama, 221, 230, 233, 237, 239, 240, 245

Mendelssohn, Moses (1728–86), 47, 94, 95

menuet, 123–28, **126,** 138, 140

Mercadante, Saverio (1795–1870), 106

merchants, 38, **232,** 244

Messiah, 108

Metastasio, Pietro (1698–1782), 187

Metternich, Clemens Wenzel Lothar Prince von (1773–1859), 4, 14–16, 18–21, **19,** 30, 32, 33, 36, 48, 50, 55, **56,** 57, **59,** 60–62, **61, 63,** 65–67, 70–76, **73, 86,** 96, 138, 172, 175, 190, 222, 229, 243, 244

Metternich, Franz Georg (1746–1818), 57

Metternich system, 222

Meyer, Ludwig. *See* Mayer, Ludwig

Michalek, Ludwig (1859–1942), **196**

Michelot, Jacques-Pierre, **105**

Middle Ages, **58,** 80, 83, 85, 144, 154, 157, 184, 218, 221, 238

middle class, 25, 26, 38–47, 49, 50, 52, 53, 54, 87, 104, 107, 108, 109, 110, 121, 123, 124, 128, 169, 175–77, 233, **234,** 243

Miethäuser. See apartments

"Mignon," 188, 189

Milan, 6, 14, 172

military bands, 3, 5, 8–10, 15, 16, 65, 67, 71–73, 75, 114, 117, 118, **162,** 240. *See also* bands

Milizia, Francesco (1725–98), 158, 172

minarets, **148**

Minorites, 144, **145**

Minotaur, 153, **153,** 159

minstrels, **99, 116**

Missa Solemnis, 103

mixing of classes, 123

Mocchi, Francesco (1580–1654), 155

Modena, 11, 71

moderns, 82–84, 87, 193. *See also* ancients and moderns

modesty, **5,** 41, 49, 50, 151

Molière (Jean-Baptiste Poquelin, 1622–73), 217

Molinara, Variations on, 106

Molitor, Simon (1766–1848), 110, 111

Mölker Bastei, 80

monasteries, **28,** 39, 146, 149, 172

Monastery Supper, The, **pl. 13**

Montagu, Lady Mary Wortley (1689–1762), 128, 139, 146, 171, 216, 244

Montet, Alexandrine Prévost de la Boutetière de St.-Mars Baroness de (1785–1866), 49

Montoyer, Louis-Joseph (1749–1811), 162, 163, **163, 166**

monumentality, 41, 144, 174, 212

monuments, 83, 154–58, **155, 157, 158, 159, 162,** 193

Moors, 230, 240, 241

Moravia, 6, 64

Moreau, Charles von (1758–1840), **122**

Moreau, Nikolaus (1805–34), **53**

Morelli, Franz (1810–59), 116

Moreto y Cavana (1618–69), 231

Mosel, Ignaz Franz von (1772–1844), 107

Moser, Johann Baptist (1799–1862), 117

Motte Fouqué, Friedrich Heinrich Karl Baron de la (1777–1843), 213

Mozart, Wolfgang Amadeus (1756–91), 11, 26, 32, 43, 47, **48,** 79, 80, 87, 90, **90,** 91, **92,** 93–97, 99, **103,** 104, 106, 107, 112, 127, 132, 166, **168,** 217, **218, 219,** 229

Mukarowsky, J., **231**

Müller, Adam Heinrich, Ritter von Nittersdorff (1779–1829), 57

Müller, Johann Heinrich Friedrich (1738–1815), 244

Müller, Sophie (1803–30), 233

Müller, Wenzel (1767–1835), 239

Müller, Wilhelm (1794–1827), 186, 192, 193, 194, 213

Müller, Wilhelm Christian (1752–1831), 109, 118

Munich, 34, 36, 54, 177, 182, 244

Murat, Joachim (1767–1815; king of Naples as Gioacchino, r. 1808–15), 63, 68, 71

musical chairs, 129

musical machines, 104

musical salons, musical soirées, **53,** 108–11, **111, 113.** *See also* Schubertiades

musicians, 47, 81, **100,** 113, 239, 246, 252

musicology, 111, 256

music societies, 99, **100,** 104, 117. *See also* Gesellschaft der Musikfreunde

Musikstadt Wien, 98

Musik und Menu, 248, **pl.23**

Nachsommer, 51, 233, 244

"Nachtstück," 204

Naples, 11, 14, 63, 64, 71

Napoleon, Franz Joseph Karl, king of Rome (1811–32), 18

Napoleon Bonaparte, 3, 8, 9, **10,** 11, 14–21, **15, 17, 19, 21,** 25, 32, 33, 35–37, 47, 48, 52, 55–58, **56, 62, 63,** 63–68, **64, 68–70,** 70, 71, **122, 136, 155,** 157, **158,** 159, 161, 162, **162, 163,** 164, 175, 177, 184, 246, **247, pl.1, pl.3**

nationalism, 16, 33, 49, 237

nature, 85, 176, 179–82, 186, 188, 189, 194, **195,** 196–99, 203–6, 209, 211, 212, 218, 225, 228, 229

Naudet, Thomas Charles (1773–1810), **15**

Nazarenes, 179

Necker, Mme. (Suzanne Curchod, 1739–94), 46

neoclassicism, **42,** 80, **81,** 82–85, 87, 89, 93, 97, 149, **150,** 151, 152, 153, **153,** 156, 157, **159,** 161, 162, **163,** 164–66, **165,** 172, 228, 230

neo-Gothic, 166, 169

neo-Grec, 152, 163, **171**

Nestroy, Johann Nepomuk (1801–62), 117, 242, **242,** 243, 245

Netherlands, 6, 9, 11, 71

Neue Burgtor, 114, 161, **162**

New Zealand, 135, 140

Nice, Josef (1782–1863), 71, 211

Nicholas I, tsar of Russia (1796–1855, r. 1825–55), 114

Nigg, Josef (1782–1863), 181, **pl.20**

"Night Thoughts," 199

Nobile, Peter von (1774–1854), **150,** 151, **161**

nobility, 26, 38, 39, 41, 54, 100, 108, 121, 182, 195

noble, 4, 25, 38, 56, 75, 124, 125, 140, 151, 228, 229, 233

noble simplicity, 151

Noireterre, Marie Thérèse (fl. late 18th c.), **64**

Normentagen, 99

North Sea, 71

Norway, 72

noseflute, 104

Novalis (Georg Philipp Friedrich Freiherr von Hardenberg, 1772–1801), 80, 85, 187

Obermeyer, Johann Georg (1733–1801), 84

oboeists, **105**

occupation, **15,** 17, **17,** 71, **103**

Octet for Strings and Winds, **249**

"old" music. *See* early music

"On Naive and Sentimental Poetry," 192

"On the Discrimination of Romanticisms," 82

opera, 14, **20,** 26, 28, 29, 31, 32, 34, 43, 45, 46, 52, 80, 95, 98, 100, 101, **102,** 103, 104, 112, 116, 166, 169, 177, 187, 215, 217, 218, 222,

224, 228, 230, 236–41, **237, 238,** 243–45, 248, **pl.22**

opera seria, 187, 215, 218, 244

Opiz, Georg Emanuel (1775–1841), **23**

Orange, 71

oratorio, **100,** 102, 103

orchestra, 47, 53, **57,** 100–102, 104, **108,** 112, 115, **115,** 116, 121, 237, 239, 254

Orcus, 87, 96

Order of St. Stephen, 4, 14, **23,** 88, 194

organists, 112, 114

organs, 112, 117

Orlando furioso, 84

orphans, 100, **100**

Orpheus, 87, 191

"Orpheus," 191

Ossian (James MacPherson, 1736–96), 187, 198

Othellerl, 222

Othello, 84, 244

Ottoman Empire 11, 74. *See also* Turks

Outing to Atzenbrugg, 177

overtures, 96, 100, 103, 106, 145, 239, 248

Overtures in the Italian Style, 96

Padua, 155

Paganini, Niccolò (1782–1840), 102, 104, 108, **110**

pagodas, 148

painters, Chapter 8, *passim;* 28, 29, 33, **45,** 58, **59, 92, 136, 251,** 255. *See also* specific names

palaces, 17, 26, 38, 39, 46, 65, 112, 114, 121, 143, 145, 146, 148, 149, **149, 150,** 151, 153, **153,** 154, **154, 155,** 159, 162, 163, **164–66,** 166, 168, 228, 237, **pl.5, pl.8, pl.9, pl.16.** *See also* specific family names

Palais. *See* palaces

Palestrina, Giovanni Pierluigi (c. 1525–94), 110

Palffy Palace, 38

Pallavicini Palace, 38, 149, **150**

Panofsky, Erwin (1892–1968), 152

pantheism, 31, 179, 182, **195**

Papageno, 166, **168,** 217, **218**

Papal States, 11, 72

parades, 80, 114, 122, 138

Paris, 8, 9, 11, 14, 17–20, 38, 46, 60, 64, 65, 67, 70, 74, 75, 96, **105,** 138, 139, **147, 163,** 182, 214, 227

Paris, Treaty of, 60, 64, 65, 67

parishes, 113, **113,** 146, 172

parks. *See* Augarten; Prater; promenades; Volksgarten

parliaments, 39, 63, 66, 71

Parma, 71

parody, 33, 190, 216, 222, 232, 245

pas de basque, 131, 139

pas de bourrée, 124, 139

pastoral poems, 82, 84, 172, 239, 240

pathos, 10, 189, 191, 193, 203, 224, 225, 227, 233, 239

patriarch, **5,** 25, **25,** 175, 182, **195**

patriotism, 9, **10,** 15, 25, 47, 49, 50, 66, **155,** 179

Pavia, 155

Pawlatschenhof, 168

peacock, 54

Peacock, Francis (1723–1807), 124, 138

peasants, 39, 40, 42, 44, 190, 216, 217, **220,** 222, 226

Pergen, Johann Anton Graf von (1725–1814), 22, **23,** 33, 36

pessimism, 184. *See also* melancholy; *Weltschmerz*

Petter the Elder, Franz Xaver (1791–1866), 181

philosophers, 47, 50, 88, **155,** 156

philosophes, 9

Pian, Antonio de (1784–1851), **219**

pianists, 100, 104

piano, **20,** 26, **27, 30,** 47, 52, 59, 96, 104, **105,** 106, 107, 109, 110, 114, 119, **120, 150,** 151, 171, 186, 211, 212, **239, 249,** 255

Piano Concerto in E-flat ("Emperor"), **249**

Piano Concerto in G, 96

piano nobile, 151, **249**

Pichler, Andreas (1764–1837), 50

Pichler, Caroline (1769–1843), 26, 28, 47, 49, 50, **51,** 54, 255, 256 picnic, **29,** 176

Piedmont, 71

piety, 157, **157,** 177, 191

pilasters, 145, 162, 163

Pillnitz, Declaration of, 8

Pindar (c. 520–c. 438 B.C.), 188, 190

Pirithous, **160**

plague, 155, **157**

Plastik, 153, 172

Plato (c. 428–c.347 B.C.), 88

Plattenstil, 168

Playford, John (1623–86), 128

Poetics, 83, 96

poetry, 16, 24, 28, 34, 44, 80, 84, 85, 109, 183, 184, 186–88, 190–92, 195, 196, 198, 199, 222, 225, 227, 235

poets, 10, 22, 23, 26, 28, 47, 49, 80, **81,** 84, 85, 146, 186, 187, 190–95, **192, 193, 195, 196,** 197–99, 205, 209, 212, 213, 247. *See also* specific names

Poland, 6, 9, 17, 60, **62,** 64–66, **64, 65, 67,** 68, 71, 74, 75, **126,** 131

police, 6, 21, 22, **23,** 24, 28, 31, 33, 36, 37, 40, 45, 52, 74, 101, 102, 107, 109, 117, 121, **121,** 122, 254

political theory, 33

polonaise, 103, 104, 106, 115, 122, 124, 126, 131

Polytechnic Institute, **148,** 165, 166, **167**

Pomerania, 72

pope, 72, 74

popular theater, **215,** 215–19, **217, 220, 221, 223, 224, 225,** 226, **227,** 230, 238, 239, **239,** 242, **242,** 243, **pl.21**

population, 37, 38, 54, 148

porcelain, 176, 180, 181, **pl.20**

portraiture, 5, 29, 66, 135, 155–58, **155, 157, 159,** 174, 176–79, 182, 226, 250, **251,** 252. *See also* specific names

Portugal, 11, 64, 67

Posen, 65

Postl, Karl. *See* Sealsfield, Charles

Potpourri for Cello, 106

Pötzleindorf, 169

Prague, 126

Prater, 52, 55, **152,** 180, **pl.18**

"Prayer," 113

préciosité, 46

Prehauser, Gottfried (1699–1769), 216

Preindl, Josef (1756–1823), 112

preromantic, 187, 193

Pressburg, Treaty of, 3, 14–17

priests, 172, 230

primitivism, 183

processions, 80, 111, 114, 126, 131, 177, **pl.7**

Prokesch, Anton (1795–1876), **51**

promenades, 115, **152, 161, 162,** 165, **167**

propylaon, 161

prostitution, 44

Protestants, 14, **150,** 166, **pl.10**

protocol, 31, 67, 70, **70,** 146

protoromanticism, 95

Prussia, 8, 9, 15, 19, 20, 47, 56, **56,** 57, 61, **61,** 62, 64–69, 71, 72, **73,** 74, 147, **pl.15**

Psalms, 113, 166, **pl.10**

publishers, 33, 115, **157,** 248, 252, 253, **253**

pyramidal, 157

Pyrker von Felsö-Eör, Johann Ladislaus (1773–1847), 182, 195, **195**

quadrilles, **58,** 115, 123–25, 127–30, **130,** 138

Quadruple Alliance, **61,** 72, 74

Quartet in C-Sharp Minor, Op. 131, **93**

quartets: string, **10,** 26, 91, **93,** 94, 98, 106, 107, **109,** 110, 164, 203, **249,** 255; vocal, **105,** 106, 110, 113, 248. *See also* Schuppanzigh

"quiet grandeur," 151

quintets, string, 79, 107

Racine, Jean (1639–99), 85

Rahl, Carl Heinrich (1779–1843), **21**

Raimund, Ferdinand Jakob (1790–1836), 26, 32, 33, 36, 117, **150,** 180, **220, 224,** 224–27, **225, 227,** 239, **239,** 241–43, **242,** 245, **pl.21**

Rambouillet, Catherine de Vivonne, Marquise de (1588–1665), 46

Rameau, Pierre (fl. early 18th c.), 127, 139

Rasumofsky, Andrei Kirillowitsch, Prince (1752–1836), **56,** 164, **166**

Rasumofsky Palace, 163, **166**

Ratner, Leonard (b. 1916), 95

reader. See *Vorleserin*

reading circles, 30, 45, 109

realism, 174–76, 178–80, 217, 225, 235, **pl.12**

recitals, 100, 103

Red Hedgehog, 106

Redouten Halls *(Redoutensäle),* 59, 102, 104, 115, 121, 122, 149

reforms, 4, 15, 16, 36, 37, 39, 73, 117, 149, 171, 172, 217, **pl.4, pl.10**

Reich, 11, 14, 33

Reichardt, Johann Friedrich (1752–1814), 192

Reichsdeputation, 11

Reichsdeputationshauptschluß, 11

Reiffenstüel, Fr. Ignaz (1664–1720), 146, 171

Reil, Johann Anton Friedrich (1773–1843), 195

Reim, Johann Vincent (1796–1858), **101**

Reinhold, Friedrich Philipp (1779–1840), **68, pl.5**

reliefs (sculpture), 156, **157,** 163, 168

religion, 24, 29, 31, 47, 72, 73, 88, **92,** 96, 99, 111, 115, 146, **148,** 155, 156, 166, 172, 179, 182, 184, **195,** 203, 230, **pl.10**

Rellstab, Heinrich Friedrich Ludwig (1799–1860), 187

Renaissance, 42, 46, 80, 82, 93, 95, 96, 111, 145, 151, 152, 172

Requiem, **64**

Restoration (of the Bourbons), **64,** 67, 175, 198

Reveries of a Solitary Wanderer, 203

reversed S-figure, 41, 125, 127, 211, 243

Revett, Nicholas (1720–1804), 152

revolution, 3, 4, 8, 9, 20–22, 33, 34, 36, 37, 40, 49, 53, 63, **63, 64,** 75, 80, 89, 95, 131, 135, **136,** 166, 174, 175, 183, 243

revolutionary classicism, 166, 168

revolution from above, 37

revolution from below, 37

Revolution of *1848,* 21, 28, 34, 54, 111, 148, 172, 175, 182, 243

Rheinbund. See Confederation of the Rhine

Rhetoric, 83, 85

Rhine, 9, 11, 14–16, 63, 66, 68, 70

Rhineland, 66, 67, 71

Rich Reveler, The, **pl.13**

riding school. See Spanish Riding School

Rieder, Wilhelm August (1796–1880), **pl.2**

"Rime of the Ancient Mariner," 213

Ritterstück, 221

Rivoli, Battle of, 36

rococo, 148, **149**

Roesler, Johann Carl (1775–1845), **91**

Roman art and sculpture, 82, 153, **136, 155,** 156

Roman Catholic Church, 6, 31, 39, 52, 96, 99, 111, 145, 166, 187, **pl.7**

Roman Elegies, 190, 191

Roman forum, 162

Roman religion, 96

romanticism, 80–82, 85–87, **86,** 89, 94, 95, 96, **145,** 183, 184, 187, 188, 194, 197–99, 212, 235; music, *see* Chapter 4, *passim;* opera, 237, 238, **238,** 240, 241; painting, 28; poetry, 80, 85, Chapter 9, *passim;* romantic longing, 88, 176, 184, 194, 203, 204, 241; theater, 227, 229. See also literary theory; romantics

romantic love, 43, 218

romantics, 16, 30, 31, 79, 95, 183, 184, 186, 187, 193, 212. See also romanticism

Roman Vienna. See Vindobona

Romberg, Bernard Heinrich (1767–1841), 106

Rome, 18, 29, 72, 153–55, **153,** 179, **192**

Romeo and Juliet, 231, 244

Rosamunde, **103,** 237, 239

Rosen, Charles (b. 1927), 91, 95, 97

Rossini, Gioacchino Antonio (1792–1868), 88, 94, 96, 100, 104, 106, 108, 230, 238, 240, 248

Rousseau, Jean-Jacques (1712–78), 82, 203

Rudolphias, 182

Ruhe und Ordnung, 20, 21

Ruhr, 66

Russia, 9, 11, 14, 18, 19, 56, 60–62, 64–66, 72–74, 155, 163; court, 163

Russians, **56, 62,** 65, 66, 68, 72, 73, **73,** 163, **166**

sacred music, 103, 107, 110–14

Sagan, Katharina Wilhelmine Friederike Benigne, Herzogin von (1781–1839), 58, 75

St. Anne, 112

St. Augustine's, 107, 112

St. Bernard Pass, 11

St. Bridget, **99.** *See also* Brigittenkirchtag

St. Charles, 112, **148.** *See also* Karlskirche

St. Genois Stolberg, Gabriele Gräfin, **215**

St. Helena, 20, 37

St. Michael, 112

St. Leopold Babenberg (r. 1095–1136), 156, 172

St. Paul, 82

St. Peter, 112

St. Petersburg, 104

St. Stephen, **23, 37,** 112, 144, **144, pl.4, pl.8, pl.9**

Sales, Carl von (1791–1870), **51**

Salieri, Antonio (1750–1825), 24, 36, 59, 112, **113**

Salis-Seewis, Johann Gaudenz Freiherr von (1762–1834), 187, 198

salons, 26, 28, 41, 46, 49, **53,** 54, 58, 65, 106–10, **111,** 114, 162, 255

Salve Regina, 113

Salzburg, 11, 55, 179, 215, 216, **pl.16**

Salzkammergut, 179, 180

Sappho, **169,** 234, 235, **236**

Sardinia, 71

Sartain, John (1808–97), **81, 193**

Saurau, Franz Josef Graf von (1760–1832), 9

"savoir et savoir vivre," 46

Savoy, 71. *See also* Eugene, prince of Savoy

Saxons, Saxony, 60, 62–68, 74, 151

Schaffer, Joseph (fl. 1780–1810), 218

Schaffer, Peter (fl. 1780–1810), 218

Scheurer von Waldheim, Josef, **99**

Schikaneder, Emanuel (1751–1812), **103, 168,** 217, **218,** 220

Schiller, Johann Christoph Friedrich von (1759–1805), 27, 85, 183, 186, 187, 191–93, **193,** 230, 231, **231,** 244

Schindler, Karl (1821–42), 177

"Schlachtgesang," 107

Schlamperei, 247, 256

Schlechta von Wschehrd, Franz Xaver (1796–1875), 195, 209, 211

Schlegel, August Wilhelm von (1767–1845), 16, 48, 50, 80, **81,** 82–85, 87, 96, 183, 184, 187, 192, 193

Schlegel, Dorothea (1764–1839), 26

Schlegel, Karl Wilhelm Friedrich von (1772–1829), 16, 26, 34, 48, 50, 57, 80, 82, 85, **86,** 87, 88, 95, 96, 187

Schleiermacher, Friedrich Ernst Daniel (1768–1834), 50

Schleifer, 132

Schlesinger, Heinrich Wilhelm (1814–93), **115**

Schlüter, Andreas (c. 1660–1714), 155

Schnitt, Mlle, 104

Schober, Franz von (1796–1882), 28, **28–30,** 30, 31, 34, 187, 195, 237, 238, **238,** 240

Schoberlechner, Franz de Paula Jakob (1797–1843), 104, 110

Schöller, Johann Christian (1782–1851), **225, 227, 247**

Schönberg, Arnold (1874–1951), 91

Schönbrunn, Treaty of, 17, 18

Schönbrunn Palace, 17, 55, 146, 148, 149, **149,** 158, **255**

schools, 16, 28, 38, 44, 59, **113,** 151, **154,** 165, **169,** 181, 195, 200

Schopenhauer, Arthur (1788–1860), 88, 89, 96

Schottenfeld, **122**

Schottenhof, 168, **169**

Schreyvogel, Josef (1768–1832), 230–33, **231, 232, 234, 235,** 241, 244

Schröder, Friedrich Ludwig (1744–1816), 229

Schröder, Sophie (1781–1868), 226, 235, **236**

Schröder-Devrient, Wilhelmine (1804–60), 212

Schubart, Christian Friedrich Daniel (1739–91), 198

Schubert, Ferdinand (1794–1859), 113, **pl.16**

Schubert, Franz (1797–1828), 4, **5**, 8, 10, **15**, 16, **17**, 19, **21**, 21, 22, 23, **23**, 24, 26–34, **27–30**, 36–41, 44, 45, 49, 50, 52, 54, 55, 59, 79–81, 85, 87–89, 94, 95, 96–100, 106, 107, 110, 112–15, 117–19, 122, 123, 125, 127, 128, 132, 135, 138, 139, 143, 144–49, 151, 153, 154, 162, 164–66, 168, 169, 171, 172, 174, 177, 179, 182–84, 186, 187, 188–200, 203, 205, 209, 211–13, 217, 219, 223, 224, 230, 234, 236–41, 245–50, 252, 253, 254–56

Schubert, Franz Theodor Florian (1763–1830), 38, 44

Schubert, Ignaz (1785–1844), 253

Schubertiades, 26, **27**, 29, 109, 125, 253–55, **254**

Schufried, Jacob (1785–1857), **167**

Schuhbladkastenhaus, 168

Schuler (Edouard, 1806–82), **92**

Schultze, Ernst Konrad Friedrich (1789–1817), 187

Schumann, Robert Alexander (1810–56), 79, 90, 94

Schuppanzigh, Ignaz (1776–1830), 107, **109**, 248, **249**

Schuster, Ignaz (1779–1835), 224

Schütz, Carl (1745–1800), **40**

Schütz, Joseph, **121**

Schütz, Ludovicus, **169**

Schwäbische Tanz, 132

"Schwammerl," 52, 54, 255, 256

Schwanengesang, 241

Schwarzenberg, Karl Philipp Fürst zu (1771–1820), 66, 68, 70, 162

Schwarzenberg Palace, 146, **pl.9**

Schweizerhof, 145

Schwind, Moritz von (1804–71), **28**, 28–31, 177, **196, 224, 238, 254**

science, 46, 49, 57, 88, 157

Scotland, 124, 131, 140, 163

Scott, Sir Walter (1771–1832), 113, 187

sculptors, 16, 143, 144, 153, **153**

sculpture, 143–45, 149, **150**, 151, 153, **153**, 154, **155**, 156, 157, **157–60**, 159, 161, **165**, **168**, 172, 182

Sealsfield, Charles (Karl Postl, 1793–1864), 114, 118

Second Peace of Paris, 70, 74

Sedlnitzky, Josef Graf von (1778–1855), 23, **23**

Seidl, Johann Gabriel (1804–75), 187, 195

Seitenstettengasse, 113

self-parody, 190, 222

Semiramide, 100

Senn, Johann (1792–1857), 22, 23, **23**, 28, 40, 41, 195

sensibility, 82, 183, 184, 187–89, **192**, 193, 194, 198, 199, 203, 204, 212

sentiment, 44, 228

sentimentality, 44, 106, 117, 186, 188, 191, 192, 194, 222, 228, 231

"Serenade," 107

serfdom, 39

1722.1822.1922, 221

sex roles, 44

sexuality, 34, 54, 96, 97, 231, 235, 238

Seyfried, Ignaz Ritter von (1776–1841), 112, 113

Shakespeare, William (1564–1616), **81**, 84, 85, 96, 217, 222, 231, **231, 232**, 238

Shelley, Percy Bysshe (1792–1822), 80

Sicily, 71

silk, **39, pl.11.** *See also* Arthaber, Rudolf von; factories; industrialization

Silvana, 106

Simrock, Nikolaus (1752–1834), 33

Singspiel, 237, 238

sketches, 138, 180, 182, 213, 237

slave, 56, 67

Slavonia, 6

social change, 15, 36, 37, 39, 45, 123, 125, 174, 175

social classes, 26, 37, 39–41, 44–47, 49, 52, **115**, 124, 164, 175, 182, 196, 246. *See also* aristocracy; lower classes; middle class; women social criticism, 222, 234, 241, 243

social dance, 25, Chapter 6, *passim*

Social Games of the Schubertians, 177

social injustice, 175

social life, **5,** 28, 45–47, **48,** 49–54, 75, 100, 109, 177, 214, 215, 222, 228, 232, 254, 255, **pl.5**

society, 4, 24, 25, **25, 27,** 30, 31, 36, 37, 39–42, 46, 49–52, 85, 89, 100, 104, 106, 107, 113, 117, 118, 125, 140, 175, 176, 229, 235, 243, 249, 250, 254

Society of the Friends of Music. *See* Gesellschaft der Musikfreunde˙

sonatas, 26, 32, 93, 94, 110, 255

songs, 9, 19, 24, 26, 28, 31, 32, 34, 44, **51,** 79, 85, 98, **105,** 107, 110, **111,** 113–17, 134, 164, 171, 182–84, 186–90, 192, 193, 196, 199, 203, 211–13, **239,** 240, 248, **249, 250,** 252, 254, 255. *See also* specific titles

Songs of Greek Antiquity, 114, 188, 190, 212

Sonnenfels, Joseph Reichsfreiherr (c. 1733–1817), 217, 228

Sonnleithner, Ignaz (1770–1831), 110, **111**

Sorrows of Young Werther, The. See "Werther"

Spain, 9, 18, 64, 67, **70,** 240

Spanish dramatists, 52, 57, 231

Spanish language, 49, 52

Spanish Riding School, 149, **154**

Spaun, Joseph Freiherr von (1788–1865), 29, **29, 30,** 31, **168,** 195, 203, 204, 248, **254**

spectacles, 66, 215, 220, 222, 227

Sperl (dance hall), 116, 135

sphinxes, 163

Spohr, Louis (1784–1859), 102

Spontini, Gaspare Luigi Pacifico (1774–1851), 106

Stabat Mater, 113

Staberl, 222, 224, 227

Stadion, Johann Philipp (1763–1824), 15, 16, 18

Stadler, Albert (1794–1888), 195

Stadtkonvikt, 16, **17, 40, 144, 242, pl.6**

Staël, Mme. de (Anne Louise Germaine, Baroness of South Holstein, *née* Necker, 1766–1817), 46, 48

Stallburg, 145

Steblin, Rita (b. 1951), 24, 33, 54, 250, 256

Stefansplatz, 24

Stein, Karl Heinrich Reichsfreiherr vom (1757–1831), 57

Steinfeld the Younger, Franz (1787–1868), 180

Stendahl (Marie-Henri Beyle, 1783–1842), 85

Stewart, Robert Vane, Viscount Castlereagh (1769–1822), **56,** 60, **61**

Stifter, Adalbert (1805–68), 50, 51, 233, 244

still life, 178, 181

Stolberg-Stolberg, Friedrich Leopold Graf zu (1750–1819), 198, 199, 203

Stranitzky, Johann (1676–1726), 215–17, **215,** 222, **223**

Strassburger, 132, **133**

Strauss, Johann, Jr. (1825–99), 117, 131, 243

Strauss, Johann, Sr. (1804–49), 52, 114, **115,** 116

string quartet. *See* quartets, string

String Quartet in A minor, **109**

String Quintet in C, 79

Stuart, James (1713–88), 152, 244

Sturm und Drang, 229

sublime, 74, 86, 143, 188

suburbs, 22, 26, **37,** 38, **39,** 54, 56, 80, 102, 113, 115, 116, **122,** 146, 169, 176, 214, 217, 219, 220, 223, 228

suicide, 32, **61, 150,** 189, 194, 196, **196,** 242

Sulzer, Salomon (1804–90), 113, 118

supernatural, 212, **pl.21**

Swabia, 132, 139

Sweden, 14, 64, 72

Swieten, Gottfried van (1734–1803), 46, 47

Switzerland, Swiss, 67, **70,** 71, 149, **150**

symphonies, 26, 32, **57,** 79, 87, 93, 94, 97, 102, **102,** 103, 106, 107, 110, 119, 164, **169,** 171, 248, 255, **pl.3;** Beethoven, 26, 79, 102, **102,** 164, **169,** 206, **pl.3;** Schubert, 79, 255

synagogue, 111, 113, 114, 166, **pl.10**

syphilis, 34, 44, **238**

"Tales of the Vienna Woods," 116

Talleyrand, Charles Maurice de, prince of Bénévent, duke of Talleyrand-Périgord (1754–1838), 56, **56,** 59, 63, **64,** 65–67, 70

Tarouca Palace, 162

Tasso, Torquato (1544–95), 84, 244

taste, 42, 46, 83, 135, 147, **149,** 188, 195, 212, 216, 230, 232, 248

taverns, **116,** 121, **123,** 144, 169

Te Deum, **112**

Teltscher, Josef (1801–37), 250

temples, 113, 159, 161, **161,** 218, **219,** 226, 230

Tencin, Claudine Alexandrine Guérin de (1682–1749), 46

tenements, 166

Teutscher, 132

Thaddädl, 223

Theater an der Wien, 26, 102, 103, **103,** 166, **168,** 220, 234, 237

Theater auf der Wieden, 218, 219

Theater in der Josefstadt, 102, 220, **221,** 224, 241

Theater in der Leopoldstadt, 26, 219, **220,** 223, **239,** 243, 244

Theater nächst dem Burg, **101,** 217, 228

Theaterzeitung, 221

theorists, drama and art, 83, 96, 152. *See also* literary theory; political theory

Theseon, 159, **161, 162**

Theseus, 153, **153,** 159, **160,** 161, **161,** 164

Theseus and the Minotaur, 153

Theseus Fighting the Centaur, 159, **160, 161,** 164

Thieck, Johann Ludwig. *See* Tieck, Johann Ludwig

Thirty Years' War, 145

Thorn, 64, 65

Thoughts on the Imitation of Works of the Greeks, 15, 151, 199, 203, 253

Thoughts on the Origin, Growth, and Decline of Decoration in the Fine Arts, 151

Thucydides (c. 460–c. 395 B.C.), 32

Thugut, Johann Amadeus Franz de Paula (1736–1818), 11

Thursday Evening Entertainments. See *Abendunterhaltungen*

Tieck, Johann Ludwig (1773–1853), 50, 80, 85, 187, 213

Tietze, Ludwig (1797–1850), 110

tolerance, 47, 51, 166, **pl.10**

Tomaschek, Wenzel Johann (1774–1850), 101

tomb, 29, 157, 158, 162

Tonkünstler Society, 99. *See also* music societies

"tradition," 247

tragedy, 83, 87, 189, 228, 231–34

Trajan, 162

"Tranquility and Order," 20

Trautson Palace, 146

Traux, 143, 146, 171

Treml, Johann Friedrich (1816–52), 177

trio, 106, 107

triple meter, 126, 128, 132, 139

Trollope, Frances, 113, 118

troubadours, trouvères, 84

tsar, 19, 61–66, **62, 63,** 72–74, **73,** 114

Tübingen, 250. *See also* International Schubert Society

Tuchlauben, 106

Turkey, 11, **148**

Turks, 4, 146, **147,** 214. *See also* Ottoman Empire

Tuscany, 4, 11, 71

Twelfth Night, 238

Über den gegenwärtigen Zustand der Musik, 96

Ukrainian, 53

Ulrichsplatz, **170**

"Undine," 213

United Provinces, 9

United States of America, 8

unities (of action, time, and place), 83, 84

university, 28, 29, 33, 34, 36, 40, **40,** 41, 57, 76, 80, 95–97, 102, 118, 139, 140, 172, 182, 212, 213, 230, 245, 256, **pl.6**

Unsinns-Gesellschaft, 24

urbanization, 38, 39, 42, 43

vague des passions, 85, 96

Valmy, Battle of, 8

variations, **10,** 103, 104, 106

Vaterländische Blätter, 25

vedute, **pl.8, pl.9**

Vega Carpio, Lope Félix de, (1562–1635), 84

Venetia. *See* Venice

Venice, 11, 71, 74, 153, 155, 182, **195, 232,**
    244, **pl.9**

Verdienstadel, 195

Verrocchio (Andrea di Michele Cioni,
    1435–88), 155

*Versuch einer kritischen Dichtkunst für die
    Deutschen,* 83

"Verwünschungen der Franzosen," 9

veterinary school, 165, 166

Vetter, Walter (1891–1967), 95

Victoria and Albert Museum, **153,** 172

Vienna, Treaty of (Vienna Settlement), 70,
    72

Vienna, Treaty of, 70

Vienna Final Act, 70, **70,** 71

"Vienna lectures," 183, 192

Villanella Rapita, 104

Vindobona, 144, 156

violinists, **45,** 98, 103, 107, **109, 110,** 225,
    pl.13

violins, 102, 104, 106, 107, 171

Vistula River, 60

Vittoria, Battle of, 18, **20**

vocal music, 106, 107, 111, **111,** 113, 246, 248.
    See also arias; folk music; Mass; oratorio;
    quartets, vocal; songs

Vogl, Johann Michael (1768–1840), **27,** 29,
    105, 110, 236, 237, **pl.16**

Völkel, Reinhold (b. 1834), **170**

Volksgarten, 114, 159, **161**

Volkslied, 10

Volksstück, 221

Vorleserin, 47

Wackenroder, Wilhelm Heinrich (1773–98),
    80

Wagner, Richard (1813–83), 241, 243, 245

Wagram, Battle of, 17

Waldmüller, Ferdinand Georg (1793–1865),
    27, 176, 178–80, 182

waltz *(Walzer),* 114–17, **115,** 122, 123, 131,
    124, 128–35, **134, 137,** 138, 139

waltz kings, 116

Wanderer Fantasie, 203, **239**

Wanderers Nachtlieder, 188, 189

"Wanderers Sturmlied," 190

Warmuth, Sebastian, **164**

Warsaw, 64

Wars of Liberation, 28, 157

Waterloo, 20, 68, 70, **70,** 72

Watteau, Louis Joseph (1731–98), **223**

Weber, Carl Maria von (1786–1826), 98,
    104, 118, 240

Webster, James (b. 1942), 95, 97

Wegmayer (Wegmayr), Sebastian
    (1776–1857), 181

Weh dem, der lügt, 234

Weimar, 212, 230, 231, 233

Weimar classicism, **193,** 230

Wellington, Arthur Wellesley, Duke of
    (1769–1852), 18, **20,** 48, **56, 57,** 59, 66,
    68–70, 164

Wellington's Victory, 18, **57,** 164

Weltschmerz, 183, 184, 190, **196,** 198, 203, 212

Wendt, Amadeus (1783–1836), 90, **90,** 91, 96

Werner, Friedrich Ludwig Zacharias
    (1768–1823), 54, 58

"Werther," 189, 190, 194, 197, 198, 211

West-östlicher Divan, 188

Whittall, Arnold (1935–), 95

widows, 100, **100**

Wigand, Balthasar (1771–1846), **pl.7**

Wilhelm Meisters Lehrjahre, 188, 190

Willemer, Marianne von (1784–1860), 188

"Willkommen und Abschied," 188

Wilson, Thomas (fl. early 19th c.), 135, 139

Winckelmann, Johann Joachim (1717–68),
    151, 153, 158, 172

wind instruments, **105, 249**

Winter, Peter von (1754–1825), 112

Winterreise, 117, 184, 186, 193, 194, 196, 213,
    241

Wohnhaus, 168

Wolf, [?], **239**

Woltener, [?], **62**

women, 26, 38, 39, 42–44, 46, 47, **48,** 49, 50,
55, 57, 108, 109, 113, 124, 125, 128, 131,
134, 135, 136, **136, 137,** 138, 189, 194, 209,
211, **218,** 224, 235

woods, 43, 52, 55, 116, 146

Wordsworth, William (1770–1850), 85, 188

workhouses, 38

World as Will and Representation, The, 88, 96

Württemberg, 14, 56, 65, 247

Young, Edward (1683–65), 199

Zauberflöte. See *Die Zauberflöte*

Zauberstück, 222, 226, 237, 239

Zauner, Franz Anton Edler von
(1746–1822), 16, 151, 154, **155,** 156, 172

Z-figure, 125, **126,** 127

Zincke (Zinke), Johann Wenzel (1797–1858),
227

zither, 116

Zseliz, 41, 113

Zum roten Igl, 106

Zumsteeg, Johann Rudolf (1760–1802),
192

Zwischenzeit, 143